UNITS

G000145666

CONTRIBUTING TO THE
MANAGEMENT OF PERFORMANCE
AND THE ENHANCEMENT OF VALUE

CONTRIBUTING TO THE PLANNING
AND CONTROL OF RESOURCES

AAT Technician NVQ/SVQ Level 4 in Accounting

British Library Cataloguing-in-Publication Data

A catalogue record for this book is available from the British Library.

Published by
Kaplan Publishing UK
Unit 2, The Business Centre
Molly Millars Lane
Wokingham
Berkshire
RG41 2QZ

ISBN 978-1-84710-814-2

Printed in the UK by CPI William Clowes Beccles NR34 7TL

We are grateful to the Association of Accounting Technicians for permission to reproduce past assessment materials. The solutions have been prepared by Kaplan Publishing.

Crown copyright material is reproduced with the permission of the Controller of HMSO.

CONTENTS

KAPLAN PUBLISHING

CONTENTS

KAPLAN PUBLISHING

PREFACE

STUDY TEXT

The study text is written in a practical and interactive style:
- key terms and concepts are clearly defined
- all topics are illustrated with practical examples with clearly worked solutions
- frequent practice activities throughout the chapters ensure that what you have learnt is regularly reinforced
- test your knowledge section at the end of each chapter helps you to check that you have really understood the topics covered.

WORKBOOK

The workbook comprises two main elements:
(a) A question bank of key techniques to give additional practice and reinforce the work covered in each chapter. The questions are divided into their relevant chapters and students may either attempt these questions as they work through the study text, or leave some or all of these until they have completed the study text as a sort of final revision of what they have studied.
(b) Two mock examinations which closely reflect the type of examination students may expect.

KAPLAN PUBLISHING

STANDARDS OF COMPETENCE – NVQ/SVQ IN ACCOUNTING

Unit 8   Contributing to the Management of Performance and the Enhancement of Value

Unit commentary

This unit is about collecting, analysing and interpreting information of help to managers in controlling costs and improving the performance of operations. There are two elements.

The first element focuses on the identification and analysis of costs that may be of help to managers. You will have to monitor and analyse costs against trends, standards and organisational needs, and explain any difference between actual and planned or expected costs. In addition, you will have to demonstrate your understanding of forecasting techniques as an aid to cost analysis and control.

The second element is concerned with monitoring the performance of an organisation or parts of an organisation and making recommendations that will enhance the organisation's value. In this element you have to identify and calculate performance indicators, monitor the performance of part or all of the organisation and make proposals that will enhance the value of the organisation.

You will have to obtain information from a variety of internal and external sources and monitor costs, performance indicators and movements in prices over an appropriate timescale. You will also be required to use the information to prepare and present management reports. As well as being familiar with manually developing information, you will also need to know how computer spreadsheets can assist you in preparing cost and performance information.

Elements contained within this unit are:

Element: 8.1
Collect, analyse and disseminate information about costs

Element: 8.2
Monitor performance and make recommendations to enhance value

---

Knowledge and Understanding

To perform this unit effectively you will need to know and understand:

Chapter

The business environment

1	External sources of information on costs and prices: government statistics, trade associations, financial press, quotations, price lists (Elements 8.1 and 8.2)	1
2	General economic environment (Elements 8.1 and 8.2)	1

Accounting techniques

3	Basic statistical methods: index numbers; sampling techniques; time series analysis (moving averages, linear regression and seasonal trends) (Element 8.1)	4
4	Use of relevant computer packages (Elements 8.1 and 8.2)	6
5	Methods of presenting information in graphical, diagrammatic and tabular form (Element 8.1)	Through out
6	Performance indicators: efficiency, effectiveness, productivity; balanced score-card, benchmarking; unit costs; control ratios (efficiency, capacity and activity), scenario planning ('what if' analysis) (Element 8.2)	7
7	Standard costing (Element 8.1)	5

Accounting principles and theory

8	Marginal and absorption costing: cost recording, cost reporting and cost behaviour (Elements 8.1 and 8.2)	2, 3
9	Cost management: life cycle costing; target costing (including value engineering); activity based costing; principles of Total Quality Management (including cost of quality) (Element 8.2)	3, 7
10	The use and limitation of published statistics (Element 8.1)	3
11	Effect of accounting controls on behaviour of managers and other employees (Elements 8.1 and 8.2)	7

The organisation

12	How the accounting systems of an organisation are affected by its organisational structure, its administrative systems and procedures and the nature of its business transactions (Elements 8.1 and 8.2)	1, 3
13	The organisation's external environment and specific external costs (Element 8.1)	Through out
14	The contribution of functional specialists in an organisation (e.g. marketing, design, engineering, quality control etc) to cost reduction and value enhancement (Element 8.2)	7

Element 8.1 Collect, analyse and disseminate information about costs

Chapter

Performance criteria

In order to perform this element successfully you need to:

A	Identify valid, relevant **information** from internal and external sources	1, 2, 4
B	Monitor and analyse on a regular basis current and forecast trends in prices and market conditions	4
C	Compare trends with previous experience and identify potential implications	4
D	Compare standard costs with actual costs and analyse any **variances**	5
E	Analyse the effect of organisational accounting policies on reported costs	2, 3
F	Consult relevant staff in the organisation about the analysis of trends and variances	4
G	Present reports to management that **summarise data**, present information using appropriate **methods** and highlight significant trends	4, 5, 6, 7

Range statement

Performance in this element relates to the following contexts:

Information:

· Movements in prices charged by suppliers, competitors and providers of services

· General price changes

Methods of summarising data:

· Time series (moving averages, linear regression, seasonal variations)

· Index numbers and sampling

Methods of presenting information in reports:

· Written analysis and explanation

· Tables

· Diagrams

Variance analysis:

· Material price and usage variances

· Labour rate and efficiency variances

· Fixed overhead expenditure, volume, capacity and efficiency variances

· Subdivision of variances

The build up of costs:

· Absorption costing

· Marginal costing

· Activity based costing

Element 8.2   Monitor performance and make recommendations to enhance value

Performance criteria

Chapter

In order to perform this element successfully you need to:

A	Analyse routine cost reports and budgets, compare then with other sources of information and identify any implications	3
B	Prepare and monitor relevant **performance indicators**, interpret the results and identify potential improvements and estimate the value of potential improvements	7
C	Consult relevant specialists and assist in identifying ways to reduce costs and enhance value	7
D	Prepare exception reports to identify matters which require further investigation	5, 6
E	Make specific **recommendations** to management in a clear and appropriate form	Through out

Range statement

Performance in this element relates to the following contexts:

Performance indicators to measure:

- Financial, customer, internal business, and learning and growth perspectives
- Efficiency, effectiveness and productivity
- Unit costs; resource utilisation
- Profitability
- Quality of service
- Cost of quality

Recommendations:

- Efficiencies
- Modifications to work processes
- Benchmarking

Unit 9   Contributing to the Planning and Control of Resources

Unit commentary

This unit focuses on the planning and control of resources in an organisation. There are three elements.

In the first element, you have to develop forecasts of demand, turnover, resources to be consumed and their cost.

The second element requires you to use forecasts to prepare draft budgets for income and expenditure. This may involve you changing your initial budget to take account of revised information about factors that limit the operations of the organisation.

The final element relates to part of the control function in organisations. You will be required to compare the actual performance of all or part of an organisation against what was planned to happen and advise managers of possible reasons for any difference.

You will need to ensure all relevant data has been included in your budgets and that all relevant staff have been consulted. In addition, you will need to ensure that transactions have been accurately recorded and appropriate accounting methods have been used for both the planning and monitoring of budgets. As well as being familiar with manually developing forecasts and budgets, you will also need to know how computer spreadsheets can help you in their development.

> **Elements contained within this unit are:**
>
> **Element: 9.1**
> Prepare forecasts of income and expenditure
>
> **Element: 9.2**
> Prepare draft budget proposals
>
> **Element: 9.3**
> Monitor the performance of responsibility centres against budgets

Knowledge and Understanding

To perform this unit effectively you will need to know and understand:

Chapter

The business environment

1	External sources of information on costs, prices, demand and availability of resources (Elements 9.1, 9.2 and 9.3)	1
2	General economic environment (Elements 9.1, 9.2. and 9.3)	1

Accounting techniques

3	Basic statistical methods: time series (moving averages, linear regression and seasonal variations), sampling techniques; index numbers (Element 9.1)	4
4	Use of relevant computer packages (Elements 9.1, 9.2 and 9.3)	6
5	Development of production, resource and revenue budgets from forecast sales data	8
6	Coordination of the budget system (Elements 9.2 & 9.3)	8
7	The effect of capacity constraints, other production constraints and sales constraints on budgets; limiting (key or budget) factor (Elements 9.2 & 9.3)	8
8	Budgets for control: flexible budgets, marginal costing	9
9	The effect of budgetary systems on the behaviour and motivation of managers and other employees (Element 9.2)	9
10	Analysing the significance of budget variances and possible responses required by managers (Element 9.3)	9
11	Presentation of budget data in a form that satisfies the differing needs of budget holders	9

Accounting principles and theory

12	Marginal and absorption costing: cost recording, cost reporting, cost behaviour (Elements 9.2 and 9.3)	2, 3
13	Uses of budgetary control: planning, coordinating, authorising, cost control (Elements 9.1, 9.2 & 9.3)	8
14	Relationship between budgets, forecasts and planning and product life cycles (Elements 9.1, 9.2 & 9.3)	8, 9
15	Different types of budgets: budgets for income and expenditure; resource budgets (production, material, labour and other resource budgets); capital budgets (Elements 9.2 & 9.3)	8

The organisation

16	How the accounting systems of an organisation are affected by its organisational structure, its administrative systems and procedures and the nature of its business transactions (Elements 9.1, 9.2 & 9.3)	1, 3
17	The structure of the organisation and its responsibility centres and an understanding of the inter-relationships between departments and functions is required (Elements 9.1, 9.2 & 9.3)	Through out
18	Responsibility centres: expense centres; profit centres; investment centres (Element 9.3)	8, 9

KAPLAN PUBLISHING

Element 9.1 Prepare forecasts of income and expenditure

Chapter

Performance criteria

In order to perform this element successfully you need to:

A	Identify relevant **data** for projecting **forecasts** from internal and external sources	1, 2, 4
B	Communicate with relevant individuals and give them the opportunity to raise queries and to clarify forecasts	Through out
C	Prepare forecasts in a clear format with explanations of assumptions, **projections** and adjustments	4, 8
D	Review and revise the validity of forecasts in the light of any significant anticipated changes	8, 9

Range statement

Performance in this element relates to the following contexts:

Data:

- Accounting information
- Wage and salary information
- Information about suppliers and availability of inputs
- Information about customers and markets
- General economic information

Forecasts:

- Income
- Expenditure

Projections:

- Trends
- Seasonal variations
- Market research

Element 9.2   Prepare draft budget proposals

Chapter

Performance criteria

In order to perform this element successfully you need to:

A	Present to management draft **budget** proposals in a clear and appropriate format and on schedule	8
B	Verify that draft budget proposals are consistent with organisational objectives and include all relevant **data** and assumptions	8, 9
C	Break down budgets into periods appropriate to the organisation	8
D	Communicate with budget holders in a manner which maintains goodwill and ensure budget proposals are agreed with budget holders	9

Range statement

Performance in this element relates to the following contexts:

Types of budgets:

· Budgets for income and expenditure

· Resource budgets (production budget, material budget, labour budget, fixed overhead budget)

· Capital budgets

Data:

· Accounting information

· Wage and salary information

· Market information

· General economic information

· Strategic plans

Element 9.3 Monitor the performance of responsibility centres against budgets

Chapter

Performance criteria

In order to perform this element successfully you need to:

A	Check and reconcile **budget** figures on an ongoing basis	8
B	Correctly code and allocate actual cost and revenue data to **responsibility centres**	9
C	Clearly and correctly identify **variances** and prepare relevant reports for management	5
D	Discuss with budget holders and other managers any significant variances and help managers take remedial action	5

Range statement

Performance in this element relates to the following contexts:

Types of budgets:

· Budget for income and expenditure

· Resource budget

· Fixed and flexible budgets

Responsibility centres:

· Expense centres

· Profit centres

Variances:

· Actual

· Potential

THE BUSINESS ENVIRONMENT

INTRODUCTION

This chapter provides general background information to the context of management accounting which is essential background knowledge and should be useful in answering tasks in examinations for both Unit 8 and Unit 9.

KNOWLEDGE & UNDERSTANDING

- External sources of information on costs and prices: government statistics, trade associations, financial press, quotations, price lists (Elements 8.1, 8.2, 9.1, 9.2 and 9.3)
- General economic environment (Elements 8.1, 8.2, 9.1, 9.2 and 9.3)
- How the accounting systems of an organisation are affected by its organisational structure, its administrative systems and procedures and the nature of its business transactions (Elements 8.1, 8.2, 9.1, 9.2 and 9.3)

CONTENTS

1. The business environment
2. Management information systems (MIS)
3. The role of the cost and management accountant
4. Organisational structure
5. General factors affecting forecasts
6. SWOT analysis

PERFORMANCE CRITERIA

- Identify valid, relevant information from internal and external sources (Element 8.1)
- Identify relevant data for projecting forecasts from internal and external sources (Element 9.1)

1 The business environment

1.1 Management accounting vs financial accounting

Accountants have to provide **information** to very diverse groups. The specific needs of each determine whether these can best be served by the financial accounting or the management accounting function of the business organisation. The main **differences between financial accounting and management accounting** are as follows:

· Financial accounting provides information to users who are **external** to the business, such as the shareholders of a company; management accounting is usually concerned with **internal** users of accounting information such as the managers of the business.

· Financial accounting draws up financial statements, the formats of which are governed by law and accounting standards for limited companies; management accounting reports can be in any format which suits the user and may differ considerably from one company to another.

· Financial accounting reports on **past** transactions; management accounting records historic transactions, compares actual figures to budget figures and hence makes **predictions for the future**.

Management VS Financial accounting	
Internal users	External users (Shareholders)
Market driven	Law governed
User-driven Format	Law-governed Format
Future	Past

Management accounting information can take many different forms as it is designed specifically to be of use to the managers of the business.

1.2 Cost accounting

Cost accounting is normally a large part of the management accounting role. It is primarily concerned with ascertainment of costs and it was developed to a great extent within a manufacturing context where costs can be difficult to isolate and analyse. In such a business there are two things which the financial accountant's profit and loss account will not disclose:

· the amount of profit attributable to each unit of a product or service;
· the amount of cost and/or revenue attributable to each manager.

The information provided by the cost accountant will be part of the **management information system** (MIS) of the business (often the major part). We shall first consider the nature of the MIS overall.

2 Management information systems (MIS)

> ☐ **DEFINITION** ☐☐☐☐
>
> A management information system (MIS) is a system using formalised procedures to provide managers at all levels with appropriate information from all relevant sources (internal and external to the business) for the purposes of planning and controlling the activities for which they are responsible.

An MIS has been defined as 'a system in which defined data are collected, processed and communicated to assist those responsible for the use of resources'.

2.1 Type of management information system

Each MIS will be determined by:
· the type of organisation or business;
· the products or services offered;
· the principal markets;
· the principal objectives;
· the organisation structure and reporting relationships;
· the principal users of information; and
· the use to which the information is put.

The information systems will operate within **different levels**, from the board of directors down to shop-floor supervisors, and within different functions (for example, production, marketing and finance).

The manner in which information is presented should depend on the recipient, so that the recipient obtains the maximum value from the information he is being given. It may be appropriate to present shop-floor supervisors with diagrams or bar charts that they can easily understand, while experienced financial managers should perhaps be presented with detailed tables of figures that they can themselves manipulate (e.g. with a spreadsheet program) to reach their own conclusions.

2.2 Why is management information needed?

Information is mainly needed:
· to assist management in **planning** the most effective use of resources, such as labour and materials;
· to assist management in **decision-making** (i.e. choosing between alternative courses of action), for example whether to make a product or purchase it from an outside supplier;
· to aid management in **controlling** day-to-day operations, for example by comparing actual results with those planned.

A manager will use resources in the light of the information that is relevant and available to him. The problem facing the chairman of a large group might be to decide how much funds to allocate to a particular activity, whereas a supervisor in the machine shop might be deciding which machine to use and which operators should be asked to operate it to produce a particular job.

Information is necessary at each level to **guide decisions** and, in due course, to **measure the effectiveness** of the action taken.

2.3 Requirements of management information

A successful business needs management capable of making decisions. In turn, a successful business manager must have the responsibility and authority to make those decisions. Irrespective of whether these decisions may dictate the future long-term policy or conduct of the business or simply its day to day routine operation, management must be equipped with **adequate and timely information.**

Management information may be of two types, as follows:
· information about the past results of the type of action envisaged – **historical information;**
· information about the future effects of decisions – **forecast information**.

2.4 Types of information

Three basic types of information have been identified:
(a) **Scorekeeping** – The accumulation of data to enable both internal and external parties to evaluate organisational performance and position. This embraces internal reporting for use in planning and controlling non-routine operations. To some extent this also embraces external reporting to shareholders, government and other external parties.
(b) **Attention-directing** – The reporting and the interpretation of information which helps managers to focus on operational problems, imperfections, inefficiencies and opportunities. This aspect of accounting assists managers with the provision of important data about the operations enabling timely decision making, whether on a long-term or a short-term basis.
(c) **Problem-solving** – This *ad hoc* aspect of accounting involves the concise quantification of the relative merits of possible courses of action, often with recommendations as to the best procedure. In this it is seen that the cost accountant is a very vital part of the management team.

2.5 Attributes of information

Since management at all levels must perform a certain amount of planning, decision-making and control, it is vital that the manager has the necessary information to perform his tasks. There are four fundamental attributes of information:
(a) **Relevance to the scope of responsibility.** A production manager will primarily be concerned with information about stocks, production levels, production performance and machine loads within his department. He will not be interested in the shortcomings of other departments unless they specifically affect his area.
(b) **Relevance to any particular decision.** This is a difficult one. Management have to be able to identify the decisions that need to be made.

This requires information that directs attention to specific problems. However, having identified the decisions, the information that enables the right decisions to be made needs to be acquired.

(c) **Production in time.** This is an area of great conflict for manager and accountant. Two of the most desirable attributes of the accountant's work are accuracy and timeliness. Of course, information to satisfy the requirements already outlined, must be accurate, but to be of use in the business it must be presented quickly. A beautiful, well written, superbly accurate report, covering and analysing all the facets of a particular problem and all the possible solutions and their consequences is useless if it cannot be prepared in time for the decision to be taken, or is delivered after the problem has been resolved.

(d) **Value.** This may be assessed by the resulting cost and benefit in the planned course of action. If a change takes place then the value is represented by the benefit in changing. The information also has a cost and the cost of obtaining information must be compared with the potential benefit arising from it.

For management information to be useful it must be provided to the appropriate manager, must be relevant, timely and cost effective.

2.6 The accounting information system

The major objective of most commercial organisations is to **make profits**. Consequently, the accounting system is a most important information system. It provides the basis for the process of budgetary planning and control and linking together the other information systems within the organisation, e.g. production, personnel, etc.

The purpose of an MIS is to determine, and to provide as efficiently, effectively and economically as possible, **what management need to know**. Since most of the information within any business is handled by the accounts department, the accountant, and particularly the cost accountant, is thus in a very important position.

3 The role of the cost and management accountant

3.1 The accountant's skills

The chief role of the accountant was traditionally **'stewardship'**. He began as the custodian of the firm's assets and the faithful recorder of their movement. Because profit is the net increase in asset values, stewardship gradually developed so that the emphasis fell on the **calculation of the organisation's profit**.

Stewardship involves the careful, effective and efficient use of assets, and so the management accountant is concerned with the pursuit of efficiency and of productivity in the use of the firm's resources, as well as with the generation of profits.

3.2 The functions of a management accountant

The management accountant helps managers to answer the following questions:

- **Score keeping** – How well have we done? The management accountant records, aggregates and presents costs so that we can see where profit has been made.
- **Control** – Did we do as well as we thought we would? Comparing actual results with the budget helps to identify where operations are not running according to plan. Investigation of the causes and subsequent action achieves effective control of the business.
- **Planning** – How well will we do next year? Primarily through preparation of a short-term annual budget, but also through long range strategic planning, planning enables all departments involved to be organised and avoids lack of goal congruence, i.e. individual managers seeking good results for their department but with a bad overall effect on the company.
- **Co-ordinating** – How can we overcome any identified problems so we can do even better next year? Bottlenecks, delays etc pinpointed by the questions above can be analysed and new strategies put in place to overcome them.
- **Decision-making** – How can we make the right decisions as new problems and opportunities come along?
- **Motivation** – How can we make sure that managers and staff are kept motivated to achieve the objectives of the organisation as measured by accounting information?

Management accounts will therefore serve a variety of purposes; it is no surprise then that they take a variety of forms. There is no set format; management accounts should include information relevant to their purpose.

4 Organisational structure

4.1 Behavioural aspects of decision-making

It is important to take account of the impact of any management decision or action on the **behavioural aspects** of the business.

Decision-making impacts on people involved in the organisation at all levels. The method of generating information on which those decisions are to be based will therefore impact on those people and may consequently influence their behaviour patterns. Therefore the management accountant must always bear in mind **how employees may react to different policies**.

This aspect will be examined later in the context of budgetary control.

4.2 Types of organisational structure

The management accountant must also be aware of the impact of his role on the **organisational structure** of the firm. A suitable organisational structure must be implemented to allow effective delegation of information-gathering roles and decision-making responsibility. This must allow for a chain of authority and information flow, and also to enable responsibility to rest at the appropriate level in the corporate hierarchy.

There are various ways in which an organisation may be structured. An important reason for imposing such structures is to make what may be a very large organisation more manageable, by breaking it down into smaller units. Here are some of the possible ways in which this might be achieved.

· A product structure: each product (or, more likely, each separate range of products) is regarded as a management unit.
· A geographical structure: separate geographical areas are regarded as management units. For example, a UK company might have a Northern Region, a Southern Region and a Midlands Region.
· A divisional structure: the organisation might be broken down into different trading units. For example, a manufacturer of computer hardware might have a Sales Division and a Maintenance Division.
· A function structure.
· A matrix structure.

These last two possibilities are discussed in more detail below.

4.3 Functional structure

There are advantages to the functional structure, mainly because it allows greater operational control at a senior level in an organisation, and linked to this is the clear definition of roles and tasks.

However, there are disadvantages, particularly as organisations become larger or more diverse. In such circumstances, senior managers can become burdened with everyday operational issues, or rely on their specialist skills, rather than taking a strategic perspective on problems. Such organisations are also likely to require co-operation between different functions since they cannot rely on lengthy vertical chains of decision-making.

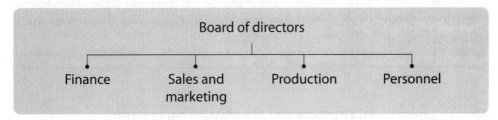

In the functional structure shown above the production department is responsible for manufacturing all the products sold by the organisation. Similarly the marketing department is responsible for marketing all the products. In principle the individual departments are separated from each other, though of course in practice a good deal of interaction will always be required.

4.4 Matrix structure

A matrix structure is a combination of structures. It usually takes the form of product and geographical divisions or functional and divisional structures operating in tandem.

Matrix organisation structures started in the US aircraft industry and gained rapid acceptance in the construction, aerospace and computer fields. A study in the UK in 1987 showed that the majority of large companies in the UK have a matrix organisation structure.

The structure can exist at departmental and company level, for example:

· *At department level* – A marketing department could have product managers on one axis, responsible for the 'total health' of respective products, whilst on the other axis there are heads of various marketing functions.
· *At company level* – A company may have managers in charge of a regional depot responsible for sales, servicing and distribution. At head office, each of these functions would be the responsibility of a senior manager.

An example is given below.

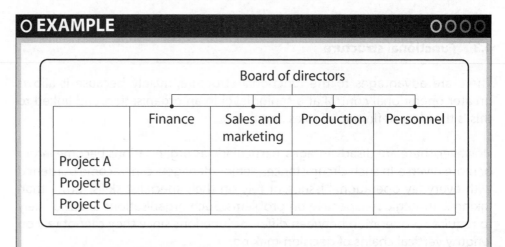

○ **EXAMPLE**   ○○○○

In the above structure, the emphasis is placed on the projects and the four functions (finance, sales, etc) have a specific responsibility to each of the projects.

4.5 Organisational structure and the accounting systems

If you compare the above two organisation charts you will see that typically the finance (or accounts) department is a separate function. However, unlike the other functions which communicate with each other but do not necessarily get involved in each other's operational affairs, the accounting function does get involved operationally with all the other functions. It is the role of the accounting function to monitor the performance of all functions in the company and report on their performance.

KAPLAN PUBLISHING

In general terms, the matrix type of structure will apply to more complex and larger organisations. The accounting function will therefore not simply have to report on the 'vertical' functions, but will also have to report on the horizontal divisions (whether they are projects or geographical areas or whatever other category suits the business).

This will require more sophisticated accounting systems, particularly coding systems. Thus, for example, the coding system will not simply have to identify costs and revenues as relating to, say, marketing, but will also have to identify them as relating to project A or B, etc. It will also require additional skills in the accounts department. These additional skills may be needed because in order to correctly evaluate the performance of let us say project A, it may be necessary to employ someone who has experience of such a project and who is therefore able to fully understand what the accounts mean and whether the results are reasonable given the typical environment and problems that such a project is likely to encounter.

5 General factors affecting forecasts

5.1 Forecasting and long-range planning

Long-range plans are often based on estimates of the future from extrapolations of the past to find trends, a method which can be fairly accurate in the short term. However, using data and relationships derived from past behaviour is limited in that such data cannot forecast something which has never happened before, nor can it accurately forecast very far ahead.

If a company were to rely solely on forecasting rather than long-range planning, it would need to operate in a very predictable environment. Planning is an attempt to control outcomes whereas forecasting is a more passive attempt to predict outcomes, making educated guesses about the future.

Long-range planning is concerned with deciding which courses of action the organisation should take for the future. Corporate long-range planning does not attempt to minimise risks as, usually, the greater the risk the higher the return, but it helps to ensure that the organisation takes the right kind of risks with the best possible knowledge of the consequences.

5.2 Forecasting economic change

Forecasting changes in the external economy is an area fraught with problems and there are various conflicting views on the appropriate model to use. However, it is still essential for a company to be aware of likely trends in, for example, gross domestic product per capita. To this end, many large organisations have their own models or adapt the findings of other models to reflect their requirements. Whatever the applicability of the models for forecasting the likely effects on a particular organisation, it would be foolish to ignore trends in consumer incomes and expenditure, and sources of long-term finance.

5.3 External sources of information for assessing economic change

- The Government's National Statistics (available on the internet).
- Government reports on particular industries.
- Reports prepared by international bodies, such as the UN, OECD and EU.
- Commercial publications dealing with economic matters of particular industries.
- Publications by trade associations and professional organisations.
- Bank reviews.
- Stockbroker reports.
- Statistics from advertising agencies.
- Special sampling surveys.
- Price lists and quotations from suppliers and competitors.

Source: National Statistics website: http://www.statistics.gov.uk

Management must monitor a wide range of external sources of information so that their decisions on managing costs and setting prices fit in with the prevailing environment.

In principle, data can either be **primary** data, gathered for the purpose in hand, or **secondary** data, gathered for another purpose but used by the business for the purpose in hand. There is an inherent limitation in using published statistics for a secondary purpose, since the statistics were not expressly gathered for the purpose they are being put to by the business.

5.4 General economic environment

As a result of government intervention the plans of companies can require revision. The government's task is to keep the economy in balance and this may well result in a stop-go type of policy, particularly towards the end of the life of a parliament. Management must therefore be prepared to rethink drastically and immediately should the situation arise.

The effective business can act in the manner of a detective and by keeping track of party political publications try to predict likely governmental changes and when they will occur. Remember that policies can change drastically with a change of government.

5.5 Social and environmental responsibility

Regularly in the media there are examples of companies that are considered to lack social responsibility because they fail to protect the area surrounding their factories from the hazards of their product or because they treat their staff or members of the public shabbily. Society today is far more socially aware and will not accept hazards which can be avoided. This developing awareness has resulted in changes in the attitudes of companies.

Awareness of the activities of pressure groups can be of critical importance to business planning. Often items that start off as aspects of consumer pressure can lead to legislative controls.

Society today is far more sensitive to environmental hazards

5.6 Indicators

Indicators of likely change in the wider environment can be identified. Thus for example problems which are occurring currently may indicate major changes, such as late payment from a customer highlighting possible trading difficulties or potential bankruptcy. Current political changes within a country may indicate future problems for the supply of raw materials and availability of markets.

The degree of influence that suppliers, markets etc have on the organisation will determine the priority which should be given to these indicators in the planning process.

5.7 The importance of trends

It is important to be able to identify trends in market competition. Increasing competition can provide the threat of likely takeover or the need to merge with another organisation in order to obtain from larger production units any economies of scale available. It is also important to realise that increasing competition, perhaps even within the context of a diminishing market, may present an opportunity. An efficient organisation should be capable of successfully competing, and where organisations go into liquidation this will free sections of the market previously served by the liquidated enterprises.

6 SWOT analysis

6.1 Introduction

Before any long-term planning decision can be made, four factors have to be taken into consideration: the organisation's **strengths** and **weaknesses**, and the **opportunities** and **threats** presented to the organisation by its environment (SWOT analysis)

·   Internal appraisal is the assessment of the strengths and weaknesses of an organisation.
·   External appraisal is the assessment of opportunities and threats.

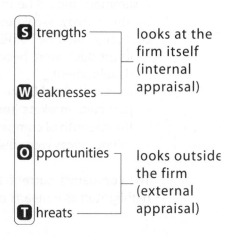

6.2 Internal appraisal – strengths and weaknesses

The object is to ascertain the company's strengths and areas where improvements can be made, and to forecast what the results may be if the company continues as it is, in the light of information at present available to it. The review should be organised and co-ordinated throughout the company and carried out in a way that motivates management to face up to the true issues and think constructively and not defensively.

6.3 Elements of the review

Such a review should include the following.

(a) A comprehensive review of the company's results.

(b) An investigation to ascertain the strengths of the company (the areas in which it has exclusive skills or does well as compared with competitive standards) and areas where significant improvements are needed. The word 'improvements' is used instead of 'weaknesses' because people are reluctant to confess to weaknesses and are likely to make a better contribution if they are asked to suggest how they think improvements can be made.

(c) Comparisons with competitors, and other industries where useful. It is this feature which gives the internal appraisal its alternative title of 'competitive audit'.

The main areas considered in a strengths and weaknesses survey would include the following:

· Products
· Marketing
· Distribution
· Production
· Research and development
· Human resources
· Finance

6.4 Presentation of the results

A summary should be made of the major strengths and weaknesses revealed by this survey. Weaknesses indicate areas of 'vulnerability'; for example, a company could be vulnerable to adverse conditions if:

· its products were becoming obsolete, and could be replaced by competitors' developments;
· it were short of liquid resources;
· particular markets (for example, overseas) ceased to be available;
· the strength of competition were augmented by amalgamations or mergers;
· selling prices were being forced below an economic level.

The company's current strengths may relate to similar areas, and should be highlighted as a means by which the company can increase its profits.

6.5   Need for continuous reviews

The absence of an objective analysis of the organisation's strengths and weaknesses may result in the selection of a strategy which is totally inadequate or inappropriate. Circumstances change rapidly and it is therefore necessary to see the process of internal appraisal as a continuous monitoring of critical aspects of the business. A single snapshot of the organisation is only relevant for one point in time and consequently continual review is essential.

6.6   External appraisal – opportunities and threats (PEST analysis)

> ## ☐ DEFINITION   ☐☐☐☐
>
> External analysis is often referred to as PEST analysis because it focuses on Politics (Government), Economics, Social policy and Technology. To this we have added competition.

6.7   Politics (Government)

Environmental legislation, concerning the control of pollution and health hazards, can affect the future plans of a company. The banning of the use of a particular substance (e.g. asbestos) will initially represent a threat to the manufacturers and to suppliers of goods that use it, but it will also present an opportunity for the development of new replacement products.

Full use needs to be made of government grants and tax concessions available in the industry. Plans for the levels and directions of government spending must be monitored carefully for business opportunities and threats.

6.8   Economics

General economic conditions and trends are critical to the success of an organisation. Wages, price changes by suppliers and competitors, and government policies affect both the costs of producing products or offering services and the market conditions under which they are sold.

Common economic indicators measure national income and national product, savings, investment, prices, wages, productivity, employment, government activities, and international transactions. All these factors vary over time, and managers can usefully devote part of their organisation's time and resources to forecasting the economy and anticipating changes.

6.9   Social aspects

Changes in demographic variables – such as age, sex, family size, income, occupation, education, nationality and social class – can have major effects upon the organisation.

People's attitudes and values are an important consideration and are reflected in their lifestyles. In recent years, change rather than stability has become the norm for lifestyle in the UK. For example, families account for a shrinking proportion of UK households and fewer of these families include married couples; households consisting of single adults and one-parent families are becoming more numerous.

Other lifestyle changes include a trend towards better education. Smaller cars, oven-ready meals and paid household help are only a few examples of new consumption patterns. Physical fitness has experienced a big surge in popularity, and other home-centred activities – notably satellite TV, video recorders and DVD players – are more and more prevalent.

All these factors will have an effect, favourable or adverse, upon businesses in the consumer sector.

6.10 Technology

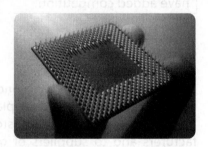

The level of technology in a particular industry determines to a large extent what products and services will be produced, what equipment will be used and how operations will be managed.

Technological development begins with basic research, when a scientist discovers some new phenomenon; other researchers then examine the breakthrough for its potential. If further development leads to a workable prototype and engineering refinements make commercial exploitation practical, then the technology is finally put to use and may be widely adopted.

6.11 Competitors

The degree of competition between organisations already operating within the market is likely to be based on:
· whether there is a dominant organisation(s) – generally the most stable markets have dominant organisations;
· whether the market is growing or declining – generally when markets are entering a 'maturity' phase and firms are trying to establish themselves as market leaders, competitive rivalry will be high;
· whether the product or service can be differentiated between competitors – generally if products and services can be clearly differentiated then competitive rivalry will be lower;
· whether the economy is in recession or booming – generally as an economy goes into recession competitive rivalry will intensify in an attempt to 'survive'.

The 'degree' competition will be reduced by the effectiveness of any barriers to entry. Typical barriers to entry are as follows:
(a) **Financial or capital requirement of entry.** The amount of capital required may not be the major barrier to entry but rather the availability and cost of raising finance.

KAPLAN PUBLISHING

(b) **The patterns of distribution or access to distribution channels.** The soft drinks industry in the UK for example, was traditionally dominated by two companies because brewers such as Bass and Whitbread owned the soft drinks companies and the distribution outlets (i.e. the public houses). This pattern of distribution, however, has been forced to change with government legislation now restricting the number of public houses that can be owned by brewers.

(c) **Government legislation** and changes in such legislation obviously have a major effect on barriers to entry. Deregulation and privatisation has meant that extensive barriers to entry have now been lowered in an attempt to make markets contestable.

There are other barriers to entry such as advertising, patents and trade secrets, but it is not possible to state which are the most important. What is important is the recognition that barriers to entry have a major impact on the threat of potential entry.

7   Test your knowledge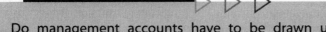

1   Do management accounts have to be drawn up in compliance with mandatory statutory formats?

2   Define a management information system.

3   State three attributes of valuable information.

4   What is the difference between planning and forecasting?

5   What is the difference between primary data and secondary data?

6   What do the four letters of SWOT analysis stand for?   [Answers on p. 16]

8   Summary

The cost accountant is mainly concerned with the proper recording and analysis of costs incurred in a business in a manner that will enable management to control current operations and plan and make decisions for the future.

Effective communication with the workforce and management is vital and will be achieved via the following:
(a) a suitable organisational structure;
(b) reports produced on a timely basis.

This chapter also considered internal and external information which affects forecasts, and then looked at SWOT and PEST analysis which are ways of assessing the company's strategic location in the business environment it is operating in.

Answers to 'test your knowledge' questions

Test your knowledge

1   No. Companies must draw up their financial accounts in statutory formats. Management accounts can use any format that management find useful.

2   A management information system is a system providing managers at all levels with the information that they need to carry out their roles.

3   Information should be relevant, timely and cost-effective. (Also reliable and understandable.)

4   Planning is an attempt to control future outcomes, while forecasting is a more passive attempt to predict what is likely to happen.

5   Primary data was collected for the purpose in hand, while secondary data was originally collected for some other purpose.

6   SWOT stands for strengths, weaknesses, opportunities and threats.

KAPLAN PUBLISHING

COLLECTION OF COST INFORMATION

INTRODUCTION

This chapter is concerned with the classification of costs by behaviour. Much of the information here has been met in previous units so should be considered to be revision of relevant areas.

Some costs change when activity levels change, whilst others do not. The ability to isolate cost elements by behaviour is essential to management who are concerned with predicting future costs as part of the planning and decision making processes. It will also be necessary to enable a marginal costing approach to be taken, as covered in the next chapter.

KNOWLEDGE & UNDERSTANDING

- Marginal and absorption costing: cost recording, cost reporting and cost behaviour (Elements 8.1, 8.2, 9.2 and 9.3)

CONTENTS

1 Cost accounting
2 The cost accounting department
3 Cost units
4 Cost centres
5 Cost classification
6 Cost behaviour
7 Cost estimation
8 The high/low method

PERFORMANCE CRITERIA

- Identify valid, relevant information from internal and external sources (Element 8.1)
- Identify relevant data for preparing forecasts and budgets from internal and external sources (Element 9.1)
- Analyse the effect of organisational accounting policies on reported costs (Element 8.1)

1 Cost accounting

1.1 The need for cost accounting

Historically, financial accounts have reflected the transactions of a business entity in its relationships with the outside world: customers, suppliers, employees, shareholders and other investors. To this end, financial accounting has been geared up to the preparation of annual and other periodic accounts, with the emphasis upon statutory requirements.

A typical profit and loss account statement follows the following general layout (in summary).

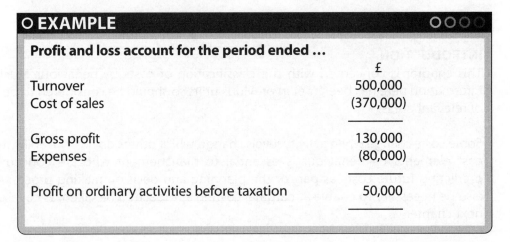

○ EXAMPLE ○○○○

Profit and loss account for the period ended ...

	£
Turnover	500,000
Cost of sales	(370,000)
Gross profit	130,000
Expenses	(80,000)
Profit on ordinary activities before taxation	50,000

Typically the profit and loss account will include a subjective analysis of expenses according to category either by function (distribution/administrative) or by nature (materials/staff costs/depreciation). Despite some recent changes, financial accounts do not readily disclose:

(a)   profit performance by individual products, services or activity; but more importantly
(b)   the responsibility of individual managers for performance.

Thus financial accounts can only provide 'scorekeeping' statistical information, rather than information that will form the basis of decision-making or control. The provision of this additional detail is one of the functions of cost accounting: cost-finding.

□ DEFINITION □□□□

Cost-finding means taking the transactions which make up the financial accounts and analysing them to turn data into information which will be more helpful to the managers of the business. This will be an 'objective' analysis, matching the expenses to the purposes for which they were incurred. This analysis may be done on a purely memorandum basis, the results being reconciled with the financial records, or it may be sometimes incorporated into the general bookkeeping system of the company.

Whichever procedure is adopted, cost accounting has two important effects on business documentation:

(a)   Additional internal documents will be needed to identify which products or departments are affected by various transactions.

(b)   Additional data regarding transactions will be needed to assist accurate classification and analysis.

○ EXAMPLE   ○ ○ ○ ○

Assume that the profit and loss account illustrated above related to a company marketing four different products during a particular month. For management a more detailed analysis is required.

Solution

From his analysis of the source documents (purchase invoices, payrolls, petty cash vouchers and so on), the cost accountant is able to provide the following detailed report.

	Product A	Product B	Product C	Product D	Total
Sales					
Quantity	315,000	32,500	80,500	28,100	–
Price per unit	£0.50	£2.50	£1.50	£5.00	–
Amount	£157,500	£81,250	£120,750	£140,500	£500,000
	£	£	£	£	£
Costs					
Materials	50,000	40,000	75,000	85,000	250,000
Wages	40,000	30,000	20,000	30,000	120,000
Expenses	22,000	25,500	17,500	15,000	80,000
Total	112,000	95,500	112,500	130,000	450,000
Net profit/(loss) before tax	45,500	(14,250)	8,250	10,500	50,000

From this 'product profit and loss account', the managers of the business can see that the total profit of £50,000 resulted from profits on products A, C and D, offset by a loss on product B, and that product A alone yielded 91% of the company total.

We do not know at this stage whether the information will lead them to take any decision to change things for the future, because we do not know whether the above result is in accordance with a deliberate plan or not. Nor can we be sure without further information whether it would be a good thing to discontinue product B since such a decision might involve some further analysis of the costs incurred, and some forecasts of future developments.

Both comparisons against plan and the preparation of special analyses for decision purposes fall within the scope of the cost accounting function.

2   The cost accounting department

2.1   Data required for reports

A company's requirements for historical information include three main types of data:

(a)   Data from the normal financial accounts of the business: the balance sheet and profit and loss account with their supporting notes and schedules, and the cash flow statement.

(b)   Data obtained by analysing the accounts of the business, identifying items with cost units and cost centres: in other words the work of the cost accounting department (details of stockholdings would come from this source).

(c)   Data derived immediately from source documents without evaluation, such as statistics on labour efficiency, material usage, sickness, absenteeism and machine breakdowns.

In addition, most reports will include comparisons with budgets, standards, targets or estimates, and the explanations of variances based on detailed investigation and close knowledge of the data used in budget preparation.

2.2 Organisation

The accounts department, therefore, comprises a financial accounting segment, a costing segment and a budgetary control segment. The extent to which these are separate departments within the organisation depends on the number and diversity of the transactions to be handled and on the management organisation of the business, including the extent of divisional autonomy. All these factors affect the required number of accounting staff and the consequent need for specialisation of effort.

2.3 Cost recording

The cost department is responsible for maintaining the cost accounting records. To be effective these records should:

(a)   analyse production, administration and marketing costs to facilitate cost and profit computations, stock valuations, forecast and budget data and decision-making data;

(b)   enable the production of periodic performance statements which are necessary for management control purposes;

(c)   permit analysis of:

    (i)   past costs for profit measurement and stock valuation;

    (ii)   present costs for control purposes;

    (iii)   future costs - forecasts, targets, budgets and decision-making.

2.4 Cost accountant and other managers

Because his job is to interpret physical facts into money values, the cost accountant is in an excellent position to ensure that all types of report are integrated and are prepared on a consistent basis. Although inevitably other departments will wish to report on their own activities, the cost accountant should maintain close liaison and build a good relationship with them so that:

(a)   the information he provides can assist them in interpreting the results of their own activities;

(b)   there is no conflict on questions of fact between reports prepared by, for example, the sales manager or the production manager and the information emerging from the costing system.

2.5   Cost accounting and computers

Whilst records can be maintained manually, computer-based data concerning sales and production quantities, stock levels, costs, etc will assist the cost accounting function in the following ways:

(a)   Reports and cost accounts can be prepared quickly.

(b)   Information for decision-making will be more plentiful and be available more speedily than would be the case with manual data.

(c)   Large volumes of data can be stored and manipulated with ease.

Computers assist the accounting function in many ways

2.6   The benefits of cost accounting

The benefits of cost accounting can be identified as:

(a)   disclosure of profitable and non-profitable activities (as might appear in the product profit and loss account already illustrated). This data could also be modified to identify locations which are unprofitable;

(b)   identification of waste and inefficiency, particularly in relation to usage of materials and labour;

(c)   analysis of movements in profit;

(d)   assistance in the determination of selling prices;

(e)   valuation of stocks (there are auditing and taxation implications here);

(f)   development of planning and control information;

(g)   evaluation of the cost effect of policy decisions.

3   Cost units

3.1   Cost units

> ☐ **DEFINITION**   ☐☐☐☐
>
> A cost unit is a quantitative unit of product or service in relation to which costs are ascertained.

○ EXAMPLE　　　　　　　　　　　　　　　○○○○

Have a look at the costing profit and loss account illustrated earlier. This showed the sales quantity of various products (A-D) and the total cost of those sales under the headings materials, wages and expenses.

Further additional calculations could be made from that example.

Solution

Calculation of cost per unit for the month ended ... 20X...

	Product A	Product B	Product C	Product D
	£	£	£	£
Materials	0.16	1.23	0.93	3.02
Wages	0.13	0.92	0.25	1.07
Expenses	0.07	0.78	0.22	0.53
Total cost per unit	0.36	2.93	1.40	4.62

We have taken the total costs attributable to each product in a month (any other period could have been used) and arrived at the average cost per unit of each product, rounded to the nearest penny, by dividing the totals by the numbers of units involved. The 'cost unit' in this instance is the unit of product sold.

The cost unit might have been a piece, a pack, a kilogram, a litre or any other measure appropriate to what was being produced.

3.2　Average unit costs

The average unit cost approach can be used in mining

In practice the business would probably have produced more units than it sold in the period, the unsold quantity being taken into stock. In such a case, the costs of production would have been collected and divided by the number of units produced to give the average unit cost. This would have been applied to the number of units sold to give the cost of sales, and to the number of units remaining to give the costs of the residual stock.

This average unit cost approach is used whenever production is continuous and leads to uniform product units, as in the case of many chemical plants, food processors or extractive operations such as mining and quarrying.

3.3　Job costs

Some businesses, however, undertake special jobs for their customers. A workshop making tools and jigs does this; and so on a much larger scale does the contractor building bridges or putting up a factory. In such cases, costs are first analysed between the various jobs or contracts, and then the costs of the jobs invoiced will be gathered together into the periodic summary profit and loss account. For such businesses, in other words, the 'cost unit' is the job or contract.

3.4 Batch costs

In the manufacture of mechanical or electrical components, such products are customarily made in batches of say 1,000 or 10,000 items, according to the circumstances of the case. In this type of business, the cost of each batch is determined and the batch is the primary 'cost unit'. Thereafter it is possible, if desired, to calculate the average cost per item in the batch.

3.5 Non-manufacturing cost units

The above examples have concentrated on cost units for production or manufacturing processes. Examples of cost units for service industries, or non-manufacturing activities within a business are as follows:

Service industry/activity	Cost unit
Accountants	Chargeable hour
College	Student enrolled
Hotel	Bed-night
Hospital	Patient-day
Transport department	kg-mile
Credit control department	Customer account
Selling	Calls made
Maintenance department	Man-hours

Note that some of these are in fact composite cost units, where a cost is considered to be dependent upon two main factors. For example, if the manager of a chain of hotels wanted to compare costs between two of the hotels, calculating costs per bed would not take account of the differing levels of occupation of the beds of the two hotels. Thus the cost can be calculated per bed-night (i.e. the cost of one bed per night of occupation).

A cost unit is a quantitative unit of product or service in relation to which costs are ascertained; the purpose of product costing is to arrive at the cost of the cost unit appropriate to the business concerned.

4 Cost centres

□ DEFINITION

A cost centre is a location, function or item(s) of equipment in respect of which costs may be accumulated and related to cost units for control purposes.

A cost centre therefore is used as an initial collection point for costs; once the total cost of operating the cost centre for a period has been ascertained, it can be related to the cost units that have passed through the cost centre.

The location, function or item of equipment referred to in the definition can be directly related to production, to a service department or to a business.

4.1 Examples of cost centres

Assembly lines are an example of a production cost centre

Production	Assembly line
	Packing machine
Service department	Stores
	Canteen
	Quality control
Service	Tax department (accountants)
	Ward (hospital)
	Faculty (college)

4.2 Responsibility for cost centres

Control can only be exercised by people, and for every cost somebody must be responsible; so whether a cost centre is impersonal or personal there must always be a manager in whose sphere of responsibility that cost centre is included.

4.3 Profit centres

> **□ DEFINITION** □□□□
>
> A profit centre is a location, function or item(s) of equipment in respect of which costs and revenues may be ascertained for the purposes of control of the resulting profit.

Thus, while the paint shop in a factory might be treated as a cost centre (to monitor the costs incurred there), a large company might treat its French operations as a profit centre (since they generate both costs and revenues).

5 Cost classification

5.1 Types of cost classification

Costs can be classified (collected into logical groups) in many ways. The particular classification selected will depend upon the purpose for which the resulting analysed data will be used.

Purpose	Classification
Cost control	By nature – materials, labour, overheads, etc.
Cost accounts	By relationship to cost units – direct/indirect costs, etc.
Budgeting, contribution analysis	By behaviour – fixed/variable costs.
Decision-making	Relevant and non-relevant costs.
Responsibility accounting	Controllable and uncontrollable costs.

You will come across these classifications in more detail as you work through this study text. At this stage, we will revise the basic classification terms used in cost accounting.

5.2 Direct and indirect costs

For cost accounting purposes, the costs of the business will be classified in quite a different way from the analysis required by a financial accountant for the profit and loss account in published accounts.

The basic classification of costs in cost accounting may be illustrated as follows.

○ EXAMPLE ○○○○

	£	£
Direct costs		
Direct materials		250,000
Direct labour		120,000
Direct expenses		10,000
		―――
Prime cost (= total of direct costs)		380,000
Indirect production costs		25,000
		―――
Production cost		405,000
Indirect non-production costs		
Administration overhead	20,000	
Selling and distribution overhead	25,000	
	―――	
		45,000
		―――
Total cost		450,000
		―――

5.3 Direct costs

□ DEFINITION ▫▫▫▫

Direct costs are costs which can be related directly to one cost unit. Direct costs comprise direct materials, direct labour and direct expenses.

For example, considering a cost unit of a chair, direct costs will include the cost of wood and screws used (direct material cost) and the cost of manufacturing labour hours per chair (direct labour cost).

In a service context, the direct costs relating to, say, a student enrolled at a college would include the costs of books provided, individual tuition and marking costs.

5.4 Indirect costs

□ DEFINITION ▫▫▫▫

Indirect costs cannot be identified directly with a cost unit and are often referred to as *overheads*.

For stock valuation purposes a distinction needs to be made between overheads incurred in the production process (factory costs, eg factory rent and rates, power etc) and non-production costs.

Non-production costs are indirect costs involved in converting finished goods into revenue, comprising:

(a)   administrative overhead costs (eg executive salaries and office costs); and

(b)   marketing, selling and distribution overhead costs.

Non-production costs are not included in stock valuation since they are not costs of making a product, but costs of selling it. Stock on hand at the end of a period is valued at total production cost only, including production overheads (in a total absorption costing system). We shall return to this point in the next chapter.

Considering the cost unit of a chair, the salaries of the sales representatives who promote and sell the chairs to retail outlets would be a selling overhead.

Indirect costs associated with a college would include premises running costs, lecturers' salaries and administrative staff costs.

Overhead costs can always be identified with cost centres; and because cost centres are the responsibility of particular functional managers one will find overheads classified according to the main functional divisions of the business.

6   Cost behaviour

6.1   The nature of costs

We mentioned earlier the need for cost classification by behaviour for budgeting purposes. In order to make predictions of future cost levels, we must determine the basis of the charge.

As an example, consider the cost of direct materials expected next month. The charge would depend on the amount used and the cost per unit. The amount used would depend, in turn, on the production anticipated for the period.

In order to derive this cost therefore we must make an estimate such as the following:

(a)   Production levels   10,000 units

(b)   Usage of materials per unit:
         Material A   2 kg
         Material B   1 kg
         Material C   0.2 kg

(c)   Costs of materials:
         Material A   30 pence per kg
         Material B   25 pence per kg
         Material C   50 pence per kg

Estimate of next month's material cost

		£
Material A	20,000 kg @ 30p/kg	6,000
Material B	10,000 kg @ 25p/kg	2,500
Material C	2,000 kg @ 50p/kg	1,000
Total estimated material cost		9,500

6.2 Variable costs

What have we done? We have set up a simple mathematical model which will, for any level of production, usage and cost of materials, enable the total level of cost in a future period to be predicted. The direct materials example was perhaps the easiest to use and, in practice, we may wish to deal with other variables which affect the cost such as wastage rates thus producing a slightly more complex model.

Direct labour costs may tend to vary due to changes in productivity and other factors in addition to the more obvious variables such as grade and rate of payment. A certain amount of estimation will still be required; if payment is on a production related basis we would expect a cost which, like materials, will vary in line with the volume of production.

At this stage, therefore, we have come to the rule-of-thumb guide that direct material, labour and expenses will probably vary roughly in line with anticipated production levels or the level of activity. We call such costs **variable costs**.

6.3 Fixed costs

This will not be the case with all costs. If we take the cost of rent and rates, for example, the charge is not determined on the basis of the intensity of usage of the premises but rather on the basis of time. Costs that are unaffected by the volume of production are called **fixed costs**. Rent and rates are an example. Labour paid on a time basis would also fall under this heading. How then can we predict the cost of such expenses for next month? Well, there is no difficulty in doing this as all we have to do is consult our rental agreement and the rates notice and we can forecast with complete certainty what these costs will be for the month.

6.4 Classification of costs by behaviour

The above example illustrates the need for cost behaviour classification. For cost prediction purposes, we must make a distinction between costs which vary with production or activity levels (variable costs) and those which do not (fixed costs). There also exists a type of cost which moves in sympathy with production levels but contains an element which does not, such as an electricity charge which contains a minimum standing charge plus an element which relates to the usage of the period. Such a cost would be described as semi-variable or mixed.

□ DEFINITIONS

Variable costs are those that vary (usually assumed in direct proportion) with changes in level of activity of the cost centre to which they relate (e.g. output volume), for example the raw material used in a product. It should be noted that the variable cost per unit may not remain constant over a wide range. It may be possible, for example, to obtain discounts for large purchases of material, reducing the cost per unit.

Fixed costs are those that accrue with the passage of time and are not affected by changes in activity level; they are therefore also known as period costs, for example rent of premises.

Stepped costs are fixed over a range of output and then suddenly increase in one big jump, for example a staffing level of up to 20 people may only require one supervisor but, if the staff level is more than 20, an extra supervisor will be needed.

Semi-variable (mixed) costs contain both a fixed and a variable element. When output is nil, the fixed element is incurred, but they also increase, like variable costs, as output increases. An example is telephone charges where there is a fixed rental to which is added the charge for calls made. These are also sometimes known as semi-fixed costs.

6.5 Graphical illustrations

Various cost behaviour patterns are illustrated in the graphs below.

(a)　**Variable cost**: direct materials, the purchase price per unit being constant

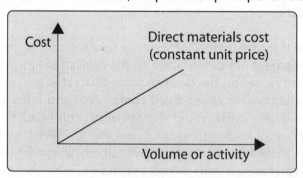

(b)　**Fixed cost**: rent of factory payable under a long-term lease

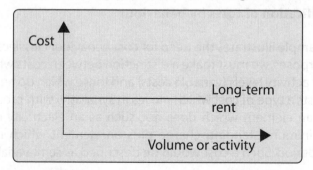

(c)   Stepped costs

   (i)   Canteen cost where additional assistants are required as increases
          in activity result in larger numbers of factory personnel

   (ii)   Rent of premises, additional accommodation eventually being
          required

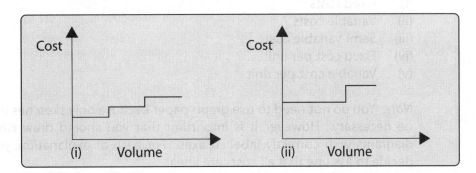

(d)   Semi-variable costs

   (i)   Direct materials cost (trade discount at higher levels of activity)

   (ii)   Salesmen's remuneration with added commission from a certain
          level of activity

   (iii) Electricity charges comprising a fixed standing charge and variable
          unit charge

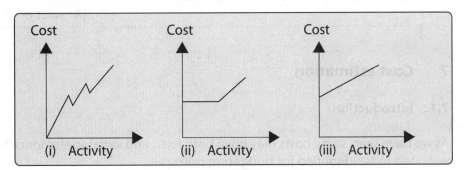

The common approach is as follows:

(a)   Treat as variable those costs which change by regular steps.

(b)   Treat as fixed those costs which only change at wide intervals of activity;
       this recognises that review will be required if there is a permanent
       change in the normal level of activity.

▷ ACTIVITY 1   ▷ ▷ ▷ ▷

AB Limited (AAT CA J94)

You have been asked to give a short talk to new employees who are attend-
ing your company's trainee induction programme. The talk will be entitled
The importance of understanding cost behaviour.

You are now in the process of preparing materials for your talk.

Required

(a) You have decided that you will use sketch graphs to demonstrate cost behaviour patterns. In preparation for your talk, produce sketch graphs which will demonstrate the way in which the following costs behave in relation to the level of activity:

(i) Fixed costs
(ii) Variable costs
(iii) Semi-variable costs
(iv) Fixed cost per unit
(v) Variable cost per unit

Note: You do not need to use graph paper because only sketches will be necessary. However, it is important that you should draw clear diagrams with correctly labelled axes. For ease of explanation, you decide to assume that all costs are linear.

(b) For each of the graphs in (a), prepare brief notes for your talk which explain the shape of the graph. Also note down **two** examples of each of costs (i), (ii) and (iii) above so that you can give them to your audience if requested.

(c) Prepare a further brief set of notes for your talk which explains why an understanding of cost behaviour patterns is necessary for effective planning and control in an organisation.

[Answer on p. 35]

7 Cost estimation

7.1 Introduction

As we have seen, some costs may have both fixed and variable elements. These will need to be identified for budgeting purposes.

If it is not easy to do this directly (as it is in the case of the telephone cost, where the bill clearly shows the fixed charge and rate per unit), then an analysis of past cost and volume data will need to be carried out.

7.2 Methods of cost estimation

It is assumed that there is a linear relationship, ie:

Total cost = Fixed cost + (Variable cost per unit × Units produced)

and that the total fixed cost and the variable cost per unit are constant at all levels of production unless told otherwise.

Possible techniques include the high/low method and linear regression.

8 The high/low method

8.1 Introduction

This is a simple method of estimating future costs from past results. It takes the costs for the highest and lowest activity levels, and assumes that a linear relationship covers the range in between.

○ EXAMPLE   ○○○

Widgets are produced by a process that incurs both fixed and variable costs.

Total costs have been recorded for the process for each of the last six months as follows.

Month	Output (units)	Total cost £
1	4,500	33,750
2	3,500	30,500
3	5,100	34,130
4	6,200	38,600
5	5,700	38,000
6	4,100	31,900

(a) What is the estimated fixed cost element and estimated variable cost per unit?

(b) What would be the estimated total cost at the budgeted activity level for month 7 of 6,000 units?

Solution

Select the months with the highest and lowest output levels as follows.

	Output (units)	Total cost £
Lowest output	3,500	30,500
Highest output	6,200	38,600
	———	———
Increase	2,700	8,100
	———	———

For an increase of 2,700 units, cost has increased by £8,100. If we assume that the fixed cost element remains constant, this cost increase must represent a change in variable costs only.

Assuming a straight-line relationship, then the variable cost per unit =

$\frac{£8,100}{2,700}$ = £3 per unit

Note that the factor determining which values to choose is the total cost at the highest output level and the total cost at the lowest output level. These are not necessarily the highest and lowest costs. The high/low observations are always based on the independent variable (in this case, output).

We can now substitute back into either of the two output levels to obtain the fixed cost.

At the 3,500 units level:

	£
Total cost	30,500
Variable cost (3,500 × £3)	(10,500)
Fixed costs	20,000

As a check on the accuracy of the calculations, at the 6,200 units level:

	£
Total costs	38,600
Variable cost (6,200 × £3)	(18,600)
Fixed costs	20,000

(a) Therefore the estimated fixed cost element is £20,000 and the estimated variable cost is £3 per unit.

(b) At an output level of 6,000 units the total estimated cost would be:

	£
Variable cost (6,000 × £3)	18,000
Fixed cost	20,000
Total cost	38,000

8.2 Advantages of high-low method

· Simple to operate.
· Easy to understand.

8.3 Disadvantages of high-low method

The problem with the high-low method is that it could give a completely inaccurate result. This is because we are only considering two sets of data, and ignoring all of the others. It is possible that the points we have chosen are completely unrepresentative of the rest of the data. This is a distinct possibility since we have chosen the two points at the extreme ends of the activity range. At these levels it is more likely that operating conditions will be atypical compared with more normal output. One way around this problem is to choose the 'next to highest' and 'next to lowest' figures, but this destroys some of the simplicity of the model.

▷ ACTIVITY 2 ▷ ▷ ▷

Production

Given below are the production quantities and production overhead costs for each of the last six months:

Month	Production quantity (units)	Production overheads £
January	10,000	58,000
February	9,000	50,000
March	12,000	65,000
April	11,000	62,000
May	8,000	45,000
June	9,500	52,000

Production in July is anticipated to be 10,500 units. What should be the amount of budgeted production overhead for July?

[Answer on p. 36]

9 Test your knowledge ▷ ▷ ▷

1   List three benefits of accurate cost accounting.

2   What is the cost unit in batch processing?

3   Give two examples of service cost centres in a manufacturing business.

4   What is a profit centre?

5   What is meant by prime cost?

6   Is direct labour typically a variable cost or a fixed cost?

7   Give an example of a stepped cost.

8   Factory costs were £80,000 in January when output was 20,000 units, and £90,000 in February when output was 30,000 units. What factory cost is expected for March when output is expected to be 32,000 units?

[Answers on p. 37]

10 Summary

Much of cost accounting is about gathering information about current costs and making predictions about future costs. Some costs, direct costs, can be allocated directly to a cost unit whereas other costs, indirect costs or overheads, are allocated initially to a cost centre.

Costs can also be usefully classified according to their behaviour. This is particularly useful when budgeting costs for future periods or for making decisions about activity levels. Costs can be classified as variable, fixed, stepped or semi-variable.

For semi-variable costs the fixed element and the variable element will need to be identified for forecasting purposes. This can be done using the high/low method.

KAPLAN PUBLISHING

Answers to chapter activities & 'test your knowledge' questions

△ ACTIVITY 1 △△△△

AB Limited

(a) (i) **Fixed costs**   (ii) **Variable costs**

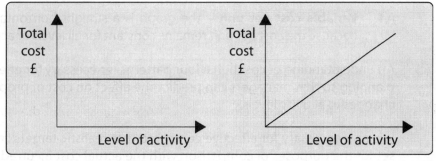

(iii) **Semi-variable costs**   (iv) **Fixed cost per unit**

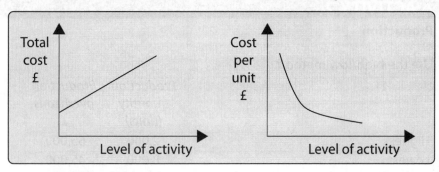

(v) **Variable cost per unit**

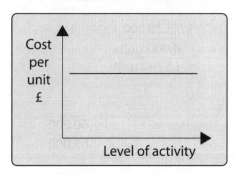

(b) (i) **Fixed costs** – the graph is a straight horizontal line because the cost remains constant for all levels of activity. Two examples could be office rent and administrative salaries.

(ii) **Variable costs** – the graph slopes upwards because each unit adds a constant amount to the total cost. Two examples could be direct materials and direct labour.

(iii) **Semi-variable costs** – the cost includes a basic amount of fixed cost, therefore the graph starts part-way up the vertical axis.

It then slopes upwards because each unit adds a constant amount of variable cost to the total cost. Two examples could be telephone costs and electricity costs.

(iv) **Fixed cost per unit** – the graph slopes downwards because the fixed cost per unit reduces as the constant amount of fixed cost is spread over more units.

(v) **Variable cost per unit** – the graph is a straight horizontal line because the cost per unit remains constant for all levels of activity.

(c) An understanding of cost behaviour patterns is necessary for effective planning so that managers can predict the effect on cost of proposed changes in activity levels.

It is also necessary for effective control so that realistic targets can be set for the purposes of comparison with the actual cost incurred.

△ ACTIVITY 2

Production

Use the high/low method.

	Production quantity (units)	Production overheads £
Highest	12,000	65,000
Lowest	8,000	45,000
Increase in activity	4,000	20,000
Variable cost =	$\dfrac{£20,000}{4,000 \text{ units}}$	
=	£5 per unit	

Substituting at 12,000 unit level:

		£
Variable cost 12,000 × £5		60,000
Total cost		65,000
Fixed cost		5,000

At a production level of 10,500 units:

		£
Variable cost 10,500 × £5		52,500
Fixed cost		5,000
Total cost		57,500

Test your knowledge △ △ △

1 Cost accounting permits the identification of profitable and non-profitable activities, the identification of waste and inefficiency, and assistance in setting selling prices.

2 In batch processing the cost unit is the batch. Costs are determined for each batch of output.

3 Service cost centres include the stores and the canteen.

4 A profit centre is a location or function for which costs and revenues are ascertained for the purpose of controlling the resultant profit.

5 Prime cost is the total of all direct costs.

6 Direct labour is typically a variable cost.

7 An example of a stepped cost is the rent of premises. At certain points a new premises will have to be rented.

8

	Costs £	Output (units)
High	90,000	30,000
Low	80,000	20,000
Difference	10,000	10,000

Therefore, the variable cost is $\dfrac{10,000}{10,000} = $ £1 per unit and the fixed cost is £60,000 per month. In March, factory cost will be £60,000 + £32,000 = £92,000.

ACCOUNTING FOR OVERHEADS

INTRODUCTION

Overhead is the general term used to describe costs which are not direct costs of production. They are also known as indirect costs and they may be indirect production costs or indirect non-production costs. When a management accountant is trying to ascertain the cost of a product or service, there are two possible approaches available for dealing with overheads.

Firstly, apportionment and allocation of all production overheads may be used to arrive at a 'full' cost per unit. This is known as absorption costing and is considered first. Remember that as well as the indirect production cost there are indirect non-production costs. These non-production costs are never included in the cost of the product, or stock or cost of sales.

Alternatively, one can use only direct costs to arrive at the cost per unit and leave indirect costs as a general overhead not related to units of output. This approach is generally known as marginal costing and will be dealt with later in the chapter.

This chapter contains the essential understanding of accounting for overheads and overhead absorption which is necessary for your further studies for Units 8 and 9.

KNOWLEDGE & UNDERSTANDING

- Marginal and absorption costing: cost recording, cost reporting and cost behaviour (Elements 8.1, 8.2, 9.2 and 9.3)
- The use and limitation of published statistics (Element 8.1)
- Cost management: life cycle costing; target costing (including value engineering); activity-based costing; principles of Total Quality Management (including cost of quality) (Element 8.2)
- How the accounting systems of an organisation are affected by its organisational structure, its administrative systems and procedures and the nature of its business transactions (Elements 8.1, 8.2, 9.1, 9.2 and 9.3)

CONTENTS

1 Allocation, apportionment and absorption of overheads
2 Activity-based costing (ABC)
3 Absorption costing and marginal costing
4 Limiting factor analysis

PERFORMANCE CRITERIA

- Analyse the effect of organisational accounting policies on reported costs (Element 8.1)
- Analyse routine cost reports, compare them with other sources of information and identify any implications (Element 8.2)

1 Allocation, apportionment and absorption of overheads

1.1 Introduction

We have already identified two types of costs that make up the full production cost of a unit:

(a) **Direct costs** are those that can be uniquely identified with an individual cost unit (e.g. direct materials, direct labour, direct expenses).

(b) **Indirect costs** (overheads) are costs incurred in production but not easily 'traced' to individual units, e.g. machine power (variable), factory rent (fixed), heat and light (semi-variable).

The problem we are considering here is how to divide indirect production costs between cost units, in order to prepare a 'standard' total cost per unit for budgeting, stock valuation and pricing purposes.

The method used to divide production overheads between production units is made up of three processes: allocation, apportionment and absorption.

Step 1 Identify the indirect cost with a cost centre

This can be done in two ways depending on the nature of the cost.

(a) **Allocation**.

> **□ DEFINITION**　□□□□
>
> Where the indirect cost is borne entirely by one cost centre, the entire cost is allocated to that cost centre.

(b) **Apportionment**.

> **□ DEFINITION**　□□□□
>
> Where the indirect cost is shared by more than one cost centre, the cost is apportioned between the cost centre.

Step 2 Identify the indirect costs of the cost centre calculated in Step 1 with the cost units produced by that centre.

This is called absorption.

> **□ DEFINITION**　□□□□
>
> Absorption is the technique of relating a cost centre's indirect costs to the units produced by the cost centre.

We shall now look at each of these in more detail.

1.2 Cost allocation

Certain cost items will be incurred entirely by one cost centre. Allocation deals with this type of cost and simply allots it to the cost centre which has incurred the cost.

Cost centre	*Allocated cost*
Canteen	Tea bags
	Spaghetti
	Chef's wages
Packing department	Cardboard
	String

1.3 Cost apportionment (primary)

More frequently, however, the benefit of an item of cost will be shared by a number of cost centres. The overhead will be split or apportioned between the relevant cost centres on an 'equitable' basis.

The rent of buildings, for example, can relate to the total floor space occupied by a number of different departments and it is usual to allot the rental charge to those departments in proportion to the floor space they occupy.

The cost of rent is shared between a number of cost centres

Nature of cost	*Possible bases of apportionment*
Rent and rates	Floor area occupied by various departments
Lighting and heating	Cubic capacity of locations or metered usage
Insurance of stocks	Value of stockholdings in various locations

O EXAMPLE   O O O O

A general cost in a manufacturing company is factory rental. Annual rental costs are £80,000. How should this cost be apportioned between production departments and service departments?

Rental costs are usually apportioned between departments on the basis of the floor space taken up by each department. For example, suppose that three departments have floor space of 10,000 square metres, 15,000 square metres and 25,000 square metres, and annual rental costs are £80,000. If we apportion rental costs between the departments on the basis of their floor space, the apportionment would be as follows.

Annual rental	£80,000
Total floor sapce (10,000 + 15,000 + 25,000)	50,000 square metres
Apportionment rate (£80,000/50,000)	£1.60/square metre

		£
Apportion to department with 10,000 square metres		16,000
Apportion to department with 15,000 square metres		24,000
Apportion to departmnet with 25,000 square metres		40,000
		80,000

○ EXAMPLE   ○○○○

The costs of heating and lighting might also be apportioned on the basis of floor space. Alternatively, since heating relates to volume rather than floor space, it could be argued that the costs should be apportioned on the volume of space taken up by each department. Yet another view is that electricity costs relate more to the consumption of electrical power by machines, therefore the apportionment of these costs should be on the basis of the number and power of the machines in each department.

A reasonable argument could be made for any of these basis of apportionment.

1.4 Cost apportionment (secondary)

After completing the allocation and primary apportionment stages, you should have assigned all costs to cost centres.

Some cost centres, however, will not have production units passing through them; these cost centres are called service departments (e.g. quality control department, works canteen). Before the final stage of absorption into cost units can be carried out, it is necessary to perform a further type of apportionment whereby the total costs of the service cost centres are reassigned to production cost centres. This is known as secondary apportionment. This should be done on a fair basis to reflect the benefit derived from the service centre.

The following example is an illustration of primary and secondary apportionment.

KAPLAN PUBLISHING

○ EXAMPLE

Overhead Analysis Sheet	Total	Production		Service	
		Assembly	Finishing	Stores	Canteen
	£	£	£	£	£
Overheads allocated directly to cost centres	133,000	49,000	36,000	27,000	21,000
Overheads to be apportioned					
Rent (apportionment basis: ....)	76,000	26,000	24,000	15,000	11,000
Equipment depreciation (Apportionment basis: ....)	15,000	8,000	1,000	5,000	1,000
Total overhead	224,000	83,000	61,000	47,000	33,000
Apportioning of stores (Apportionment basis: ....)		31,000	16,000	(47,000)	
Apportioning of canteen (Apportionment basis: ....)		14,000	19,000		(33,000)
		128,000	96,000	–	–

1.5 Absorption

Having collected all indirect costs in the production cost centres via overhead allocation and apportionment, the cost has to be spread over the output of the production cost centre.

The allotment of accumulated overhead costs to cost units is called overhead absorption. The absorption rate is normally calculated at the start of the period and therefore based on budgeted quantities. Various methods of absorption exist and the one most fitting should be chosen.

The following are the most common methods you will encounter.

(a) **Rate per unit**

The simple unit rate is obtained by dividing total budgeted overheads by the number of units budgeted to be produced. However, where more than one product is produced, this is an unsatisfactory basis for absorbing overheads as it will not reflect the relative demands of each product on the production departments through which they pass.

(b) **Alternative bases of absorption**

There are a number of bases commonly used as an alternative to the simple unit rate:
- rate per direct labour hour;
- rate per machine hour;
- percentage of material cost;
- percentage of wage cost;
- percentage of total direct cost (prime cost).

It is important to appreciate, however, that whichever method or combination of methods is used, the result will only be an approximate estimate of what that product actually costs.

In practice, many businesses use a 'direct labour hour rate' or 'machine hour rate' in preference to a rate based on a percentage of direct materials cost, direct wages or prime cost, as it may be possible to associate some overheads either with labour time or with machine time.

It may be possible to analyse the total overhead apportioned to each production department into fixed and variable elements. In this case a variable overhead rate per unit and a fixed overhead rate per unit can be calculated.

The absorption rates will normally be calculated at the beginning of a period and hence be based on budgeted costs and production levels. This can lead to problems when actual costs and volumes are not the same as budgeted leading to over- or under-absorption.

○ EXAMPLE   ○ ○ ○ ○

For the year ended 31 December 20X4 the planned overhead for the Machining Cost Centre at Cuecraft Ltd was:

Overhead   £132,000
Volume of activity   15,000 machine hours

In January 20X4 the cost centre incurred £12,000 of overhead and 1,350 machine hours were worked.

Task

Calculate the pre-determined overhead rate per machine hour and the overhead under or over-recovered in the month.

Solution

Absorption rate, based on the budget:

$$\frac{\text{Planned overhead}}{\text{Machine hours}} = \frac{£132,000}{15,000 \text{ machine hours}} = £8.80 \text{ per machine hour}$$

KAPLAN PUBLISHING

	£
Overhead absorbed	
1,350 machine hours at £8.80	11,880
Overhead incurred	12,000
Under-absorption	120

Here, the amount of overheads actually charged to production are £11,880, which is less than actual expenditure. We therefore have under-absorption of overhead.

Under-recovery of overheads is shown as a separate item in the costing profit and loss account. Since production has been charged with less over-heads than the amount of overheads incurred, an adjustment to profit for under-absorption is downwards. In other words, under-absorption is a 'loss' item.

○ EXAMPLE ○○○○

The following example covers all stages of overhead allocation, apportion-ment and absorption summarised above. Work through it carefully to ensure you have fully understood this area.

SB Limited has two production departments (Assembly and Finishing) and two service departments (Maintenance and Canteen). The following costs are expected to be incurred during the next time period.

	£
Indirect materials	20,000
Rent	15,000
Electricity	10,000
Machine depreciation	5,000
Building depreciation	10,000
Direct labour	55,000

The following information is available.

	Assembly	Finishing	Maintenance	Canteen
Area (square metres)	1,000	2,000	500	500
Kw hours consumed	1,000	4,000	Nil	5,000
Machine value	£45,000	£35,000	£11,000	£9,000
Number of staff	20	30	10	4
Indirect materials consumed	7,000	8,000	3,000	2,000
Direct labour hours	10,000	2,000	500	200
Machine hours	1,000	5,000	–	–

The maintenance department spends 60% of its time servicing equipment for the assembly department and 40% of its time servicing equipment for the finishing department. The canteen equipment is serviced by outside specialist contractors.

(a) Calculate the total overheads in each cost centre.
(b) Reapportion the service centre costs to production cost centres.
(c) Calculate appropriate absorption rates for each production department.
(d) One of SB Ltd's products is the JK. Production details for each unit of JK are:

	Assembly	Finishing
Direct labour hours	4	1
Machine hours	0.5	2.5

How much overhead should be absorbed into each unit of JK?

Solution

(a)

Overhead	Total	Basis of apportionment (note)	Assembly	Finishing	Maintenance	Canteen
	£		£	£	£	£
Indirect materials	20,000	Allocate (i)	7,000	8,000	3,000	2,000
Rent	15,000	Area (ii)	3,750	7,500	1,875	1,875
Electricity	10,000	Kw hours (iii)	1,000	4,000	–	5,000
Machine depreciation	5,000	Machine value (iv)	2,250	1,750	550	450
Building depreciation	10,000	Area (v)	2,500	5,000	1,250	1,250
Direct labour	55,000	- (vi)	–	–	–	–
Total	60,000		16,500	26,250	6,675	10,575

Notes

(i) We are given the amount of indirect materials used by each cost centre. This allows us to allocate the cost straight to each cost centre.

(ii) Rent is something that is shared by the whole factory and therefore the cost must be apportioned between the cost centres. The first thing to decide is what basis to use. Since rent is related to area, floorspace would be a sensible basis to use (the bigger the area of a cost centre the more rent will be apportioned to it). The apportionment is carried out as follows.

· Calculate the total floor area for the factory.
· For each cost centre calculate what fraction of the total floor area this represents.
· Multiply this fraction by £15,000.

In the present case this would be as follows:
Total floor area = 1,000 + 2,000 + 500 + 500 = 4,000 square metres.

Assembly is 1,000 square metres, i.e. 1,000/4,000 of the total area. Assembly is apportioned £15,000 × 1,000/4,000 = £3,750.

Similarly, finishing is apportioned £15,000 × 2,000/4,000 = £7,500 and Maintenance and Canteen are apportioned £15,000 × 500/4,000 = £1,875 each.

(iii) The most appropriate basis for apportioning the electricity between the cost centres will be the Kw hours consumed since these are a measure of the amount of electricity used.

The total Kw hours consumed = 1,000 + 4,000 + 0 + 5,000 = 10,000.

Assembly will be apportioned £10,000 × 1,000/10,000 = £1,000 etc.

(iv) Machine depreciation will be based on the value of the machinery and again needs to be apportioned between the cost centres.

The total machine value is £45,000 + £35,000 + £11,000 + £9,000 = £100,000.

This results in Assembly being apportioned £5,000 × 45/100 = £2,250 etc.

(v) Since the whole building is being depreciated, building depreciation should be related to the area of each cost centre. It does not matter that we have already used area once. There is no restriction against using it again if it is the most appropriate basis for apportioning this cost.

(vi) You may have thought that using number of employees was a good way to share out the direct wages bill, but remember that we are only interested here in overheads. Direct wages will already be included in the costs of the products that are made by the company. (Similarly direct materials are ignored for overheads.) If the question had included indirect labour then that would be included as an overhead and could be apportioned using the number of people working in each cost centre.

(b)   A suitable basis for sharing out canteen costs is the number of employees. A suitable basis for sharing out the maintenance costs is the time spent servicing equipment.

First re-apportion canteen costs since the canteen provides services for maintenance but maintenance do not work for the canteen. Then re-apportion the maintenance work, which include a share of the canteen.

Overhead	Basis		Assembly	Finishing	Maintenance	Canteen
			£	£	£	£
Total from above			16,500	26,250	6,675	10,575
Canteen	Personnel	20:30:10	3,525	5,288	1,762	(10,575)
Sub-total			20,025	31,538	8,437	
Maintenance	Time	60:40	5,062	3,375	(8,437)	
Total			25,087	34,913		

Total overhead = £60,000

(c)   The assembly department seems to be labour based, therefore overhead is absorbed on the basis of labour hours:

$$\text{Overhead absorption rate} = \frac{£25,087}{10,000 \text{ hours}} = £2.51 \text{ per direct labour hour}$$

The finishing department seems to be machine based, therefore overhead is absorbed on the basis of machine hours:

$$\text{Overhead absorption rate} = \frac{£34,913}{5,000 \text{ hours}} = £6.98 \text{ per machine hour}$$

(d)   Overhead absorbed per unit of JK:
(£2.51 × 4 hours) + (£6.98 × 2.5 hours) = £27.49

▷ ACTIVITY 1   ▷ ▷ ▷ ▷

Lorus Limited

Lorus Limited makes cupboards. This involves three production departments (Sawing, Assembly and Finishing) together with two service departments (Maintenance and Materials Handling).

Last year 4,000 cupboards were made.

Costs incurred:

	Sawing	Assembly	Finishing
	£	£	£
Materials	120,000	80,000	20,000
Wages	50,000	25,000	40,000
Overheads	75,000	50,000	20,000

Materials Handling wages:	£9,000
Maintenance wages:	£20,000

The benefits derived from the service departments are estimated to be as follows:

	Sawing	Assembly	Finishing	Materials Handling
	%	%	%	%
Maintenance	30	40	20	10
Materials Handling	50	20	30	

Required

(a)   Prepare a memorandum to the managing director, copied to each production head, showing the overheads allotted to each production department.

(b)   Calculate the unit cost of a cupboard.   [Answer on p. 68]

2   Activity-based costing (ABC)

2.1   Criticisms of absorption costs

Historically a direct labour rate for absorption of all fixed overheads was a verycommon method, as production tended to be highly labour-intensive. Such items as rent would be apportioned using the area involved, but the absorption rate would usually be labour hours. It was reasonable to assume that the more labour time spent on a product, the more production resources in general were being used. Thus the product should be charged with a higher share of the overheads.

However, nowadays, production is far more mechanised. This has two impacts as follows:

(a)   A higher proportion of the overheads is accounted for by machine-related costs (power, depreciation, maintenance, etc).

(b)   The amount of labour time spent upon a unit is far less representative of its final significance in the use of production resources.

To take a simple example, Product A may use 9 machine hours and 1 labour hour, whilst Product B requires 1 machine hour and 4 labour hours. The traditional approach would charge B with four times as much production overhead (including machine costs) as A, even though it takes half the time overall.

In this example, one solution would be to use machine hours as a basis. However, this still tries to relate all overhead costs, whatever their nature, to usage of machines. This would not necessarily be appropriate for, say, costs of receiving and checking materials going into the production process. This will be more likely to depend upon the number of times an order of material is received into stores for a particular product.

2.2   Activity-based costing (ABC) approach

Professors Robin Cooper and Robert Kaplan at the Harvard Business School have developed a costing system called activity-based costing (ABC) which avoids the problems experienced by traditional costing methods. If management are keen to control costs, then it is vital that they should know the activities that cause costs to arise.

(a)   **Cost drivers**

Those activities that are the significant determinants of cost are known as cost-drivers. For example, if production-scheduling cost is driven by the number of production set-ups, then that number is the cost-driver for the cost of production-scheduling. The cost-drivers represent the bases for charging costs in the ABC system, with a separate cost centre established for each cost-driver.

(b)   **Cost pools**

Where several costs are 'driven' by the same activity (e.g. engine oil, machine breakdown and repairs) then these costs are put into 'cost pools' and the total of the cost pool is absorbed by, say, machine hours.

2.3   Mechanics of ABC

The mechanics of operating an ABC system are similar to a traditional costing system. The significant cost drivers need to be ascertained and a cost centre is established for each cost driver. Costs are allocated to products by dividing the cost centre costs by the number of transactions undertaken.

For example, in Plant Y a set up of a production run would be a cost driver. The cost of the engineers who do the set ups would be a cost centre. If the cost of the engineers is say £280,000 and the number of sets ups is 500, then the charging out rate is $\frac{280,000}{500}$ = £560. A product which has a number of small production runs will thus have a greater proportion of these costs relative to the quantity of the product produced, than a product with large production runs.

Other overheads will be allocated to products in a different way; which way depends upon the cost drivers which have been ascertained.

○ **EXAMPLE**   ○ ○ ○ ○

Plant Y produces about one hundred products. Its largest selling product is Product A; its smallest is Product B. Relevant data is given below.

	Product A	Product B	Total products
Units produced pa	50,000	1,000	500,000
Material cost per unit	£1.00	£1.00	
Direct labour per unit	15 minutes	15 minutes	
Machine time per unit	1 hour	1 hour	
Number of set ups pa	24	2	500
Number of purchase orders for materials	36	6	2,800
Number of times material handled	200	15	12,000
Direct labour cost per hour			£5

Overhead costs:

	£
Set up	280,000
Purchasing	145,000
Materials handling	130,000
Machines	660,000
	1,215,000

Total machine hours are 600,000 hours.

Traditional costing (absorbing overheads on machine hours):

Unit cost	A	B
	£	£
Material cost	1.00	1.00
Labour cost	1.25	1.25
Overhead per machine hour		

$$\frac{1,215,000}{600,000} = 2.025$$

	A	B
	2.025	2.025
	4.275	4.275

The above costings imply that we are indifferent between producing Product A and Product B.

Using an ABC approach would show:

Step 1 Calculate the direct material and labour costs as for the traditional approach.

Unit cost	A £	B £
Material cost	1.00	1.00
Labour cost	1.25	1.25
	2.25	2.25

Step 2 Calculate the overheads that will be charged to each product by:

(a) Calculating the overhead cost per cost driver for each type of overhead (e.g. cost per set-up).

(b) Charge cost to each unit by calculating the unit cost accordingly.

Overheads:	A £	B £

Set up

$$\frac{280,000}{500} = £560 \text{ per set up}$$

$\dfrac{560 \times 24}{50,000}$	0.27	
$\dfrac{560 \times 2}{1,000}$		1.12

Purchasing:

$$\frac{145,000}{2,800} = £51.786 \text{ per purchase order}$$

$\dfrac{36 \times 51.786}{50,000}$	0.04	
$\dfrac{6 \times 51.786}{1,000}$		0.31

Materials handling:

$$\frac{130,000}{12,000} = 10.833 \text{ per time}$$

$\dfrac{200 \times 10.833}{50,000}$	0.04	
$\dfrac{15 \times 10.833}{1,000}$		0.16

Machines:

$$\frac{660,000}{600,000} = £1.10 \text{ per machine hour} \qquad 1.10 \qquad 1.10$$

	1.45	2.69
Add: Direct material and labour costs	2.25	2.25
	£3.70	£4.94

Common-sense would lead us to conclude that ABC is a more accurate representation of the relative real costs of the two products.

What must be considered, however, is whether the benefits of this approach outweigh the costs of implementing and applying the system.

The following example again contrasts a traditional product costing system with an ABC system and shows that an ABC system produces much more accurate product costs.

○ EXAMPLE ○○○○

Mayes plc has a single production centre and has provided the following budgeted information for the next period.

	Product A	Product B	Product C	Total
Production and sales (units)	40,000	25,000	10,000	75,000
Direct material cost	£25	£20	£18	£1,680,000
Direct labour hours	3	4	2	240,000
Machine hours	2	4	3	210,000
Number of production runs	5	10	25	40
Number of component receipts	15	25	120	160
Number of production orders	15	10	25	50

Direct labour is paid £8 per hour.

Overhead costs in the period are expected to be as follows:

	£
Set-up	140,000
Machine	900,000
Goods inwards	280,000
Packing	200,000
Engineering	180,000
	1,700,000

What are the unit costs of each product using:
(a)   the traditional approach?
(b)   the ABC method?

Solution

(a) A traditional costing approach would cost each product as follows:

	Product A	Product B	Product C
	£	£	£
Direct materials	25.00	20.00	18.00
Direct labour (@ £8 per hour)	24.00	32.00	16.00
Overhead (@ £7.08 per hour – see below)	21.24	28.32	14.16
Total cost	70.24	80.32	48.16

$$\text{Overhead recovery rate} = \frac{£1,700,000}{240,000} = £7.08 \text{ per direct labour hour}$$

(b) An ABC system needs to investigate the cost determinants for the indirect overheads not driven by production volume. Assume that these are as follows.

Cost	Cost driver
Set-up	Number of production runs
Goods inwards	Number of receipts
Packing	Number of production orders
Engineering	Number of production orders

The machine overhead of £900,000 is likely to be related primarily to production volume, so it will be recovered on the basis of machine hours used $= \dfrac{£900,000}{210,000} = £4.29$ per machine hour (after rounding)

The cost per activity for each of the other cost centres is as follows.

Set-up cost	$\dfrac{£140,000}{40} =$	£3,500 per set-up
Goods inwards	$\dfrac{£280,000}{160} =$	£1,750 per receipt
Packing	$\dfrac{£200,000}{50} =$	£4,000 per order
Engineering	$\dfrac{£180,000}{50} =$	£3,600 per order

An ABC approach would allocate overheads to each of the product groups as follows:

	Product A £	Product B £	Product C £
Set-up costs			
5 × £3,500	17,500		
10 × £3,500		35,000	
25 × £3,500			87,500
Machine costs (rounded down)			
(2 × 40,000) × £4.29	343,000		
(4 × 25,000) × £4.29		429,000	
(3 × 10,000) × £4.29			128,000
Goods inwards costs			
15 × £1,750	26,250		
25 × £1,750		43,750	
120 × £1,750			210,000
Packing costs			
15 × £4,000	60,000		
10 × £4,000		40,000	
25 × £4,000			100,000
Engineering costs			
15 × £3,600	54,000		
10 × £3,600		36,000	
25 × £3,600			90,000
Total overhead	500,750	583,750	615,500
Average overhead per unit			
£500,750/40,000	£12.52		
£583,750/25,000		£23.35	
£615,500/10,000			£61.55
This compares to the traditional overhead absorption of:			
	£21.24	£28.32	£14.16

It can be seen that product C is significantly under-costed under the traditional system, while products A and B are over-costed. This situation arises because the large proportion of costs driven by product C is not picked up under the traditional costing system. Since it is the cost-drivers identified in the ABC system which generate the costs in the first place, the ABC system will produce a more accurate final analysis.

▷ **ACTIVITY 2**   ▷ ▷ ▷ ▷
Products X and Y

Calculate the unit cost of products X and Y, where products X and Y are sole output of the business:

	Product X	Product Y
Units produced	45,000	5,000
Material cost per unit	£1.50	£4.00
Direct labour per unit	£7.00	£3.50
Direct labour time per unit	1 hr	30 mins
Number of set ups	30	10
Number of purchase orders for materials	70	10
Overhead costs:		£
Set up		20,000
Purchasing		16,000
Labour supervision		23,750

[Answer on p. 69]

3 Absorption costing and marginal costing

3.1 Introduction

We have discussed the idea of the collection of costs initially in cost centres and then attributing them to the cost units passing through those cost centres. But should all costs eventually be attributed to (absorbed by) cost units?

Two points should be noted regarding the absorption of costs into cost units:

· **Production/selling costs** – in a manufacturing context, we have already seen that stocks of finished goods will never include an element of selling costs. The stocks will be valued at production costs only (including overheads). However, for pricing or profitability purposes, the cost of units sold may well include a selling cost element.

· **Fixed/variable costs** – whether or not all production costs will be absorbed into cost units for stock valuation will depend upon the particular system being used.

   (i)   A total absorption costing (TAC) system absorbs all production costs (direct or indirect, fixed or variable) into cost units.

   (ii) A marginal costing (MC) system only absorbs variable production costs (direct and indirect) into cost units. Fixed costs are treated as period costs, and deducted as a 'lump sum' from the profits of the period concerned.

3.2 The main difference between absorption and marginal costing

The main difference between absorption and marginal costing is that under absorption costing the fixed production overheads are absorbed into the production cost of the units produced. They are thus treated as part of the cost per unit and are shown as part of the cost of sales.

Because the absorption rate for these costs is determined from the budgeted figures for output and the cost of the fixed overheads, there may be a difference between the amount absorbed into the units produced (which is based on the budgeted amounts) and the amount that should have been absorbed into the units produced if it had been based on the actual amounts. This may result in an over- or under-absorption of the production overheads which has to be corrected by an entry in the profit statement.

○ EXAMPLE ○ ○ ○ ○

A business has the following actual results (there are no opening or closing stocks)

Units produces and sold	5,000 (units)
Sales price per unit	£15
Direct materials (£4 per unit)	£20,000
Direct labour (£3 per unit)	£15,000
Variable production costs (£1 per unit)	£5,000
Fixed production costs incurred	£12,000
Admin and selling costs	£8,000

The budgeted production was 4,800 units.
Budgeted fixed overheads were £14,400.

Task

Prepare operating statements under absorption and marginal costing.

Solution

	Absorption		Marginal	
	£	£	£	£
Sales (5,000 x £15)		75,000		75,000
Less cost of sales				
Materials	20,000		20,000	
Labour	15,000		15,000	
Variable overhead	5,000		5,000	
Fixed overhead absorbed (W 2)	15,000			
		55,000		40,000
		20,000		35,000
Over-absorbed overhead (W 3)		3,000		–
		23,000		
Fixed production costs		–		12,000
Admin and selling costs		8,000		8,000
		15,000		15,000

Workings

1   Calculate the fixed production overhead absorption rate

   = £14,400/4,800 = £3 per unit

2   Calculate the fixed production overhead absorbed into production under absorption costing

   = actual units produced x absorption rate = 5,000 x £3 = £15,000

3   Calculate the overabsorbed fixed overhead

Actual overhead	12,000
Absorbed overhead	15,000
Overabsorbed	3,000

The overhead was overabsorbed by £3,000 and this amount has to be added back to profit in the absorption statement to restore the figure to the actual amount.

3.3   The effect of changes in stock levels

The above example illustrated the difference between the two types of accounting but note that the profit figure at the end of the period was the same under both systems.

However if stock levels change in the period for which the statement is prepared, the two systems will give a different figure for profit. This occurs because if stock is carried forward under absorption costing, the stock value will include some of the overheads incurred in the period. This effectively carries those overheads forward into the next period which reduces the over-heads charged to profit in the first period thereby increasing the reported profit.

In the example above, if there had been no opening stock but 500 units of stock at the end of the period, the absorption statement would carry forward the production cost of this stock to the next period including the fixed over-head element. The marginal statement would also carry forward the production cost of the stock but there would be no fixed cost element carried forward.

○ EXAMPLE   ○○○○

Consider the previous example with the business manufacturing 5,000 units, selling 4,500 units and carrying forward 500 units of stock to the next period. All other facts are the same.

Task

Prepare operating statements under absorption and marginal costing.

Solution

	Absorption		Marginal	
	£	£	£	£
Sales (4,500 x £15)		67,500		67,500
Less cost of sales				
Materials	20,000		20,000	
Labour	15,000		15,000	
Variable overhead	5,000		5,000	
Fixed overhead absorbed	15,000			
	———		———	
	55,000		40,000	
less closing stock (W1)	(5,500)		(4,000)	
	———		———	
		49,500		36,000
		———		———
		18,000		31,500
Over-absorbed overhead		3,000		–
		———		
		21,000		
Fixed production costs		–		12,000
Admin and selling costs		8,000		8,000
		———		———
		13,000		11,500
		———		———

Working

Value of closing stock

	Absorption	Marginal
	£	£
Cost per unit		
Materials	4	4
Labour	3	3
Variable overhead	1	1
Fixed overhead	3	Nil
	—	—
Unit cost	11	8
	—	—
Cost of 500 units	5,500 (500 x £11)	4,000 (500 x £8)

○ EXAMPLE ○○○○

Tivoli Limited has produced the following budgeted figures for a new product it hopes to launch.

Direct material	£10 per unit
Direct labour	£5 per unit
Variable production overheads	£8 per unit
Fixed production costs	£27,000 per month
Budgeted output	9,000 units per month
Sales price	£30 per unit

	Month 1	Month 2	Month 3
Production	6,500	9,000	10,000
Sales	5,000	8,500	9,500

Required

Prepare a profit statement for each of the three months on each of the following bases:
(a)   marginal costing;
(b)   absorption costing.

Solution

(a)   Marginal costing

Cost of production (per unit)

	£
Direct materials	10
Direct labour	5
Variable production overheads	8
Total variable cost	23

	Month 1		Month 2		Month 3	
	£	£	£	£	£	£
Sales @ £30		150,000		255,000		285,000
Opening stock	–		34,500		46,000	
Cost of production @ £23	149,500		207,000		230,000	
	149,500		241,500		276,000	
Closing stock (W) £23	(34,500)		(46,000)		(57,500)	
Variable cost of sales		(115,000)		(195,500)		(218,500)
Contribution		35,000		59,500		66,500
Fixed costs		(27,000)		(27,000)		(27,000)
Profit		8,000		32,500		39,500

Working

	Month 1 (units)	Month 2 (units)	Month 3 (units)
Opening stock	–	1,500	2,000
Production	6,500	9,000	10,000
Sales	(5,000)	(8,500)	(9,500)
Closing stock	1,500	2,000	2,500

(b) **Absorption costing**

Fixed costs are allocated to units of production based on the budgeted rate of activity, i.e. 9,000 units per month. Therefore the fixed cost per unit is £3 (£27,000/9,000).

Cost of production (per unit)

	£
Direct materials	10
Direct labour	5
Variable production overheads	8
Fixed production costs	3
Total cost	26

However, actual production levels are not known until the end of the period, by which time each product has been charged with standard fixed costs per unit.

So an adjustment for over or under absorption of overheads has to be made at the end of each period, as follows.

Month 1 (9,000 – 6,500) × £3 = £7,500 under absorbed.
Month 2 Production is equal to budget, so no adjustment necessary.
Month 3 (9,000 – 10,000) × £3 = £3,000 over absorbed.

	Month 1		Month 2		Month 3	
	£	£	£	£	£	£
Sales @ £30		150,000		255,000		285,000
Opening stock	–		39,000		52,000	
Cost of production @ £26	169,000		234,000		260,000	
	169,000		273,000		312,000	
Closing stock @ £26	(39,000)		(52,000)		(65,000)	
Fully absorbed cost of sales		(130,000)		(221,000)		(247,000)
Gross profit		20,000		34,000		38,000
(Under)/overabsorption		(7,500)		–		3,000
Profit		12,500		34,000		41,000

Notice that the profit figure under both methods would have been the same if there had been no change in stock levels in each month.

○ EXAMPLE ○○○○

Let us assume that Tivoli has the same budgeted monthly output for the new product but it sells everything it produces every month.

Direct materials	£10 per unit
Direct labour	£5 per unit
Variable production overheads	£8 per unit
Fixed production costs	£27,000 per month
Budgeted output	9,000 units per month
Sales price	£30 per unit

	Month 1	Month 2	Month 3
Production and sales	5,000	8,000	10,000

Produce a profit statement for each of the three months under (a) marginal costing and (b) absorption costing.

Solution

(a) **Marginal costing**

Unit cost of production (10 + 5 + 8) £23

	Month 1	Month 2	Month 3
	£	£	£
Sales @ £30	150,000	240,000	300,000
Variable cost of sales @ £23	(115,000)	(184,000)	(230,000)
Contribution	35,000	56,000	70,000
Fixed costs	(27,000)	(27,000)	(27,000)
Marginal costing profit	8,000	29,000	43,000

(b) **Absorption costing**

Fixed cost to be absorbed per unit is at £27,000/9,000 = £3. Unit cost of production is still £26 therefore.

Adjustment for over/under absorption

Month 1	(9,000 – 5,000) × £3	= £12,000 under absorbed
Month 2	(9,000 – 8,000) × £3	= £3,000 under absorbed
Month 3	(9,000 – 10,000) × £3	= £3,000 over absorbed.

	Month 1	Month 2	Month 3
	£	£	£
Sales @ £30	150,000	240,000	300,000
Variable cost of sales @ £26	(130,000)	(208,000)	(260,000)
Gross profit	20,000	32,000	40,000
(Under)/over absorption	(12,000)	(3,000)	3,000
Absorption costing profit	8,000	29,000	43,000

In this example stock levels remained constant at zero, therefore marginal costing profit and absorption costing profit were the same. The only reason for differences in profit under the two methods is any increase or decrease in stock levels and the fixed overhead absorbed in those units of stock.

4 Limiting factor analysis

4.1 Marginal costing and decision-making

In the section on overheads we compared total absorption costing (TAC) with marginal costing (MC), where only directly attributable variable overheads are absorbed into cost units. The key reason for using MC is to assist in decision making. If a decision has to be made it is sensible only to take into account those costs which will actually be affected by the decision. Since most overheads are fixed the decision to make one extra unit of production will not affect that cost, so it should be ignored. Only the marginal cost of making one extra unit should be considered in decision making and therefore be absorbed into cost units.

This approach to costing has two key uses:
- It affects stock valuation (stock valued under an MC approach is of lower value than that under TAC since fixed overheads have not been absorbed).
- It enables us to make decisions when there is a scarcity of resources, that is when the shortage of one resource means that that resource limits the entire capacity of the operation: it is the limiting factor.

4.2 Single limiting factor

A company may have two products, each requiring materials and labour. There may be a limit as to the amount of labour or materials that is available for the coming month. How can the company make the most possible profit subject to such a constraint?

Since fixed costs are independent of production they are irrelevant (they will have to be paid however many units of each product are manufactured). The above problem therefore requires us to maximise contribution taking into account the limiting factor.

○ EXAMPLE ○○○○

Barbecue Limited manufactures two products for which the following details are available.

	Product X		Product Y
Selling price	£38		£38
Direct materials 8 units @ £1	£8	4 units @ £1	£4
Labour 4 hours @ £2	£8	6 hours @ £2	£12
Variable overhead 4 machine hours @ £3	£12	3 machine hours @ £3	£9
Fixed overheads	£5		£7

Maximum demand for X is 2,500 units.

Maximum demand for Y is 2,000 units.

Calculate the optimum production plan for Barbecue in each of the following two situations:

(a)   Labour in the next period is limited to 16,000 hours, with no limit on machine hours.

(b)   Machine hours in the next period are limited to 12,000 hours, with no limit on labour hours.

Solution

We would like to produce Xs and Ys up to the point where maximum demand is reached. (There is no point producing beyond this, because customers do not want any more.) So ideally we would like to produce 2,500 X and 2,000 Y. To do this we would require the following resources.

	Labour hours	Machine hours
2,500 X	10,000	10,000
2,000 Y	12,000	6,000
	22,000	16,000

If labour is limited to 16,000 hours we will not have enough labour hours to achieve this. Similarly, if machine hours are limited to 12,000 our production will be restricted.

To tackle this problem we begin by calculating the contribution earned per unit of each product.

Contribution for each unit of X = £ (38 – 8 – 8 – 12) = £10 per unit
Contribution for each unit of Y = £ (38 – 4 – 12 – 9) = £13 per unit

(a)   Labour is limited so we calculate the contribution earned per labour hour for each product.

X = £10/4 = £2.50 per labour hour
Y = £13/6 = £2.17 per labour hour

You get more contribution per labour hour for X than for Y so make as many Xs as possible.

Available hours = 16,000
2,500 Xs require 10,000 hrs

The remaining hours are all used to make as many Ys as possible.

Remaining Ys will take six hours each to make so produce 6,000/6 = 1,000 Ys.

Contribution = (2,500 × £10) + (1,000 × £13) = £38,000

(b) In this case, machine hours are the scarce resource so we calculate contribution per machine hour.

$$X = £10/4 = £2.50 \text{ per machine hour}$$
$$Y = £13/3 = £4.33 \text{ per machine hour}$$

Now it is better to make Ys. Making 2,000 Ys requires 2,000 × 3 = 6,000 machine hours. That leaves us a further 6,000 machine hours for making Xs.

6,000 remaining hours for X means making 6,000/4 = 1,500 Xs

Contribution = (1,500 × £10) + (2,000 × £13) = £41,000

Note that in the examination, if you are told the maximum demand for a product it is a big hint that this method should be used.

▷ ACTIVITY 3 ▷▷▷▷

Luda Limited

Luda Limited manufactures three products: P, Q and R. Each product is started in the machining area and completed in the finishing shop. The direct unit costs associated with each product forecast for the next trading period are as follows.

	P	Q	R
	£	£	£
Materials	18.50	15.00	22.50
Wages			
Machining area @ £5 per hour	10.00	5.00	10.00
Finishing shop @ £4 per hour	6.00	4.00	8.00
	34.50	24.00	40.50

There are machines in both departments and the machine hours required to complete one of each product are:

	P	Q	R
Machining area	4.0	1.5	3.0
Finishing shop	0.5	0.5	1.0
Budgeted output in units	6,000	8,000	2,000
Fixed overheads			
Machining area		£100,800	
Finishing shop		£94,500	

Required

(a)   Calculate the overhead absorption rate for fixed overheads using:
(i)   a labour hour rate for each department.
(ii)   a machine hour rate for each department.

(b)   Calculate the total cost of each product using:
(i)   the labour hour rate.
(ii)   the machine hour rate.
as calculated in (a) above.

(c)   Set out your comments to the factory manager who has suggested that one overhead rate for both departments would simplify matters.

[Answer on p. 69]

5   Test your knowledge

1   Which gives the higher closing stock valuation – marginal costing or total absorption costing?

2   State a fair basis for apportioning the factory rental cost between the various cost centres in the business.

3   Which basis of absorbing factory overheads has traditionally been the most common?

4   What is meant by a cost driver?

5   Does ABC or traditional absorption costing give more accurate product costings?

[Answers on p. 71]

6   Summary

This chapter has revised several fundamental cost accounting topics from your earlier studies, in particular the treatment of overheads including:
·   allocation/apportionment/absorption;
·   service departments;
·   over-/under-absorption;
·   activity based costing approach;
·   limiting factor analysis.

Answers to chapter activities & 'test your knowledge' questions

△ ACTIVITY 1   △ △ △ △

Lorus Limited

(a)   *Memorandum re overheads*

> **MEMORANDUM**
>
> **To:**   Managing Director
>
> **Copy:**   Production heads – sawing, assembly, finishing, materials handling (MH), maintenance
>
> **From:**   Management Accountant
>
> **Date:**   X-X-XX
>
> **Subject:** Statement to show allotment of overhead
>
> | | Sawing £ | Assembly £ | Finishing £ | MH £ | Maintenance £ |
> |---|---|---|---|---|---|
> | Overhead | 75,000 | 50,000 | 20,000 | 9,000 | 20,000 |
> | Apportion maintenance department overhead | 6,000 | 8,000 | 4,000 | 2,000 | (20,000) |
> | Apportion MH overhead | 5,500 | 2,200 | 3,300 | (11,000) | – |
> | Total allotted | 86,500 | 60,200 | 27,300 | – | – |
>
> *Note:*   Service department overhead has been apportioned to production departments on the basis of percentage estimates of relative benefit, as specified.

(b)   4,000 cupboards were produced with the following costs incurred:

	Sawing £	Assembly £	Finishing £	Total £	Unit cost £
Materials	120,000	80,000	20,000	220,000	55.00
Wages	50,000	25,000	40,000	115,000	28.75
Overheads	86,500	60,200	27,300	174,000	43.50
	256,500	165,200	87,300	509,000	127.25

The unit cost of a cupboard is £127.25.

△ ACTIVITY 2 △ △ △ △

Products X and Y

	X	Y
	£	£
Material cost	1.50	4.00
Labour cost	7.00	3.50
	8.50	7.50

Overhead cost:

Set-up

$$\frac{20,000}{40} = £500 \text{ per set - up}$$

$$\frac{500 \times 30}{45,000} \qquad 0.33$$

$$\frac{500 \times 10}{5,000} \qquad\qquad 1.00$$

Purchasing

$$\frac{16,000}{80} = £200 \text{ per order}$$

$$\frac{70 \times 200}{45,000} \qquad 0.31$$

$$\frac{10 \times 200}{5,000} \qquad\qquad 0.40$$

Labour supervision

$$\frac{23,750}{47,500} = £0.50 \text{ per labour hour} \qquad 0.50 \qquad 0.25$$

Total unit cost	£9.64	£9.15

△ ACTIVITY 3 △ △ △ △

Luda Limited

(a)   *Fixed overhead absorption rates*

				Machine area	Finishing shop
				£	£
	Fixed overhead			100,800	94,500
				Hours	Hours
(i)	Labour hours	P	6,000 units × 2, 1.5	12,000	9,000
		Q	8,000 units × 1, 1	8,000	8,000
		R	2,000 units × 2, 2	4,000	4,000
				24,000	21,000
	Overhead absorption rate per labour hour			£4.20	£4.50

(ii)	Machine hours	P	6,000 × 4, 0.5	24,000	3,000
		Q	8,000 × 1.5, 0.5	12,000	4,000
		R	2,000 × 3, 1	6,000	2,000
				42,000	9,000

Overhead absorption rate per machine hour £2.40   £10.50

(b)   *Product costs*

	P	Q	R
	£	£	£
Materials	18.50	15.00	22.50
Wages	16.00	9.00	18.00
Prime cost	34.50	24.00	40.50

(i)   *Labour hour rate absorption*

	P	Q	R
	£	£	£
Prime costs as above	34.50	24.00	40.50
Fixed overheads:			
Machine area £4.20 × 2, 1, 2	8.40	4.20	8.40
Finishing shop £4.50 × 1.5, 1, 2	6.75	4.50	9.00
	49.65	32.70	57.90

(ii)   *Machine hour rate absorption*

	P	Q	R
	£	£	£
Prime costs as above	34.50	24.00	40.50
Fixed overheads:			
Machine area £2.40 × 4, 1.5, 3	9.60	3.60	7.20
Finishing shop £10.50 × 0.5, 0.5, 1	5.25	5.25	10.50
	49.35	32.85	58.20

(c)   The alternatives shown in (b) above produce very similar results. If a labour hour rate were used in total, the rate to be applied would be (£195,300/45,000) – £4.34 per hour – not greatly different from either of the two rates calculated separately. However, the same cannot be said of the machine hour rate which in total would be (£195,300/51,000) £3.83 per hour, compared with rates of £2.40 and £10.50 calculated separately.

Test your knowledge △ △ △

1 TAC gives a higher stock valuation than MC since it includes fixed production costs which MC does not.

2 Factory rental could be apportioned on the basis of the floor area occupied by the various cost centres.

3 Traditionally, overheads have been absorbed as a rate per labour hour.

4 A cost driver is a factor that causes a change in the cost of an activity.

5 ABC gives more accurate product costings than traditional TAC costing.

4

TIME SERIES, SAMPLING AND INDEX NUMBERS

INTRODUCTION

Using time series analysis in order to forecast future figures is a favourite examination topic. You only need to use the time series techniques to forecast future trends.

In Unit 8 and 9 you may also be asked to use the results of the linear regression technique to produce a trend for a series of data.

You should be able not only to use the time series techniques to forecast future trends and seasonal variations but also understand the weaknesses of time series analysis and the problems of using historical data to predict the future.

Sampling and index numbers are also important topics and are covered in this chapter.

KNOWLEDGE & UNDERSTANDING

· Basic statistical methods: index numbers; sampling techniques; time series analysis (moving averages, linear regression and seasonal trends) (Element 8.1)
· Basic statistical methods: index numbers; sampling techniques; time series analysis (moving averages, linear regression and seasonal trends (Element 9.1)

CONTENTS

1 Time series analysis
2 Isolating the trend
3 Moving averages
4 Linear regression
5 Finding the seasonel variations
6 Forecasting with time series analysis
7 Collecting information
8 Index numbers

PERFORMANCE CRITERIA

· Identify valid, relevant information from internal and external sources (Element 8.1)
· Monitor and analyse on a regular basis current and forecast trends in prices and market conditions (Element 8.1)
· Compare trends with previous experience and identify potential implications (Element 8.1)
· Consult relevant staff in the organisation about the analysis of trends and variances (Element 8.1)
· Present reports to management that summarise data, present information using appropriate methods and highlight significant trends (Element 8.1)
· Identify relevant data for projecting forecasts from internal and external sources (Element 9.1)
· Prepare forecasts in a clear format with explanations of assumptions, projections and adjustments (Element 9.1)

1 Time series analysis

1.1 Introduction

The process of forecasting will inevitably involve some analysis of historic data (sales, costs, share prices, etc) in order that future values may be predicted.

The data may concern the economy as a whole, the particular industry with which the organisation is involved (or wants to be) or the organisation itself.

> ☐ **DEFINITIONS** ☐☐☐☐
>
> A **time series** is a set of values for some variable (e.g. monthly production) which varies with time. The set of observations will be taken at specific times, usually at regular intervals. Examples of figures which can be plotted as a time series are:
> - monthly rainfall in London;
> - daily closing price of a share on the Stock Exchange;
> - monthly sales in a department store.
>
> **Time series analysis** takes historic data and breaks it down into component parts that are easier to extrapolate (predict future values of). In particular, it will isolate the underlying trend.

1.2 Plotting the graph of a time series

The basic pattern of a time series can be identified by plotting the recent points of the values on a graph, such as below.

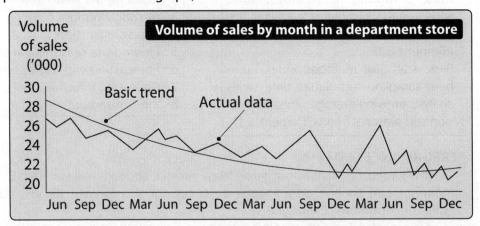

In such a graph time is always plotted on the horizontal x axis. Each point is joined by a straight line hence the typically 'jagged' appearance. Don't try to draw a smooth curve which will pass through all the points on a time series graph. You will find it practically impossible and, in any case, it is incorrect to do so. The only reason for joining the points at all is to give a clearer picture of the pattern, which would be more difficult to interpret from a series of dots.

On the graph above you will see that, having completed the time series graph, we have sketched in a 'basic trend' line. But what does it tell us? We need to look in more detail at what factors are at play in a time series.

1.3   Characteristic time series components

Analysis of time series has revealed certain characteristic movements or variations, the components of the time series. Analysis of these components is essential for forecasting purposes.

The four main types of component are as follows:
·   basic trend (long-term);
·   cyclical variations (not so long-term);
·   seasonal variations (short-term);
·   irregular or random variations (short-term).

1.4   Basic trend

The basic trend refers to the general direction in which the graph of a time series goes over a long interval of time once the short-term variations have been smoothed out. This movement can be represented on the graph by a basic trend curve or line.

1.5   Cyclical variations

Cyclical variations refer to long term oscillations or swings about the basic trend. These cycles may or may not be periodic; they do not necessarily follow exactly similar patterns after equal intervals of time. In business and economic situations movements are said to be cyclical if they recur after time intervals of more than one year. A good example is the trade cycle, representing intervals of boom, decline, recession, and recovery.

1.6   Seasonal variations

Seasonal variations are the identical, or almost identical, patterns which a time series follows during corresponding intervals of successive periods. Such movements are due to recurring events such as the sudden increase in department store sales before Christmas. Although, in general, seasonal movements refer to a period of one year, this is not always the case and periods of hours, days, weeks, months, etc may also be considered depending on the type of data available.

1.7   Random variations

Random variations are the sporadic motions of time series due to chance events such as floods, strikes, elections, etc.

By their very nature they are unpredictable and therefore cannot play a large part in any forecasting, but it is possible to isolate the random variations by calculating all other types of variation and removing them from the time series data. It is important to extract any significant random variations from the data before using them for forecasting.

Random variations will not concern you in your examination.

2 Isolating the trend

As we shall now see, there are three ways of isolating the trend:

· drawing a scattergraph;
· using moving averages;
· using linear regression.

2.1 Scattergraph – sketching a basic trend line

A basic trend line was drawn in on the time series graph shown earlier in this chapter. Indeed one way of isolating the trend is simply to draw it in freehand on the graph. This is called a 'scattergraph'.

This is actually a very helpful method. Once a time series has been prepared as a graph, it is usually a fairly simple matter to sketch in a basic trend line which manages to echo the overall long-term trend of the time series. There are some advantages to doing it this way:

· It is quick and easy.
· It allows one to interpolate a value easily. If you have monthly data for, say, Months 1, 3, 5, 7, 9 and 11 only, plotting those values and sketching a trend line will allow you to see what the likely value for the even-numbered months might have been. On the graph below you will see that we have interpolated the values of £125,000 for Month 6 of 20X4, and £175,000 for Month 12 of 20X4.
· It is possible to extrapolate a figure past the end of the data available (see the dotted line on the graph below). It is always worth bearing in mind, however, that data cannot be extrapolated very far ahead. Common sense suggests, for instance, that the trend line in the graph below is unlikely to continue in a horizontal line for very long - it is bound either to rise or fall. So the extrapolation of £175,000 for Month 7 in 20X5 is not unreasonable, but it would not be helpful to extrapolate the line and make the same prediction for, say, Month 1 of 20X6.

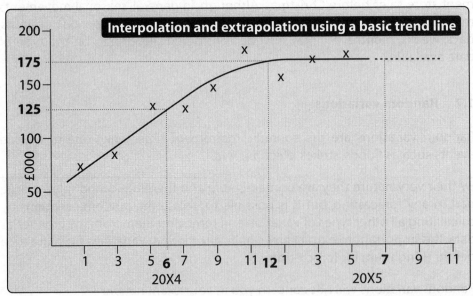

Two other common methods for isolating the trend are as follows:
· using moving averages
· calculating the 'line of best fit' using regression analysis (for a linear trend).

We shall consider these in more detail.

3 Moving averages

3.1 Introduction

By using moving averages, the effect of any seasonal variation in a time series can be eliminated to show the basic trend. This elimination process will only work if the moving average is calculated over the correct number of values (being the number of values in one complete cycle). For instance, if a seasonal variation present in a time series is repeated every fourth period, then moving averages with a cycle of four should be used.

This will become clearer as you follow through this simple example.

○ EXAMPLE   ○○○○

The following time series shows a set of sales figures for eight quarters which are clearly increasing. At first sight, however, this increase appears to be quite erratic. We can however produce this trend by the use of moving averages.

Year	Quarter	Sales
		£000
20X4	1	3
	2	5
	3	5
	4	5
20X5	1	7
	2	9
	3	9
	4	9

Solution

Because we are told that the sales figures are for quarters of a year, it is necessary to calculate a moving average for all the sets of four quarters.

Year	Quarter	Sales	4-quarter moving average
		£000	£000
20X4	1	3	
	2	5	
			4½ (W1)
	3	5	
			5½
	4	5	
			6½
20X5	1	7	
			7½
	2	9	
			8½
	3	9	
	4	9	

Workings

The moving average for the first four quarters is calculated as

$$\frac{3+5+5+5}{4} = 4½$$

Each moving average value is calculated and then placed in the centre of the numbers that were used in the calculation. For example, the first 4value moving average is calculated as the average of the first four numbers, and then placed mid-way between the 2nd and 3rd quarter values of 2004

The moving average of four values captures the steadily increasing basic trend.

It will usually be fairly obvious which is the appropriate order in an examination question due to the way in which the data are presented, e.g. in 'quarters' (order 4) or days of the working week (order 5).

Be sure that you have understood the positioning of the moving averages in the above table. Each average has been written exactly opposite the middle of the figures from which it has been calculated. This results in the moving averages for even numbers of values (four in this case) being suspended halfway between two of the original figures.

Where you have a moving average for an even number of values, it is necessary to realign the moving averages so that they fall opposite the original values by calculating a centred moving average for every two moving average values.

Year	Quarter	Original time series	Moving average (4 values)	Centred moving average order 4
20X4	1	3		
	2	5		
			4½	
	3	5		5 (W)
			5½	
	4	5		6
			6½	
20X5	1	7		7
			7½	
	2	9		8
			8½	
	3	9		
	4	9		

As you can see by the centring process, the centred moving average is the basic trend.

(W) (4½ + 5½) ÷ 2 = 5

○ EXAMPLE 2   ○ ○ ○ ○

The following data represents the sales for TS Limited for the eight quarters shown.

	Quarter			
	1	2	3	4
Year 1	74	100	94	127
Year 2	84	106	120	141

Calculate the trend using moving averages.

Solution

Year	Qtr	Value	4-quarter moving total	4-quarter average	Trend
1	1	74			
	2	100			
			395	99	
	3	94			100
			405	101	
	4	127			102
			411	103	
2	1	84			106
			437	109	
	2	106			111
			451	113	
	3	120			
	4	141			

3.2 Disadvantages of moving averages

· Values at the beginning and end of the series are lost – therefore the moving averages do not cover the complete period.

· The moving averages may generate cycles or other variations that were not present in the original data.

· The averages are strongly affected by extreme values. To overcome this a 'weighted' moving average is sometimes used giving the largest weights to central items and small weights to extreme values.

▷ ACTIVITY 1 ▷ ▷ ▷ ▷

Ski Fun Ltd

Ski Fun Ltd owns a number of chalets in Switzerland that it lets out for holidays. Given below is data showing the number of people who stayed in the chalets each quarter for a period of five years.

	Quarter 1	Quarter 2	Quarter 3	Quarter 4
20X1			92	195
20X2	433	324	95	202
20X3	486	347	98	218
20X4	499	360	104	236

Calculate the trend of the number of visitors. Use a four-period moving average and round to the nearest whole number where necessary.

[Answer on p. 97]

4 Linear regression

4.1 Introduction

The third way of isolating a trend is to use a mathematical technique called 'linear regression'. Only a broad understanding of linear regression is required in the context of producing a trend for a time series.

Regression analysis is a technique for estimating the line of best fit, given a series of data. It is essentially a statistical technique, and the description that follows is only a working guide for applying the technique.

Regression analysis is based on the concept of 'drawing the line that minimises the sum of the squares of the deviations of the line from the observed data' (so it is sometimes referred to as the least squares method). The regression line of y on x is used when an estimate of y (the **dependent** variable) is required for a given value of x (the **independent** variable).

4.2 Equation of the regression line

The general equation for the regression line is given as:

$$y = a + bx$$

Where:

       x is the independent variable
       y is the dependent variable
       a is the fixed element
       b is the variable element

You do not have to understand how this equation is calculated, but you do need to be able to use it.

In particular, you must understand that the independent variable (x) in some way causes the dependent variable (y) to have the value given by the equation.

Thus, if we were calculating the value of umbrellas sold for given amounts of monthly rainfall, the rainfall would be the independent variable (x) and the sales value would be the dependent variable (y) (rainfall causes umbrella sales and not vice versa).

○ EXAMPLE   ○ ○ ○ ○

X Ltd is forecasting its sales for the four quarters of 20X5. It has carried out a linear regression exercise on its past sales data and established the following:

    a = 20
    b = 0.7

The equation of the regression line is therefore:

    y = 20 + 0.7x

When x is number of the quarter and y is the sales value in £000s.

Calculate the sales for each of the quarters in 20X5.

Solution

		£000
Quarter 1	y = 20 + (0.7 × 1) =	20.7
Quarter 1	y = 20 + (0.7 × 2) =	21.4
Quarter 1	y = 20 + (0.7 × 3) =	22.1
Quarter 1	y = 20 + (0.7 × 4) =	22.8

▷ ACTIVITY 2   ▷ ▷ ▷ ▷

Regression line

A regression line has been calculated as y = 192 + 2.40x, where x is the output and y is the total cost. You are required to:
(a)   Explain this formula.
(b)   Use it to predict the total cost for (i) 500 units and (ii) 1,500 units.

[Answer on p. 97]

4.3   The assumptions of regression analysis

Regression analysis is based on sample data and if we selected a different sample it is probable that a different regression line would be constructed. For this reason, regression analysis is most suited to conditions where there is a relatively stable relationship between cost and activity level.

Assumptions we are making:
·   The relationship is a linear one.
·   The data used is representative of future trends.

 KAPLAN PUBLISHING

5 Finding the seasonal variations

5.1 Introduction

Having isolated the trend we need to consider how to deal with the seasonal variations. We will look at two models – the additive model and the multiplicative model.

The additive model is the simplest model and is satisfactory when the variations around the trend are within a constant band width. If, as is more usual, the variations around the trend increase as the trend itself rises, it is better to use the multiplicative model.

5.2 The additive model – finding the seasonal variations

The additive model we will use expresses variations in absolute terms with above and below average figures being shown as positive or negative.

The four components of a time series (T = trend; S = seasonal variation; C = cyclical variation; R = random variation) are expressed as absolute values which are simply added together to produce the actual figures:

Actual data (time series) = T + S + C + R

For unsophisticated analyses over a relatively short period of time cyclical variations (C) and random variations (R) are ignored. Random variations are ignored because they are unpredictable and would not normally exhibit any repetitive pattern, whereas cyclical variations (long-term oscillations) are ignored because their effect is negligible over short periods of time. The model therefore simplifies to:

Actual data = T + S

The seasonal variation is therefore the difference between the computed trend figure and the original time series figure. Thus:

S = Actual – T

○ EXAMPLE   ○○○○

The seasonal variations can be extracted by subtracting each trend value (using the moving averages method) from its corresponding time series value.

Solution

Quarter	Original time series	Underlying trend	Seasonal variation (S)
	(a)	(b)	(a) – (b)
3	94	100	(6)
4	127	102	25
1	84	106	(22)
2	106	111	(5)

6 Forecasting with time series analysis

6.1 Introduction

Earlier we noted that the analysis of a time series into its component parts would make extrapolation easier for forecasting future values for planning purposes.

In general, for short-term forecasts, only the trend and seasonal variations will be used; the cyclical variations will only have a significant effect over quite a long period of time and the random variations are, by their very nature, unpredictable.

Thus the approach to forecasting will be to:
·   extrapolate the trend to the appropriate future time; and
·   adjust the extrapolated trend value by the appropriate seasonal variation.

6.2 Extrapolating the trend

There is no unique method for extrapolation of the basic trend, as it will very much depend upon its particular shape (if, indeed, it has a discernible one).

In practice, computers will be of great help in producing various possible equations for the trend, which can be rapidly tested against the data available to determine which fits best.

If the moving averages method has been used, a certain amount of judgement will be necessary. Possible approaches include the following:
·   Plot the trend values on a graph and extrapolate by eye. (In fact, an initial sketch graph can be useful anyway to get a visual impression of the trend, before using one of the following methods to predict it.)
·   Look at the increments between each trend value for any approximate pattern (e.g. roughly equal, which makes the trend approximately linear or steadily increasing) and continue this pattern to the future time required.
·   If the increments appear to vary randomly, an average increment for the period may be calculated and used in the forecast.
·   If the pattern of the trend appears to change significantly over the period, you may restrict your prediction technique to later data values only, as being more representative of future values.

○ EXAMPLE   ○○○○

We will now use the time series analysis from paragraph 5.2 to forecast the sales value for quarter 4 of year 3, given that the time series figures are the quarterly sales in £000.

Solution

The trend values obtained by moving averages have been plotted on a graph (unless specifically required, it is unlikely that you would have time to do this in an examination).

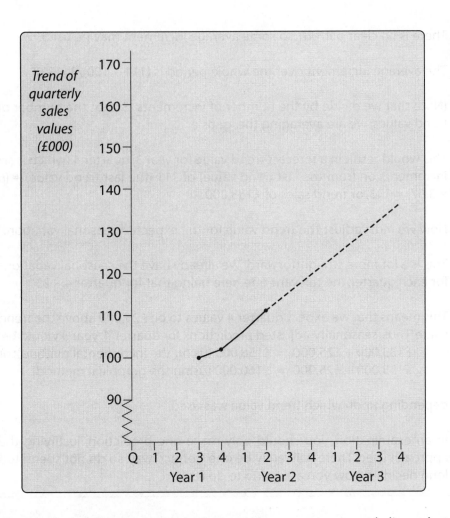

The graph shows an upward sloping trend, very approximately linear, but which becomes increasingly steep.

If we were to use the graphical approach to extrapolation, one approach would be to extend the line using the later, steeper gradient (although it should be noted that the earlier part of the curve shows that this may, in fact, revert to a shallower gradient). This approach may be over-optimistic. Perhaps it would be more prudent to assume that the earlier gradient will continue. The dashed line on the above graph shows a compromise between the two and produces a forecast for Q4 of Year 3 of approximately 135, indicating a trend value for sales of £135,000.

Now consider the increments (the differences between each successive pair of trend values). Note that you do not need to work these out exactly; they will just be used to detect any pattern or change.

From previous quarter to		Trend	Approximate increment
Year	Quarter		
1	3	100	–
	4	102	2
2	1	106	4
	2	111	5

There is no clear pattern, so some average increment may be used.

The average increment over the whole period is $(111 - 100)/3 \cong 3.67$

(Note that we divide by the number of increments (3), not the number of trend values; we are averaging the 'gaps'.)

This would result in a forecast trend value for year 3, quarter 4 (which is six increments on from the last trend value) of 111 (the last trend value) + (6 × 3.67) = 133, or trend sales of £133,000.

Now we must adjust the trend value for the expected seasonal variation.

This is a lot more straightforward! We already have the seasonal variations for each quarter, the relevant one here being that for quarter 4: +25

This means that we expect quarter 4 values to be £25,000 above the trend value. Thus, seasonally-adjusted predictions for quarter 4, year 3 would be:
         £133,000 + £25,000 = £158,000 (using the incremental method); or
         £135,000 + £25,000 = £160,000 (using the graphical method)

depending upon which trend value was used.

In an examination, you should only make one prediction, justifying the approach used. There will rarely be one 'correct' way, so do not spend too long deciding how you are going to do it.

▷ ACTIVITY 3   ▷ ▷ ▷ ▷

Your organisation (AAT CA D94)

Your organisation is about to commence work on the preparation of the forthcoming year's annual budget.

As assistant management accountant, you have been asked to assist budget-holders and to respond to any queries which they may raise in the course of submitting their budget proposals.

Your organisation's sales analyst had made some progress in preparing the sales forecasts for year 5 when she unexpectedly needed to take leave for personal reasons.

She has left you the following memo.

MEMORANDUM

To:	Assistant Management Accountant
From:	Sales Analyst
Date:	12 December 20X4
Subject:	Sales forecasts for year 5

In preparing the sales volume forecasts for year 5, I have got as far as establishing the following trend figures and average seasonal variations.

	Quarter 1 units	Quarter 2 units	Quarter 3 units	Quarter 4 units
Year 3 – trend figures	3,270	3,313	3,358	3,407
Year 4 – trend figures	3,452	3,496	3,541	3,587
Average seasonal variation	(50)	22	60	(32)

As a basis for extrapolating the trend line, I forecast that the trend will continue to increase in year 5 at the same average amount per quarter as during year 4.

Sorry to leave you with this unfinished job, but it should be possible to prepare an outline forecast for year 5 with this data.

Required

(a) Briefly explain what is meant by the following:
   (i) seasonal variations;
   (ii) extrapolating a trend line.

   Use the data from the memorandum to illustrate your explanations.

(b) Prepare a forecast of sales volumes for each of the four quarters of year 5, based on the data contained in the analyst's memo.

   [Answer on p. 98]

6.3 Seasonal variations and the multiplicative model

In some examinations you may be given the trend figures and seasonal variations but, instead of the seasonal variations being given in absolute figures as in the additive model that we have used so far, the seasonal variations may be given as percentage figures. This is the case if the multiplicative model is used for the time series analysis.

In order to find the forecast figures in this case, simply multiply the trend figure by the seasonal variation percentage and either add it to the trend or deduct it from the trend.

○ EXAMPLE ○○○○

Given below are the estimated trend figures for a company's sales for the next four quarters:

20X3	Trend
	£
Quarter 1	560,000
Quarter 2	580,000
Quarter 3	605,000
Quarter 4	632,000

The seasonal variations using the multiplicative model have been calculated as:

Quarter 1	+ 15%
Quarter 2	+ 10%
Quarter 3	– 5%
Quarter 4	– 20%

Calculate the forecast sales figures for each of the next four quarters.

Solution

Quarter 1	£560,000 + (560,000 × 0.15)	=	£644,000
Quarter 2	£580,000 + (580,000 × 0.10)	=	£638,000
Quarter 3	£605,000 – (605,000 × 0.05)	=	£574,750
Quarter 4	£632,000 – (632,000 × 0.20)	=	£505,600

6.4 Problems with forecasting

There are a number of problems with using time series analysis in order to estimate or forecast future results.

· The main problem is the inherent weakness of extrapolation. In order to estimate the trend for the future the trend line is extended on the graph and the figures read off. However, although the time series has moved in that particular manner in the past, it does not necessarily mean that it will continue to do so in the future.
· The seasonal adjustments used to find the forecast for the future are again based upon historic figures that may well already be out of date. There is no guarantee that the seasonal variations will remain the same in the future.
· If the time series has a large residual or random variation element, then this will make any forecasts even less reliable.

▷ ACTIVITY 4 ▷▷▷▷

Star Fuel (AAT Specimen paper)

Star Fuel is a multinational oil company selling oil for industrial and domestic purposes through a network of distributors. Distributors purchase fuel oil from Star Fuel and then sell it on to their own customers.

A regular complaint of the distributors is that they either have to pay for fuel on delivery to their storage tanks or be charged interest on a daily basis on the amount owed. This problem could be reduced if the distributors were able to forecast their demands more accurately.

You are employed as the Assistant Management Accountant to Northern Fuel Distributors Ltd, a major distributor of Star Fuel's fuel oils. You recently attended a meeting with Mary Lamberton, a member of Star Fuel's central staff. At the meeting, she demonstrated a statistical software package used for estimating the demand for fuel oil. The user enters sales volumes per period, and the package then calculates the least-squares regression equation for the data. This is in the form $y = a + bx$ where x is the time period, y is the forecast and a and b are terms derived from the original data. Following further inputs by the user the package can also estimate seasonal variations. Two forms of seasonal variation are calculated: the first calculates the seasonal variance as an absolute amount, the second as a percentage.

One week after the meeting, your copy of the software arrives at the head office of Northern Fuel Distributors Limited and you immediately set about testing its capability. Purely for the purpose of testing, you assume seasonal variations occur quarterly. You enter this assumption along with the sales turnover figures for fuel oil for the last 20 quarters. Within moments, the software outputs the following information.

Regression line $y = £2,000,000 + £40,000x$

Seasonal variations

Quarter	A	B	C	D
Amount	+£350,000	+£250,000	−£400,000	−£200,000
Percentage	+15%	+10%	−15%	−10%

Quarter A refers to the first quarter of annual data, B to the second quarter, C to the third and D to the fourth. The pattern then repeats itself. In terms of the specific data you input, seasonal variation A refers to Quarter 17, B to Quarter 18, C to Quarter 19 and D to Quarter 20.

Actual results

Quarter	17	18	19	20
Sales turnover	£3,079,500	£3,002,400	£2,346,500	£2,490,200

Task 1
Making use of the formula derived by the software package, calculate the forecast sales turnover for quarters 17 to 20 using:
(a)   the absolute seasonal variations;
(b)   the percentage seasonal variations.

Task 2
(a)   From your answers to Task 1, determine which method of calculating seasonal variations gives the best estimate of actual sales turnover.

(b)   Having identified the preferred method, use that method to forecast the sales turnover for quarters 21 to 24.

Task 3

Write a memorandum to your Managing Director. The memorandum should:

(a)   explain what is meant by seasonal variations and seasonally adjusted data. Illustrate your explanation with examples relevant to Northern Fuel Distributors;

(b)   suggest why your chosen method of seasonal adjustment might be more accurate;

(c)   show how an understanding of seasonal variations and seasonally adjusted data can help Northern Fuel Distributors to be more efficient;

(d)   identify two weaknesses within your approach to forecasting undertaken in Tasks 1 and 2.   [Answer on p. 99]

7   Collecting information

7.1   Introduction

As we have seen, the purpose of the management information system and the management accountant is to provide useful information to the management of the business. In order to do this the management accountant will have to collect the information in the first place. However, before collecting information, it will be necessary to determine what the population is that we are interested in.

□ DEFINITION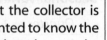

The population is simply all of the items of information that the collector is interested in. For example, if the management accountant wanted to know the proportion of defective units produced by a machine in a day then the population would be all of the units of product produced by the machine in the day.

7.2   Census or sampling approach

If information is required about a particular topic then there are two main approaches to obtaining the information, the census approach or the sampling approach.

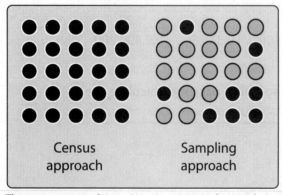

Census approach   Sampling approach

The census approach examines every item in the population

The question here is whether we examine every item in the population, the census approach, or take a sample of the population. In business contexts it is rare to use the census approach so some form of sampling technique will be used. When sampling is used only a small number of items in the population are examined or tested.

Care must be taken when selecting a sample as the reliability of the results will be dependent upon how unbiased the sample is.

7.3 Random sampling

Random sampling is the best method of producing a totally unbiased sample; each item in the population has an equal chance of being included in the sample. In order for random sampling to be used each item in the population must be known and must have a consecutive number assigned to it. The sample is then chosen by random numbers taken from random number tables or a random number generator.

It is rare in practice for all items of the population to be known and for pure random sampling to be used. Therefore there are a number of other quasi-random methods of sampling that could be used:
·   systematic sampling;
·   stratified sampling;
·   multi-stage sampling.

7.4 Systematic sampling

Systematic sampling is a simpler method of random sampling where again all of the items in the population must be known and each item must have a consecutive number assigned to it. Under systematic sampling the first item in the sample is chosen using a random number. Thereafter, every nth item in the population is taken to make up the sample. For example, the 14th item followed by every 50th item would produce a sample of 20 items from a population of 1,000 items.

7.5 Stratified sampling

Stratified sampling can be used if the population falls into distinct layers or groups. The population is split into these groups and the sample is then chosen from each group in proportion to the size of the group compared to the total population.

7.6 Multi-stage sampling

Again this is a method that can be used if the population naturally fall into fairly large groups or areas. Initially a number of groups or areas are selected randomly. The next stage is to take each group that has been selected and to split them into smaller groups from which again a sample is chosen randomly. This can be done any number of times until the final sample has been chosen.

7.7 Non-random sampling methods

In some instances it may not be cost effective to carry out random sampling techniques and therefore some form of non-random sampling is used. These methods will not produce such accurate results as the random sampling methods but the information collected can still be useful. Typical non-random sampling methods that can be used are:
·   quota sampling;
·   cluster sampling.

7.8 Quota sampling

This is particularly useful when market research is being carried out. Quota sampling can be used when there are a number of different groups in the population, for example men under 30, women over 30, etc. The number of sample members required from each group is determined and these samples are taken on a non-random basis from the group until the required number has been reached.

7.9 Cluster sampling

Cluster sampling is where one or more areas of the population are determined to be representative of the population as a whole and therefore the sample is taken from that group alone. For example, if a business was carrying out market research into the buying habits of supermarket shoppers countrywide then it may be decided that customers shopping at three different supermarkets in Birmingham are representative of nationwide supermarket shoppers and the sample can then be taken from shoppers at these three supermarkets only.

8 Index numbers

8.1 Introduction

We have seen that the trend of income or costs can be estimated using time series analysis. However, this method is quite complex and time-consuming. There are other methods of indicating the trend of figures for income or costs and one of these is to use index numbers.

8.2 Use of index numbers

A time series of figures for costs or income can be easily converted into an index. This is done firstly by choosing a base year and allocating to this year's figure an index of 100. Each subsequent period's figure is then converted into a relevant index number using the formula:

$$\text{Index} = \frac{\text{Current year's figure}}{\text{Base year figure}} \times 100$$

O EXAMPLE   O O O O

The materials costs for a business for the last six months have been as follows:

	£
March	427,000
April	442,000
May	460,000
June	433,000
July	447,000
August	470,000

If the index for March is 100, what are the index numbers of the costs for each of the subsequent months and what do these index numbers tell us?

Solution

Month		Index
March		100.0
April	$\frac{442{,}000}{427{,}000} \times 100$	103.5
May	$\frac{460{,}000}{427{,}000} \times 100$	107.7
June	$\frac{433{,}000}{427{,}000} \times 100$	101.4
July	$\frac{447{,}000}{427{,}000} \times 100$	104.7
August	$\frac{470{,}000}{427{,}000} \times 100$	110.1

The index shows that the materials costs are generally rising although there is a fall back in June which has been made up for by the highest level yet in August.

8.3 Indices to measure inflation

Published indices that can be useful to the management accountant are the Consumer Price Index (CPI) and the Retail Price Index (RPI). These indices published on a monthly basis by the Government and are used as measures of general price changes and inflation.

If we have a series of cost or income figures measured over a fairly long time period then they could have been distorted by price changes over the period and may not necessarily show the correct position.

We can use the RPI to adjust all of the figures in the time series into current day prices by using the formula:

$$\text{Current price adjusted figure} = \text{Actual sales} \times \frac{\text{RPI in current year}}{\text{RPI in year of sales}}$$

○ EXAMPLE   ○ ○ ○ ○

Suppose that a company has recorded annual sales over the last six years as follows:

	£
20X0	735,000
20X1	764,000
20X2	791,000
20X3	811,000
20X4	833,000
20X5	856,000

The average RPI for each of those years was as follows:

	RPI
20X0	144.3
20X1	149.8
20X2	153.0
20X3	157.2
20X4	161.9
20X5	170.0

Show the sales for the last six years in terms of current year (20X5) prices and explain what this shows.

Solution

	Actual sales £	RPI adjustment	Price adjusted sales £
20X0	735,000	× 170.0/144.3	865,900
20X1	764,000	× 170.0/149.8	867,000
20X2	791,000	× 170.0/153.0	878,900
20X3	811,000	× 170.0/157.2	877,000
20X4	833,000	× 170.0/161.9	874,700
20X5	856,000		856,000

Whereas the original, unadjusted figures indicated a fairly substantial increase in sales over the period, once the sales are adjusted to current day prices, a different picture appears. In fact the sales increased very gradually until 20X2 and have been in decline for the last three years.

When comparing costs or income over time the management accountant should consider the effects of either general inflation by using the RPI or more specific price changes that affect the cost or income by using a price index specifically related to that cost or income.

▷ ACTIVITY 5   ▷ ▷ ▷ ▷

Price indices

A product which cost £12.50 in 20X0, cost £13.65 in 20X1. Calculate the simple price index for 20X1 based on 20X0.   [Answer on p. 101]

▷ **ACTIVITY 6**   ▷▷▷▷

Restating sales figures

Given below are the sales figures of an organisation and the Retail Price Index for a number of years.

	Sales £000	Retail Price Index
20X1	500	131
20X2	510	139
20X3	540	149
20X4	580	154
20X5	650	164

Restate the sales figures for each year on the following bases:

(a)   deflating each year's sales in order to take out the effect of inflation;

(b)   restating each year's figures in terms of 20X5 prices.

Briefly comment on the figures that are revealed.   [Answer on p. 101]

9   **Test your knowledge** ▷ ▷ ▷

1   What is a time series?

2   Calculate the moving average of the following sales figures to:
(a)   order 3;
(b)   order 4.

Month	Value £
1	10
2	12
3	14
4	17
5	21
6	19
7	17
8	17

3   What is random sampling?

4   Why is cluster sampling an example of non-random sampling?

5   If a machine costs £2,000 on 1 January 20X2 and the relevant cost index has risen from 125.0 to 133.4 from January to April 20X2, how much would the machine be expected to cost in April 20X2?

6   In what circumstances should the multiplicative model of time series analysis be used rather than the additive model?   [Answers on p. 102]

10 Summary

Forecasts of future events are normally based on historical information. Information may be available from a wide variety of sources both internal and external to the business.

Time series analysis helps with the isolation of trends, although these still may not be easy to extrapolate into the future. Remember that you are using historic data which will not reflect future economic and environmental changes.

Also, you must be able to calculate the seasonal variations and be able to de-seasonalise data if required.

In this chapter we also look briefly at sampling techniques and you should be aware of the definitions of the main sampling methods. Finally, we studied index numbers. This is a simple technique but does frequently appear in examinations.

KAPLAN PUBLISHING

Answers to chapter activities & 'test your knowledge' questions

△ **ACTIVITY 1** △△△△

Ski Fun Ltd

Quarter		Numbers	Four-period moving total Step 1	Four-period moving average Step 2	Trend Step 3
20X1 –	3	92			
	4	195			
			1,044	261	
20X2 –	1	433			262
			1,047	262	
	2	324			263
			1,054	264	
	3	95			271
			1,107	277	
	4	202			280
			1,130	283	
20X3 –	1	486			283
			1,133	283	
	2	347			285
			1,149	287	
	3	98			289
			1,162	291	
	4	218			293
			1,175	294	
20X4 –	1	499			295
			1,181	295	
	2	360			298
			1,199	300	
	3	104			
	4	236			

△ **ACTIVITY 2** △△△

Regression line

(a) In the formula y represents total cost (the dependent variable), x represents the units of activity (the independent variable), 192 represents the fixed cost element (£), 2.40 represents the variable cost per unit (£).

The formula is estimating a linear relationship between activity level and total cost.

(b)	(i)	x	=	500
		y	=	192 + 2.40 (500)
			=	£1,392
	(ii)	x	=	1,500
		y	=	192 + 2.40 (1,500)
			=	£3,792

△ ACTIVITY 3   △ △ △ △

Your organisation

(a) (i) Seasonal variations are regular patterns of fluctuations which occur over the year. For example, the seasonal variation for quarter 1 is minus 50 units. This indicates that the sales volume for quarter 1 is on average 50 units below the general trend in sales. Similarly, the sales volume for quarter 2 is generally 22 units above the general trend.

(ii) A trend line is the underlying direction in which a time series of data is moving. The trend is determined by removing the effect of seasonal variations, usually by using the technique of moving averages.

In the data provided, the monthly sales volume appears to be increasing by an average of 45 units in each quarter, after eliminating the seasonal variations. This is the underlying trend in the data, which the analyst suggests should be used to project the sales data into the future. This is known as extrapolating the trend (i.e. continuing its general direction as a basis for the sales forecast).

(b) **Sales volume forecasts**

Working: calculating the average quarterly increase in the trend

Year	Quarter	Trend (units)	Increase in trend (units)	
3	4	3,407		
4	1	3,452	45	
	2	3,496	44	
	3	3,541	45	
	4	3,587	46	
			180	Average = 180/4 = 45 units

Sales volume forecast for year 5

	Quarter 1 units	Quarter 2 units	Quarter 3 units	Quarter 4 units
Trend	3,632	3,677	3,722	3,767
Seasonal adjustment	−50	+22	+60	−32
Forecast	3,582	3,699	3,782	3,735

Quarter 1 trend = Year 4 Quarter 4 trend + average quarterly trend
 = 3,587 + 45
 = 3,632

△ ACTIVITY 4 △△△△

Star Fuel

Task 1

Quarter	Season	Trend	Absolute variance	(a) Forecast (absolute)	Percentage variance	(b) Forecast (percentage)
17	A	2,680,000	350,000	3,030,000	115	3,082,000
18	B	2,720,000	250,000	2,970,000	110	2,992,000
19	C	2,760,000	−400,000	2,360,000	85	2,346,000
20	D	2,800,000	−200,000	2,600,000	90	2,520,000

Working

Trend for quarter 17
Trend (y) = 2,000,000 + (40,000 × 17) = 2,680,000

Task 2

Quarter	Actual	Forecast (absolute)	Error forecast	Forecast (percentage)	Error forecast
17	3,079,500	3,030,000	−49,500	3,082,000	+2,500
18	3,002,400	2,970,000	−32,400	2,992,000	−10,400
19	2,346,500	2,360,000	+13,500	2,346,000	−500
20	2,490,200	2,600,000	+109,800	2,520,000	+29,800

(a) Examining the residual errors from using the two different methods of measuring seasonal variations, the percentage seasonal variation always results in a lower error than the absolute variance. On the basis of the sample of four quarters, the percentage seasonal variation thus appears to be the more accurate method for calculating seasonal variations.

(b)

Quarter	Season	Trend	Seasonal variation %	Forecast
21	A	2,840,000	115	3,266,000
22	B	2,880,000	110	3,168,000
23	C	2,920,000	85	2,482,000
24	D	2,960,000	90	2,664,000

Task 3

MEMORANDUM

To: The Managing Director
From: The Assistant Management Accountant
Date: X June 20X7
Subject: Seasonal variations and seasonally adjusted data

Seasonal variations are regular, predictable and consistent changes in activity that occur over a period of time, normally one year. For oil distribution, the demand will be higher in winter months than summer months, and this is reflected in the seasonal variations for Northern Fuel Distributors. Quarter A is likely to include the winter months, with demand being 115% of the average quarter. Quarter C, with demand only being 85% of the average quarter, is likely to include mainly summer months.

Seasonally adjusted data is the actual data from which the seasonal variations have been removed. It comprises two elements; the trend, or general direction in which the data is moving, plus any random variations. For example, the forecast seasonal variation for quarter 17 was 15/115 × £3,082,000 or +£402,000. Deducting this from the actual demand of £3,079,500 leaves an underlying figure of £2,677,500. As the trend was forecast as £2,680,000, the random error is -£2,500. Possible reasons for this error might be an unusually mild winter or insufficient stock of fuel to meet customers' needs. Provided that these random variations are small, the seasonally adjusted data allows the general direction of the demand for fuel oil over time to be seen.

Seasonal variations can be viewed in two ways: as an absolute amount or as a percentage. Doubling the activity being considered is likely to double the seasonal variation. Therefore, when the trend is either an increasing or decreasing one, measuring seasonal variations as a percentage is likely to be more accurate. As the demand for Northern Fuel Distributors' fuel oil is increasing through time, the percentage method has been used to forecast demand.

An awareness of seasonal variations and seasonally adjusted data enables future trends to be determined, along with variations around that trend. Not only does this help Northern Fuel Distributors to forecast future profits, but it also helps in stock control. By accurate forecasting of demand, excessive stocks are minimised. This helps cash flow in two ways: it reduces cash tied up in stocks and minimises the interest charged on amounts owing to Star Fuel.

There are, however, limitations to the forecasting technique demonstrated. First, the assumption implicit in linear regression is that demand is a linear function of time. Secondly, it assumes that demand is based only on time, whereas there might be other variables influencing demand (such as other competitors and the prices they charge for their energy). Thirdly, the data used is measured in monetary terms. Part of any increased demand may be due to rising prices rather than increased volume. It might, therefore, be better to measure demand in litres rather than value. Fourthly, quarterly measurement may hide peaks and troughs of demand; forecasting by the week is likely to reduce this problem.

△ ACTIVITY 5 △△△△

Price indices

$$\text{Simple price index} \quad = \quad \frac{p_1}{p_0} \times 100$$

$$= \quad \frac{13.65}{12.50} \times 100$$

$$= \quad 1.092 \times 100$$

$$= \quad 109.2$$

This means that the price has increased by 9.2% of its base year price of £12.50.

△ ACTIVITY 6 △△△△

Restating Sales Figures

(a)   Deflation of figures

20X1 $£500,000 \times \dfrac{131}{131} = £500,000$

20X2 $£510,000 \times \dfrac{131}{139} = £480,647$

20X3 $£540,000 \times \dfrac{131}{149} = £474,765$

20X4 $£580,000 \times \dfrac{131}{154} = £493,377$

20X5 $£650,000 \times \dfrac{131}{164} = £519,207$

(b)   Inflation to current year prices

20X1 $£500,000 \times \dfrac{164}{131} = £625,954$

20X2 $£510,000 \times \dfrac{164}{139} = £601,727$

20X3 $£540,000 \times \dfrac{164}{149} = £594,362$

$20X4 \quad £580,000 \times \dfrac{164}{154} = £617,662$

$20X5 \quad £650,000 \times \dfrac{164}{164} = £650,000$

Comment

The sales figures alone show increases year after year. However, once inflation is taken into account the result is different.

Both sets of figures, once deflated by one method or the other, show that in real terms sales values decreased in 20X2 and 20X3 and increased again in 20X4 and 20X5. By 20X5, even in real terms, sales were higher than in 20X1.

Test your knowledge △ △ △

1 A time series is a set of values recorded for a variable (e.g. sales) over a period of time.

2

Month	Value £000	Moving average order 3	Moving average order 4
1	10		
2	12	12.0	
			13.25
3	14	14.3	
			16.00
4	17	17.3	
			17.75
5	21	19.0	
			18.50
6	19	19.0	
			18.50
7	17	17.6	
8	17		

3 Random sampling is a method of sampling whereby each item in the population has an equal change of being included in the sample.

4 Cluster sampling makes the assumption that specific groups of the population will be representative of the population as a whole and selects items from specified groups rather than the entire population.

5 $£2,000 \times \dfrac{133.4}{125.0} = £2,134.40.$

6 The multiplicative model should be used when the variations about the trend increase in absolute size as the size of the trend figure increases.

STANDARD COSTING AND VARIANCE ANALYSIS

INTRODUCTION
In this chapter, we examine how standards costs are set for the various inputs that go into production. This is called 'standard costing'. We then examine how and why the actual results may vary from the standard.

Examinations for Unit 8 will tend to concentrate on the calculation of variances for materials, labour and fixed overheads and the intelligent interpretation of these variances. Note that variances for variable overheads are not examined in Unit 8.

KNOWLEDGE & UNDERSTANDING
· Standard costing (Element 8.1)

PERFORMANCE CRITERIA
· Compare standard costs with actual costs and analyse any variances (Element 8.1)
· Present reports to management that summarise data, present information using appropriate methods and highlight significant trends (Element 8.1)
· Prepare exception reports to identify matters which require further investigation (Element 8.2)
· Clearly and correctly identify variances and prepare relevant reports for management (Element 9.3)
· Discuss with budget holders and other managers any significant variances and help managers take remedial action (Element 9.3)

CONTENTS

1 Standard costing

1.1 Introduction

Standard costing provides us with a system that provides more immediate and detailed information to management as to why actual performance differs from expected performance.

Standard costing systems are widely used because they provide cost data which can be used for many different purposes, including the following:
(a) To assist in budget setting and evaluating performance.
(b) To act as a control device by highlighting those activities that do not conform to plan and thus alerting managers to those situations which may be 'out of control' and hence in need of corrective action.
(c) To provide a prediction of future costs to be used in decision-making.
(d) To simplify the task of tracing costs to products for stock valuation.
(e) To provide a challenging target that individuals are motivated to achieve.

An effective standard costing system relies on standard cost reports, with variances clearly identified, to be presented in an intelligible form to management as part of the overall cost reporting cycle.

☐ DEFINITIONS ☐☐☐☐

A **standard cost** is a predetermined cost which is calculated from management's standards of efficient operation and the relevant necessary expenditure. It may be used as a basis for fixing selling prices, for valuing stock and work in progress, and to provide control over actual costs through the process of variance analysis.

Standard costing is the preparation and use of standard costs, their comparison with actual costs, and the analysis of variances to their causes.

2 Methods of developing standards

2.1 The nature of standards

Whenever identical operations are performed or identical products are manufactured time and time again, it should be possible to decide in advance not only what they are likely to cost but also what they ought to cost. In other words, it is possible to set a standard cost for each operation or product unit, taking account of:

(a) technical standards for the quantities of material to be used and the working time required;
(b) cost standards for the material prices and hourly rates that should be paid.

2.2 Standards from past records

Past data can be used to predict future costs if operating conditions are fairly constant between past and future time periods. This method may not be appropriate for newly introduced operations.

The main disadvantage with this method is that past data may contain inefficiencies which would then be built into the standards.

2.3 Engineering standards

This involves engineers developing standards for materials, direct labour and variable overheads by studying the product and the production process, possibly with the help of time and motion studies. This method is particularly useful when managers are evaluating new products.

The main disadvantage is that engineering standards may be too tight as they may not allow for the behaviour of the workers.

3 Setting standards

3.1 Standard material usage

In setting material usage standards, the first stage is to define what quantity of material input is theoretically required to achieve one unit of measured output.

In most manufacturing operations the quantity or volume of product emerging will be less than the quantity of materials introduced. This type of waste is normal to most operations and the usage figure would be increased by an allowance for this normal waste.

Usually the final product is less than the materials used

3.2 Standard time allowed

The standard or allowed time for an operation is a realistic estimate of the amount of productive time required to perform that operation based on work study methods. It is normally expressed in standard hours.

Various allowances may be added to the theoretical operating time, to take account of operator fatigue and personal needs and periodical activities such as machine setting, clearing up, regrinding tools and on-line quality inspection. An allowance may also be made for spoilt work, or for rectification of defects appearing in the course of processing.

3.3 Basic approach to price standards

When setting cost standards, there are two basic approaches:

(a)   **To use the prices or rates which are current at the time the standards are set.**
This has the advantage that each standard is clearly identifiable with a known fact. On the other hand, if prices are likely to change then the standards based on them will have a limited value for planning purposes.

The standards would have to be revised in detail from time to time to ensure that they are up to date. If this is not done, then any differences between standard and actual costs are likely to be largely due to invalid standards.

(b)   **To use a forecast of average prices or rates over the period for which the standard is to be used.**
This can postpone the need for revision, but has the disadvantages that the standard may never correspond with observed fact (so there will be a price variance on all transactions) and that the forecast may be subject to significant error.

3.4   Material price standards

In setting material price standards, a particular item of material may be purchased from several suppliers at slightly different prices; which price shall be adopted as standard? There are three possible approaches:

(a)   **To identify the major supplier and to use their price as the standard**
This is particularly appropriate where there is no intention of buying large quantities from the alternative suppliers, but merely to use them as a means of ensuring continuity of supply should there be any delay or failure by the principal supplier.

(b)   **To use the lowest quoted price as the standard**
This method can be used if it is desirable to put pressure on the buyer to obtain price reductions from other suppliers.

(c)   **To forecast the proportion of supplies to be bought from each supplier and to calculate a weighted average price as the costing standard**
This is the most satisfactory method for control purposes if the required forecast can be made with reasonable accuracy.

Carriage cost should be included in the standard

Another question in relation to material price standards is whether to include the cost of carriage inwards and other costs such as non-returnable packing and transit insurance.

The objective always will be to price incoming goods at their total delivered cost, so the costs such as those instanced above should be included in the standards.

3.5   Standard labour rates

When setting standard labour rates, one can either use basic pay rates only, or incorporate overtime premiums as well. The nature of the overtime work and the approach to cost control adopted by management will decide this issue.

(a)   If a normal level of overtime work can be identified and is accepted as necessary, or if overtime is planned for the company's convenience, then the relative overtime premium payments will normally be included in the standard labour rate.

(b)   If it is a management objective to reduce or eliminate overtime working, the standard rate may be restricted to basic pay.

4   Standard cost card – absorption costing

A standard cost card is built up using the technical specification for one unit.

A simple standard cost card is as follows:

Standard cost card – absorption costing	
	£
Direct material: 1.5 sq m @ £28 per sq m	42.00
Direct labour: 4 hours @ £5.25 per hour	21.00
Fixed overheads: 4 hours @ £7 per hour	28.00

Total standard cost	91.00

You can see that:

(a)   Standard direct material cost
       = Standard quantity of material × standard material price.
(b)   Standard direct labour cost
       = Standard direct labour hours × standard labour rate.
(c)   Fixed overheads are absorbed using the direct labour hour overhead absorption rate.

(Note that variable overheads are not in the syllabus.)

5   Types of standard

5.1   Introduction

The way in which control is exercised and the interpretation and use of variances from standards will depend on which type of standard is used.

5.2   Ideal standards

In some cases standards are established on the assumption that machines and employees will work with optimal efficiency at all times, and that there will be no stoppages and no losses of material or services. Such standards would represent an ideal state of affairs and therefore the objectives they set are never achieved.

Managers who are responsible for the costs can hardly approve of targets which they can never reach and which, therefore, result in large adverse variances from the standards. This is demotivating for managers, particularly if there is an element of performance-related pay in their remuneration.

5.3 Attainable (expected) standards

In other cases the standards set will be those which are reasonably attainable, consideration being given to the state of efficiency which can be achieved from the existing facilities. There is no question of assuming, as for ideal standard costs, that production resources will be used at maximum efficiency.

A positive effort is still made to achieve a high level of efficiency, but there is no question of going beyond what is attainable.

5.4 Basic standards

A basic standard is one which, having been fixed, is not generally revised with changing conditions, but remains in force for a long period of time. It may be set originally having regard to either ideal or expected conditions. Under circumstances of rapid technological change or of significant price changes, basic standards are of limited value in relation to the achievement of the benefits outlined above.

There may be variations on these methods, but the aim should be to select the standard cost which is likely to be the most realistic for the business concerned. It should be remembered that standards are the yardstick against which efficiency is measured and therefore, if they are unrealistic then the variances will be of little meaning.

6 Advantages and disadvantages of standard costing

6.1 Advantages

The advantages of standard costing fall into two broad categories: planning and control.

Planning

Predetermined standards make the preparation of forecasts and budgets much easier. If the standards are to be used for these operational decisions then they must obviously be as accurate as possible. This again means that standards should be revised on a frequent basis.

Control

Control is primarily exercised through the comparison of standard and actual results, and the isolation of variances. This will highlight areas of apparent efficiency and inefficiency, and as necessary investigations as to the causes of the variance can be made. If these investigations discover the causes of the variances, then corrective action can be taken to improve efficiency in the future or alter the standards if necessary.

In addition to the above, there are subsidiary advantages such as:
(a)   if the standards are perceived to be attainable, then they will serve to motivate the employees concerned;
(b)   a standard costing bookkeeping system can be set up that will fulfil all requirements, for both internal and external reporting;
(c)   recording of stock issues is simplified, as it is done at the standard price.

6.2   Disadvantages

A standard costing system is costly to set up and maintain, and standards must be revised on a regular basis to retain effectiveness. It is for this reason that standard costing is most effective for well-established and repetitive processes, so that the revisions of standards are kept to a minimum.

7   Cost variances

7.1   Introduction

> □ **DEFINITION**   □□□□
>
> A cost variance is the difference between the standard cost of a product and its actual cost.

Cost variances are usually calculated for each element of cost separately, e.g. material, labour and fixed overheads.

We have seen how management will develop standard costs in advance of the period under review. During the course of that period actual costs will then be compared with standard costs, and any differences isolated for investigation as to their causes. This will then enable any corrective action to be taken as soon as possible.

If we consider top level management within the firm, perhaps the board of directors, then they will want to see a clear and succinct summary of the results for a given period. In particular they will wish to see a reconciliation between budgeted profit and actual profit that highlights the factors causing the difference (note that in Units 8 and 9, we are only concerned with cost variances, not sales or profit variances).

7.2   Diagrammatic view of cost variances

Consider the cost of materials for producing 1,000 units of product X.

The standard cost of one unit is calculated as 2 kg of material at £2 per kg = £4 per unit.

To produce 1,000 units in period 1, the process actually uses 2,200 kg which cost £2.30 per kg.

The actual and standard costs for materials can be calculated as follows:
Standard cost of 1,000 units = 2,000 kg × £2   £4,000
Actual cost of 1,000 units = 2,200 kg × £2.30   £5,060
Total cost variance (adverse)   £1,060

This can be shown in a diagram as follows:

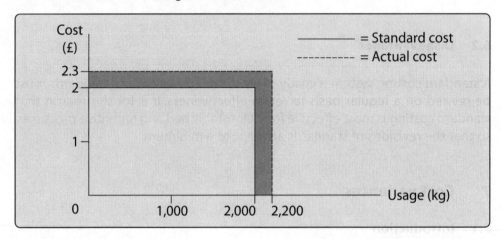

The shaded area shows the excess of the total actual cost over the total standard cost.

We need to analyse this into two parts:
(a)   the price variance, i.e. the amount of the excess cost caused by actually paying £2.30 rather than standard £2.00 per unit;
(b)   the usage variance, i.e. the amount of the excess cost caused by actually using 2,200 kg rather than the standard 2,000 kg.

This is shown in the diagram by dividing the shaded area of total excess cost into two parts as shown below:

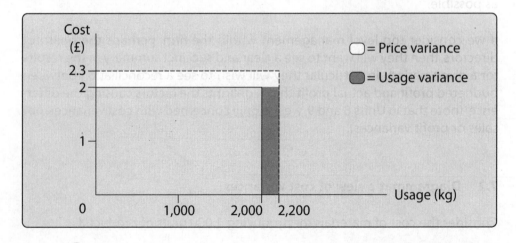

(a)   The price variance is calculated as:

Total amount actually purchased	×	The difference between what was actually paid and the standard price that should have been paid
2,200 kg	×	£(2.30 – 2.00) = £660

This is an adverse variance as we actually paid more than we should have paid.

(b)   The usage variance is calculated as:

The difference between the standard amount that should have been used and the actual amount that was used	×	The standard cost
(2,200 – 2,000) kg	×	£2.00 = £400

This is an adverse variance as we actually used more than we should have used.

The two variances give the total variance as follows:

	£
Price variance	660 (adverse)
Usage variance	400 (adverse)
Total material variance	£1,060 (adverse)

7.3   A commonsense approach

The important thing to realise is that variances are quite easy if you understand what you are calculating.

All you are calculating is the difference between what something **should have cost** and what it **actually did cost**.

We shall see this time and time again as we work through the variances.

8   Variance analysis – absorption costing

8.1   Illustration

The following illustration will be used to show the computation of all necessary cost variances.

Katzman Ltd produces soap in bulk.

The standard cost per drum of soap is made up as follows:

Raw materials	100 kg costing £2 per kg
Labour	12 hours costing £3 per hour

Fixed production costs per month are budgeted at £90,000. For April 20X8, budgeted production was 7,500 drums.

The actual costs incurred in the month were:

Raw materials (900,000 kg purchased)	£1,755,000
Labour (110,000 hours paid)	£341,000
	£2,096,000
Fixed production costs	£86,000
	£2,182,000

During April 7,800 drums of soap were actually produced. There were no raw materials stocks at the start or end of the period.

8.2 Standard cost card

When standards have been set for individual operations or items of material, they can be combined to give the standard costs for products, components or other units of output.

The standard cost card for a drum of soap would appear as below:

	£
Raw materials (100 kg × £2)	200
Labour (12 hours × £3)	36
Fixed production overheads (12 hours × £1) (see working below)	12
Standard cost per drum	248

Working

The only figure requiring explanation here is the hourly fixed production overhead rate.

Based on our budgeted output, we planned to produce 7,500 drums, each taking 12 hours. Thus, budgeted hours are (7,500 × 12) = 90,000.

This gives us a standard fixed overhead absorption rate per hour of $\frac{£90,000}{90,000} =$ £1/hour

Notice here that we have assumed two things:
· we are operating a total absorption costing system, so that all production costs are absorbed into units produced; and
· the basis for absorbing fixed overheads is labour hours.

8.3 A simplistic comparison

Let us now compare the standard total costs with the actual total costs incurred.

	Standard cost	Actual cost	Variance	
Output (drums)	7,500	7,800		
	£	£	£	
Direct materials	1,500,000 (W1)	1,755,000	255,000	A
Labour	270,000 (W2)	341,000	71,000	A
Fixed production overheads	90,000	86,000	4,000	F
	1,860,000	2,182,000	322,000	A

(A = Adverse, F = Favourable)

Workings

W1 Total direct materials at standard = 7,500 drums × (100 kg × £2)   = £1,500,000
W2 Total labour cost at standard   = 7,500 drums × (12 hours × £3) =   £270,000

Why is this a simplistic comparison?

Quite simply because the standard and actual costs are not directly comparable. The budgeted activity level was 7,500 drums, but 7,800 were actually produced. It is not surprising therefore that total actual costs exceed the budget.

It would be much more useful to management to compare the actual costs of producing 7,800 drums with the standard costs of producing that same quantity.

8.4   A better comparison

A better comparison as suggested above is to compare the standard and actual costs of the actual quantity produced.

This is done by what is known as 'flexing the budget', as the following table shows:

	Standard cost of budgeted output	Standard cost of actual output	Actual cost of actual output	Variance	
Output (drums)	7,500	7,800	7,800	–	
	£	£	£	£	
Direct materials	1,500,000	1,560,000 (W1)	1,755,000	195,000	A
Labour	270,000	280,800 (W2)	341,000	60,200	A
Fixed production overheads	90,000	90,000 (W3)	86,000	4,000	F
	1,860,000	1,930,800	2,182,000	251,200	A

Workings

W1 7,800 drums × 100 kg × £2 = 1,560,000
W2 7,800 drums × 12 hours × £3 = 280,800
W3 Remember that the definition of a fixed cost is a cost that does not change as the output changes.

The above table shows the revised variances caused by comparing the standard and actual costs for the actual output of 7,800 drums.

Note: The preparation of variances may be beginning to seem a little arbitrary; we appear to be able to compare different things and produce a different version of what the variances are - surely there must be a right way of doing it? The important point to remember is that you are producing the most useful information for management. There is no right or unique way of doing this. The most useful way to produce the variances is to 'flex the budget' and that is how variances are always produced.

9   Raw material variances

9.1   Introduction

Let us now begin our detailed analysis of the difference between standard and actual cost, by looking at raw materials.

9.2   Total material cost variance

(a)   To produce 7,800 drums we should have used (7,800 × 100 kg) = 780,000 kg. The material should have cost £2 per kg.

		£
	Therefore, 7,800 drums should have cost 780,000 kg × £2 =	1,560,000
(b)	To produce 7,800 drums we actually used 900,000 kg. This actually cost	1,755,000
	Total cost variance (adverse)	195,000

The budgeted level of 7,500 drums is irrelevant here, since we must compute the standard cost for **actual** production.

We shall now analyse this total variance into a price and usage variance.

9.3   Materials price variance

We actually purchased 900,000 kg.

The price variance is simply the difference between what 900,000 kg should have cost and what they did actually cost.

	£
At standard price per kg, they should have cost (900,000 × £2)	1,800,000
At actual price per kg, they did cost	1,755,000
Price variance (favourable)	45,000

Therefore, there is a favourable price variance of £45,000.

This means that the actual price per kg purchased must have been less than standard. We can compute the actual price as follows:

$$\frac{\text{Actual cost}}{\text{Quantity purchased}} = \frac{£1,755,000}{900,000} = £1.95/\text{kg}$$

Thus, for every kg we purchased, we actually paid £0.05 less than the standard price. Clearly, since this is a cost saving, it gives rise to a favourable variance.

9.4 Materials usage variance

We actually produced 7,800 drums.

		£
At standard usage, this should have used (7,800 × 100) = 780,000 kg which should have cost £2/kg	=	1,560,000
We actually used 900,000 kg which should have cost £2/kg	=	1,800,000
Usage variance		240,000

Remember, this over-usage is valued at the standard price per kg.

Clearly, the variance is adverse, since the additional usage above standard incurs extra cost.

Reconciliation

We can summarise the above computations as follows:

	Calculations			£	
Step 1	Actual quantity purchased at actual cost	900,000 kg		1,755,000	Price variance £45,000 F
Step 2	Actual quantity purchased at standard cost	900,000 kg × £2		1,800,000	
Step 3	Standard quantity that should have been used at standard cost	780,000 kg × £2		1,560,000	Usage variance £240,000 A

This tabulation is the method that we will use to compute the variances.

Thus, what we have really done is the following:

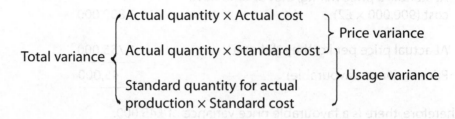

9.5 The style of examination question – materials

The examiner tends to examine variance analysis in a particular way, leading you through the task bit by bit. Thus rather than asking you to just calculate the variances, the examiner may lead you through the answer and ask you to calculate some of the key figures you need and then ask you to calculate the variances. There are many variations that the examiner can use but a typical example is shown below for materials.

○ EXAMPLE ○○○○

Materials Ltd makes boxes and the budget and actual results for June 2008 were as follows.

		Budget		Actual
Production (units)		1,000		1,200
Direct materials	500 kgs	£5,000	530 kgs	£5,700

Calculate the following

(a) Standard price of materials per kilogram
(b) Standard usage of materials for actual production
(c) Direct materials price variance
(d) Direct materials usage variance

Solution

(a) Standard price of materials per kilogram

£5,000/500kg = £10 per kg

(b) Standard usage of materials for actual production

Standard usage for one unit = 500kg/1,000 = 0.5 kg
Standard usage for actual production = 0.5 x 1,200 = 600kg

(c) Direct materials price variance

530 kg should have cost 530 x £10	£5,300
530 kg did cost	£5,700
Price variance	400 (A)

(d)   Direct materials usage variance

1,200 units should have used 600 kg	
which should have cost at standard price 600 x £10	£6,000
1,200 units did use 530 kg	
which should have cost at standard price 530 x £10	£5,300
Usage variance	£700 (F)

Tutorial note

You are not asked to reconcile the total materials variance, but you could do this as follows.

Total material budget cost of 1,200 units from data in question =	
(£5,000/1,000 units) x 1,200 units =	£6,000
Total actual cost from data in question	£5,700
Total variance	£300 (F)
Variances per answer	
Price	£400 (A)
Usage	£700 (F)
	£300(F)

9.6   Interpretation of the variances

The variances computed in 9.4 above act as error signals to management. They in no way explain why we have used more material than the standard allowed, or why we have succeeded in purchasing material more cheaply than the standard price.

If management decided that these exceptional performances (compared to budget) demanded explanation, then investigation would have to be carried out as to their causes. This would enable responsibility for the variance to be identified, and management could then take any corrective action considered necessary.

Some possible causes of the variances in 9.4 above are listed below.

Price variance

·   Purchase of a cheaper substitute than the material per the standard cost and specification. Such an action may be a deliberate policy of the buying department (and therefore controllable), or may result from uncontrollable external factors such as market shortages.

Bulk buying leads to discounts

· Bulk buying leading to discounts that the standard had not envisaged.
· Market factors leading to a lower price than anticipated (this would apply for example where raw materials depend upon random factors such as the weather affecting harvests).
· Using different suppliers from normal.
· The standard may have been set at a 'mid-year' price, anticipating future price rises. Thus we would expect favourable variances initially.

Usage variance

· Sub-standard raw materials. Notice the possibility here of interdependence between the variances. If the favourable price variance is due to buying a cheaper substitute, this may well cause operating inefficiencies leading to an adverse usage variance. Thus, in allocating responsibility for the variances, after investigation we may hold the purchasing manager responsible for the usage variance!
· Mechanical breakdown leading to spoilage of raw materials.
· The standard itself could be too tight (is it an ideal standard that is unattainable in practice?).
· Measurement errors. For example, if there are raw materials closing stocks that have not been recorded, this would overstate actual usage for the current period, but underestimate usage in the next period. Widely fluctuating variances from period to period may be indicative of such errors.
· Operating inefficiencies.

▷ **ACTIVITY 1** ▷ ▷ ▷ ▷

Total material variance

The standard direct material cost of product A is £5. During August 600 units of product A were made and the actual direct material cost was £3,200. Calculate the direct material total cost variance for the period.

[Answer on p. 140]

▷ **ACTIVITY 2** ▷ ▷ ▷ ▷

Materials price variance

A raw material, used in the manufacture of product F has a standard price of £1.30 per litre. During May, 2,300 litres were bought and used at a cost of £3,128. Calculate the direct material price variance for May.

[Answer on p. 140]

KAPLAN PUBLISHING

10 Labour variances

10.1 Total labour cost variance

Referring back to the original example, you will see that the standard for labour per drum of soap is 12 hours at £3 per hour.

The actual results were:

Hours paid	110,000	costing £341,000
Actual production	7,800 drums	

Total labour cost variance

To produce 7,800 drums we should have taken (7,800 × 12 hours) = 93,600 hours

	£
This should have cost, at the standard rate, (93,600 × £3)	280,800
This did cost	341,000
Total cost variance (adverse)	60,200

Note that, just as for materials variances:

· the variance is adverse because the actual labour cost exceeds the standard cost for actual production;
· the budgeted production level of 7,500 drums is again irrelevant;
· again, we would obtain more useful management information if we could analyse the total cost variance further into the rate of pay and efficiency variances.

10.2 Rate of pay variance

We actually paid for 110,000 hours.

	£
At standard rate per hour, this should have cost (110,000 × £3)	330,000
This did cost	341,000
Rate variance (adverse)	11,000

This means that the actual rate of pay per hour must have been more than the standard.

The actual rate is $\dfrac{\text{Actual cost}}{\text{Hours paid}} = \dfrac{£341,000}{110,000} = £3.10/\text{hour}$

Thus, for every hour paid for, we have actually paid £0.10 more than the standard price, and so the labour rate of pay variance is adverse.

10.3 Labour efficiency variance

We actually produced 7,800 drums.

£

At standard efficiency, this should have taken (7,800 × 12) =
93,600 hrs which should have cost £3/hr   =   280,800
This did take 110,000 hrs which should have cost £3/hr   =   330,000

Efficiency variance   49,200

This variance is adverse, because we have taken more hours, and therefore incurred more cost, to produce 7,800 drums than the standard allowed.

Reconciliation

We can summarise the above computations as follows:

			£	£
Step 1	Actual hours paid at actual rate (actual cost)	110,000 hrs	341,000	
Step 2	Actual hours paid at standard rate	110,000 hrs × £3	330,000	11,000 A Rate of pay variance
Step 3	Standard hours that should have been paid at standard rate (standard cost)	93,600 hrs × £3	280,800	49,200 A Efficiency variance

Again, we can show the above in 'shorthand' as:

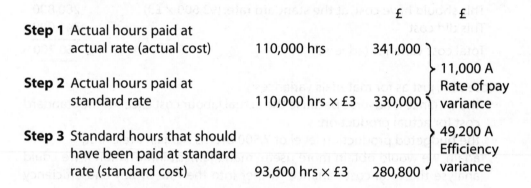

10.4   Examination style questions – labour

As we noted when dealing with material variances, the examiner may test variances in any manner he thinks fit. However he may lead you through the answer and ask you to calculate some of the key figures you need and then ask you to calculate the variances. There are many variations that the examiner can use but a typical example is shown below for labour.

○ **EXAMPLE**   ○○○○

Labour Ltd makes boxes and the budget and actual results for June 2008 were as follows.

		Budget		**Actual**
Production (units)		1,000		1,200
Direct labour	300 hrs	£4,500	340 hrs	£5,440

Calculate the following

(a) Standard labour rate per hour
(b) Standard labour hours for actual production
(c) Direct labour rate variance
(d) Direct labour efficiency variance

Solution

(a) Standard labour rate per hour

  £4,500/300hr = £15 per hr

(b) Standard labour hours for actual production

  Standard labour hours for one unit = 300/1,000 = 0.3 hrs
  Standard labour hours for actual production = 0.3 x 1,200 = 360 hrs

(c) Direct labour rate variance

  340 hrs should have cost 340 x £15 =   £5,100
  340 hrs did cost   £5,440
                                                   ———
  Labour rate variance   £340 (A)
                                                   ———

(d) Direct labour efficiency variance

  1,200 units should have used 360 hrs
  which should have cost at standard rate 360 x £15   £5,400
  1,200 units did use 340 hrs
  which should have cost at standard price 340 x £15   £5,100
                                                        ———
  Labour efficiency variance   £300 (F)
                                                        ———

Tutorial note

You are not asked to reconcile the total materials variance, but you could do this as follows.

Total labour budget cost of 1,200 units from data in question = (£4,500/1,000 units) x 1,200 units =	£5,400
Total actual cost from data in question	£5,440
Total variance	£40 (A)
Variances per answer	
Labour rate	£340 (A)
Labour efficiency	£300 (F)
	£40(A)

10.5 Interpretation of labour variances

Some possible causes of labour variances may be:

· Rate of pay variances
   (i)   Failure to include overtime premiums in the standard, or failure to allow for pay increases during the period.
   (ii)   Rush orders necessitating costly overtime working.
   (iii) Using different grades of labour compared to that budgeted for, which could of course lead to an adverse or favourable variance.

· Efficiency variances
   (i)   Good quality raw materials could lead to favourable labour efficiency, or of course sub-standard materials could cause inefficiencies. Time could be lost in setting up machines after breakdowns, or rectifying poor quality output.

   (ii)   Random fluctuations such as high morale due to the local football team's winning streak.

         Although this last example is somewhat flippant, it does illustrate an important point. We are dealing here with labour – a human asset. As such its efficiency will depend greatly upon behavioural factors.

   (iii) The plan itself could be wrong! Remember that to compute the variance we compare standard labour time with actual labour time. If the standard represents an ideal time, then adverse variances are inevitable. Alternatively, if the standard is outdated due to technical innovations or revised working practices, then again we would expect to see variances.

▷ ACTIVITY 3   ▷ ▷ ▷ ▷

Compute variances for the following examples.

Labour

(a)	Standard	2 hours per unit at £3 per hour
	Hours paid and worked	5,000 hours, cost £14,000
	Units produced	2,800 units
(b)	Standard	3 hours per unit, £12 per unit
	Original budget	20,000 units
	Production	18,000 units
	Hours paid	50,000 hours, cost £210,000

[Answer on p. 140]

---

11 Fixed overheads

11.1 Introduction

Remember that, in order to set a fixed overhead absorption rate per hour, we had to make an estimate of activity level in hours, as well as of the fixed cost itself.

The relevant information from the example is:

Budgeted fixed production costs	=	£90,000
Standard hours per drum	=	12 hours
Budgeted production	=	7,500 drums

The actual results were:		
Labour	=	110,000 hours paid
Fixed production costs	=	£86,000
Production	=	7,800 drums

From these estimates we obtained the standard fixed overhead absorption rate per hour:

$$\frac{\text{Budgeted cost}}{\text{Budgeted hours}} = \frac{£90,000}{(7,500 \times 12)} = £1/\text{hour}$$

This means that, as units are produced, we will absorb £12 (12 hours at the standard of £1) per unit. Thus, there may be a variance due to the over or under absorption of fixed overheads.

For example, if actual fixed costs were exactly as per budget of £90,000, but we actually produced 8,000 units, then we would absorb 8,000 × 12 hours × £1 = £96,000.

Thus we would have over-absorbed £6,000, due to the increased production compared to budget. Finished goods will therefore be valued at £6,000 more than actual cost, and so a favourable variance would be needed to reduce this standard cost back to actual cost. This variance is called the volume variance, and only arises because we have chosen to absorb fixed overheads into production.

11.2 Fixed overheads – total cost variance

		£
In producing 7,800 drums we have absorbed (7,800 × £12)		93,600
The actual cost was		86,000
Total cost variance (favourable)		7,600

11.3 Fixed overhead expenditure variance

Since fixed costs do not vary with the level of production, the expenditure variance is simply a comparison of budgeted and actual fixed costs.

	£
Actual total cost	86,000
Budgeted cost	90,000
Expenditure variance (favourable)	4,000

Thus we have actually incurred, regardless of activity level, £4,000 less fixed costs than budgeted. The variance is therefore favourable.

11.4 Fixed overhead volume variance

We actually produced 7,800 drums.

	£
Actual absorption (7,800 × £12)	93,600
Budgeted absorption (7,500 × £12)	90,000
Volume variance (favourable)	3,600

Remember that the variance is favourable because we have over absorbed fixed overheads. We thus require a favourable variance to compensate for this over-absorption.

We have produced 300 units more than budget, thus over-absorbing fixed overheads by 300 × the standard rate of £12 per unit i.e. £3,600 favourable volume variance.

11.5 Sub-division of the volume variance

The volume variance as computed above can be subdivided further to explain why the level of activity was different from budget. In other words, how did we manage to produce 300 units more than the budget of 7,500:

· Capacity variance

This compares actual hours worked with the budgeted hours, and is favourable where actual hours exceed budgeted hours since squeezing more hours out of our factory enables us to make extra units.

· Efficiency variance

This compares standard hours that should have been worked with actual hours worked, and so is the usual measure of efficiency seen already for both labour and variable overheads.

These sub-variances can be calculated as shown below:

Capacity variance

	Hours	£
Budgeted hours at the standard rate	90,000	90,000
Actual hours worked at the standard rate	110,000	110,000
Capacity variance (favourable)	20,000	20,000

Efficiency variance

	Hours	£
Actual hours worked at the standard rate	110,000	110,000
Standard hours that should have been worked at the standard rate	93,600	93,600
Efficiency variance (adverse)	16,400	16,400

Reconciliation

	Hours	£
Budgeted hours at actual total cost	90,000	86,000
Expenditure variance (favourable)	–	4,000
Budgeted hours at standard cost	90,000	90,000
Capacity variance (favourable)	20,000	20,000
Actual hours at standard cost	110,000	110,000
Efficiency variance (adverse)	16,400	16,400
Standard hours at standard cost	93,600	93,600

Thus, if we absorb fixed overheads on the basis of labour hours it enables us to split the volume variance further into capacity and efficiency elements. The total cost variance must remain the same. The 'variance tree' below may help as a convenient way of remembering this.

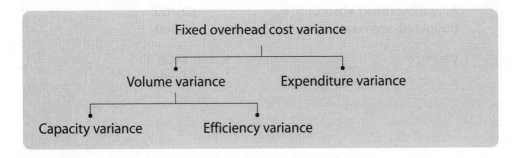

11.6 Examination style questions – fixed overheads

As we noted when dealing with labour variances, the examiner may test variances in any manner he thinks fit. However he may lead you through the answer and ask you to calculate some of the key figures you need and then ask you to calculate the variances. There are many variations that the examiner can use but a typical example is shown below for fixed overheads.

EXAMPLE

Fixed Ltd makes boxes and the budget and actual results for June 2008 were as follows.

		Budget		Actual
Production (units)		1,000		1,200
Fixed overheads		£2,000		£2,500

Calculate the following

(a) Budgeted overhead absorption rate per unit
(b) Fixed overheads absorbed into actual production
(c) Fixed overhead expenditure variance
(d) Fixed overhead volume variance

Solution

(a) Budgeted overhead absorption rate per unit

£2,000/1,000 = £2 per unit

(b) Fixed overheads absorbed into actual production

Units actually produced = 1,200 units
Overheads absorbed into actual production = 1,200 x £2 = £2,400

(c) Fixed overhead expenditure variance

£2,000 – £2,500 = £500 (A)

(d) Fixed overhead volume variance

Actual overhead absorbed =	£2,400
Budgeted overhead =	£2,000
Varaince	£400 (F)

Tutorial note

You are not asked to reconcile the fixed overhead variance, but you could do this as follows.

Overhead absorbed	2,400
Actual overhead	2,500
Total variance	£100 (A)
Variances per answer	
Expenditure variance	£500 (A)
Volume variance	£400 (F)
	£100(A)

11.7 Usefulness of fixed overhead variances

The problem

We must be clear throughout the above analysis that we are dealing with a fixed cost. Refer back to the earlier sections on materials and labour, and you will see that there are no volume variances for these items. The volume variance arises for fixed overheads purely because of our desire to absorb fixed costs into production, and the consequent setting up of an arbitrary absorption basis such as labour hours.

Conflict

Thus we are really seeing a conflict between the use of standard costing for control purposes, and the use of standards for product costing. We may for example base our selling price on cost plus a fixed mark-up, in which case a production cost inclusive of fixed costs may be desired. However, for control purposes the only variance of any real significance is the expenditure variance. Since we are dealing with a fixed cost, then the cost will not change simply because we are operating at something other than budgeted output level.

Thus the volume variance is really uncontrollable, and arises due to our failure to operate at the budgeted activity level.

A partial solution

One solution to this criticism is to sub-divide the volume variance into capacity and efficiency. The capacity variance compares actual hours worked with budgeted hours that should have been worked. When actual hours exceed budgeted hours, the capacity variance is favourable, because we are making better use of our facilities than expected. In other words, we have obtained more productive hours worth of output for the same fixed cost.

If the capacity variance is of some use in terms of explaining utilisation of facilities, then how can we use the efficiency variance? The answer is that the fixed overhead efficiency variance is very different from the efficiency variances computed for labour. Efficient use of the latter can reduce actual cost, but fixed overhead cost cannot be affected by efficiency in the short-run. Further, there is little to be gained in terms of information to management since they are already aware of inefficiencies through the variable cost reports.

▷ **ACTIVITY 4** ▷▷▷▷

PD

PD has the following data concerning its fixed production overheads:

Budget cost	£50,000
Budget production	10,000 units
Budget labour hours	20,000
Actual cost	£47,500
Actual production	8,450 units
Actual labour hours	16,600

Calculate the fixed overhead total variance assuming an absorption system based upon labour hours.   [Answer on p. 141]

---

12 Comparison of budgeted and actual results – operating statements

The Operating Statement with absorption costing is a statement that reconciles

the total standard cost of actual output (production), with
the total actual cost of actual output (production).

Note that the 'total standard cost of actual production' is not the same as the original budgeted cost (£1,860,000 in the example per paragraph 8.4) or even the flexed budgeted cost (£1,930,800 in that example).

It is the standard cost per unit x the actual output of the period, i.e.
£248 x 7,800 units = £1,934,400

The reason for this difference is that the total standard cost of actual output includes the fixed overhead absorption rate for all units produced (£12 x 7,800 = £93,600) whereas the original and flexed budget only includes the fixed overhead budget figure of £90,000.

		£	£	£
Total standard cost of actual output (7,800 × £248)				1,934,400
Cost variances		*Adverse*	*Favourable*	
Materials	price		45,000	
	usage	240,000		
Labour	rate of pay	11,000		
	efficiency	49,200		
Fixed overheads	expenditure		4,000	
	capacity		20,000	
	efficiency	16,400		
Net variances (adverse, there-fore increase costs)		316,600	69,000	247,600
Actual cost				2,182,000

13   Marginal costing

13.1 Standard cost card

So far in this chapter we have dealt exclusively with the calculations for absorption costing. We shall now look at the calculations for marginal costing.

There is only one very important difference between the two. As we have seen, with absorption costing we absorb the fixed overheads into the units produced at a standard absorption rate based on labour hours.

With marginal costing, we don't attempt to absorb the fixed overheads into the units produced.

The standard cost card will look as follows.

Standard cost card – marginal costing	
	£
Raw material: 100g × £2	200.00
Labour: 12 hours @ £3 per hour	36.00
Total standard cost	236.00

You can see that the standard costs for direct material and labour are calculated exactly as before:

(a) Standard direct material cost = Standard quantity of material × standard material price.

(b) Standard direct labour cost = Standard direct labour hours × standard labour rate.

The only difference is that there is no standard amount for fixed overheads absorbed into the units.

13.2 Variance analysis – marginal costing

Having mastered the sometimes tricky calculations in this chapter so far, you will be delighted to know that the calculations of the material and labour variances are exactly the same as before (and so we don't calculate them again here). Even better, if you struggled a little with the fixed overhead variances, the calculation of the fixed overhead variance in marginal costing is breathtakingly easy.

13.3 The fixed overhead variance

Taking the same example as before, the fixed overhead variance is simply the expenditure variance (the difference between the budgeted fixed cost and the actual fixed cost incurred). There is no volume or other variance because we are not attempting to absorb the fixed overheads into the units – hence no volume variance can arise.

Budgeted fixed cost	£90,000
Actual fixed cost	£86,000
Fixed cost variance	£4,000

13.4 Comparison of budgeted and actual results – marginal costing

Having computed all of the variances, we can now reconcile the budgeted and actual cost. Remember that we are dealing here with marginal costing.

		£	£	£
Budgeted cost (7,800 × £236)				1,840,800
Cost variances		*Adverse*	*Favourable*	
Materials	price		45,000	
	usage	240,000		
Labour	rate of pay	11,000		
	efficiency	49,200		
		300,200	45,000	255,200
				2,096,000
Add budgeted fixed overhead				90,000
Fixed overheads variance	expenditure		4,000	(4,000)
Actual cost				2,182,000

14 Sales variances

The purpose of calculating **sales variances** is to show their effect when a comparison is made between budget and actual profit for actual sales volume. There are two causes of sales variances, a difference in the selling price and a difference in the sales volume.

14.1 Sales price variance

The **sales price variance** shows the effect on profit of selling at a different price from that expected. The following example is used to illustrate its calculation.

○ **EXAMPLE**   ○○○○

Budgeted sales   1,000 units
Budgeted selling price   £10/unit
Standard variable cost   £6/unit
Budgeted fixed cost   £2/unit*

*Based upon annual fixed costs and activity levels

Actual sales   940 units
Actual selling price   £10.50/unit

Calculate the sales price variance.

Solution

If the actual sales volume had been sold at the budgeted selling price, the sales revenue would have been:

940 units × £10.00   £9,400

But actual sales revenue was:

940 units × £10.50		£9,870
Variance		470 (F)

The variance is favourable because the higher actual selling price causes an increase in revenue and a consequent increase in profit.

14.2 Sales volume variance

The purpose of the sales volume variance is to calculate the effect on profit of the actual sales volume being different from that budgeted. The effect on profit will differ depending upon whether a marginal or absorption costing system is being used.

Under absorption costing, all production costs are attributed to the cost unit, and the fixed production overhead volume variance accounts for the effects of actual volumes differing from those expected. Under marginal costing contribution is emphasised (i.e. the difference between the selling price and the variable cost).

This affects the calculation of the sales volume variance. Under absorption costing, any difference in units is valued at the standard profit per unit, whereas under marginal costing such a difference in units is valued at the standard contribution per unit.

14.3 Sales volume variance – absorption costing

Using the data from the example above:

Budgeted sales	1,000 units
Actual sales	940 units
Difference	60 units

These 60 units are valued at the standard profit of £2/unit (£10 – £6 – £2):

60 units × £2 = £120 (A)

The variance is adverse because actual sales volume was less than expected.

14.4 Sales volume variance – marginal costing

The difference of 60 units (as above) is valued at the standard contribution of £4/unit (£10 – £6):

60 units × £4 = £240 (A)

14.5 Reconciling the sales volume variances under absorption and marginal costing

Using the above example:

Variance under absorption costing	£120 (A)
Variance under marginal costing	£240 (A)
Difference between these variances	£120 (A)

Earlier in this chapter we learnt how to calculate fixed overhead variances. These too were affected by the choice of costing method. Absorption costing required the calculation of both an expenditure and a volume variance, whereas marginal costing only required an expenditure variance.

Continuing with the data from the above example, there is a volume difference of 60 units. The fixed cost is absorbed at a rate equivalent to £2/unit.

Thus, the fixed production overhead volume variance would be:
60 units × £2/unit = £120 (A)

The variance would be adverse because actual volume was less than expected.

Thus, when reconciling the profits, the absorption and marginal systems would show:

	Absorption	Marginal
Variances:		
Sales volume	£120 (A)	£240 (A)
Fixed production overhead volume	£120 (A)	N/A
	£240 (A)	£240 (A)

All other cost variances and the sales price variance would be identical under both systems. The reconciliation of profits is covered in more depth in the next chapter.

▷ ACTIVITY 5 ▷▷▷▷

A company makes and sells widgets which have a fully absorbed cost of £14 per unit. Widgets are expected to sell for £19 per unit. Budgeted sales are 276,000 units each year, with the same volume of sales in each month.

During November, 23,650 widgets were sold for £425,100.

Required:
Calculate the sales price variance and the sales volume variance for October.

[Answer on p. 141]

15 Materials variances with stock

15.1 Introduction

So far we have only considered an example where all the materials purchased were used so that there is no stock at the end of the period.

We need to consider cases where all the materials purchased are not used and stock therefore remains at the end of the period.

15.2 Materials price variance calculated on purchases

The most important thing to understand is that the materials price variance is calculated on the total of all the materials purchased in the period, whether they are used or not.

This means that any stock carried to the next period is carried at its standard cost.

Note that the materials usage variance is based on the quantity of materials used as before.

○ **EXAMPLE**   ○ ○ ○ ○

X Ltd purchases 4,000 kg of material at a cost of £8,400. It uses 3,300 kg to produce 600 of product A. Product A's standard cost card for material is as follows:

	Standard cost per unit
	£
Material – 5 kg at £2 per kg	10.00

Calculate:
(a)   the price variance;
(b)   the usage variance;
(c)   the value of closing stock in the cost records.

Solution

(a)   **Price variance**

This is calculated on all the materials purchased whether they are used in production or not.

			£	
Standard cost of 4,000 kg	= 4,000 × £2	=	8,000	
Actual cost of 4,000 kg		=	8,400	
			―――	
Price variance (adverse)			400	(A)
			―――	

(b)   **Usage variance**

			£	
Standard cost of producing 600 units	= 600 × 5 kg × £2	=	6,000	
Actual cost of producing 600 units	= 3,300 kg × £2	=	6,600	
			————	
Usage variance (adverse)			600	(A)
			————	

(c)   **Closing stock**

Closing stock will be valued at standard cost.

Purchased	4,000 kg
Used	3,300 kg
Closing stock	700 kg

Value per cost accounts = 700 × £2 = £1,400.

▷ **ACTIVITY 6**   ▷ ▷ ▷ ▷

Y Ltd
Y Ltd produces a product B which has the following standard cost for materials.

	Standard cost per unit
	£
Material – 5 kg at £3 per kg	15.00

Y Ltd produces 100 units of B in a period. It purchased 750 kg of material at a cost of £2,500 and uses 600 kg for production.

Calculate:
(a)   the price variance;
(b)   the value of closing stock of material in the cost records. [Answer on p. 142]

16   Using variances backwards

16.1   Introduction

So far, variance calculations have started with standard and actual costs given in the question and you have been required to calculate the variances.

The examiner may also set questions where the question will, for example, give the standard and the variance and ask you to calculate the actual.

The examiner has indicated that this will only be required for price variances and not for usage or overheads.

○ EXAMPLE 1   ○○○○

A Ltd purchases 1,000 kg of material at a cost of £550.

The adverse price variance is £50. What was the standard cost of 1 kg of material?

Solution

	£	
Actual cost of 1,000 kg	550	
Adverse variance	(50)	(A)
Therefore, standard cost of 1,000 kg	500	
Therefore, standard cost of 1 kg	0.50	

○ EXAMPLE 2   ○○○○

Alternatively, you could be given data on the standard cost and variance and be asked to calculate the actual cost paid.

For example, B Ltd purchases 200 litres of oil which should have cost £1 per litre at standard. The adverse price variance is £0.10 per litre. Calculate the actual cost of the 200 litres purchased.

Solution

	£	
200 litres should have cost 200 × £1	200	
Price variance = 200 × £0.10	20	(A)
Therefore, 200 litres did cost	£220	

○ EXAMPLE 3   ○○○○

An added complication could involve a change in stock, for example.

C Ltd produces 600 widgets in March.

The standard cost card for a widget shows the following:

	Standard cost per unit
	£
Material – 3 kg at £2 per kg	6.00

There was no materials usage variance.

There was no opening stock but closing stock of material was 200 kg.

There was a £200 adverse price variance.

Calculate the actual amount paid for materials purchased in March.

Solution

	kg
Standard amount of material used (600 x 3kg)	1,800
No usage variance, therefore actual amount used	1,800
Closing stock	200
Total purchased	2,000

	£
Standard cost of purchases 2,000 × £2	4,000
Price variance	200 (A)
Actual cost	4,200

16.2 Exam style questions

In December 2007 the examiner set a variance question which required the use of the techniques in this chapter. The following is an example that illustrates the main features of this type of question.

○ EXAMPLE ○○○○

The accountant of Back Ltd has calculated the fixed overhead capacity variance as £8,000 adverse for the month of July 2008.

Fixed overhead incurred in the month was £90,000.
Budgeted production for the month was 85,000 boxes
Actual production was 80,000 boxes.
The overhead recovery rate was £1 per box

Calculate
(a) Budgeted overheads
(b) Fixed overhead expenditure variance
(c) Fixed overhead volume variance
(d) Fixed overhead efficiency variance

Solution

(Tutorial note – most of the question is normal variance analysis. It is in part (d) (step 4 below) that you have to use details of the capacity variance given in the question to work back to the efficiency variance asked for).

(a) Budgeted overhead was £85,000. Budgeted production was 85,000 boxes and the recovery rate was set as £1.

(b) **Calculate the expenditure variance**

	£
Actual overhead	90,000
Budgeted overhead	85,000
	5,000 (A)

(c) **Calculate the volume variance**

	£
Budgeted overhead	85,000
Actual overhead absorbed (80,000 x £1)	80,000
	5,000 (A)

(The business fell short of budgeted absorption by £5,000)

(d) **Calculate the overhead efficiency variance**

Volume variance = capacity + efficiency variance

	£
Volume variance =	5,000 (A)
Capacity variance = (per question)	8,000 (A)
Efficiency variance	3,000 (F)

(The volume variance shows that the business did not produce as much as budget and under-absorbed £5,000 of overhead. The capacity variance shows that £8,000 was under-absorbed due to insufficient hours being worked. This means that £3,000 was recovered by the workforce producing more goods in the time worked).

17 Test your knowledge

1 State three objectives of a standard costing system.

2 Would the setting of ideal standards be motivational to managers?

3 The standard direct material usage per unit of product K is 0.4 tonnes. The standard price of the material is £30/tonne.

   During April, 500 units of K were produced using 223 tonnes of material costing £6,913. Calculate the direct material usage variance.

4 The standard direct labour cost of product H is £7. During January 450 units of product H were made and the actual direct labour cost was £3,450. Calculate the direct labour total cost variance of the period.

5 The following data relates to product C:

Actual production of C (units)	700
Standard wage rate/hour	£4
Standard time allowance per unit of C (hours)	1.50
Actual hours worked	1,000
Actual wage cost	£4,200

   Calculate (a) the direct labour rate variance and (b) the efficiency variance from the above data.

6 From the information below calculate (a) the fixed overhead variance and (b) all the sub-variances, using absorption costing.

   TP has the following data concerning its fixed production overheads:

Budget fixed overhead	£44,000
Budget production	8,000 units
Budget labour hours	16,000
Actual fixed overhead	£47,500
Actual production	8,450 units
Actual labour hours	16,600

   [Answers on p. 142]

18 Summary

In this chapter we have looked at the various ways of establishing standard costs within a standard cost reporting system. We have also examined the causes of variances and outlined techniques which may be used to decide whether to investigate them.

We have revised the computation and interpretations of variances; in particular, fixed overhead variances which are a little more taxing.

Remember that the fixed overhead expenditure variance simply compares the budgeted cost with the actual cost. The volume variance compares the budgeted activity level with the standard activity level and can be split further into a capacity and efficiency variance.

Answers to chapter activities & 'test your knowledge' questions

△ ACTIVITY 1 △△△△

Total material variance

	£
Standard direct material cost of 600 units i.e. standard cost of actual production £5 × 600	3,000
Actual direct material cost	3,200
Direct material total cost variance – Adverse	200

△ ACTIVITY 2 △△△△

Materials price variance

	£
Standard cost of 2,300 litres:	
2,300 litres × £1.30/litre	2,990
Actual cost of 2,300 litres	3,128
Direct material price variance – Adverse	138

or actual cost per litre – £3,128/2,300 = £1.36/litre
thus (1.30 – 1.36) × 2,300 = £138 adverse.

△ ACTIVITY 3 △△△△

(a)

	Hours	£
Actual hours paid at actual rate per hour	5,000	14,000
Actual hours paid at standard rate per hour	5,000	15,000
Direct labour rate variance	–	1,000 F
Actual hours worked at standard rate per hour	5,000	15,000
Standard hours for production achieved at standard rate per hour	5,600	16,800
Direct labour efficiency variance	600	1,800 F

(b)

	Hours	£
Actual hours paid at actual rate per hour	50,000	210,000
Actual hours paid at standard rate per hour	50,000	200,000
Direct labour rate variance	–	10,000 A

Actual hours worked at standard rate per hour	50,000	200,000
Standard hours for production achieved at standard rate per hour	54,000	216,000
Direct labour efficiency variance	4,000	16,000 F

△ ACTIVITY 4 △△△△

PD

$$\text{Absorption rate} = \frac{\text{Budgeted cost}}{\text{Budgeted hours}} = \frac{£50,000}{20,000} = £2.50 \text{ /std hour}$$

$$\text{Actual output in standard hours} = 8,450 \times \frac{20,000}{10,000} = 16,900 \text{ standard hours}$$

Amount absorbed = 16,900 × £2.50 =	£42,250
Actual cost =	£47,500
Variance – under-recovery	£5,250 A

△ ACTIVITY 5 △△△△

Sales price variance

		£
23,650 units sold	should sell for (× £19)	449,350
	did sell for	425,100
Sales price variance		24,250 (A)

The sales price variance is adverse because the units were sold at a lower price than expected.

Sales volume variance

	Units
Budgeted sales (276,000/12)	23,000
Actual sales	23,650
Sales volume variance in units	650 (F)

Standard profit per unit (£19 – £14)	£5
Sales volume variance in £	£3,250 (F)

The sales volume variance is favourable because actual sales were higher than budget.

△ ACTIVITY 6   △ △ △ △

Y Ltd

(a)

		£	
Standard cost of materials purchased = 750 × £3 =		2,250	
Actual cost of materials purchased =		2,500	
		250	(A)

(b)

Closing stock (kg)	=	Purchase – quantity used
	=	750 – 600
	=	150 kg

Valued at standard cost, this gives a closing stock valuation of 150 × 3 = £450

Test your knowledge △ △ △

1 A standard costing system will assist in:
   · evaluating managers' and divisional performance;
   · highlighting areas that are out of control and need attention;
   · motivating employees.

2 It is impossible to be 100% certain, since different managers will react in different ways, but generally ideal standards will demotivate since adverse variances will continually be reported.

3 Standard usage of 500 units of K:

500 × 0.4 tonnes	200 tonnes
Actual usage	223 tonnes
Excess usage	23 tonnes

Valued at standard price of £30/tonne:

Direct material usage variance is:

23 tonnes × £30/tonne = £690 Adverse

i.e.: (Standard usage – actual usage) × standard price = (200 – 223) × £30 = £690 Adverse.

4		£
Standard direct labour cost of 450 units:		
£7 × 450		3,150
Actual direct labour cost		3,450
Direct labour total cost variance – Adverse		300

5 (a) Actual hours worked should cost

	£
1,000 x £4 =	£4,000
Acual hours worked did cost	£4,200
Rate variance	£200 (A)

    (b) Standard hours produced:

       700 units × 1.50 standard hours = 1,050 standard hours

      Actual hours worked = 1,000, thus efficiency variance

       = (standard hours produced – actual hours worked) × standard rate

       = (1,050 – 1,000) × £4 = £200 favourable – the hours worked were less than those allowed.

6 Fixed overhead recovery rate $\dfrac{\text{Budget overhead}}{\text{Budget hours}} = \dfrac{£44,000}{16,000} = £2.75/\text{hr}$

Standard hours per unit $= \dfrac{16,000}{8,000} = 2$ hrs per unit

    (a) Fixed overhead variance

      Fixed overhead recovered in production achieved

      = 8,450 x 2 = 16,900 hours

	£
Fixed overhead recovered = 16,900 × £2.75/hr =	46,475
Actual fixed overhead incurred =	47,500
Variance (under-recovered)	1,025 (A)

    (b) Sub-variances

       (i) Fixed overhead expenditure variance:

	£
Budgeted overhead	44,000
Actual cost	47,500
	£3,500 A

         £3,500 adverse, represents an overspend

       (ii) Fixed overhead volume variance:

Budget production (labour hours)	16,000
Actual production (standard hours)	16,900
Over-recovery	900
900 hours × £2.75 =	£2,475 F

The volume variance can be analysed into a capacity and efficiency variance.

(iii) Fixed overhead capacity variance:

Budgeted labour hours	16,000
Actual hours worked	16,600
	600 F
600 hours × £2.75	£1,650 F

(iv) Fixed overhead efficiency variance:

Standard hours produced	16,900
Actual hours worked	16,600
	300 F
300 hours × £2.75	£825 F

Summary

Overall fixed overhead variance summary:

	£
Expenditure variance	3,500 A
Volume variance	2,475 F
Fixed overhead variance	1,025 F

Volume variance summary	
Capacity variance	1,650 F
Efficiency variance	825 F
Volume variance	£2,475 F

INVESTIGATING AND REPORTING VARIANCES

INTRODUCTION

In this chapter we shall start by revising the variances we calculated in the previous chapter. We shall then concentrate on the ways in which management uses these variances. This will include investigating the causes of the variances, seeking ways to control the variances and ways in which the variances can be reported.

KNOWLEDGE & UNDERSTANDING

· Use of relevant computer packages (Elements 8.1 and 8.2)

CONTENTS

1 Example
2 Measuring the significance of variances
3 Investigation of variances
4 Responsibility accounting and the interdependence of variances
5 Exchange rates and price variance
6 Spreadsheets

PERFORMANCE CRITERIA

· Present reports to management that summarise data, present information using appropriate methods and highlight significant trends (Element 8.1)
· Prepare exception reports to identify matters which require further investigation (Element 8.2)

1 Example

1.1 Introduction

We have seen that standard costs are developed in advance of the period under review. During the course of that period, actual costs are compared with standard costs. Any variances are isolated for investigation as to their cause, enabling corrective action to be taken as soon as possible.

Management will wish to see a clear and succinct summary of the results for the period and in particular will want any unusual or unexpected items to be brought to their attention (exception reporting). In general, this will take the form of a reconciliation between budgeted and actual profits which highlights the variances between them. To be useful as a management tool, the reconciliation should be part of an overall report to management.

○ EXAMPLE   ○○○○

You have already covered in the previous chapter the calculation of basic cost variances.

The following budgeted and actual data for TJB Limited for 20X1 will be used to revise the principles and computations, and lead on to reporting these variances.

TJB Limited – Budgeted profit for the year ending 31 December 20X1			
Produce and sell 10,000 units			
		Produce and sell 10,000 units	
		£	£
Budgeted sales	10,000 units		100,000
Production cost	*£/unit*		
Direct materials – 10,000 tons @ £1 per ton (1 ton per unit)	1.00	10,000	
Direct labour – 20,000 hours @ 50p per hour (2 hours per unit)	1.00	10,000	
Fixed production overhead – 20,000 hours @ 75p per hour	1.50	15,000	
	——	——	
Total budgeted production cost	3.50		35,000
	——		——
Budgeted profit for the period			65,000
			——

During the year to 31 December 20X1, the following actual results were obtained.

TJB Limited – Actual profit for the year ending 31 December 20X1		
Production and sales 8,000 units		
	£	£
Sales		96,000
Production cost		
Direct materials – 7,750 tons purchased and used (£1.0968 per ton)	8,500	
Direct labour – 16,500 hours paid (£0.4545 per hour)	7,500	
Fixed production overhead incurred	15,500	
Total actual production cost		31,500
Total profit		64,500

The purpose of a cost analysis is to reconcile the budgeted costs of £35,000 to the actual costs of £31,500.

Such a reconciliation is a budgetary control statement or budgetary control report.

Solution

Cost variances

	Flexed budget cost of producing 8,000 units	Actual cost of producing 8,000 units	Difference (variance)	
	£	£	£	
Direct materials	8,000	8,500	500	A
Direct labour	8,000	7,500	500	F
Fixed production overhead	12,000	15,500	3,500	A
Total	28,000	31,500	3,500	A

All these total variances can be analysed into at least two further types of variance:
(a)   a price variance;
(b)   a usage or utilisation variance, which in some cases can be broken down further.

Total direct material cost variance

		£	
(a)	The actual amount of material used at the actual price	8,500	
(b)	The standard amount of material that should have been used for the actual production at the standard price – 8,000 tons × £1	8,000	
	Total variance	500	A

To analyse this further we need first to get the actual amount of material used at the standard price: the direct materials price variance.

Direct materials price variance

	Tons	£	
Actual materials purchased, at actual price	7,750	8,500	
Actual materials purchased, at standard price per ton (£1)	7,750	7,750	
Materials price variance	–	750	A

We next need to compare this with the standard materials that should have been used for that level of production: the direct materials usage variance.

Direct materials usage variance

	Tons	£	
Actual materials used at standard price	7,750	7,750	
Standard materials allowed for production achieved at standard price	8,000	8,000	
Materials usage variance (@ £1 per ton)	250	250	F

Total direct material cost variance	=	£750 A + £250 F
	=	£500 A

Total direct labour cost variance

		£	
(a)	The actual hours paid at the actual rate per hour	7,500	
(b)	The standard time allowed to produce the output, priced at the standard rate per hour (16,000 × £0.50)	8,000	
	Total variance	500	F

The total variance can be analysed into rate and efficiency variances as with materials.

Labour rate variance

	Hours	£	
Actual hours paid at actual rate per hour	16,500	7,500	
Actual hours paid at standard rate per hour (50p/hour)	16,500	8,250	
Direct labour rate variance	–	750	F

Total labour efficiency variance

	Hours	£	
Actual hours paid at standard rate per hour	16,500	8,250	
Standard hours allowed for production achieved at standard rate per hour (50p)	16,000	8,000	
Direct labour usage variance		250	A

Total direct labour cost variance	=	£750 F + £250 A
	=	£500 F

Total fixed overhead cost variance

	£	
Actual fixed overhead cost	15,500	
Standard cost absorbed into actual production (8,000 × £1.50 per unit)	12,000	
Total fixed overhead cost variance	3,500	A

This is then analysed into price (expenditure) and volume variances. The volume variance is then sub-analysed into usage (efficiency) and capacity variances.

Fixed overhead price variance

	£	
Actual fixed overhead cost	15,500	
Budgeted fixed overhead cost	15,000	
Fixed overhead price variance	500	A

This variance is also known as the fixed overhead expenditure variance.

Fixed overhead volume variance

This is the under-absorption (at standard rates) due to the lower actual production level than that budgeted.

	Units	£	
Actual production	8,000		
Budgeted production	10,000		
Fixed overhead volume variance (in units)	2,000		
Valued at standard absorption rate (£1.50 per unit)		3,000	A

The variance is adverse because we have under-absorbed fixed overhead by 2,000 units' worth. We thus require an extra charge to the cost account to compensate for this under-absorption. The £3,000 adverse volume variance can be analysed further.

Fixed overhead efficiency variance

	Hours
Actual hours worked for actual production	16,500
Standard hours allowed for actual production achieved	16,000
Efficiency variance @ £0.75 per hour	500 = £375 A

Fixed overhead capacity variance

	Hours
Actual hours worked	16,500
Budgeted hours for the period	20,000
Capacity variance @ £0.75 per hour	3,500 = £2,625 A

The two variances add up to the volume variance (£375 + £2,625 = £3,000 adverse), and shows that the principal reason for our under-production was a failure to devote sufficient hours to production (3,500 hours short).

Having computed all the variances, we can now reconcile budgeted costs with actual costs.

		Adverse	Favourable	
		£	£	£
Total budgeted cost				35,000
Cost variances				
Materials	Price	750		
	Usage		250	
Labour	Rate		750	
	Efficiency	250		
Fixed overheads	Expenditure	500		
	Usage	375		
	Capacity	2,625		
Total/net cost variances		4,500	1,000	(3,500)
Total actual cost				31,500

▷ ACTIVITY 1   ▷ ▷ ▷ ▷

Attainable and ideal standard

(a)   Explain the terms 'attainable standard' and 'ideal standard', and explain briefly why attainable standards tend to be used in preference to ideal standards.

(b)   The budget for product A for a period is as follows:
        Production   2,000 units
        Sales   2,000 units: £15 per unit
        Direct material cost   6,000 kg of XYZ: £2 per kg
        Direct labour cost   4,000 hours: £2 per hour

        Actual results for the period were:
        Production   2,500 units
        Sales   2,250 units: £15 per unit
        Direct materials   5,000 kg purchased and consumed at a total cost of £12,000
        Direct labour   6,000 hours at a total cost of £9,000

There were no opening stocks. It is company policy to value stocks at standard cost.

(i)   Prepare a statement of actual profit for the period.
(ii)   Calculate the following:
·   Material price variance
·   Material usage variance
·   Labour rate variance
·   Labour efficiency variance   [Answer on p. 181]

1.2   Marginal costing

The previous example of TJB Limited was based upon total absorption costing as the fixed production overhead was absorbed into the standard cost of the product. Under marginal costing the fixed overhead is charged to the profit and loss account as a period cost and is not absorbed into the cost of the product.

For the purpose of variances this means that the only fixed overhead variance that exists is the fixed overhead price or expenditure variance. There is no volume variance.

1.3   Materials price variance and price changes

In some examination tasks you may be given information about specific price indices that have affected the materials prices during the period. In these circumstances it is then possible to split the materials price variance into that element that relates to the price increase and any other cause of the variance.

○ EXAMPLE   ○ ○ ○ ○

The standard material cost for a business' single product is 4 kg at a price of £12.00 per kg. The standard price was set when the index for this material price stood at 120. During August, 10,000 units of the product were made using 42,000 kgs at a total cost of £525,000. The August price index for this material is 122.

What is the total materials price variance, the element relating to the price increase and the element relating to other causes?

Solution

Total materials price variance

		£
Standard cost of actual materials	42,000 × £12.00	504,000
Actual cost		525,000
		———
		21,000 Adverse
		———

This adverse variance of £21,000 can then be split into the element relating to the price increase and the element relating to other factors:

Variance relating to price increase

		£
Standard cost of actual materials	42,000 × £12.00	504,000
Adjusted price for actual materials	42,000 × (£12.00 × 122/120)	512,400
		———
		8,400 Adverse
		———

Variance relating to other factors

		£
Adjusted price for actual materials	42,000 × (£12.00 × 122/120)	512,400
Actual cost		525,000
		———
		12,600 Adverse
		———

2 Measuring the significance of variances

2.1 Introduction

As we have seen, the key tool for management control within a standard costing system is some form of variance analysis report or budgetary control statement. The aim is to prepare a report to management on a routine basis in which variances are clearly identified and can be acted upon as appropriate.

In exercising control, it is generally impracticable to review every variance in detail at each accounting period and attention will usually be concentrated on those variances which have the greatest impact on the achievement of the budget plan.

2.2   Identifying significant variances

One method of identifying significant variances is to express each variance as a percentage of the related budget allowance or standard value. Those showing the highest percentage deviation would then be given the most urgent attention.

This method, however, could result in lack of attention to variances which, although representing a small percentage of the standard value, nevertheless involve significant sums of money. Both percentages and absolute values should be looked at in deciding where the priorities for control actually lie.

In practice, management will review the variance report presented to them and decide which variances should be investigated on the basis of whether the costs of investigation are outweighed by the benefits. Management will often request a more detailed analysis and explanation of specific variances to be produced as the decision as to whether or not a variance merits investigation may need more information than is provided in the original variance report.

2.3   Fluctuating variances – looking at trends

The variances of a particular period may not be representative of a general trend. Items like stationery costs can fluctuate widely from month to month, dependent on the amount of stationery that has been invoiced. Sometimes the

accountant will make estimated adjustments to either the budget or the actual figures in an attempt to give a better picture of the underlying trend but this is not a completely satisfactory way of dealing with the matter. The simplest way of getting the month's figures into context is to show also the accumulated cost for the year to date. High cost and low cost periods will then be revealed but will balance out in the cumulative figures.

Items like stationery costs can fluctuate widely from month to month

A development of the above idea is also to report each period the manager's latest forecast compared with the annual budget. It will then be possible to see whether variances from budget currently being reported are likely to continue to accumulate during the remainder of the year, or whether they will be offset by later opposite variances. Although this technique of forecasting is dependent on managers' subjective assessments, it is a good way of ensuring that the correct control action gets taken on the current figures.

○ EXAMPLE ○○○○

You might like to spend a few minutes considering what the report below tells you about the business.

Profit and loss account – Seven periods cumulative to ... 20...

	Period 7			Cumulative			Whole year	
			Variances			Variances		Latest
	Budget	Actual	For (A)	Budget	Actual	For (A)	Budget	forecast
	£000	£000	£000	£000	£000	£000	£000	£000
Sales	500	600	100	3,500	3,420	(80)	6,000	6,200
Direct cost of sales	280	322	(42)	1,960	1,951	9	3,500	3,850
Factory overhead	58	69	(11)	420	400	20	700	750
Administration and selling costs	122	123	(1)	840	800	40	1,320	1,147
Total costs	460	514	(54)	3,220	3,151	69	5,520	5,747
Operating profit	40	86	46	280	269	(11)	480	453
Profit: Sales %	8	14.3	–	8	7.9	–	8	7.3

Solution

(a) Sales, which had obviously been below budget for the first six periods of the year, are significantly in excess of budget for period 7 (reducing the cumulative shortfall to £80,000), and are now expected to exceed the budget for the year as a whole.

(b) Direct costs are naturally higher when sales are higher. The percentage of direct costs to sales value is not consistent, however, as the following calculations show:

	Budget	Actual
Period 7	56.0%	53.7%
Cumulative to date	56.0%	57.0%
Forecast for whole year	58.3%	62.1%

For the seven periods as a whole, direct costs have been in excess of the budgeted percentage and even though the budget for the twelve months provides for an increase in that percentage the forecast actual increase is still higher. Period 7 in isolation shows an anomalous result, perhaps due to some peculiarity in sales mix.

(c) The variance on factory overhead, which is favourable over the seven periods as a whole, has become adverse in period 7 and is forecast as adverse for the year as a whole (though not at the rate experienced in period 7). Failure to budget adequately for inflationary increases is one possibility.

(d) Administration and selling costs have a cumulative favourable variance to date of £40,000 against a budget of £840,000, i.e. 4.8%. By the end of the year a favourable variance of £173,000 (13.1% on budget) is expected. It would appear that considerable economies are planned, and have already commenced. The fact that period 7 above shows a small adverse variance is not significant. Such results can emerge in administration costs, which can be influenced by random occurrences like a large purchase of stationery or a major visit overseas by the managing director.

2.4 Comparing against forecasts

Some large organisations in the UK have taken the idea of comparing against forecasts a step further. Many companies employ the following comparisons.

	Comparison	Information
1	Budget v actual	What progress have we made towards achieving objectives?
2	Budget v forecast	Will we continue to progress towards achievement of objectives?
3	Budget v revised forecast	Will suggested corrective actions lead us back to achievement of objectives?
4	Latest forecast v previous	Why are the forecasts different and are circumstances getting better or worse?
5	Actual v past forecast	Why were forecasts incorrect and can they be improved?

It may not be necessary to perform each of these control comparisons every month or quarter. The actual versus past forecast may only be necessary annually or less frequently.

It must be remembered that managers will need to be motivated to produce these forecasts and use them. They must be educated to recognise why and how they can use them to enable them to do a better job and not feel that they are just another means for higher level management to check on them and apply pressure.

Finally, this year's results are sometimes compared with those for the corresponding period last year. In some cases this may be helpful in establishing a trend, but it must never be forgotten that the budget is this year's plan, and it is against that plan that performance must be controlled.

3 Investigation of variances

3.1 Introduction

Variance analysis, if properly carried out, can be a useful cost-controlling and cost-saving tool. However, the traditional variance analysis seen so far is only a step towards the final goal of controlling and saving costs.

3.2 Generalised reasons for variances

The causes of variances can be classified under four headings:
· Planning errors
· Measurement errors
· Random factors
· Operational causes

Planning errors lead to the setting of inappropriate standards or budgets. This may be due to carelessness on the part of the standard setter (not taking account of known changes in the production process or expected price rises, for example) or due to unexpected external changes (a market shortage of a resource leading to increased price. These need to be isolated from hindsight information and a revision of the standard considered for future budgets.

Measurement errors include errors caused by inaccurate completion of timesheets or job cards, inaccurate measurement of quantities issued from stores, etc. The rectification of such errors or errors caused by random factors will probably not give rise to any cost savings (though this is a generalisation).

Random factors are by definition uncontrollable, although they need careful monitoring to ensure that they are not, in fact, one of the other types of variance.

3.3 Operational causes of variances

Examples of some specific reasons for individual variances are shown below.

Variance		Possible causes
Materials:	Price	Bulk discounts
		Different suppliers
		Different materials
		Unexpected delivery costs
		Different buying procedures
	Usage	Different quality material
		Theft, obsolescence, deterioration
		Different quality of staff
		Different mix of material
		Different batch sizes and trim loss

Variance		Possible causes
Labour:	Rate	Different class of labour
		Excessive overtime
		Productivity bonuses
		National wage negotiations
		Union action
	Efficiency	Different levels of skill
		Different working conditions
		The learning effect
		Lack of supervision
		Works to rule
		Machine breakdowns
		Lack of material
		Lack of orders
		Strikes (if paid)
		Too long over coffee breaks
Overhead:	Price	Change in nature of overhead
		Unforeseen price changes
	Volume	Excessive idle time
		Increase in workforce

It will nearly always be useful to consult staff working in operational departments to resolve any queries in the data as they will have 'local' knowledge of the day-to-day operations.

○ EXAMPLE ○○○○

An adverse materials usage variance of £50,000 arose in a month as follows:

Standard cost per kg	£10
Actual cost per kg	£12
Units produced	2,000
Standard quantity per unit	25 kg
Actual quantity used	55,000 kg

	£
Standard cost of actual usage (55,000 kg × £10)	550,000
Standard cost of standard usage (2,000 × 25 kg × £10)	500,000
Adverse usage variance	50,000

On further investigation, the following is ascertained.

1. The actual quantity used was based on estimated stock figures. A stocktake showed that 53,000 kg were in fact used.

2. 3,000 kg is the best estimate for what might politely be called the monthly 'shrinkage' but, in less polite circles, theft.

3   2,000 kg of stock were damaged by hoodlums who broke into the stores through some of the shaky panelling.

4   The supervisor feels that existing machinery is outmoded and more efficient machinery could save 1,000 kg a month.

Additional considerations

1   A security guard would cost £9,000 a year to employ and would stop 20% of all theft. Resultant dissatisfaction amongst works staff might cost £20,000 per annum.

2   Given the easy access to stores, vandals might be expected to break in every other month; £10,000 would make the stores vandal-proof.

3   New machinery would cost £720,000.

Analyse the usage variance in the light of this information and comment on your results.

Solution

The original £50,000 usage variance could be analysed as follows:

		Adverse/(favourable) variance £
(a)	Bad measurement (53,000 – 55,000) × £10	20,000
(b)	Theft (3,000 × £10)	30,000
(c)	Damage (2,000 × £10)	20,000
(d)	Obsolete machinery (1,000 × £10)	10,000
(e)	Other operational factors (balance)	(30,000)
		50,000

In each case, the variances should be studied and compared with the cost of rectification.

(a)   **Bad measurement** – Assuming no costly decisions were made, or are likely to be made in the future, such as over-stocking, the component is of no future consequence.

(b)   **Theft** – Annual cost due to theft is 12 × £30,000 or £360,000; 20% of this saved would amount to £72,000 at a cost of £9,000 + £20,000, thus the security guard is worth employing.

(c)   **Damage** – Annual cost due to vandalism is 6 × £20,000 or £120,000; this would presumably be avoided by spending £10,000 now; again worthwhile.

(d)   **Obsolete machinery** – Annual cost of using old machines is 12 × £10,000 or £120,000; the cost of making this saving (the saving would increase as purchase prices increased or if production increased) is £720,000; the decision over this investment would require further consideration such as discounted cash flow analysis.

(e)   **Other factors** – We now see a favourable usage variance once all known factors above have been accounted for. This may need further investigation, particularly if it affects the quality of goods produced.

3.4 Fixed overhead variances

These are worth a special note, due to the particular nature of the fixed overhead volume variance.

We have seen that the volume variance is a product of the TAC system, and represents the adjustment for over-/under-absorption of fixed costs due to actual production being higher or lower than budgeted. Unlike the other variances, it does not actually represent a cost saving or overspend.

If this is the case, is it worth spending any time on the investigation of fixed overhead volume variances? Does it really matter if overheads are under-/over-absorbed, since it will all be adjusted for in the end?

The problem with having an inappropriate absorption rate is that decisions may have been taken on a unit cost that is too high or too low - for example, in setting the price of a product. If this is too high, sales may have been unnecessarily lost; if it is too low, profit margins may have been significantly eroded.

To minimise such effects of over-/under-absorption, regular reviews should be conducted of expenditure and activity levels arising throughout the period. The absorption rate can then be adjusted if it is felt necessary to reflect more recent estimates of expenditure and activity levels.

3.5 The cost of variance analysis

The provision of any information involves the costs of collecting the basic data, processing it, and reporting the results. Variance analysis is no exception and, as with other forms of management information, the benefits to which it gives rise must be commensurate with the costs incurred.

(a) Variance analysis allows 'management by exception' and it is presumably for this purpose that a standard costing system has been introduced.
(b) When variances are known to exist, failure to make adequate investigations, even on a random basis, will weaken the control system and thus the motivation of managers.
(c) The amount of analysis required can sometimes be reduced by defining levels of significance below which detailed investigation is not required.
(d) The costs of clerical work can be over-estimated. In most working days there will be some spare capacity that can be utilised without extra cost.

What has to be considered, therefore, is the amount of detail that can be incorporated usefully in variance analysis. This will fall into two categories:
(a) **Including more detailed codings** in source documents indicating causes and responsibilities. Such coding is likely to involve people outside the accounts department, who may be unwilling to give time to the task. How useful the analysis will be, will depend on whether or not it is practicable to identify causes and responsibilities at the time the document is initiated.

(b) **Investigations and re-analysis of variances after the event.** This can involve the time of quite senior people, but the process of investigation may well be more useful from the point of view of the management of the business than any quantity of formal variance calculations.

▷ ACTIVITY 2   ▷ ▷ ▷ ▷

Excelsior Manufacturing Company

Excelsior Manufacturing Company produces a single product on an assembly line. As budget officer you have prepared the following production budgets from the best information available, to represent the extremes of high and low volume of production likely to be encountered by the company over a three month period.

	Production of 4,000 units £	Production of 8,000 units £
Direct materials	80,000	160,000
Indirect materials	12,000	20,000
Direct labour	50,000	100,000
Power	18,000	24,000
Repairs	20,000	30,000
Supervision	20,000	36,000
Rent, insurance and rates	9,000	9,000

Supervision is a 'step function'. One supervisor is employed for all production levels up to and including 5,000 units. For higher levels of production, an assistant supervisor (£16,000) is also required. For power, a minimum charge is payable on all production up to and including 6,000 units. For production above this level, there is an additional variable charge based on the power consumed.

Other variable and semi-variable costs are incurred evenly over the production range.

Required

(a) Prepare a set of flexible budgets for presentation to the production manager to cover the following levels of production over a period of three months:
- (i) 4,000 units
- (ii) 5,000 units
- (iii) 6,000 units
- (iv) 7,000 units
- (v) 8,000 units

(b) During the three months July to September (covering most of the summer holiday period) 5,000 units were produced. Costs incurred during the three-month period were as follows:

	£
Direct materials	110,000
Indirect materials	14,000
Direct labour	70,000
Power	18,000
Repairs	30,000
Supervision	20,000
Rent, insurance and rates	8,000

Note that **price variances** have been eliminated from the figures for direct and indirect materials and **rate variances** have been eliminated from the labour and supervision costs.

Required

You are preparing a budget report for presentation to the production manager. For each variance suggest any further investigations which might be required and any action which might be taken by the production manager.

[Answer on p. 182]

4 Responsibility accounting and the interdependence of variances

4.1 Introduction

It is part of any system aimed at improving the performance of a business or any part of the business, that actions shall be traced to the person responsible. This may give the impression of 'laying the blame', but it is equally possible to award praise (and remunerate accordingly).

We have seen that responsibility accounting is a system which recognises various decision centres within a business and traces costs (and possibly revenues) to the individual managers who are primarily responsible for making decisions about the items in question.

○ EXAMPLE   ○○○○

An opportunity arises for a buying department to obtain a consignment of a particular material at an exceptionally low price. The purchase is made; a favourable price variance is recorded and the buying department is duly praised.

Subsequently, when products are being manufactured using this type of material, significant adverse material usage variances and labour efficiency variances are recorded, and are initially regarded as the responsibility of the department where the work is done.

Is it fair to blame the adverse variances on the operational departments?

Solution

Investigations may reveal a number of relevant facts, for example:

· The 'cheap' material was of poor quality, and in consequence much of it was wasted in the process of machining. The resultant material usage and labour efficiency variances should presumably be regarded as the responsibility of the buying department, to offset the favourable price variance.

· Due to an employee leaving it had been necessary to use an operator who was not familiar with the job. At least part of the excess usage of materials could be attributed to this cause; but whether it should be regarded as the responsibility of the operating department or of the personnel department (for failing to recruit a replacement) is still open to question. If the employee who left had been highly paid, his removal might cause a favourable wage rate variance in the period under review - an offset to the adverse efficiency variance.

· The tools used had been badly worn, thus causing excessive time on the job. It would be necessary to consider whether this condition was attributable to the operating department (failing to sharpen tools or to requisition replacements) or to the tools store-keeper or to the buying department (for failing to buy on time or for buying poor quality items again).

The important points to bear in mind are as follows:

· Different types of variance can be inter-linked by a common cause.

· In many cases, the responsibility for variances cannot be identified merely by reference to the cost centre where the variance has been reported. Responsibility may be shared by several managers or may lie completely outside the cost centre in which the variance has arisen.

5 Exchange rates and price variances

5.1 Introduction

Material price variances are sometimes caused by movements of the exchange rate of a currency when the materials are imported from an overseas country.

The following table illustrates the effect on the Sterling price in the UK of good which is imported from the United States if the exchange rate of the pound and dollar changes:

Price of good in US	Exchange rate	Price of good in UK
$1	£1 = $1.50	£ $\frac{1}{1.50}$ = £0.67
$1	£1 = $2.00	£ $\frac{1}{2.00}$ = £0.50

The price of the good in the US does not change, but as the exchange rate changes, the UK price also changes.

Thus, when £1 = $1.50, the imported good costs £0.67. But when the pound strengthens against the dollar (so that you now buy $2 rather than $1.50 for every pound), the imported good becomes cheaper – it now only costs £0.50.

The dollar price of course remains the same. However, because £1 buys more dollars, UK importers get more for their money so that the UK price in pounds falls.

5.2   Price variances

How does this affect price variances?

The first thing to note is that it doesn't affect the total variance – that can still be calculated as before. However, a changing exchange rate does affect the way we can analyse and explain a price variance.

Consider the following example.

○ **EXAMPLE**   ○○○○

D Ltd buys 2,000 kg of material for £2,000 in March 20X5. The standard cost of the material was set at £1.05 per kg when the standards were set in May 20X4. The material is imported from the US. The exchange rate has changed from £1 = $1.50 in May 20X4 to £1 = $1.65 in March 20X5.

(a)   **Calculating the price variance using the traditional method.**

Amount that should have been paid for 2,000 kg = 2,000 × £1.05 = £2,100
Amount actually paid   = £2,000
Price variance   £100(F)

(b)   **Calculating the price variance taking account of the changed exchange rate.**

The person responsible for purchasing the materials may feel pleased if they are given credit for the £100 favourable variance.

However, things may not be as they seem.

Hence, we shall separate out the effect of the exchange rates. We do this by altering the standard cost in line with the exchange rate and calculating **two** price variances.

(i)   a price variance caused by the exchange rate (sometimes referred to as a 'planning variance' because a factor outside the company control has caused the original standard to be wrong);

(ii)   a price variance caused by the way the company actually bought the materials (sometimes called an 'operating variance' because it is caused by the normal operations of the company).

The relevant prices and variances can be set out as follows:

Original standard cost = 2,000 kg × £1.05		= £2,100	
			£191 (F) (Planning)
Exchange rate adjusted = 2,000 kg × $\left[£1.05 \times \dfrac{1.50}{1.65}\right]$ = £1,909			
			£91 (A) (Operating)
Actual cost = 2,000 x £1.00		= £2,000	
Total variance			£100 (F)

The total variance is still £100 (F) but this is due to a movement in the exchange rate. The company's operations have resulted in an unfavourable price variance of £91.

▷ ACTIVITY 3   ▷▷▷▷

WH Limited (AAT CA D94)

WH Limited uses a standard costing system which produces monthly control statements to manufacture product M, a perishable, high quality raw material which is carefully weighed by direct employees. Some wastage and quality control rejects occur at this stage. The employees then compress the material to change its shape and create product M.

All direct employees are paid a basic hourly rate appropriate to their individual skill level and a bonus scheme is in operation. Bonuses are paid according to the daily rate of output achieved by each individual.

A standard allowance for all of the above operational factors is included in the standard cost of product M. Standard cost data for one unit of product M is as follows:

		Standard cost £ per unit
Direct material X:	4.5 kg × £4.90 per kg	22.05
Direct labour:	10.3 hours × £3.50 per hour	36.05
Standard direct cost		58.10

The production manager has approached you for further explanations concerning the standard costing control system. He is particularly interested in understanding how the standard price is set per kg of material used.

Task 1

Write a memo to the production manager, explaining the following:

(a)   what information would be needed to determine the standard price per kg of material X;

(b)   the possible sources from which this information might be obtained.

Further data

During November, the following costs were incurred producing 400 units of product M:

		Actual costs
		£
Direct material X:	2,100 kg @ £4.60 per kg	9,660
Direct labour:	4,000 hrs@ £4.00 per hr	16,000
Actual direct cost		25,660

Task 2

(a)   Calculate the following direct cost variances for product M for November:
(i)   direct material price;
(ii)   direct material usage;
(iii)   direct labour rate;
(iv)   direct labour utilisation or efficiency;

(b)   Present the variances in a statement which reconciles the total standard direct cost of production with the actual direct cost for product M in November.

Further data

The production manager receives a copy of the standard costing control statement for product M every month. However, he has recently confessed to you that he does not really have a clear understanding of the meaning of the variances.

He has also been baffled by the following statement made by the finance director at a recent meeting of senior managers:
'Assigning responsibility for variances can be complicated if the variances are interdependent, for example if an adverse variance in one part of the organisation is caused by a favourable variance elsewhere.'

Task 3

As assistant accountant for WH Limited, you are asked to write a memo to the production manager which explains the following:
(a)   the meaning of each of the direct cost variances calculated for product M;
(b)   two possible causes of each of the variances which you have calculated for product M for November;
(c)   two examples of interdependence which may be present in the variances which you have calculated for product M for November. Explain clearly why the variances may be interdependent, so that the manager can better understand the meaning of the finance director's statement.

[Answer on p.184]

▷ ACTIVITY 4   ▷ ▷ ▷ ▷

Revamp Furniture Limited

Revamp Furniture Limited manufacture a lounge chair by subjecting plasticised metal to a moulding process, thereby producing the chair in one piece.

(a)   From the information provided below, you are required to analyse the cost variances and prepare a reconciliation of budgeted with actual cost incorporating the result of your analysis.

Standard/budget data

Unit variable costs:	
Direct material	6 lb at 50p per lb
Direct labour	2 hours at 160p per hour
Budgeted fixed overhead for the year (240 working days)	£30,000
Budgeted production/sales for the year	60,000 chairs
Actual data for period 1	
Number of working days	20
Production/sales	5,200 chairs

Direct material received and used:

Delivery No 1	12,000 lb	Cost	£5,880
Delivery No 2	14,000 lb	Cost	£6,790
Delivery No 3	6,000 lb	Cost	£3,060
Direct labour hours worked	10,080	Cost	£17,540
Fixed overhead			£2,550

(b)   'Cost variances are often found, upon investigation of causes, to be interdependent.'

Briefly explain this statement using as illustrations:
(i)   material price and usage variances;
(ii)   labour rate and efficiency variances;
taken from your answer to (a) above and comment briefly on any possible interdependence between material cost variances and labour cost variances.   [Answer on p. 188]

6   Spreadsheets

It is a requirement of Unit 8 and 9 that you should be able to produce information for reports using appropriate computer software. For most purposes that will mean a spreadsheet. Here we will consider how to set up, run and produce output from a spreadsheet.

For those unfamiliar with spreadsheet packages, this chapter will provide the basic introduction needed to feel confident to 'get into' Microsoft Excel and carry out simple information analysis tasks. This package has been chosen because it is the most popular and therefore the most likely to be used in your college or work environment. The editions and programs that you are using may not be the same as those used in this text. In that case, the screens you produce will not be identical to those shown here. However, all spreadsheet packages will perform the basic functions covered in this chapter and access to a different package will not cause too many problems.

If you are at all unsure, you should read the manual that accompanies your chosen spreadsheet.

6.1 The use of spreadsheets

What is a spreadsheet used for?

Much of the data of a company is likely to be held on a number of spreadsheets. They are a convenient way of setting up all sorts of charts, records and tables, including:
· profit and loss accounts
· sales forecasting
· budgeting charts
· breakeven point analysis
· stock valuation.

Spreadsheets can be used for anything with a **rows and columns format**.

Spreadsheets

A spreadsheet is used to manipulate data. You could define it as a table of rows and columns that intersect to form cells. Each row is identified by a number and each column by a letter (or letters). Each cell has a unique identifier formed by a letter (or letters) and a number.

The word **spreadsheet** has its origins in the large sheets of paper used by accountants, over which they spread their figures and calculations in neat rows and columns. The little boxes made by the horizontal and vertical lines have their counterpart in the PC's spreadsheet and are called **cells**.

Into these cells may be entered numbers, text or a **formula**. Formulae are not visible when you are entering data but reside in the background. A formula normally involves a mathematical calculation on the content of other cells, the result being inserted in the cell containing the formula.

The size of spreadsheets, in terms of the number of columns and rows, varies greatly between packages. Spreadsheets with millions of cells are possible. Because most business worksheets are quite large, extending beyond the edge of the computer screen, the screen is in effect a 'window' into the worksheet. Some or all of the spreadsheet can be printed out directly or saved on disk for insertion into reports or other documents using a word processing package.

The power of these systems is that the data held in any one cell on the 'paper' can be made dependent on that held in other cells, so changing a value in one cell can set off a chain reaction of changes through other related cells. This means that a model can be built in which the effect of changing key parameters may be observed (so called 'what if?' analysis).

Three-dimensional spreadsheets have the advantage of consolidation that the two dimensional ones do not have. An example to highlight this facility might be sales figures by region, where the top sheet (All products) might be a total of the sales of all the products that the company has (whilst Products 1 to 4 have separate sheets behind).

6.2   Accessing a spreadsheet

Excel

In the instructions that follow you will be using the Excel for Windows® (or similar) package to create a worksheet, make calculations, enter formulae and copy data.

The following should be read and attempted in full if you are unfamiliar with the use of spreadsheets. If you are confident using spreadsheets check through the notes and exercises for any areas you may not have covered previously.

If you do not have access to Excel it will be assumed that you can use a similar package and you should refer to your manual for the basic mouse clicks.

As you are introduced to more commands, the worksheet will provide more information and give you a way to make business forecasts, 'What if?' analysis. When you have completed your report, you will print out a copy to present to your manager.

Running the program

The way to gain access to the spreadsheet package depends upon the type of computer system in use. A **menu** may be available to allow access to the chosen software by entering a single number or letter or by use of a cursor or mouse.

If you are using the spreadsheet at work, you must check first with your supervisor that it is allowed and that you are using the right version of the software.

If you are working in a **Windows** environment, you will access the spreadsheet package using the mouse. Click on the Start button in the bottom left hand corner of the Window. Keeping the mouse button depressed move to highlight the 'Programs' and then to the package that you want to use. Click on the icon.

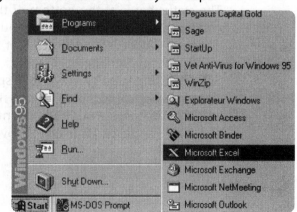

The opening screen in Microsoft Excel might look like this:

(Yours might look a little different if you have a different version of Excel)

On the screen you will see the **title bar**, the **menu bar,** the **function tool bar** and in the top right corner the buttons to **minimise, maximise**/restore and close the worksheet. As with most Windows programs you can change the size and move the Excel Window.

If your screen does not have a formula bar, a formatting bar or a toolbar you can show these by accessing **View** and then Toolbars from the menu at the top of the screen. You can then select (or deselect) what you want to show on the screen. A tick signifies that it is switched on.

The toolbars are below the menu bar. Clicking on any of these buttons provides a shortcut to selecting options from the menu bar. If you pause the pointer over a button a label will appear and, in the **status bar**, Excel will tell you what that button does.

The formula bar is between the spreadsheet and the toolbar. This provides you with information about the contents of the active cell. The co-ordinates of the active cell are displayed on the left-hand side of the formula bar.

The status bar is at the bottom of the screen. It gives you information about your spreadsheet, such as when you are opening or saving a file and whether you have CAPS LOCK, NUM LOCK or SCROLL LOCK on.

Scroll bars are used to move your spreadsheet both up and down and left to right. The vertical scroll bar (on the right hand side of the spreadsheet) is used to move up and down. The horizontal scroll bar (below the spreadsheet and above the status bar) is used to move left and right.

Vocabulary

The spreadsheet is now ready to go to work, but first you will need to know some basic terms and some spreadsheet vocabulary, so that you can give instructions.

- **Worksheet**: a worksheet or spreadsheet (as shown above) is the basis of all the work you do. It could be considered to be the electronic equivalent of an accountant's ledger.
- **Workbook**: is a collection of worksheets. The workbook is simply a folder that binds together your worksheets. When you open a new workbook, it automatically contains three worksheets.
- **Cells**: the worksheet is divided into columns and rows. The intersection of a column and a row is known as a 'cell'. To refer to a particular cell, use its column and row location. This is called a 'cell address', for example A1, B22, etc.
- **Columns**: each column is referenced by one or two letters in the column heading. The whole worksheet consists of 256 columns, labelled A through IV.
- **Rows**: each row is referenced by the row number shown in the row heading to the left of a row. There are 65,536 rows in Excel.
- **Sheet tabs**: these are between the worksheet and the status bar and are used to move between worksheets in your workbook.
- **Window**: you can only see part of the worksheet at any time; you could consider the screen to be a window onto the worksheet. You have the facility to move this window, so that you can view any part of the spreadsheet.
- **Cell pointer**: look at the cell that is highlighted; this highlighted area is known as the cell pointer. It indicates the cell in which you are currently working. The current cell location is also displayed on the edit line above the spreadsheet.

Creating and saving a new file

When you first open Excel, a blank spreadsheet appears on the screen and you can start typing straight away. At this point you can work on an established spreadsheet or start on a new one by creating a file as described below.

From the file menu choose the NEW option, and a new Excel workbook will appear on the screen. Once you have created a document, you must save it if you wish to use it in the future. To save a file:

- From the **FILE** menu choose the **SAVE AS** option.
- A dialogue box will appear.
- If necessary, use the DRIVE drop down menu to select the relevant drive.
- In the **FILE NAME** text box type in the name you wish to use. All spreadsheet packages automatically add a three-digit extension to your filename. In Lotus it will begin with wk and in Excel it will begin with xl.
- Click on the **OK** button.

When you have saved a file once, you do not need to choose the **SAVE AS** option again, but simply choose **SAVE** from the **FILE** menu or click on the icon on the tool bar (picture of a floppy disk).

Closing a file/Quitting

When you have finished working on a spreadsheet and you have saved it, you will need to close it down. You can do this by either pressing the button at the top right hand side of the worksheet with a cross on it or by choosing the CLOSE or EXIT option from the FILE menu.

If you only want to exit Excel briefly and prefer not to close down the whole package you can switch to another application or back to the Windows Program Manager by pressing <Alt><Tab> repeatedly. This allows you to step through all the opened packages in rotation.

If you have changed the file, Excel will ask if you wish to save the changes you made before closing. Click on the appropriate button.

6.3 Moving around the spreadsheet

Cell pointer

The whole worksheet consists of many columns and rows. On opening the spreadsheet, you can only see a small part of it – generally columns A to H and rows 1 to 16. The screen is like a window onto the worksheet and you have the facility to move this window so that you can view any part of the worksheet. The cell pointer highlights the cell you are currently in.

By moving the cell pointer you are able to enter information into any cell of the worksheet. There are a number of ways of moving the cell pointer, but the easiest way is to use the mouse. You can move around the spreadsheet by positioning the **mouse pointer** over the appropriate cell and clicking to select that cell. If the cell address you want is outside the range shown in the current window, it is possible to move down or across the spreadsheet by clicking on the scroll bars to the side or below the Window. Alternatively, you can use the arrow keys on the keyboard.

Moving directly to a cell: the GOTO command

Type 'D19' in this field

Sometimes we want to move to a specific address in the spreadsheet that is too far from our present position to warrant using the arrow keys to get there. On the top of the keyboard you can see a row of keys labelled F1 through to F12; these are known as 'function keys'. When these keys are pressed, a special function is invoked. For the moment we will explore the F5 key. This is the **GOTO key** in both Excel and Lotus 123.

Let us assume you wished to go to D19. Press F5 and a dialogue box appears. You are prompted to enter an address or range. Enter D19 and the cell pointer will go directly to cell D19.

KAPLAN PUBLISHING

Try moving around your worksheet now. You can find where the end is because the spreadsheet will beep whenever you attempt to go beyond the worksheet boundaries.

The help facility

Excel has a comprehensive help facility, which provides both **general** help and **context sensitive** help.

To invoke the help command press the 'Help' button on the menu bar, the ? box on the toolbar or the shortcut key F1. To obtain information on any particular subject shown, move the mouse pointer over the required topic and click (or you may be prompted to type in a question).

Context sensitive help is available either when a help button is displayed in a dialogue box or when an error message is flashed onto the screen. Asking for help at this stage by either clicking on the help button, ? box or by pressing F1 will result in the help window appearing at the topic relevant to the problem encountered.

6.4 Entering data

Putting data onto the worksheet

Entering data on the worksheet is very easy. You simply type your entry at the keyboard, press return and whatever you typed will be placed in the current cell, ie where the cell pointer is.

As you type, each character will be displayed on the edit line at the top of the screen. The entry is not put onto the worksheet until you press the return key.

Move to cell A1. Type ABCDEF <Enter>

Now move to Cell A3. Type 123 <Enter>

When you have finished entering data you can either press the <Enter> key on the keyboard or click on the Enter Box (a green tick) on the formula bar.

If you change your mind about entering the data then either press the <Esc> key on the keyboard or click on the Cancel Box (a red cross) on the formula bar.

If you have made a mistake, you can press the 'backspace key' (the key above the ENTER key) to delete what you have done one character at a time. If you have already pressed the ENTER key, you can delete it by highlighting the cell or cells and pressing the Delete key.

There are three types of data that can be entered into your worksheet – text, numbers and formulae.

Entering text

Text is entered by simply typing into a cell. Typing any letter at the beginning of a cell entry causes it to be accepted as a 'label', rather than a 'value'. If the text you enter is longer than the width of the cell then the text will 'run over' into the next cell. But if the next cell also contains data/information then you will only see part of the text you entered, i.e. the label will be truncated.

There will be times when you want the spreadsheet to treat a number or a formula as text. To do this you must type an apostrophe in front of the number or formula you are entering, e.g. '01707 320903 or '=A4+D5.

Entering numbers

Numbers can be entered on the spreadsheet by simply typing into a cell. If the space in the cell is insufficient, the number will be shown in an exponential form on the spreadsheet, but the number will still be retained in full in the formula bar. If you want to see the contents of cells in full, the columns can be widened to accommodate the number (or text).

It is not necessary to put the commas in manually when entering large numbers (1,000 or more), because it is easy to format the data to display commas and decimal places to make the data easier to understand.

Entering formulae

The arithmetic operations and method of writing the basic formulae are very similar in all packages.

The BODMAS (Brackets, Of, Division, Multiplication, Addition, Subtraction) rule must be used to evaluate an arithmetic problem:
· Use brackets to clarify the correct order of operation and evaluate expressions within the brackets first.
· Calculate 'of' expressions (e.g. 20% of the total).
· Perform division and multiplication before addition and subtraction.
· Work from left to right if the expression contains only addition and subtraction.

The basic commands for statistical functions that calculate lists of values are also very similar throughout the range of spreadsheet packages. Examples of these are:

SUM	The sum of the values in list
AVG	The average of the values in list
COUNT	The number of non-blank entries in list
MAX	The maximum value in list
MIN	The minimum value in list

A formula always starts with an equal sign (=) in Excel. If you start it with an equal sign (=) in Lotus 123®, it automatically converts it to a plus (+) sign. Formulae consist of numbers, cell co-ordinates (e.g. A2, F7), operators and functions. Operators perform actions on numbers and co-ordinates. Examples of operators are plus, minus, divide and multiply. Functions perform more advanced actions on numbers and co-ordinates.

To enter a formula:

· Select the cell where you want to enter the formula.
· Press the equal sign (=) on the keyboard [or click on the sign in the formula bar, if you have one].
· Key in the formula directly from the keyboard or use the mouse to select the cells you want in the formula. There are no spaces in a formula.
· Press the <Enter> key.

When you have entered a formula, the resulting value appears in that cell. The formula is only visible in the formula bar.

Typical formulae:

=(A6+C10)-E25	Adds A6 with C10 and subtracts E25
=(H19*A7)/3	Multiplies H19 with A7 and divides the total by 3
=SUM(L12:L14)	A quick way of adding L12 + L13 + L14

An even quicker way to add a row or column of numbers is to click the [4] button in the toolbar for Lotus 1-2-3.

The equivalent button in MS Excel is the Greek symbol sigma Σ .

Exercise 1 – Basic data entry

In Excel, open a new blank worksheet and enter the following data. Leave plenty of space so that the titles are distinct. You will probably be putting the first invoice number in row 6.

Sales Invoices	August 20X0		
Invoice	Firm	Items	Price
1001	AB Plastics Ltd	10	0.2
1002	J Cables Ltd	21	0.2
1003	DC Covers Ltd	45	0.2
1004	DC Covers Ltd	42	0.2
1005	J Cables Ltd	500	0.2
1006	AB Plastics Ltd	25	0.2
1007	J Hoggs Ltd	300	0.2
1008	L Quick Ltd	1000	0.2
1009	DC Covers Ltd	50	0.2
1010	AB Plastics Ltd	12	0.2
1011	AB Plastics Ltd	15	0.2
1012	J Hoggs Ltd	350	0.2
1013	L Quick Ltd	1500	0.2
1014	J Hoggs Ltd	400	0.2

1015	L Quick Ltd	1250	0.2
1016	DC Covers Ltd	90	0.2
1017	F Browns Ltd	48	0.2
1018	L Quick Ltd	500	0.2
1019	F Browns Ltd	52	0.2
1020	F Browns Ltd	25	0.2

Adding basic formulae

Excel allows you to build up mathematical formulae to perform many useful functions, eg add up data, find average values, produce variances, add or subtract VAT, etc.

It has the capability of producing complex analyses and as your experience grows you can pick up more of these using a manual or the on-screen help function.

We will look at building up some basic formulae, which are commonly used in financial spreadsheets. In this exercise, we are going to calculate the Net price, the VAT and the Gross. You need to add three more columns after Price and label them: Net, VAT and Gross respectively.

(a)   **Multiply** - in the 'Net' column we are going to put a formula to multiply the Items by the Price.
·   Click on first entry in Net column (E6 probably)
·   Type an = in the formula bar
·   Click on first entry in the Items column (or type the address in – C6 probably)
·   Type a * (to multiply)
·   Click on first entry in the Price column (D6 probably)
·   Press <Return> or OK

(b)   Using the same type of multiply formula in the VAT column (F6 probably), calculate the VAT on the Net figure: this will be =E6*0.175.

(c)   **Add** – we want to add the VAT to the Net to give us the Gross figure in G6

·   Click on G6
·   Type an = in the formula bar (or click on the = sign)
·   Click on E6
·   Type a +
·   Click on F6
·   Press <Return> or OK

(d)   Another useful function is SUM. This can be used to total a list of values in a row or column without specifying each one individually.

We need to copy these formulae to the rest of the entries in the worksheet before we can total the columns.

Copying

Shown below are the Cut, Copy and Paste buttons toolbar at the top of the screen on both Excel (left) and Lotus

(If you can't find all of these on your toolbar, click on the >> button – this will display more buttons.)

Cut then **paste** is used to move cells from one area of the spreadsheet to another.

Copy then **paste** is used to copy cells from one area to another.

Copying and pasting or cutting and pasting operations always have two parts:
·   define the range you want to copy or cut **from**; then
·   define the range that you want to copy or move **to**.

Click on cell D5 and key in '£, press Enter. Go back to D5 and click on the ☰ button to place the text in the centre of the cell.

This is the range you want to copy from. (Here the range is a single cell.)

Click the **copy** button on the toolbar (next to scissors). The border of D5 will start to shimmer.

Position the cursor over cell D5, hold down the mouse button and drag to the right until cells D5 to G5 have been highlighted (D5 will be white, E5 to G5 will be black or blue). This is the range to copy to.

Click on the **paste** button on the toolbar. The '£' sign has been copied from D5 and should now appear in E5 to G5.

You can copy formulae to different cells by the same method. Try to copy the formula from E6 to E25. Then from F6 to F25 and G6 to G25.

Note that the cell references change automatically when formulae are copied.

6.5   Producing reports

Assumptions

Although the spreadsheet that you have completed is very simple, you still have the basis of a powerful planning and analysis tool. Assumptions and figures can be changed and the spreadsheet will automatically recalculate the results. The main benefit of the spreadsheet is the ability to do 'What if?' experiments.

This allows you to see what happens if, for example, the prices are raised with a subsequent reduction in sales. It can also be used to calculate the overdraft facility if different variables are changed in a cash flow calculation.

Another facility is 'goal seeking'. This is different from seeing what results you get from changing the variables. It gives you the opportunity to state the result you want and make changes until you get that result.

Changing the variables

In your spreadsheet, you are going to change some of the entries.

Charts and graphs

Most spreadsheet packages make it easy to draw charts and graphs from the data in your worksheet. In Excel, the Chart Wizard is the icon that looks like a chart.

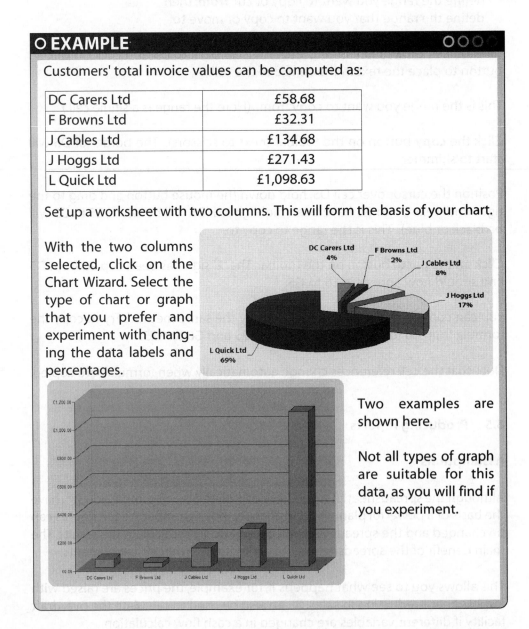

○ EXAMPLE

Customers' total invoice values can be computed as:

DC Carers Ltd	£58.68
F Browns Ltd	£32.31
J Cables Ltd	£134.68
J Hoggs Ltd	£271.43
L Quick Ltd	£1,098.63

Set up a worksheet with two columns. This will form the basis of your chart.

With the two columns selected, click on the Chart Wizard. Select the type of chart or graph that you prefer and experiment with changing the data labels and percentages.

Two examples are shown here.

Not all types of graph are suitable for this data, as you will find if you experiment.

6.6 Transferring to another document

Under Windows, you can transfer (or copy) a chart or other diagrams from your worksheet to another document, such as a word processing package. You do this by using the copy and paste facilities.

It is easier if you have both files open at the same time so that you can switch from one to the other using the task bar at the bottom of the screen showing the windows that are currently open. For example, if you are switching from Excel to Word, you just click on the icon with the W on it. Vice versa, it has an X on it.

To copy a chart from Excel to a file in Word:
· Access the correct area of your worksheet.
· Highlight the area you want to transfer or copy to another document.
· Click on Copy.
· Switch to the other document by clicking onto it on the task bar.
· Position the cursor where you want the chart to be and click on Paste. You can alter this position by grabbing the picture and dragging it to its position.

Report design

The appearance of reports is very important and the design should incorporate the following:
· A clear **heading** to indicate what the report is about.
· A **date** that the report relates to.
· A **date** that the report was **printed** (in case it is amended and printed again).
· **Page numbers** to help control large reports over several pages (possibly also the total number of pages).
· **Column headings** to explain what each column contains.
· **Units** for data to ensure that monetary amounts are clearly stated as being in £, £'000 or £m.

Printing a report

When you are required to produce a report, you should try to concentrate on important information, starting and stopping at relevant points. However, this need to limit the scope of a report should not be at the expense of accuracy, and items that are necessary should not be omitted.

To print from your computer make sure that it is connected to a printer and that it is switched on and loaded with the correct paper.

The quickest way to print anything in a Windows environment is to press the **Print** icon on the toolbar. If you want to print more than one copy, specific pages or a highlighted area you must select the Print option from the File menu. If necessary, change the number of copies required or change the page range to specify which pages to print.

To print an area from your worksheet, highlight the area that you want to print. Select **Print Area** then **Print Preview**. This shows you what your print will look like on the page.

The worksheet might be compressed if the page is set up in Portrait. To change to Landscape, click on Page Set Up and change the orientation.

When you are ready to print, click the OK button.

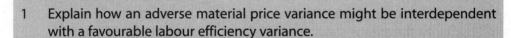

7 **Test your knowledge**

1   Explain how an adverse material price variance might be interdependent with a favourable labour efficiency variance.

2   State four categories of reasons why variances might arise.

[Answers on p. 190]

8   Summary

In this chapter we have examined ways of measuring the significance of variances and the way in which management might introduce controls based on the variance reports provided to them. The investigation of variances is a part of this process and it is important that you understand the causes of variances and their typical remedies.

We then considered briefly responsibility accounting and the possible interaction of variances. This is a very important area in the context of management appraisal. As we have seen, purchasing of cheap materials may cause a knock-on effect into the working of those materials thereby giving the impression that the workforce (and by implication the managers of the workforce) are inefficient. This will not be the case as the problems are caused by poor purchasing of materials rather than inefficient labour.

Finally, we examined very briefly how spreadsheets can be used to simplify report preparation.

Answers to chapter activities & 'test your knowledge' questions

△ **ACTIVITY 1**   △ △ △ △

Attainable and ideal standard

(a)   An **attainable standard** is a standard which can be attained if a standard unit of work is carried out efficiently, a machine properly operated or material properly used. The standard makes allowances for normal shrinkage, waste and machine breakdowns. It is intended to have a positive motivational impact on employees.

An **ideal standard** is a standard which can be attained under the most favourable conditions. The standard makes no provision for shrinkage, spoilage or machine breakdowns.

Ideal standards are not widely used in practice because of their adverse effect on employee motivation. Unfavourable variances usually result making them less useful for planning purposes.

(b)   (i)   *Actual profit for the period*

	£	£
Sales (2,250 units × £15)		33,750
Production cost (2,500 units)		
Direct materials	12,000	
Direct labour	9,000	
	21,000	
Less: Closing stock		
(250 units at £10 per unit) (W1)	2,500	
Cost of sales		18,500
Actual profit		15,250

Working

Standard cost data per unit	£
Direct materials ($\frac{6,000 \text{ kg}}{2,000 \text{ units}}$ @ £2/kg)	6.00
Direct labour ($\frac{4,000 \text{ hours}}{2,000 \text{ units}}$ @ £2/hour)	4.00
	10.00

(ii)   *Material price variance*

	£
Actual usage (5,000 kg) at actual cost	12,000
Actual usage (5,000 kg) at standard cost (£2/kg)	10,000
Material price variance	2,000(A)

		£
Actual usage (5,000 kg) at standard cost (£2/kg)		10,000
Standard usage for actual production (7,500 kg) at standard cost (£2/kg)		15,000
Material usage variance		5,000(F)

Labour rate variance

	£
Actual hours (6,000 hours) at actual rate (£1.50/hour)	9,000
Actual hours (6,000 hours) at standard rate (£2/hour)	12,000
Labour rate variance	3,000(F)

Labour efficiency variance

	£
Actual hours (6,000 hours) at standard rate (£2/hour)	12,000
Standard hours for actual production (5,000 hours) at standard rate (£2/hour)	10,000
Labour efficiency variance	2,000(A)

△ ACTIVITY 2

Excelsior Manufacturing Company

(a)

	Production level (units)				
	4,000	*5,000*	*6,000*	*7,000*	*8,000*
	£	£	£	£	£
Direct materials	80,000	100,000	120,000	140,000	160,000
Indirect materials	12,000	14,000	16,000	18,000	20,000
Direct labour	50,000	62,500	75,000	87,500	100,000
Power	18,000	18,000	18,000	21,000	24,000
Repairs	20,000	22,500	25,000	27,500	30,000
Supervision	20,000	20,000	36,000	36,000	36,000
Rent, insurance and rates	9,000	9,000	9,000	9,000	9,000
Total cost	209,000	246,000	299,000	339,000	379,000

(b)

	Budget (5,000)		Actual (5,000)		Variance
	£		£		£
Direct materials	100,000		110,000		10,000(A)
Indirect materials	14,000		14,000		–
Direct labour	62,500		70,000		7,500(A)
Power	18,000		18,000		–
Repairs	22,500		30,000		7,500(A)
Supervision	20,000		20,000		–
Rent, insurance and rates	9,000		8,000		1,000(F)
Total cost	246,000		270,000		24,000(A)

Comments on variances
- Direct materials: more was used than expected. Possibly waste in production, poor quality materials, operatives need more training. Is a particular department or machine at fault?
- Direct labour: again more was used than expected. Investigate reasons. Excessive overtime (should not be needed at a low level of production)?
- Repairs: needs investigation. Possible exceptional item. Do some pieces of capital equipment need replacing?
- Rent, insurance and rates: this is probably a price variance. Is this a one-off item or does the budget need to be altered in future?

WH Limited
MEMORANDUM

To: Production Manager

From: Assistant Accountant

Date: 12 December 20X4

Subject: Determining the standard price per kg of material X

As requested I detail below the information which would be needed to determine the standard price of material X and possible sources of the information.

(a) *The information which is needed*	(b) *Possible sources*
· Type and quality of material	Technical specification
· Quantity and timing of purchases, for determining any bulk discounts	Production and purchasing schedules
· Past trend in prices	Historical records in company Supplier records Government statistics Trade association statistics Movements in price indexes
· Future trend in prices	Discussions/negotiations with suppliers Trade association forecasts Financial press forecasts Government forecasts of key indexes
· Carriage costs to be added	Historical records in company Supplier records
· Type of standard to be set, e.g. average for year, or increasing with inflation	Company policy on standard setting

Task 2

(a)   (i)   Direct material price variance = (£4.90 – £4.60) × 2,100
                                                  = £630 favourable

        (ii)   Direct material usage variance = [(400 × 4.5) – 2,100] × £4.90
                                                  = £1,470 adverse

        (iii)   Direct labour rate variance = (£3.50 – £4) × 4,000
                                                  = £2,000 adverse

        (iv)   Direct labour efficiency variance = [(400 × 10.3) – 4,000] × £3.50
                                                  = £420 favourable

(b)   Reconciliation of standard direct cost of production with actual direct cost for November:

			£	£
Standard direct cost of production (400 × £58.10)				23,240
Direct cost variances:				
Direct material	-	price	630 (F)	
	-	usage	(1,470) (A)	
				(840) (A)
Direct labour	-	rate	(2,000) (A)	
	-	efficiency	420 (F)	
				(1,580) (A)
Actual direct cost of production				25,660

Note that adverse variances are added to the standard cost to give the actual cost.

Note: A = adverse variance; F = favourable variance

Task 3

(a) – (c)

WH Limited
MEMORANDUM

To: Production Manager

From: Assistant Accountant

Date: 12 December 20X4

Subject: Direct cost variances for November

As requested I detail below explanations of the direct cost variances and possible suggestions as to their cause in November.

Page 1 of 3

(a) *The meaning of the variances*

Direct material price variance

This variance shows the saving or overspending which resulted from paying a lower or higher price than standard for the direct material used in the period. The favourable variance indicates that a lower than standard price was paid.

Direct material usage variance

This variance shows the saving or overspending, at standard prices, which resulted from using less or more material than standard to manufacture the production for the period. The adverse variance indicates that more material was used than standard.

Direct labour rate variance

This variance shows the saving or overspending which resulted from paying a lower or higher hourly rate than standard for the hours worked in the period. The adverse variance indicates that a higher than standard hourly rate was paid.

Direct labour efficiency variance

This variance shows the saving or overspending, at standard rates, which resulted from working less or more hours than standard to manufacture the production for the period. The favourable variance indicates that less hours were worked than standard.

(b) *Possible causes of the variances*

Favourable direct material price variance

Bulk discounts were received which were not allowed for in the standard.
The standard price of material was set too high.
A lower quality material was purchased, at a lower price than standard.
Effective negotiations by the buyer secured a price lower than the standard.

Adverse direct material usage variance

Material wastage was higher than allowed in the standard.
The standard usage was set too low.
There was a higher than standard level of rejects.
Theft of material.

KAPLAN PUBLISHING

Adverse direct labour rate variance

High levels of overtime were paid for compared with the standard allowance.
The standard wage rate was set too low.
A higher grade of labour was used.
Bonus payments were higher than standard.

Favourable direct labour efficiency variance

Employees were working faster than standard.
More skilled employees were used.
There were savings through the learning effect.
The standard labour time was set too high.
The material was easy to process, leading to savings against the standard time.

(c) Two examples of interdependence, where one variance can be related to others, could include the following.

The savings made on material price (favourable material price variance) may indicate that poor quality material was purchased, leading to high wastage, rejects and an adverse usage variance.

Bulk discounts may have resulted in the saving on material price. However, the consequent excessive stocks may have led to deterioration and write-offs, hence the adverse usage variance.

Direct workers may have been of a higher grade than standard, resulting in higher hourly rates and the adverse rate variance. However, the higher skill level may have led to time savings and the favourable efficiency variance.

Higher than standard bonus payments may have caused the adverse labour rate variance, but the bonuses may have resulted from faster working and hence the favourable efficiency variance.

Faster working resulted in the favourable efficiency variance, but less care may have been taken over weighing and handling the material, hence the adverse material usage variance.

Page 3 of 3

△ ACTIVITY 4

Revamp Furniture Limited

(a)   Reconciliation for Period 1 (see workings)

	Favourable £	Adverse £	£
Flexed budgeted cost (W1)			34,840
Cost variances			
Materials (W2)			
Price	270		
Usage		400	
Labour (W3)			
Rate of pay		1,412	
Efficiency	512		
Fixed overhead (W4)			
Expenditure		50	
Efficiency	80		
Capacity	20		
	882	1,862	980
Actual cost (W5)			35,820

(b)   (i)   Although standard costing has, as one of its purposes, the allocation of responsibility for cost variances, it is often found in practice that the analysis of variances is merely the beginning of a further task of investigation before ultimate responsibility can be fairly assigned.

On the operating statement submitted for part (a) of this question there is disclosed a favourable material price variance and an adverse usage variance. Theoretically this should indicate that the buyer is operating efficiently and the production manager inefficiently. This need not necessarily be true, however. The buyer could have taken advantage of a special offer of material at less than standard price, not appreciating that the material was slightly below standard quality. It is very likely that the inferior material would give rise to production problems of machining, handling and possibly others which could well result in excess usage; hence the adverse usage variance.

(ii)   As regards labour, the payment of higher than standard rates (suggested by the adverse rate of pay variance in the operating statement) may well have had the effect of providing greater motivation, and hence speedier work, which is reflected in the favourable efficiency variance.

There may well be interdependence between the material and labour cost variances; for instance, the speedier work suggested by the favourable labour efficiency variance may have been accomplished by disregarding material usage standards.

KAPLAN PUBLISHING

From the foregoing it will be seen that not only is there possible interdependence between the variances of each element of cost, but also cross-interdependence between the elements of cost.

Workings

1   *Standard cost per unit*

		£
Materials (6 × 50p)		3.00
Labour (2 × £1.60)		3.20
Fixed overhead $\frac{£30,000}{120,000}$ = 25p per hour × 2 hours		0.50
		6.70

Flexed budgeted cost 5,200 × £6.70   £34,840

(Fixed overhead is budgeted to be absorbed over (60,000 x 2 hours) = 120,000 hours

2   *Materials*
    (i)   *Price variance*

	£
Actual cost of 32,000 lb (5,880 + 6,790 + 3,060)	15,730
Standard cost	16,000
	270 (F)

    (ii)   *Usage variance*

	lb
Expected usage for 5,200 chairs (5,200 x 6)	31,200
Actual usage	32,000
Excessive usage	800
@ 50p per lb	£400 (A)

3   *Labour*
    (i)   *Rate of pay*

	£
Actual cost of 10,080 hours	17,540
Standard cost (10,080 x £1.60)	16,128
	1,412 (A)

    (iii)   *Efficiency*

	Hrs
Standard time for 5,200 chairs	10,400
Actual time taken	10,080
Hours gained through efficiency	320
@ 160p per hour	512 (F)

4   Fixed overhead
(i)   *Expenditure variance*

	£
Budgeted cost (30,000 x 20/240)	2,500
Actual cost	2,550
	50 (A)

(ii)   *Efficiency variance*

320 hours @ 25p	80 (F)

(The absorption rate is calculated by dividing the budgeted cost by the budgeted number of hours to be worked: £30,000/(60,000 × 2 hours) = 25p.)

(iii)   *Capacity variance*

	£
Actual hours worked	10,080
Budgeted 20/240 × 120,000	10,000
	80
@ 25p per hour	20 (F)

5   *Actual cost statement*

	£
Materials (5,880 + 6,790 + 3,060)	15,730
Labour	17,540
Fixed overhead	2,550
	35,820

Test your knowledge △ △ △

1   An adverse material price variance might mean that better quality material was bought than standard. The employees found it easier to work with this high quality material, so worked more efficiently than standard.

2   Variances might arise due to:
· planning errors;
· measurement errors;
· random factors;
· operational causes.

PERFORMANCE INDICATORS

INTRODUCTION

Cost variances, covered earlier, give one type of performance indicator – how individual operational managers perform against pre-set budget and standard cost targets. Here we continue this theme, but look at measures for productivity, efficiency etc; ratios that assist in assessment of resource utilisation; and overall profitability measures that may be applied to operating divisions and the business as a whole. We also look at the particular performance evaluation aspects of service industries, in particular the measurement of quality of service. The objective will always be to highlight activities, processes, products and business units that need some attention in order to enhance their value to the business.

KNOWLEDGE & UNDERSTANDING

· Performance indicators: efficiency, effectiveness, productivity; balanced scorecard, benchmarking; unit costs; control ratios (efficiency, capacity and activity), scenario planning ('what if' analysis) (Element 8.2)
· Cost management: life cycle costing; target costing (including value engineering); activity-based costing; principles of Total Quality Management (including cost of quality) (Element 8.2)
· The contribution of functional specialists in an organisation (e.g. marketing, design, engineering, quality control, etc) to cost reduction and value enhancement (Element 8.2)
· Effect of accounting controls on the behaviour and motivation of managers and other employees (Elements 8.1 and 8.2)

CONTENTS

1 Types of performance indicator
2 Ratio analysis
3 Profitability
4 Liquidity
5 Manufacturing industries
6 Service departments
7 Service sectors
8 Total quality management (TQM)
9 The balanced scorecard
10 Cost reduction and value enhancement

PERFORMANCE CRITERIA

· Present reports to management that summarise data, present information using appropriate methods and highlight significant trends (Element 8.1)
· Prepare and monitor relevant performance indicators, interpret the results, identify potential improvements and estimate the value of potential improvements (Element 8.2)
· Consult relevant specialists and assist in identifying ways to reduce costs and enhance value (Element 8.2)

1 Types of performance indicator

1.1 Introduction

Performance indicators may be categorised as quantitative or qualitative.

1.2 Quantitative performance indicators

Quantitative measures are expressed in numerical terms which include the following:
(a) variances;
(b) profit, sales, costs, etc;
(c) ratios and percentages;
(d) indices.

1.3 Qualitative performance indicators

Qualitative indicators are far more subjective and cannot be expressed as an objective, numerical measure. Examples relevant to business and managerial performance would include the following:
(a) level of customer satisfaction: expressed as a subjective level 'very satisfied' … to …'not at all satisfied';
(b) staff performance grades: 'excellent', 'average', 'poor', etc;
(c) company performance: 'steady', 'volatile results', 'disappointing', etc.

1.4 Efficiency and effectiveness

Performance indicators can be used to measure the efficiency and effectiveness of organisations.

□ DEFINITIONS   □□□□

Efficiency can be defined as the relationship between inputs and outputs achieved. The fewer the inputs used by an organisation to achieve any given output, the more efficient is that organisation. In commercial organisations, efficiency is usually measured in terms of profitability, often in relation to assets employed.
Effectiveness is the degree to which an objective or target is met.

---

2 Ratio analysis

2.1 Introduction

Ratio analysis is one of the main tools utilised in appraising the performance of a company, the main advantage being that the magnitude of the individual figures is eliminated allowing the appraiser to concentrate on relative movements.

Ratio analysis is generally utilised in two ways as follows:

(a)   comparison of performance year to year;

(b)   comparison with other companies.

The techniques covered here occur in many branches of accountancy and it is important that you can calculate and interpret appropriate ratios.

2.2   Types of ratios

The main types of ratio used are:

(a)   profitability ratios;

(b)   liquidity ratios;

(c)   gearing ratios;

(d)   investment ratios.

Of these, profitability and liquidity ratios are of the greatest significance to the management accountant and it is those we shall examine in more detail.

○ EXAMPLE   ○○○○

In order to illustrate the most common ratios, let's look at some calculations based on the summarised accounts of Knotty plc. The information from Knotty plc's financial statements will be used in the following sections.

Profit and loss account for the year ended 31 July 20X9

	Notes	20X9		20X8	
		£000	£000	£000	£000
Turnover			37,589		30,209
Cost of sales			(28,380)		(22,808)
Gross profit			9,209		7,401
Distribution costs		(3,755)		(3,098)	
Administrative expenses		(2,291)		(2,030)	
			(6,046)		(5,128)
			3,163		2,273
Other operating income			108		279
Operating profit			3,271		2,552
Interest receivable			7		28
			3,278		2,580
Interest payable			(442)		(471)
Profit on ordinary activities before taxation			2,836		2,109
Tax on profit on ordinary activities			(1,038)		(650)
Profit on ordinary activities after taxation			1,798		1,459
Preference dividend			(6)		(6)
			1,792		1,453
Ordinary dividends			(606)		(441)
Retained profit for the year			1,186		1,012

Balance sheet as at 31 July 20X9

	Notes	20X9 £000	20X9 £000	20X8 £000	20X8 £000
Fixed assets					
Tangible assets			8,687		5,669
Investments			15		15
			8,702		5,684
Current assets					
Stocks		8,486		6,519	
Debtors	1	8,836		6,261	
Cash at bank and in hand		479		250	
		17,801		13,030	
Creditors: amounts falling due within one year					
Bank loans and overdrafts		(929)		(511)	
Other amounts falling due within one year		(9,178)		(6,645)	
		(10,107)		(7,156)	
Net current assets			7,694		5,874
Total assets less current liabilities			16,396		11,558
Creditors: amounts falling due after more than one year					
Debentures			(2,840)		(2,853)
Net assets			13,556		8,705
Capital and reserves					
Called up share capital					
Ordinary shares of 20p each	2		2,003		1,762
4.2% cumulative preference shares of £1 each			150		150
			2,153		1,912
Share premium account			123		123
Other reserves			2,576		–
Profit and loss account			8,704		6,670
			13,556		8,705

Notes

1 Debtors at 31 July 20X9 include trade debtors of £8,233,000 (20X8 £5,735,000).

2 The number of ordinary shares in issue at 31 July 20X9 was 10,014,514 (20X8 8,808,214).

3 Profitability

3.1 Return on capital employed (ROCE)

Return on capital employed (ROCE) expresses profit as a percentage of the assets in use (the capital employed in the business) and can be further sub-divided into profit margin and asset turnover (use of assets):

Profit margin $\times$ Asset turnover = Return on capital employed (ROCE)

$$\frac{\text{Profit}}{\text{Turnover}} \quad \times \quad \frac{\text{Turnover}}{\text{Assets}} \quad = \quad \frac{\text{Profit}}{\text{Assets}}$$

The equation helps to demonstrate how management can influence the rate of return on capital employed:

(a)   By increasing profit margins:
  (i)   increase sales prices;
  (ii)   reduce costs.

(b)   By increasing asset turnover (use of assets):
  (i)   increase sales;
  (ii)   reduce assets (capital employed).

3.2   Year-end or average capital employed

Ideally, the profits for the year ended 31 July 20X9 should be related to the assets in use throughout the year (the average capital employed). In practice, the ratio is usually computed using the assets at the year-end (the year-end capital employed). Using year-end figures of capital employed can distort trends and inter-company comparison; if new investment has been under-taken near to the year-end and financed (for example) by the issue of new shares, the capital employed will have risen by the total finance raised, whereas the profits will only have a month or two of the new investment's contribution.

A range of different acceptable measures of the assets in use is available; the matter of principle should be that the profit figure which is related to the capital employed should include all types of return on those assets.

Solution

For Knotty plc, a suitable calculation would be as follows.

	20X9	20X8
	£000	*£000*
Capital and reserves	13,556	8,705
Add: Debentures	2,840	2,853
Year-end capital employed	16,396	11,558

	20X9	20X8
	£000	*£000*
Operating profit	3,271	2,552
Interest receivable	7	28
Profit before interest payable and tax	3,278	2,580

So the return on capital employed is calculated as:

$$\frac{\text{Profit before interest and tax}}{\text{Capital and reserves and long-term debt}} \times 100\%$$

20X9 $\dfrac{3,278}{16,396} \times 100 = 20.0\%$

20X8 $\dfrac{2,580}{11,558} \times 100 = 22.3\%$

The capital employed figure includes the long-term debt, the debentures. Therefore, the profit used must be that available to these providers of capital, the profit before interest payable.

The rate of return on year-end capital employed has fallen in 20X9 compared with 20X8, and might indicate less effective management. To comment further, we need to sub-analyse the ratio into profit margin and asset turnover.

3.3 Profit margin

If the profitability ratios are to interlock perfectly, the profit margin will be calculated expressing the same profit before interest payable and tax as a percentage of turnover:

$$\frac{\text{Profit before interest and tax}}{\text{Turnover}} \times 100\%$$

A small problem with the approach in this example is that the profit includes interest receivable which is not represented in turnover; however, as the amount is small, this can be ignored.

In order that the profit can be related more fairly to turnover, profit margin is sometimes calculated using operating profit.

Solution

For Knotty plc: 20X9 $\dfrac{3,278}{37,589} \times 100 = 8.7\%$

20X8 $\dfrac{2,580}{30,209} \times 100 = 8.5\%$

Profit margins have improved slightly over the last year, possibly due to better cost control.

Sectors which have traditionally generated relatively high margins include publishing, electronics manufacturing, distillers and brewers, whereas food retailing and motor vehicle distribution are examples of low margin businesses.

Low margins within a sector may arise from a policy designed to increase market share by cutting selling prices, or may be due to high development costs associated with new products, both of which may be positive factors for the future. However, low margins are often associated with inefficiency and poor quality management.

Distillery has traditionally generated relatively high margins.

Conversely, high margins relative to competitors, or improving margins, are usually taken as indicators of efficiency and good management. High margins achieved by dominating a particular market may, however, attract competitors into that market and imply lower margins in the longer term.

3.4   Asset turnover

Another aspect of efficient management is to 'make the assets work'. This may involve disposing of those 'underperforming' assets which cannot be made to generate sales, as well as developing and marketing the company's products or services.

Solution

Once again, the simplest method of computing the ratio is to relate turnover to the same figure of year-end capital employed used in calculating return on capital employed:

$$\text{Asset turnover} = \frac{\text{Turnover}}{\text{Capital employed}}$$

20X9 $\dfrac{37,589}{16,396}$ = 2.3 times   20X8 $\dfrac{30,209}{11,558}$ = 2.6 times

---

However, as with profit margins, certain assets represented by capital employed have no turnover implications. One method of avoiding this illogicality is to exclude long and short-term investments from capital employed. For companies with substantial investments this will make a considerable difference.

Asset turnover will tend to be lower in capital-intensive manufacturing industries, which carry substantial tangible fixed assets, stocks and trade debtors, than in service industries where the principal resource is people rather than plant and machinery, and where stocks are low.

There are often trade-offs between asset turnover and profit margins in different sectors. For example, food retailers have relatively low profit margins compared to electronic equipment manufacturers, but asset turnover is higher. Typical numbers might be:

	Profit margin	×	Asset turnover	=	ROCE
	%				%
Food retailer	3.7	×	6.7	=	24.8
Electronic equipment manufacturer	10.3	×	2.3	=	23.7

3.5 Gross profit margin

The profit margin given above used a profit figure that included non-productive overheads and sundry items of income. The gross profit margin looks at the profitability of the pure trading activities of the business:

$$\frac{\text{Gross profit}}{\text{Turnover}} \times 100\%$$

Solution

For Knotty plc: 20X9 $\quad \dfrac{9,209}{37,589} \times 100 = 24.5\%$

20X8 $\quad \dfrac{7,401}{30,209} \times 100 = 24.5\%$

The company has maintained its gross profit margin; thus the slight rise in net profit margin must be due to overhead costs being better controlled.

▷ **ACTIVITY 1** ▷ ▷ ▷ ▷

WH Limited (AAT D94)

WH Limited is a member of a trade association which operates an inter-company comparison scheme. The scheme is designed to help its member companies to monitor their own performance against that of other companies in the same industry.

At the end of each year, the member companies submit detailed annual accounts to the scheme organisers. The results are processed and a number of accounting ratios are published and circulated to members. The ratios indicate the average results for all member companies.

Your manager has given you the following extract, which shows the average profitability and asset turnover ratios for the latest year. For comparison purposes, WH Limited's accounts analyst has added the ratios for your company.

	Results for year 4	
	Trade association average	WH Limited
Return on capital employed	20.5%	18.4%
Net (operating) profit margin	5.4%	6.8%
Asset turnover	3.8 times	2.7 times
Gross margin	14.2%	12.9%

Required

As assistant accountant for WH Limited, your manager has asked you to pre-pare a report for the senior management committee. The report should cover the following points:
(a)   an explanation of what each ratio is designed to show;
(b)   an interpretation of WH Limited's profitability and asset turnover com-pared with the trade association average;
(c)   comments on any limitations of these ratios and of comparisons made on this basis.   [Answer on p. 228]

4   Liquidity

4.1   Current ratio and quick ratio

When analysing a company's balance sheet without access to management information, it is customary to calculate two ratios as indicators of the company's ability to pay its way:

$$\text{Current ratio} = \frac{\text{Current assets}}{\text{Creditors due within one year}}$$

$$\text{Quick ratio (or acid test ratio)} = \frac{\text{Current assets less stocks}}{\text{Creditors due within one year}}$$

Solution

For Knotty plc:

		20X9	20X8
(a)	Current ratio	$\frac{17,801}{10,107} = 1.76$	$\frac{13,030}{7,156} = 1.82$
(b)	Quick ratio	$\frac{9,315}{10,107} = 0.92$	$\frac{6,511}{7,156} = 0.91$

4.2 Cash and funds flow analysis

Although current and quick ratios are used to measure liquidity, they are limited insofar as they concentrate on only one area of the balance sheet. If the company needs adequate cash to meet its obligations, there are sources other than the sale of stocks and the collection of amounts owed by debtors.

Analysis of cash flows is a more comprehensive method of assessing liquidity, although significant variations in the liquidity ratios may indicate important changes.

4.3 Other working capital ratios

A more detailed analysis of the movement in the elements of working capital can be made with the help of the following ratios.

4.4 Stock holding period (stock days)

Stock holding periods can be compared if they relate costs of sales as a measure of activity to stocks which are usually included at cost:

$$\frac{\text{Stocks}}{\text{Cost of sales}} \times 365$$

Solution

20X9 $\dfrac{8,486}{28,380} \times 365 = 109$ days

20X8 $\dfrac{6,519}{22,808} \times 365 = 104$ days

There has been a slight increase in the holding period, indicating stock is taking longer to sell. A review of stocks may be necessary to determine whether levels of obsolete or damaged stocks are increasing. There may be a deliberate policy to increase stocks.

4.5 Average debtors collection period (debtor days)

This calculation is always made using turnover since trade debtors includes the profit element:

$$\frac{\text{Trade debtors}}{\text{Turnover}} \times 365 \text{ days}$$

Solution

20X9 $\dfrac{8{,}233}{37{,}589} \times 365 = 80$ days

20X8 $\dfrac{5{,}735}{30{,}209} \times 365 = 69$ days

The company is taking approximately 11 days longer, on average, to collect its debts.

As the year-end figures may be unrepresentative (due perhaps to season-ality of sales), an average debtors figure for the year might be used if this were available.

4.6 Average creditors payment period (creditor days)

A similar calculation can be made to determine the creditors payment (settle-ment) period:

$$\frac{\text{Trade creditors}}{\text{Purchases or Cost of sales}} \times 365$$

Purchases should normally be used for this ratio but if it is not available from the information then cost of sales can be used as a substitute.

▷ ACTIVITY 2   ▷ ▷ ▷ ▷

Homely Limited

Data

Stately Hotels plc is considering making an offer to buy a small privately owned chain of hotels, Homely Limited. In order to carry out an initial appraisal, you have been provided with an abbreviated set of their accounts for 20X4.

Homely Limited – Profit and loss account for the year ended 31 December 20X4 (extract)

	£000
Turnover	820
Operating costs	754
Operating profit	66
Interest payable	4
Profit before tax	62
Taxation	18
Profit after tax	44
Dividends	22
Retained profits	22

Homely Limited – Balance sheet as at 31 December 20X4 (extract)

	£000
Fixed assets at net book value	230
Net current assets	70
Total assets less current liabilities	300
Long-term loans	50
Shareholders' funds	250
Number of employees (full-time equivalents)	20
Number of rooms, each available for 365 nights	18
Number of room nights achieved in 20X4	5,900

Stately Hotels plc uses a number of key accounting ratios to monitor the performance of the group of hotels and of individual hotels in the chain. An extract from the target ratios for 20X4 is as follows:

Stately Hotels plc - target ratios for 20X4 (extract)

(i) Return on capital employed, based on profit before interest and tax   26%

(ii) Operating profit percentage   13%

(iii) Asset turnover   2 times

(iv) Working capital period $= \dfrac{\text{Working capital}}{\text{Operating costs}} \times 365$ 20 days

(v) Percentage room occupancy $= \dfrac{\text{Number of room nights let}}{\text{Number of room nights available}} \times 100\%$ 85%

(vi) Turnover per employee (full-time equivalent)   £30,000

Required

(a) Calculate the six target ratios above based on Homely Limited's accounts and present them in a table which enables easy comparison with Stately Hotels' target ratios for 20X4.

(b) Prepare a memorandum for the management accountant of Stately Hotels plc, giving your initial assessment of Homely Limited based on a comparison of these ratios with Stately Hotels' target ratios. Your memorandum should provide the following information for each of the six ratios.

    (i) Comments on the performance of Homely Limited and suggestions about the management action which might be necessary to correct any apparent adverse performance.

    (ii) A discussion of any limitations in the use of the ratio for this performance comparison.   [Answer on p. 230]

○ EXAMPLE ○○○○

Work through the following example to ensure that you understand how to calculate and interpret basic ratios.

The outline balance sheets of the Nantred Trading Co Limited were as shown below.

Balance sheets as at 30 September

	20X6		20X5	
	£	£	£	£
Fixed assets (at written-down values)				
Premises	98,000		40,000	
Plant and equipment	162,000		65,000	
		260,000		105,000
Current assets				
Stock	95,300		31,200	
Trade debtors	30,700		19,700	
Bank and cash	26,500		15,600	
	152,500		66,500	
Current liabilities				
Trade creditors	55,800		23,900	
Corporation tax	13,100		11,400	
Proposed dividends	17,000		17,000	
	85,900		52,300	
Working capital		66,600		14,200
Net assets employed		326,600		119,200
Financed by				
Ordinary share capital	200,000		100,000	
Reserves	26,600		19,200	
Shareholders' funds		226,600		119,200
7% debentures		100,000		–
		326,600		119,200

The only other information available is that:

· turnover for the years ended 30 September 20X5 and 20X6 was £202,900 and £490,700 respectively;

· profit before tax and interest (operating profit) for the years to 30 September 20X5 and 20X6 was £21,500 and £44,500 respectively.

(a)   Calculate, for each of the two years, two suitable ratios to highlight the liquidity and two suitable ratios to highlight the profitability of the company.

(b)   Comment on the situation revealed by the figures you have calculated in your answer to (a) above.

Solution

(a)

		20X6	20X5
(i)	$\dfrac{\text{Current assets}}{\text{Current liabilities}}$	$\dfrac{152{,}500}{85{,}900} = 1.78{:}1$	$\dfrac{66{,}500}{52{,}300} = 1.27{:}1$
(ii)	$\dfrac{\text{Quick assets}}{\text{Current liabilities}}$	$\dfrac{57{,}200}{85{,}900} = 0.67{:}1$	$\dfrac{35{,}300}{52{,}300} = 0.67{:}1$
(iii)	$\dfrac{\text{Profit before tax and interest}}{\text{Capital (net assets) employed}}$	$\dfrac{44{,}500}{326{,}600} \times 100 = 13.6\%$	$\dfrac{21{,}500}{119{,}200} \times 100 = 18.0\%$
(iv)	$\dfrac{\text{Profit before tax and interest}}{\text{Sales}}$	$\dfrac{44{,}500}{490{,}700} \times 100 = 9.1\%$	$\dfrac{21{,}500}{202{,}900} \times 100 = 10.6\%$

(b)   The situation revealed by the ratios calculated in (a) above may be summarised as follows.

Liquidity ratios (i) and (ii)

The current ratio indicates a substantial surplus of current assets over current liabilities and this has improved over the year. The liquid assets (debtors and bank) to current liabilities ratio shows no change and based on past experience does not signify any liquidity difficulties.

Profitability ratios (iii) and (iv)

The overall return on capital employed has decreased by a substantial amount. This may be because full benefit has not yet been received from the additional investment of £100,000 from the debentures issued during the year. The level of net profit per £ of sales has also decreased and this may be due to the same reasons. Fortunately the overall return is high enough to mean that the 7% paid to the debenture holders is still easily achieved and the surplus return will improve returns to the ordinary shareholders, compensating them for the risk they have undertaken in introducing gearing (the debentures) into the organisation.

4.7 Comparing entities using performance indicators

Comparing an entity with a similar one may come up as a very practical task in an examination. The likely situation is where you have two firms in competition with each other, and one of them sets itself a performance indicator as a target to help it achieve a competitive advantage. The other firm must try to match or better that target.

4.8 What if? analysis

'What if? analysis' or 'scenario planning' is a technique used to test the effect on a set of figures of altering one of the variables that produced those figures. Flexible budgeting is a form of what if? analysis – what if we produce 20,000 units rather than 15,000, say?

O EXAMPLE   O O O O

Theta division makes only one product, the Devon. In the year to 30 June 20X5, its results were as follows:

	£
Sales	500,000
Debtors at 30 June 20X5	105,000
Cash at 30 June 20X5	20,000

The main competitor in the Devon market is Gamma Co, which sells Devons at a 15% higher price than Theta. It has been estimated that Theta could also charge a higher price without reducing sales volume. Gamma's results for the same period as Theta are as follows:

	£
Sales	700,000
Debtors	72,500
Cash	10,000

What would be the effect on the cash balance of Theta achieving Gamma's success?

Solution

The requirement in this example can be read as – what if Theta raised its prices and implemented credit controls to achieve Gamma's levels of sales and debtors?

	Theta	Gamma
Debtor days	$\dfrac{£105,000}{£500,000} \times 365 = 77$	$\dfrac{£72,500}{£700,000} \times 365 = 38$

Theta's revised figures

	£	£
Existing cash		20,000
Sales increase (£500,000 × 1.15) – £500,000		75,000
Change in debtors: Revised debtors (£500,000 × 1.15) × $\frac{38}{365}$	59,863	
Existing debtors	105,000	
		45,137
Revised cash balance		140,137

Therefore Theta division would increase its cash balance by £120,137 by raising its prices and reducing its debt collection period.

▷ ACTIVITY 3 ▷ ▷ ▷ ▷

Diamond Limited (AAT specimen paper)

Diamond Limited is a retail jeweller operating 30 branches in similar localities. Common accounting policies operate throughout all branches, including a policy of using straight-line depreciation for fixed assets.

All branches use rented premises. These are accounted for under 'other costs' in the operating statement. Fixed assets are predominantly fixtures and fittings.

Each branch is individually responsible for ordering stock, the authorising of payments to creditors and the control of debtors. Cash management, however, is managed by Diamond's head office with any cash received by a branch being paid into a head office bank account twice daily.

You are employed in the head office of Diamond Limited as a financial analyst monitoring the performance of all 30 branches. This involves calculating performance indicators for each branch and comparing each branch's performance with company standards. Financial data relating to Branch 24 is reproduced below.

Diamond Limited – Branch 24 – Year ended 31 December 20X7

Operating statement	£000	£000	Operating net assets at year end	£000	£000
Turnover		720.0	Fixed assets		
Opening stock	80.0		Cost		225.0
Purchases	340.0		Accumulated depreciation		(90.0)
Closing stock	(60.0)				
		360.0	Net book value		135.0
Gross profit		360.0	Working capital		
Wages and salaries	220.6		Stocks	60.0	
Depreciation	45.0		Debtors	96.0	
Other costs	36.8		Creditors	(51.0)	
					105.0
		302.4	Net assets		240.0
Operating profit		57.6			

Task 1

Prepare a statement showing the following performance indicators for Branch 24:

(a) the return on capital employed;
(b) the gross profit margin as a percentage;
(c) the asset turnover;
(d) the sales (or net profit) margin as a percentage;
(e) the average age of debtors in months;
(f) the average age of creditors in months;
(g) the average age of the closing stock in months.

Data

The financial director of Diamond Limited is Charles Walden. He is concerned that Branch 24 is not performing as well as the other branches. All other branches are able to meet or exceed most of the performance standards laid down by the company.

Charles is particularly concerned the branches should achieve the standards for return on capital employed and for asset turnover. He also feels that managers should try to achieve the standards laid down for working capital management. The relevant standards are:

Return on capital employed   40%
Asset turnover   4 times per annum

Average age of debtors	0.5 months
Average age of creditors	3 months
Average age of closing stock	1 month

Charles Walden has recently attended a course on financial modelling and scenario planning. Charles explains that scenario planning shows the likely performance of a business under different assumed circumstances. It requires an understanding of the relationship between the different elements within the financial statements and how these change as the circumstances being modelled change. As an example, he tells you that if the volume of branch turnover was to increase then the cost of sales would also increase but that all other expenses would remain the same as they are fixed costs.

He believes scenario planning would be particularly helpful to the manager of Branch 24, Angela Newton. Charles had previously discussed the performance of the branch with Angela and emphasised the importance of improving the asset turnover and maintaining control of working capital. However, Angela raised the following objections:

· Turning over assets is not important; making profit should be the main objective.
· Branch 24 has been in existence for two years less than all the other branches.

Task 2

Charles Walden asks you to write a memo to Angela Newton. Your memo should:

(a) show the return on capital employed that Branch 24 would have achieved had it been able to achieve the company's asset turnover during the year to 31 December 20X7 while maintaining prices and the existing capital employed;

(b) show the return on capital employed and the asset turnover for the year if Branch 24 had been able to achieve the company's standards for the average age of debtors, the average age of creditors and the average age of finished stock while maintaining its existing sales volume;

(c) using the data in task 1 and your solution to task 2 (a), address the issues raised by Angela Newton.   [Answer on p. 233]

5 Manufacturing industries

5.1 Introduction

The performance of a manufacturing business and its constituent activities will commonly be measured in quantitative terms, mainly monetary. However, we shall also consider relevant non-monetary and qualitative factors that can be useful.

5.2 Productivity

This is a measure of the efficiency of resource usage and expresses the rate of output in relation to resource used, often in non-financial terms.

Examples include the following:
(a)   units produced per labour or machine hour;
(b)   productive hours to total hours paid;

(c)   actual output to full capacity output;
(d)   sales units per salesperson;
(e)   value added, in total or per employee.

Productivity is closely linked with both efficiency and resource utilisation (which is considered later).

5.3   Labour activity, capacity and efficiency ratios

Three control ratios are often used to measure productivity, as follows:

Activity ratio: $\dfrac{\text{Actual output measured in standard hours}}{\text{Budgeted production hours}}$

Capacity ratio: $\dfrac{\text{Actual hours worked}}{\text{Budgeted hours}}$

Efficiency ratio: $\dfrac{\text{Actual output measured in standard hours}}{\text{Actual production in hours}}$

○ **EXAMPLE**   ○○○○

	Budget	Actual
Output (units)	10,000	9,000
Hours worked	200	190

Calculate:
(a)   the activity ratio;
(b)   the capacity ratio;
(c)   the efficiency ratio.

Solution

(a)   Output per standard hour $= \dfrac{10,000}{200} = 50$ units

    Actual output in standard hours $= \dfrac{9,000}{50} = 180$

    Activity ratio: $\dfrac{180}{200} = 90\ \%$

    In other words, the production level was only 90% of the budgeted level.

(b)   Capacity ratio: $\dfrac{190}{200} = 95\ \%$

    Only 95% of budgeted hours were actually worked and used to produce units.

(c)   Efficiency ratio: $\dfrac{180}{190} = 94.74\ \%$

According to the budget, 50 units should have been produced in an hour and therefore in the 190 hours that were actually worked, 9,500 units should have been produced. Only 94.74% of that quantity (9,000) were actually produced.

Note that the three ratios are related to each other:

Efficiency ratio	×	Capacity ratio	=	Activity ratio
94.74%	×	95%	=	90%

5.4 Value added

□ DEFINITION

Value added is the pool of wealth created, out of which a business provides for:
· payment of wages, salaries and other employee benefits;
· reward for providers of capital, in the form of interest and dividends;
· payment of government taxation;
· maintenance and expansion of assets.

It is also defined as:
· the value of turnover less the cost of bought in materials and services.

○ EXAMPLE

Value added statement

Horn Ltd

	£m
Turnover	1.35
Bought in materials and services	0.55
Value added	0.80
Applied as:	
To pay employee wages and other benefits	0.28
Providers of capital dividends	0.13
Government taxation	0.04
Maintenance and expansion of assets	
Depreciation	0.15
Retained profit	0.20
	0.80

Number of employees = 20

· Value added per '£' of employee costs

$$\frac{£0.80}{£0.28} = 2.86$$

· Value added per employee

$$\frac{£0.80}{20} = £0.04m \text{ or } £40,000$$

· Value added per '£' of employee costs and depreciation

$$\frac{£0.80m}{£0.43m} = 1.86$$

or, in a highly mechanised process, related to use of machinery:
· production per machine hour;
· production per machine.

5.5 Unit costs

Unit costs are the actual average cost of production of each unit of product in the period. Management will attempt to drive down unit costs over time.

5.6 Resource utilisation

This is a measure of the extent to which resources were used in relation to maximum capacity. Examples of utilisation and related measures for different resources include the following:

Machines	–	utilisation (hours used : potential hours)
	–	down time (machine down hours : total hours)
Materials	–	wastage (normal/abnormal loss percentage)
	–	stock turnover (linked to levels of slow-moving stocks)
Labour	–	utilisation (productive : total hours)
	–	absenteeism, lateness
	–	mix variances (where different grades are used)
	–	idle time (non-productive hours : total hours)
	–	labour turnover (leavers replaced : total employed)

5.7 Quality of service

For a manufacturing business, this can be categorised into quality of service to customers and quality of service from service departments. The latter is covered in the section on the service departments.

Quality of service to customers is essentially a subjective, qualitative measure, although some quantitative measures can be used in connection with it – for example, ratios such as customer returns to total sales and customer complaints per units sold. Speed of service can be measured in retail outlets or numbers waiting per checkout in a supermarket.

The main source of measure of customer satisfaction will generally be through some sort of questionnaire. This is all considered in more detail later in this chapter.

5.8   Other non-monetary measures

Quality is a particular area in which such indicators are required; two others that have recently been identified as important attributes of world-class manufacturing are innovation and flexibility.

5.9   Innovation

Innovation is concerned with the business's ability to beat their competitors in developing new products, improvements to existing ones or additional customer services.

Measurement of innovation must concentrate on its effectiveness as well as its existence – counting the number of new products developed is of little help without knowing the extent to which they have been accepted by the market. Possible measures include the following:

(a)   research and development expenditure related to new sales (in value and timing, i.e. payback);

(b)   viable new products to existing products;

(c)   percentage of total profits relating to new products/ improvements.

5.10 Flexibility

Flexibility is concerned with the business's ability to respond to customers' needs, in terms of speed of delivery of existing products, speed of reaction to changes in demand patterns and ability to respond to particular customer requests or specifications.

In a manufacturing context, it is often the case that flexibility is connected with the amounts of products using common parts. If demand for one type of product falls, it is easier to switch stock and processing to another if there is a common base between them.

6   Service departments

6.1   Introduction

Many of the measures discussed above will be relevant in the assessment of the performance of service departments within a business. Unless an internal charge-out system operates (for example, the charging of user departments per hour of computer department time spent on their work), the emphasis will be on costs rather than profits.

6.2   Types of performance indicator

As well as the normal cost variances (with activity levels based on the departments' own cost unit, e.g. maintenance hours, meals served, data processing hours), other cost ratios will be appropriate, for example:

KAPLAN PUBLISHING

(a)   meal cost per employee per period (canteen);
(b)   running costs per van-mile (deliveries);
(c)   cost per call-out (maintenance department).

O EXAMPLE   OOOO

Consider a transport/distribution department. What type of cost perform-ance indicators might be appropriate?

Solution

(a)   **Standing costs** (ascertained as a rate per day), including:
  (i)   Road tax
  (ii)   Insurance
  (iii)   Garage and administration costs
  (iv)   Drivers' wages
  (v)   Depreciation

(b)   **Running costs** (ascertained as a rate per ton/mile), including:
  (i)   Fuel and lubricants
  (ii)   Tyres
  (iii)   Repairs
  (iv)   Maintenance

Standing costs will be incurred for vehicles owned whether or not they are in use and are in the nature of stepped fixed costs. Fixed because, for each vehicle, they do not vary in amount and 'stepped' because for each additional vehicle required, costs, on a graph, will rise by a further step and remain fixed for a further range of activity until another vehicle is required.

In addition to these, there will be depot administration and establishment costs to be absorbed. These should be ascertained in total and related to the activity of the depot. Statistical information such as mileage run, loaded and empty, and tonnages carried should also be collected so that a reasonable method of absorption may be derived.

The analysis of expenditure between fixed and variable costs (standing and running costs) gives potential for the use of marginal costing and the consequent improvements in management information.

With such information available, management will be better equipped to deal with:
(a)   control over costs for each vehicle or group of similar vehicles;
(b)   pricing;
(c)   choice of most economic vehicle for specific tasks;
(d)   acceptability of contracts;
(e)   vehicle purchase and replacement decisions;
(f)   many other day-to-day decisions.

7 Service sectors

7.1 Introduction

Service organisations include the following:

(a) **Professional services**, such as firms of accountants, architects, surveyors, solicitors, whose main assets will be their employees and who provide individual, personalised services to their customers.

(b) **Mass services**, such as transport, which are highly capital asset based and provide a standard range of services to a wide range of customers.

Firms of architects are professional service organisations

(c) **Public sector services**, such as health, education and local authorities.

7.2 Types of performance indicators

Service sector measures can be considered under very similar headings as those for manufacturing organisations, although there will be a different emphasis on their relative importance.

The main difference between the two types of organisation is the nature of their output.

Output from manufacturing businesses comprises tangible, clearly identifiable products, usually of a standard design and quality which can be rejected by a customer if not required or unsuitable, and produced in advance of demand and stored until needed.

Think about a service provided to you – can it be said to have any of these characteristics? This leads to a different approach needed for performance measurement where costs per product or units per hour are of little relevance or meaning. However, in earlier chapters, we have seen that cost units do not have to be in terms of products and that measures may be activity rather than product based.

So, using similar headings as before, particular areas to be considered about the performance indicators of service organisations are productivity, unit costs, resource utilisation, profitability and quality of service.

In examinations the tasks will ask for performance indicators which are tailored to the scenario set. Make sure that you read the scenario information carefully and actually calculate the indicators that are asked for.

7.3 Productivity

Productivity can be difficult to measure, because services rarely have a standard unit of output. For example, it would be meaningless to measure a conveyancing solicitor's productivity on the basis of 'property purchase completions per month', as each will have a different degree of complexity and value to the business. Similarly, it would be inappropriate to assess a bus line on the basis of 'journeys per day', as the contribution to the company's profits would depend upon the number of people carried at each stage of the journey and how many buses were operating on the line.

Meaningful measures of productivity or efficiency for a service depend upon a clearly defined measure of activity and resources.

So, for example, the measure of activity for the bus line might be 'passenger miles' and of the resource might be 'driver hours'.

Professional firms, such as accountants and solicitors, will generally use 'chargeable hours' as a measure of activity and employees' productivity will be judged by 'chargeable hours per employee'.

7.4 Unit costs

Again, the difficulty here is in defining an appropriate unit for the activity being measured. Once this has been established, appropriate costs need to be attributed to it. So the cost of a professional chargeable hour would mainly consist of employee costs (salaries, NICs, benefits, etc.) but will also include a recovery of general overheads.

The cost of a 'passenger mile' for a transport company will include driver costs, vehicle running costs and overheads.

7.5 Resource utilisation

Resource utilisation is the extent to which available resources are used for productive service. Examples of suitable measures for various types of service businesses are illustrated by the following ratios:

Professional	Chargeable hours : Total hours available
Transport	Passenger miles : Total train miles available
Hotel	Rooms occupied : Rooms available
Car hire	Car-days hired : Car-days available

7.6 Profitability

Clearly, for the service business overall, the usual measures can apply – ROCE, profit margins, etc. Unit profitability measures will again depend upon the clear definition of the cost unit or unit of activity. The profit can then be determined by comparison of the cost per unit (as discussed above) with the income generated (e.g. the charge-out rate for a professional chargeable hour or the average fare per mile on a bus/train route).

▷ ACTIVITY 4   ▷ ▷ ▷ ▷

Transport company (AAT J94)

A transport company is reviewing the way in which it reports vehicle operating costs to the company management. In particular, it is interested in the use of performance ratios which will help to assess the efficiency and effectiveness of the use of its vehicles.

Information on the following items is available for each vehicle for the period as follows:

Costs

Variable costs
Fuel   Tyres
Oil   Other parts
Hydraulic fluid   Repairs and maintenance

Fixed costs
Road fund licence   Cleaning
Insurance   Depreciation
Drivers' wages

Activity measures

Miles driven   Number of days available for use
Tonnes carried   Number of days vehicle actually used
Journeys made

Required

You are asked to indicate six suitable performance ratios which could be used to monitor the effectiveness and efficiency of the usage of each vehicle.

Three of your ratios should relate to the efficient control of costs and three should relate to the effective usage of vehicles.   [Answer on p. 234]

7.7   Quality of service

This has arguably more significance in the service sector than in the manu-facturing sector. Customers will make their buying decisions in the service sector on the basis of how well they expect the service to be provided.

The factors contributing to quality of service will vary according to the nature of the business. As an illustration, consider the service provided to trainee accountancy students by a private college. Possible factors that would influ-ence a potential student in their choice of college and the ways in which these might be measured are as follows:

Factor	Possible measures
Technical expertise	Pass rates
Communication	Clarity of lectures, study material and administrative information
Access	Staff/student ratios Availability of tutorial help outside lecture hours Ease of finding department/member of staff required Location of college
Friendliness	Approachability of staff
Flexibility	Ability to tailor service to individual student's needs
Facilities	Availability and standard of canteen, library, phones, etc
Aesthetics	Appearance of college Staff presentation
Comfort	Roominess of classrooms Heating/air-conditioning Comfort of seats, size of desks

You can no doubt think of some more factors and different ways in which those given could be measured. For example, it is perhaps a little glib to use pass rates as a measure of the college's technical expertise, as these are also likely to be significantly influenced by the abilities and commitment of the students themselves.

7.8 Quantitative and qualitative performance indicators

Having identified what needs to be measured, how can this be achieved? Some are a matter of fact or record – like pass rates or the existence of facilities; most of the rest are qualitative judgement and would need to be measured by the use of examination forms completed by students.

An overall measure of the quality of service provided by the college could be the trend in the number of students enrolling for courses, although again this can be affected by other factors, such as the location of the college and students, the policy of the students' employers and the size of the market for trainee accountants.

8 Total quality management (TQM)

☐ DEFINITION ☐☐☐☐

Total quality management (TQM) can be defined as 'a continuous improvement in quality, efficiency and effectiveness'.

·   It aims towards an environment of zero defects at a minimum cost – the principle of 'get it right first time'.
·   It requires an awareness by all personnel of the quality requirements with supplying the customer with products of the agreed design specification.
·   It aims towards the elimination of waste where waste is defined as anything other than the minimum essential amount of equipment, materials, space and workers' time.
·   It must embrace all aspects of operations from pre-production to post-production stages in the business cycle.

Total quality management will, therefore, seek method changes which will help in achieving such objectives. Examples include the use of Just-in-time (JIT) production procedures whereby each component or product is produced or purchased only when needed by production or by a customer, rather than for stock.

8.1   Quality circles

An important element of TQM is that every employee is involved and anyone with an idea about how to improve quality should be heard. This is done by forming groups of employees known as quality circles. These groups normally consist of about 10 employees of differing levels of seniority and with different skills who meet regularly to discuss quality problems and put forward ideas.

8.2   The cost of quality

Traditionally failure rates, scrap and reworking were subsumed within the costs of production while other aspects of poor quality were accounted for in either production or marketing overheads. TQM does not accept the cost of poor quality as inevitable and requires that the cost of quality is highlighted in management reports. This enables alternative approaches (such as built-in quality at the design stage) to be developed.

Quality-related costs are the expenditure incurred in defect prevention and appraisal activities and the losses due to internal and external failure of a product or service through failure to meet agreed specifications.

8.3   Types of quality-related costs

Quality-related costs may be classified as follows:

(a)   **Failure costs** are the costs required to evaluate, dispose of, and either correct or replace a defective or deficient product.

(i)   Internal failure costs are costs discovered before the product is delivered to the customer. Examples include the following:
·   Rework costs
·   Net cost of scrap
·   Disposal of defective products
·   Downtime due to quality problems

(ii)   External failure costs are costs discovered after the product is delivered to customers.
Examples include the following:
· Complaint investigation and processing
· Warranty claims
· Cost of lost sales
· Product recalls

(b)   **Appraisal costs** are costs of monitoring and inspecting products in terms of specified standards before the products are released to the customer. Examples include the following:
· Measurement equipment
· Inspection and tests
· Product quality audits
· Process control monitoring
· Test equipment expense

(c)   **Prevention costs** include investments in machinery, technology and education programs designed to reduce the number of defective products during production. Examples include the following:
· Customer surveys
· Research of customer needs
· Field trials
· Quality education and training programmes
· Supplier reviews
· Investment in improved production equipment
· Quality engineering
· Quality circles

○ EXAMPLE   ○○○○

Carlton Limited make and sell a single product.

The following information affects its costs and revenues.

1   5% of incoming material from suppliers is scrapped owing to poor receipt and storage organisation.

2   4% of material X input to the machine process is wasted owing to processing problems.

3   Inspection of storage of material X costs 10 pence per square metre purchased.

4   Inspection during the production cycle, calibration checks on inspection equipment and other checks cost £25,000 per period.

5   Production quantity is increased to allow for the downgrading of 12.5% of product units at the final inspection stage. Downgraded units are sold as 'second quality' units at a discount of 30% on the standard selling price.

6   Production quantity is increased to allow for returns from customers which are replaced free of charge. Returns are due to specification failure and account for 5% of units initially delivered to customers. Replacement units incur a delivery cost of £8 per unit. 80% of the returns from customers are rectified using 0.2 hours of machine running time per unit and are re-sold as 'third quality' products at a discount of 50% on the standard selling price. The remaining returned units are sold as scrap for £5 per unit.

7   Product liability and other claims by customers are estimated at 3% of sales revenue from standard product sales.

8   Machine idle time is 20% of gross machine hours used (ie running hours = 80% of gross hours).

9   Sundry costs of administration, selling and distribution total £60,000 per period.

10   Carlton Limited is aware of the problem of excess costs and currently spends £20,000 per period on training staff in efforts to prevent a number of such problems from occurring.

Give examples of internal and external failure costs, appraisal costs and prevention costs borne by Carlton Limited.

Solution

Internal failure costs. The machine processing losses, downgrading of products, and materials which are scrapped due to poor receipt and storage.

External failure costs. Product liability claims and the costs of making free replacements, including delivery costs.

Appraisal costs. Inspection during the production process, inspection of materials in storage and calibration checks.

Prevention costs. Training costs.

9   The balanced scorecard

9.1   Introduction

The balanced scorecard approach to performance indicators recognises that historically too much emphasis has been placed on financial ratios in assessing an entity's performance. A successful business will only succeed in the long-term if it keeps its customers happy as well as by making profits. The approach therefore combines financial measures with operational, organisational innovation and customer service measures. All of these perspectives must be managed by managers if the business is to prosper in the long-term.

The balanced scorecard becomes the manager's instrument panel for managing the complexity of the organisation within a dynamic external environment.

9.2   Four perspectives of the balanced scorecard

The table below is an example of a balanced scorecard performance management system which demonstrates the role of critical success factors (CSFs) and key performance indicators (KPIs) in this process.

The balanced scorecard

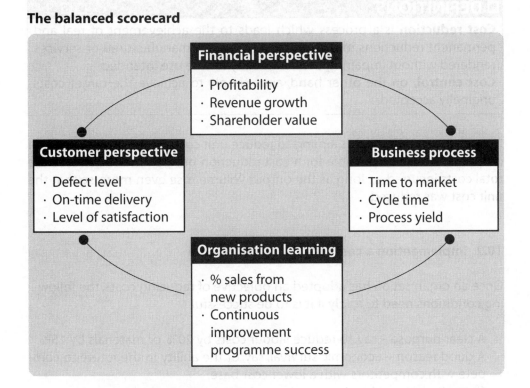

9.3   Key performance indicators

Typical key performance indicators for the balanced scorecard approach are illustrated below.

	Financial aspect	*Customer aspect*	*Business process aspect*	*Organisational learning aspect*
Strategic objective	Shareholder satisfaction	Customer satisfaction	Manufacturing excellence	New product innovation
Critical success factor	Grow shareholder wealth	Achieve preferred supplier status	State-of-the-art process plant	Successful new product development
Key performance indicators	ROCE	Number of new customers	Cycle times Unit cost % yield	% of sales represented by new products

10 Cost reduction and value enhancement

10.1 Introduction

There are few organisations which would not benefit from real efforts to keep costs to a minimum. Businesses will make more money that way, assuming quality is not compromised.

Not-for-profit organisations will make their funds go further in providing necessary services, and will be better able to meet the requirements for 'good stewardship' normally imposed on them.

□ DEFINITIONS   □□□□

Cost reduction is a process which leads to the achievement of real and permanent reductions in the unit costs of goods manufactured or services rendered without impairing their suitability for the use intended.

Cost control, on the other hand, aims simply to achieve the target costs originally accepted.

Note that cost reduction is aiming to reduce unit costs, ie the cost per item of output. It would be possible for a cost reduction programme to increase the total costs incurred, as long as the output volume rose even more, so that the unit cost was reduced.

10.2 Implementing a cost reduction programme

Once an organisation has adopted an objective of reducing costs, the following conditions need to apply if it is to be successful.

- A clear purpose – say, to reduce labour costs by 20%, or materials by 15%.
- A good reason – economic survival, say, or the ability in the future to compete with competitors with a lower cost base.
- Commitment and involvement by senior managers.
- Excellent and positive communication with workforce and, if possible, consultation.
- Gradual introduction.

10.3 Application of cost reduction techniques

Virtually all areas of businesses and not-for-profit organisations are open to the use of cost reduction techniques, including product design, production, purchasing, marketing, distribution, finance and personnel.

Two important cost reduction techniques are target costing and value engineering.

(a) **Target costing**
    Target costing starts by subtracting a desired profit margin from the market price at which an item could be sold; this gives the target cost. It

is then up to the designers to plan how the product can be manu-factured for that cost. If the product is currently planned to cost more than the target cost, then the plan must be modified.

(b) **Value engineering**

Value engineering is a philosophy of designing products which meet customer needs at the lowest cost while assuring the required standard of quality and reliability. The idea is to understand what it is that customers want from your products, and save costs by eliminating items that add no value in customers' eyes. For example, a manufacturer of computer components may decide that its customers place no value on a paper instruction manual or on fancy packaging, and will decide to sell its products with no manual and in a plain cardboard box.

10.4 Value enhancement

The 'flip side' of cost reduction is value enhancement namely, getting the best value from the resources that are used in the organisation. Use of the per-formance indicators that we have seen in this chapter will provide useful comparative measures to assess value enhancement before and after an active 'value-for-money' programme.

It should be emphasised that cost reduction and value enhancement are not just the responsibility of the accounts department of a business. All the func-tional specialists (designers, marketing, engineering, quality control, etc) must pool their knowledge and work side-by-side to achieve the required objectives.

10.5 Benchmarking

One way of closely monitoring one's own business is to compare the results in your business with those of closely related businesses. **Benchmarking** is the establishment of targets and comparators, through whose use relative levels of performance (particularly areas of under-performance) can be identified. By the adoption of identified best practices it is hoped that performance can be improved.

One common example is internal benchmarking, where a company is split up into business divisions, all operating in more or less the same industry, and per-formance indicators are calculated and compared for each division. Perhaps it is then found that one division has debtors of four months sales, while all the other divisions have debtors of less than two months sales. The division with abnormally high debtors should be able to improve its liquidity by tightening up its credit control procedures.

▷ ACTIVITY 5   ▷ ▷ ▷ ▷

Gransden Limited (AAT J96)

Gransden Limited makes and retails a variety of furniture products. One year ago, the directors realised that their traditional financial accounting system was not providing sufficient information for the managers. As a result, they established a management accounting department headed by William Jones. He quickly established standard costing throughout the organisation as well as introducing performance reports for each division in the company. Both techniques have been effective and, as a result, you were recently appointed as the Assistant Management Accountant to the company.

Some managers, however, are still having difficulty understanding the meaning of the standard costing reports prepared each month. One manager, Helen Dale, particularly feels that the report for May was misleading. Her department manufactures high quality wooden display cabinets. She wrote to William Jones about the report, and an extract from the letter is reproduced below.

'In May, my department produced 5,000 cabinets, 500 more than required in my budget. According to your own figures each cabinet requires five metres of wood at a standard price of £100 per metre, a total cost of £2,500,000. For some reason, you show the result of this as being an overall adverse material variance of £200,000, which you then break down into price and usage, despite my department only using 22,500 metres of wood in May.

Also, only yesterday, I read that the Retail Price Index stood at 168 compared with an index of 160 when the standards were agreed. This shows inflation at 3% and so the £200,000 overspend on standard cost is entirely due to price inflation, which is out of my control. Your standard costing information is not therefore particularly helpful to me as a manager.'

Required

William Jones plans to discuss with Helen the issues raised in her letter. Before doing so, however he has asked you to:
(a) (i) determine the material price and usage variances within the overall adverse variance;
    (ii) check the accuracy of the index of inflation calculated by Helen Dale.
(b) Identify three difficulties which might be experienced in interpreting the price variance, including the inflation element.

Further data

Another problem faced by William Jones has arisen from the splitting of the company into separate divisions. This restructuring had the full agreement of the Board of Directors, who viewed it as a way of giving responsibility to operating managers. Two functions, however, were deliberately retained at the centre: capital investment decisions and cash management.

Gransden's cash management system operates through a central account-ing unit within the head office finance department. Divisions inform the unit when a creditor is to be paid. The unit then makes the necessary arrange-ments for the payment to be made. Similarly, although the divisions retain overall responsibility for credit control, all remittances from debtors are handled directly by the central accounting unit. As a result of this, each division's capital employed is defined as fixed assets plus current assets (other than cash) less current liabilities.

Two divisions, the Northern Division and the Southern Division, are entirely retailing operations. Over the last year, anxieties have been expressed about the Southern Division not adequately contributing to overall company profitability. Details of their results for the year to 31 May 20X6 and the relevant management ratios for the Northern division are reproduced below.

Operating results for the year ending 31 May 20X6

	North		South	
	£000	£000	£000	£000
Turnover		135,000		191,000
Opening stocks	25,000		55,000	
Purchases	75,000		105,000	
Closing stocks	(20,000)		(40,000)	
Cost of sales		80,000		120,000
Gross profit		55,000		71,000
Wages and salaries	10,000		12,000	
Depreciation	10,000		16,000	
Other costs	9,688		8,620	
		29,688		36,620
Operating profit for the year		25,312		34,380
Net assets				
Fixed assets		100,000		160,000
Depreciation		40,000		48,000
Net book value		60,000		112,000
Finished stocks		20,000		40,000
Debtors		16,875		46,750
Creditors		(12,500)		(8,750)
Capital employed		84,375		190,000

Management ratios for the North Division

Return on capital employed	30.00%	Average age of debtors	1.5 months
Gross profit margin	40.75%	Average age of stock	3 months
Sales margin (operating profit/turnover)	18.75%	Average age of creditors	2 months
Asset turnover	1.6 times		

Required

You are informed by the Management Accountant that the Board plans to investigate ways of improving the efficiency of the Southern Division and a meeting has been called for this purpose in one week's time. William Jones has asked you to:

(c)   Calculate the relevant management ratios for the Southern Division.

(d)   Estimate what the return on capital employed would have been for the Southern Division if:

   (i)   it has achieved the same asset turnover as the Northern Division;

   (ii)   it had the same average age of debtors, stock and creditors as the Northern Division.

   Note: for the purpose of Task (d)(i) only, you should assume that the wages and salaries, the depreciation and the other costs are all fixed costs and that stock, debtors and creditors remain unaltered.

(e)   Identify two limitations to your analysis in parts (c) and (d).

[Answer on p. 235]

11 Test your knowledge

1   State two liquidity ratios.

2   Show how the return on capital employed can be divided up into two component ratios.

3   How is the debtors collection period calculated as a number of months?

4   What is value added?

5   State two external failure costs.

6   State the four perspectives of the balanced scorecard.

7   What is target costing?   [Answers on p. 237]

KAPLAN PUBLISHING

12 Summary

As you have seen, there are numerous possible performance indicators and their relevance will depend upon the type of organisation and the aspect of performance being assessed.

The most important ratios for you to be able to compute (and interpret) are as follows:

Profitability: Return on capital employed (ROCE)
Gross and net profit margins

Liquidity: Current ratio
Quick (acid test) ratio
Stock turnover
Debtors' collection period
Creditors' payment (settlement) period

Remember that a ratio on its own is not particularly useful information; it needs to be compared, internally or externally. This gives rise to problems of comparability, which you should be able to discuss.

Many of the ideas covered in earlier chapters will have relevance here (e.g. variance analysis and the use of indices).

Make sure you are quite clear about the necessary attributes of a cost unit (or unit of activity) in order for it to provide a useful basis for measurement. This is particularly important for service activities. Try to think of services you have had experience of yourself and how the various aspects may be measured.

There will rarely be a unique right or wrong answer, so do not be afraid to use your imagination!

Answers to chapter activities & 'test your knowledge' questions

△ ACTIVITY 1 △ △ △ △

WH Limited
REPORT

To: Senior Management Committee

From: Assistant Accountant

Date: 12 December 20X4

Subject: Profitability and asset turnover ratios

We have received the Trade Association results for year 4 and this report looks in detail at the profitability and asset turnover ratios.

(a) **What each ratio is designed to show**

(i) *Return on capital employed (ROCE)*

This ratio shows the percentage rate of profit which has been earned on the capital invested in the business (i.e. the return on the resources controlled by management). The expected return would vary depending on the type of business and it is usually calculated as follows:

$$\text{Return on capital employed} = \frac{\text{Profit before interest and tax}}{\text{Captial employed}} \times 100\%$$

Other profit figures can be used, as well as various definitions of capital employed.

(ii) *Net operating profit margin*

This ratio shows the operating profit as a percentage of sales. The operating profit is calculated before interest and tax and it is the profit over which operational managers can exercise day to day control. It is the amount left out of sales value after all direct costs and overheads have been deducted.

$$\text{Net operating profit margin} = \frac{\text{Operating profit}}{\text{Sales value}} \times 100\%$$

Page 1 of 3

(iii) *Asset turnover*

This ratio shows how effectively the assets of a business are being used to generate sales:

$$\text{Asset turnover} = \frac{\text{Sales}}{\text{Capital employed}}$$

If the same figure for capital employed is used as in ROCE, then ratios (i) to (iii) can be related together as follows.

(i) ROCE = (ii) Net operating profit margin × (iii) Asset turnover

(iv) *Gross margin*

This ratio measures the profitability of sales:

$$\text{Gross margin} = \frac{\text{Gross profit}}{\text{Sales value}} \times 100\%$$

The gross profit is calculated as the sales value less the cost of goods sold and this ratio therefore focuses on the company's manufacturing and trading activities.

(b) **WH Limited's profitability and asset turnover**

WH Limited's ROCE is lower than the trade association average, indicating either poor profitability (as measured by the net profit margin) or poor asset utilisation (as measured by the asset turnover) or both.

WH Limited's operating profit margin is higher than the trade association average, despite a lower than average gross profit margin. This suggests that overheads are lower relative to sales value in WH Limited.

WH Limited's asset turnover ratio is lower than the trade association average. This may mean that assets are not being used as effectively in our company and it is the cause of the lower than average ROCE.

WH Limited's gross profit margin is lower than the trade association average. This suggests either that WH's direct costs are higher than average, or that selling prices are lower.

(c) **Limitations of the ratios and of inter-company comparisons**

There are a number of limitations of which management should be aware before drawing any firm conclusions from a comparison of these ratios:

(i) The ratios are merely averages, based on year-end balance sheet data, which may not be representative.

Page 2 of 3

(ii) One particular factor which could affect these ratios is if there has been any new investment towards the end of the financial year. This investment would increase the value of the assets or capital employed, but the profits from the investment would not yet have accumulated in the profit and loss account. Generally, newer assets tend to depress the asset turnover and hence the ROCE in the short term. It is possible that this is the cause of our company's lower asset turnover and ROCE.

(iii) Although the trade association probably makes some attempt to standardise the data, different member companies may be using different accounting policies, for example in calculating depreciation and valuing stock.

(iv) Our company's analyst may have used a different formula for calculating any of the ratios. For example, as noted above, there is a variety of ways of calculating capital employed. However, it is likely that the trade association would provide information on the basis of calculation of the ratios.

(v) The member companies will have some activities in common, hence their membership of the trade association. However, some may have a diversified range of activities, which will distort the ratios and make direct comparison difficult.

Page 3 of 3

△ ACTIVITY 2   △ △ △ △
Homely Limited

(a)   *Target ratios*

$$\text{Return on capital employed} = \frac{66}{300} \times 100\% = 22\%$$

$$\text{Operating profit percentage} = \frac{66}{820} \times 100\% = 8\%$$

$$\text{Asset turnover} = \frac{820}{300} = 2.7 \text{ times}$$

$$\text{Working capital period} = \frac{70}{754} \times 365 = 34 \text{ days}$$

$$\text{Percentage room occupancy} = \frac{5,900}{18 \times 365} \times 100\% = 90\%$$

$$\text{Turnover per employee} = \frac{820,000}{20} = £41,000$$

Key ratios for 20X4

	Stately Hotels plc target	*Homely Limited actual*
Return on capital employed	26%	22%
Operating profit percentage	13%	8%
Asset turnover	2.0 times	2.7 times
Working capital period	20 days	34 days
Percentage room occupancy	85%	90%
Turnover per employee	£30,000	£41,000

WH Limited
MEMORANDUM

To: Management Accountant, Stately Hotels plc

From: Assistant to the Management Accountant

Date: 21 June X5

Subject: Initial assessment of the performance of Homely Limited

I have carried out an initial assessment of Homely Limited, based on an extract from their accounts for 20X4. I have calculated their key accounting ratios and compared them with our company's target ratios and my conclusions and recommendations are as follows.

Return on capital employed (ROCE)

At 22% the ROCE is below the target which we set for the hotels in our chain. Management action will be necessary to improve the return on capital employed, through improved profitability of operations, increased asset turnover, or both.

The main limitation in the use of this ratio is that the valuation of the capital employed can have a considerable effect on the apparent ROCE. For example, if the capital employed is undervalued, this will artificially inflate the ROCE.

Operating profit percentage

This is considerably below the target ratio set by Stately Hotels plc and it is the cause of the depressed ROCE. Management action will be necessary to improve this, either by increasing prices or by controlling operating costs relative to sales revenue. Since the former action may depress demand in Homely Limited's market, it is likely that management will need to focus on the control of operating costs.

A limitation in the use of this ratio is that Homely's operations may not be comparable to the average hotel in the Stately group. For example, they may not have conference facilities, which would affect the profile of their costs.

Page 1 of 2

Asset turnover

At 2.7 times this is higher than the target ratio, indicating that, although Homely's operations are not as profitable, they generate more turnover per £ of capital employed. It may be that Homely has a different basis of operating, i.e. charging lower prices, and thus reducing the profitability of sales, but in the process generating a higher turnover for the level of capital employed.

The main limitation of this ratio stems from the limitation of the ROCE, i.e. its accuracy relies on the correct valuation of capital employed.

Working capital period

This is 34 days of operating costs, almost double the level which we require in our target performance ratios. Working capital levels are probably unacceptably high and need to be reduced. This will require more attention to debtor control, reduction in stocks of, for example, consumable materials and foodstuffs, and an investigation into whether full use is being made of available credit facilities.

A limitation of this ratio is that it relies on the accurate valuation of working capital. For example, although stocks should not account for a high proportion of working capital in a hotel, their valuation can be very subjective.

Another major limitation is that the ratio is based on balance sheet data, which depicts the working capital level on a single day. This may not be representative of the year as a whole and therefore incorrect conclusions may be drawn from the analysis.

Percentage room occupancy

Homely Limited is achieving a room occupancy rate which is above the level expected in our organisation's target ratios. This is a healthy sign which is encouraging.

Turnover per employee

Homely Limited's turnover per employee is also healthy. However, we must ensure that customer service and quality are not suffering as a result of operating with a lower level of staffing.

Overall, Homely Limited seems to have some strengths which would be worth exploiting. However, their control of operating costs and of working capital needs some attention.

Page 2 of 2

△ ACTIVITY 3   △ △ △ △
Diamond Limited

Task 1

Diamond Ltd
Performance report – Branch 24
Year ended 31 December 20X7

(a)	Return on capital employed	57.6/240.0	24%
(b)	Gross profit margin	360.0/720.0	50%
(c)	Asset turnover	720.0/240.0	3 times
(d)	Sales margin	57.6/720.0	8%
(e)	Average age of debtors	(96.0/720.0) × 12	1.6 months
(f)	Average age of creditors	(51.0/340.0) × 12	1.8 months
(g)	Average age of stock	(60.0/360.0) × 12	2.0 months

Task 2

Workings

(a)

		£
Revised turnover	£240,000 × 4	960,000
Cost of sales = 50%		480,000
Gross profit		480,000
Fixed costs		302,400
Operating profit		177,600
Revised return on capital employed	£177,600/£240,000	**74%**

(b) *Revised working capital*

		£
Revised debtors	(0.5 × £720,000)/12	30,000
Revised stock	(1× £360,000)/12	30,000
Revised creditors	(3 × £340,000)/12	(85,000)
Revised working capital		(25,000)
Add fixed assets		135,000
Revised capital employed		110,000
Return on capital employed	£57,600/£110,000	52%
Asset turnover	£720,000/£110,000	6.5 times

MEMORANDUM

To: Angela Newton

From: Financial analyst

Date: 5 January 20X8

Subject: Branch 24 performance indicators

Charles Walden has asked me to write to you concerning the performance indicators of Branch 24 and the extent of improvement possible if the branch was able to achieve the performance standards established by the company.

Had Branch 24 been able to achieve the same asset turnover as other branches, the return on capital employed would have been 74 per cent, comfortably in excess of the standard return on capital employed.

Likewise, had the branch controlled its working capital at standard levels, not only would the return on capital employed have been 52 per cent but it would also have achieved an asset turnover of 6.5 times.

You are quite correct to emphasise the need for profitability. If the asset turnover can be improved while maintaining the existing level of net assets, then turnover will increase. If the cost of this increased turnover is less than its value, then this will lead to both increased profits and an increase in the return on capital employed.

The suggestion that your performance might be less than other branches because your branch has been established for less time may be valid. From the financial data related to your branch, it would appear that Branch 24 was only opened two years ago. (The annual depreciation is £45,000 and the accumulated depreciation is £90,000.) If other branches have been established longer, then the accumulated depreciation will be greater, leading to a lower net book value and a lower capital employed. It is also possible that the older fixtures and fittings would have been purchased at a lower price, resulting in the annual depreciation charge also being less and hence increasing operating profit.

△ ACTIVITY 4   △ △ △ △

Transport company

Cost control performance ratios

Cost per mile
Cost per tonne carried   } each of these ratios could be calculated for
Cost per journey   fixed and variable costs separately
Cost per tonne/mile

Fixed cost per available day
Fixed cost per working day

Usage performance ratios

Tonne/miles per period
Days available as a percentage of total working days
Days used as a percentage of available days
Tonnes carried per available day
Journeys made per available day
Tonnes/miles per journey

△ ACTIVITY 5   △△△△

Gransden Limited

(a)   (i)   *Material price and usage variances*

	£		
Standard cost	2,500,000	*Material price variance*	
Total variance	200,000 (A)	(£120 - £100) × 22,500 metres =	£450,000 (A)
Actual cost	2,700,000	*Material usage variance*	
		Standard metres: £2,500,000/£100	25,000
Actual usage (metres)	22,500	Actual metres	22,500
Actual cost per metre	£120	Physical variance (metres)	2,500 (F)
		2,500 metres × £100 =	£250,000 (F)

(ii)   *Increase in RPI*

Current index	168
Index at beginning of period	160
Price inflation (168/160 – 1) × 100	5%

(b)   **Difficulties in interpreting the price variance**

(i)   The original standard may not have been appropriate.

(ii)   There might be a link between the adverse price variance and the favourable usage variance. This might occur if a superior, but more expensive, material has been used.

(iii)   The Retail Price Index is a measure of the cost of living for the average household in the UK. It may not be an appropriate index for measuring price rises in manufacturing generally nor price rises for wood in particular.

(c) Return on capital employed $\dfrac{34{,}380}{190{,}000} \times 100 =$ 18.09%

Gross profit margin $\dfrac{71{,}000}{191{,}000} \times 100 =$ 37.17%

Sales margin $\dfrac{34{,}380}{191{,}000} \times 100 =$ 18.00%

Asset turnover $\dfrac{191{,}000}{190{,}000} =$ 1 time

Average age of debtors $\dfrac{47{,}750}{191{,}000} \times 12 =$ 3 months

Average age of stock $\dfrac{40{,}000}{120{,}000} \times 12 =$ 4 months

Average age of creditors $\dfrac{8{,}750}{105{,}000} \times 12 =$ 1 month

(d) (i) Southern Division's return on capital employed with an asset turnover of 1.6 times:

	£
Sales = £190,000 × 1.6	304,000
Gross profit @ 37%	112,480
Less fixed costs	36,620
Operating profit	75,860
Capital employed	£190,000
Return on capital employed	40%

(ii) Southern Division's return on capital employed with Northern's working capital ratios:

	£
Fixed assets	112,000
Stock £120,000 × 3/12 =	30,000
Debtors £191,000 × 1.5/12 =	23,875
Creditors £105,000 × 2/12 =	(17,500)
Capital employed	148,375
Operating profit	£34,380
Return on capital employed	23%

(e) (i) Both divisions appear to be charging straight-line depreciation at 10 per cent per annum. On that basis, the average age of Northern's fixed assets is four years old (£40,000/£10,000) while the comparable figure for the Southern Division is only three years (£48,000/£16,000). Because of this, Southern will have lower accumulated depreciation in relative terms and hence a higher capital employed.

(ii) Although the average age of creditors and debtors result from past activity – buying and selling respectively – the average age of stock has a different perspective. Although the cost of sales is backward looking in the same way as purchases and sales, the stock level at the year end may not be a direct consequence of this activity. Stock could be being built up in anticipation of higher sales next year.

(iii) Southern Division may be paying its creditors more quickly to obtain cash discounts.

Test your knowledge △ △ △

1 Two liquidity ratios are the current ratio and the acid test ratio.

2 $\text{ROCE} = \dfrac{\text{Profit}}{\text{Net assets}} = \dfrac{\text{Profit}}{\text{Sales}} \times \dfrac{\text{Sales}}{\text{Net assets}} = \text{Profit margin} \times \text{Asset turnover}$

3 Debtors collection period $= \dfrac{\text{Debtors}}{\text{Sales}} \times 12 \text{ months}$

4 Value added equals sales revenue less the cost of bought-in materials and services.

5 External failure costs include the costs of warranty claims and the costs of product recalls.

6 The balanced scorecard encompasses:
   · the financial perspective;
   · the customer perspective;
   · the business perspective;
   · the innovation and learning perspective.

7 Target costing is the idea of identifying the cost at which a product must be made, and then choosing a design and production method that will meet that cost. This differs from the traditional idea of producing an item, seeing how much it has cost, and then adding a profit margin to set the selling price.

BUDGET PREPARATION

INTRODUCTION

Having considered the ways in which cost, revenue and other business data may be collected, processed and analysed, we now turn to the task of putting this information to use in the future planning of the business.

The planning process starts with the identification of long term corporate objectives, based upon which a strategy is designed, resource utilisation and capital expenditure planned and ultimately short-term, quantified budgets are prepared. This chapter looks at this overall process.

In all Unit 9 examinations you will be required to prepare budgets. You should also be prepared to discuss the budget preparation process and to suggest improvements to budget presentation.

KNOWLEDGE & UNDERSTANDING

- Development of production, resource and revenue budgets from forecast sales data
- Co-ordination of the budget system (Elements 9.2 and 9.3)
- The effect of capacity constraints, other production constraints and sales constraints on budgets; limiting (key or budget) factor (Elements 9.2 and 9.3)
- Uses of budgetary control: planning, co-ordinating, authorising, cost control (Elements 9.1, 9.2 and 9.3)
- Relationship between budgets, forecasts and planning and product life cycles (Elements 9.1, 9.2 and 9.3)
- Different types of budgets: budgets for income and expenditure; resource budgets (production, material, labour and other resource budgets); capital budgets (Elements 9.2 and 9.3)
- Responsibility centres: expense centres: profit centres; investment centres (Element 9.3)

CONTENTS

1 The approach to budgetary control
2 The administration of budgetary control
3 Budget preparation
4 Problems in exam questions
5 Practical aspects of functional budgets
6 The master budget

PERFORMANCE CRITERIA

- Prepare forecasts in a clear format with explanations of assumptions, projections and adjustments (Element 9.1)
- Review and revise the validity of forecasts in the light of any significant anticipated changes (Element 9.1)
- Present to management draft budget proposals in a clear and appropriate format and on schedule (Element 9.2)
- Verify that draft budget proposals are consistent with organisational objectives and include all relevant data and assumptions (Element 9.2)
- Break down budgets into periods appropriate to the organisation (Element 9.2)
- Check and reconcile budget figures on an ongoing basis (Element 9.3)

1 The approach to budgetary control

1.1 The purpose of budgeting

One commentator has suggested that 'Budgets are a means of attaining organisational control, that is the achievement of organisational objectives'. Within this context, he then went on to consider the various functions which a budget may fulfil.

· **Authorisation**

A budget may act as a formal authorisation to a manager to spend a given amount on specified activities. If this is applied to an operating budget, however, it must be appreciated that over-strict enforcement would not be in the best interests of the business.

· **Forecasting**

Forecasting refers to the prediction of events over which little or no control is exercised. Some parts of all budgets are, therefore, based on forecasts. Budget figures may also be used by one part of an organisation to forecast the likely effect on it of the activities of other parts.

· **Planning**

Planning is an attempt to shape the future by a conscious effort to influence those factors which are open to control.

· **Communication and co-ordination**

Budgets communicate plans to managers responsible for carrying them out. They also ensure co-ordination between managers of sub-units so that each is aware of the others' requirements.

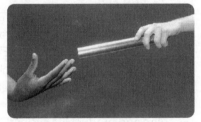

Budgets ensure co-ordination between managers

· **Motivation**

Budgets are often intended to motivate managers to perform in line with organisational objectives. The problem in this area is that unless budgets are made relevant and are properly designed to act as motivational devices, the attitude of managers using them tends to be negative.

· **Evaluation**

The performance of managers and organisational units is often evaluated by reference to budgetary standards as these are quite possibly the only quantitative reference points available. The way in which performance is evaluated will be a dominating influence on how a manager behaves in the future and is therefore worthy of separate consideration.

1.2 Objectives

Pre-requisites of budgetary control are the definition of objectives and the existence or creation of an organisational structure through which plans may be put into effect. In particular, forecasts on which budgets are based should be made available to operational departments in a clear, easily understood format with explanations of assumptions, projections and adjustments.

The objectives of the business will be defined in the long-term strategic plan and any short-term budget must be framed in such a way as to contribute towards the achievement of these objectives.

The budget, therefore, will incorporate its own short-term objectives, probably expressed in the form that a financial analyst would use when interpreting the final results as follows (we shall look at these ratios further in a later chapter):

· rate of return on total capital employed;
· net profit percentage (i.e. net profit: sales);
· asset turnover ratio (i.e. sales: capital employed);
· rate of growth in sales value;
· liquidity and asset management ratios supporting the above.

2   The administration of budgetary control

2.1   Budget centres

The organisational structure through which control will be exercised so that budget objectives are achieved must be based on manager responsibilities.

It is only when the functions to be carried out by each manager have been defined that it becomes possible to define the following:

· the output he should achieve;
· the resources he can justifiably employ;
· the costs he is expected to control.

The particular segments of the business for which individuals are allocated budget responsibility are known as budget centres or responsibility centres.

Some budget centre managers will be responsible for profitability, either profit in relation to output or profit in relation to capital employed under their control. These centres are known as profit centres or investment centres, depending upon the amount of autonomy given.

2.2   Issue of budget instructions

Budgets need to be prepared by all managers on a consistent basis in a form which facilitates combination into the master budget. The information needed includes the following:

· The organisational structure of the business, setting out clearly the responsibilities of each manager and the limits of his authority.
· The classification and coding of the various items of income and expenditure to be covered by the budget.
· A statement of the period to be covered by the budget and of the shorter accounting periods into which it is to be subdivided (or 'phased') for purposes of control.

- Copies of the forms to be used in submitting budgets.
- Instructions on what is to be shown on the various forms, and the manner in which particular items are to be calculated. Examples of practical points to be clarified are:
    (i) whether 'sales' are to be budgeted initially on the basis of order intake or of invoiced amounts;
    (ii) when costs are expected to increase, whether uniform percentages for particular items are to be used;
    (iii) what rates of salary increase, if any, are to be budgeted by managers;
    (iv) what types of cost are to be budgeted centrally and not included in departmental budgets.
- The timetable for the preparation of the budgets. In particular, draft budget proposals, presented in a clear and appropriate format, must be completed and submitted to management on schedule to allow the budget-setting process to proceed in a timely manner.

Instructions which are to be binding on all managers must clearly be issued on the authority of the managing director or chief executive; but somebody must be responsible for drafting them, explaining them when necessary, and ensuring that they are being complied with as the work of budgeting progresses.

2.3 The budget officer

The term budget officer is used to describe a role which must be played by somebody in the organisation to get the budget processed to completion (even if he or she is actually called something else). This will involve the following duties:
- the issue of the budget instructions;
- the co-ordination of the budgets;
- checking and reconciling the budget figures on an ongoing basis;
- valuing and combining the various departmental budgets;
- submitting the final company budget to the board.

After the budgets have been approved, the budget officer will continue the task of budgetary control.

In a large business all these activities may be brought together under a budget officer or 'controller' having equal or senior status to the chief accountant.

In the smaller company a chief accountant may be responsible directly to the managing director, and have under his control all the functions outlined above, including budgetary control.

To facilitate the budget-setting process, it is important that all discussions with budget-holders are conducted in a manner which maintains goodwill.

2.4 Co-ordination of budgets

So that an acceptable master budget can be prepared, the various subsidiary budgets must be co-ordinated. The most obvious example of this is the need to ensure that the quantities which the sales department are forecasting that they will sell are in line with the quantities which production are budgeting to produce.

Co-ordination of activities can be carried out by a budget committee which can include the main functional managers under the chairmanship of the budget officer.

2.5 Approval of budgets

Budgets must be approved ultimately by the board of the company. The management accountant or MD will recommend approval by the board. Before doing so, however, he will need to be satisfied that all budgets have been properly co-ordinated and that the budgets are in line with the company's objectives.

To ensure that this is achieved from the outset the draft budget proposals agreed with budget-holders must be consistent with organisational objectives and must be potentially achievable.

After being prepared, the individual draft budgets will therefore pass through the following stages before being finally approved by the board:
·   approval in principle by the manager of the function to which the budget relates;
·   examination by the budget controller who will ensure that the principles laid down for preparation of the budgets have been adhered to;
·   consideration of the budget in the light of all the other budgets by the budget committee before it recommends to the managing director that the master budget should be submitted to the board for approval.

3 Budget preparation

3.1 Limiting factors

The level of activity at which a business can operate will very seldom be unlimited. Limitations may be imposed, for example, by:
·   market demand for its products or services;
·   the number of skilled employees available;
·   the availability of material supplies;
·   the space available either as a working area or for the storage of goods;
·   the amount of cash or credit facilities available to finance the business.

Therefore, when a manager starts to prepare a budget he should review the elements in it and identify where limiting factors (or governing factors) exist.

They will not all be equally significant; but where one particular limitation is of major importance it may be necessary to budget for that item first and to construct the rest of the budget around it. This can happen not merely in one department but for the company as a whole, when the item concerned may be referred to as the principal budget factor or key factor.

Quite commonly, the rate of growth in sales is the principal budget factor and this would have to be forecast before any other budget plans were made.

It is essential to identify the principal budget factor and any other limiting factors at an early stage in the budgeting process so that management may consider whether:

- it is possible to overcome the limitation which they impose (e.g. by finding new markets for sales or by obtaining alternative supplies or substitute raw materials);
- the limitations imposed must be accepted and the business's budgets must be produced within those limitations.

▷ ACTIVITY 1

Your organisation (AAT CA D94)

Your organisation is about to commence work on the preparation of the forthcoming year's annual budget.

As assistant management accountant, you have been asked to assist budget-holders and to respond to any queries which they may raise in the course of submitting their budget proposals.

The following notes are extracts taken from your organisation's budget manual.

'*The key or principal budget factor in our organisation's budgetary process is sales volume ... The need for co-ordination in the budgetary process is paramount ...*'.

The marketing manager is a budget holder and she has approached you with a number of queries concerning the above extract.

Required

Prepare a memo for the marketing manager which provides brief answers to the following queries:

(a)   What is meant by the term *key factor* and why is the determination of this factor so important in the budgetary process?

(b)   How can co-ordination be achieved?

[Answer on p. 262]

3.2   Budgets to be produced

The budgets that a business produces will generally be a standard set of budgets that starts with the sales budget and progresses through budgets for the costs associated with those sales.

You will typically be asked to produce the following budgets for a business that manufactures the goods that it sells. Note that generally you will produce the budgets for the number of units bought and sold before translating those into revenues and costs.

(a) The sales budget
(b) The production budget of finished goods. This will follow from the sales budget. It will be the same as sales budget unless there are changes in the stocks held of finished goods.
(c) The raw materials purchases budget. This will follow from the production budget.
    The raw materials purchased will in general terms be:
    the number of finished goods produced x the raw material per unit, (after adjustments for changes in stocks of materials and process losses).
(d) The labour budget, and
(e) The overheads budget.

3.3 Sales, production, materials, labour and overheads budgets

We shall first of all look at a simple budget example.

○ EXAMPLE ○○○○

Toys Ltd budgets to sell 10,000 play cubes at £10 per cube in the month of July 20X8.

Stocks of finished cubes were 3,000 tins at the start of the month and were budgeted to be 4,000 cubes at the end of the month.

Each cube requires 0.5 kg of material that costs £1 per kg. Opening stocks of material were 1,000 kg at the start of the month and are budgeted to be 750 kg at the end of the month.

Each cube requires 0.25 hours of direct labour. The labour rate is £12 per hour.

Production overheads are absorbed into production at the rate of £15 per hour.

Task

Produce the budgets for sales, production, materials, labour and over-heads.

Solution

Step 1 – the sales budget

Number of cubes budgeted to be sold = 10,000 cubes
Budgeted sales revenue 10,000 x £10 = £100,000

Step 2 – the production budget

The standard layout for this is as follows – always work in units (cubes) first

	cubes
Sales budget	10,000
Closing stock	4,000
	14,000
Opening stock	3,000
Production of finished goods	11,000 cubes

(Tutorial note. There are no costs associated with the finished goods because the company manufactures them. The cost of the goods will be found when we deal with the budgets and costs of raw materials, labour and overheads. However we have to prepare the production budget in order to be able to prepare the raw materials budget.)

Step 3 – the raw materials budget

The standard layout for this is as follows – always work in units (kg) first. In this case remember that 1 cube requires 0.5 kg of raw material.

	Kg
For production budget 11,000 x 0.5kg	5,500
Closing stock	750
	6,250
Opening stock	1,000
Purchases of raw material	5,250 kg

Budgeted purchases of raw materials = 5,250 x £1 = £5,250

Step 4 – the labour budget

To calculate the cost of labour we have to return to the production budget because the cost of labour is determined by the level of production.

Number of labour hours budgeted for month = 11,000 cubes x 0.25 hours = 2,750hrs
Cost of direct labour = 2,750hrs x £12 = £33,000

Step 5 – the overhead budget

To calculate the cost of overheads we have to return to the labour budget because the cost of the overhead is based on the number of hours worked.

Number of labour hours budgeted for month =	2,750 hrs
Cost of overhead = 2,750hrs x £15 =	£41,250

4 Problems In Exam Questions

4.1 The raw materials budget with losses

A question may be set where the there is a percentage loss of raw materials in the production process. In practice this may be due to such things as evaporation, faulty materials supplied or materials damaged in the process.

Consider the example above, changing the raw material details read:

Each cube requires 0.5 kg of material that costs £1 per kg. Opening stocks of material were 1,000 kg at the start of the month and are budgeted to be 750 kg at the end of the month. 5% of materials are lost during the manufacturing process.

The calculation of raw materials purchased budget would be changed as follows:

	kg
For production budget 11,000 x 0.5kg	5,500
Closing stock	750
	6,250
Opening stock	1,000
Material required for production	5,250
Process loss 5,250 x (5/95) =	276
Purchases	5,526 kg

Budgeted cost of purchases of raw materials = 5,526 x £1 = £5,526

Note that the loss is 5/95 x the material required for production.
It is not 5/100 x the material required for production.

The reason for this is that the process loses 5% of the 'gross' amount purchased. We therefore have the following percentages

Purchases	100%
Losses	5%
Material required production	95%

The losses are therefore 5/95 of what is left after the loss (5,250kg) which is what is required for production.

4.2 The production budget with losses

A question may be set where the there is a percentage loss of finished goods. In practice this may be due to such things as items rejected as inferior by quality control, items damaged in the warehouse or theft.

Consider the example above, changing the finished goods details to read:

Stocks of finished cubes were 3,000 tins at the start of the month and were budgeted to be 4,000 cubes at the end of the month. 4% of finished goods are rejected as unsuitable.

The calculation of the production budget would be changed as follows:

	cubes
Sales budget	10,000
Closing stock	4,000
	14,000
Opening stock	3,000
Finished goods required	11,000
Loss 11,000 x (4/96) =	458
Production required	11,458

As before, note that the loss is 4/96 x the finished goods required It is not 4/100 x the finished goods required.

The reason for this is that the business loses 4% of the 'gross' amount produced. We therefore have the following percentages

Produced	100%
Losses	4%
Finished goods required	96%

The losses are therefore 4/96 of what is left in the warehouse after the loss (11,000 units) which is what is required for sales and stock.

4.3 Calculating the sales budget and stocks of finished goods

Exam questions will frequently present information regarding sales and stocks as follows.

> ○ **EXAMPLE**   ○ ○ ○ ○
>
> XYZ has 13 accounting periods of four weeks during the year. It had sales of £40,000 in accounting period 5 and budgets for sales to increase by 3% for each accounting period.
>
> The company budgets to have closing stock at the end of an accounting period equal to two weeks sales of the following period.
>
> Produce the budget for sales and stock for accounting periods 6, 7 and 8.

Solution

	Period 6	Period 7	Period 8	Period 9
	£	£	£	£
Sales 40,000 x 1.03	41,200			
41,200 x 1.03		42,436		
42,436 x 1.03			43,709	
43,709 x 1.03				45,020
Opening Stock	20,600(W1)	21,218	21,854	
Closing stock	21,218(W2)	21,854(W3)	22,510(W4)	

Workings

1   £41,200 x 0.5 (ie two weeks sales of a 4 week period) = £20,600
2   £42,436 x 0.5 = £21,218
3   £43,709 x 0.5 = £21,854
4   £45,020 x 0.5 = £22,510

The example below illustrates the preparation of the functional budgets, starting with projected sales information.

○ EXAMPLE   ○○○○

The following data will be used to explain the technique of budget preparation:

Hash Ltd makes two products – PS and TG. Sales for next year are budgeted at 5,000 units of PS and 1,000 units of TG. Planned selling prices are £100 and £140 respectively.

Hash Ltd has the following opening stock and required closing stock.

	PS units	TG units
Opening stock	100	50
Projected closing stock	1,100	50

You are also given the following data about the materials required to produce PS and TG and the machining and finishing processes involved in production.

	PS	TG
Finished products:		
Kg of raw material X, per unit of finished product	12	12
Kg of raw material Y, per unit of finished product	6	8
Direct labour hours per unit of finished product	8	12

Standard rates and prices:

Direct labour	£6.00 per hour
Raw material X	£0.72 per kg
Raw material Y	£1.56 per kg

Production overheads:

Variable	£1.54 per labour hour
Fixed	£0.54 per labour hour
	£2.08 per labour hour

You are required to prepare the functional budgets.

Solution

(a)   The sales budget

The sales budget represents the plan in terms of the quantity and value of sales, for sales management. In practice this is often the most difficult budget to calculate.

What is next year's sales budget?

The sales budget would be:

	Total	PS	TG
Sales units	6,000	5,000	1,000
Sales value	£640,000	£500,000	£140,000

In practice a business would market many more than two products. Moreover, the sales budget would probably be supported by subsidiary budgets to show analysis according to:
(i)   responsibility e.g. Northern area, Western area, etc.;
(ii)   type of customer e.g. wholesale, retail, government, etc.

(b)   The production budget

The production budget is usually expressed in quantity and represents the sales budget adjusted for opening/closing finished stocks and work in progress.

The production budget would be:

	PS units	TG units
Sales budget	5,000	1,000
Add projected closing stock	1,100	50
	6,100	1,050
Less opening stock	100	50
Production in units	6,000	1,000

The production budget needs to be translated into requirements for:

(i)   raw materials;
(ii)   direct labour;
(iii)   factory overheads;
(iv)   closing stock levels.

(c)   **The raw materials and purchases budget**

(Remember that Hash Ltd is going to produce 6,000 units of PS and 1,000 units of TG.)

		PS		TG
		kg		kg
Raw material usage				
X	6,000 × 12 kg	72,000	1,000 × 12 kg	12,000
Y	6,000 × 6 kg	36,000	1,000 × 8 kg	8,000

		PS		TG
		£		£
Budgeted purchases:				
X	72,000 x £0.72	51,840	12,000 x £0.72	8,640
Y	36,000 x £1.56	56,160	8,000 x £1.56	12,480
		108,000		21,120

(d)   **The direct labour budget**

		PS		TG
Usage	6,000 × 8 hrs	48,000 hrs	1,000 x 12 hrs	12,000 hrs
Cost	48,000 x £6	£288,000	12,000 x £6	£72,000

(f)   **Production overheads**

		PS		TG
Variable costs	48,000 hours × £1.54	73,920	12,000 x £1.54	18,480
Fixed costs	48,000 hours × £0.54	25,920	12,000 x £0.54	6,480
		99,840		24,960

One of the most important points illustrated by this example is how the budgets are inter-related.

It is a simple example and you should be aware that in practice budgeting can be more than simply an arithmetical exercise. The practical problems are discussed later.

4.4 The budgeted profit and loss account

The budgeted profit and loss account shows the net profit by deducting the budgeted costs from the budgeted sales revenue.

Using the example above the budgeted profit and loss account would be as follows.

	PS £	TG £
Sales	500,000	140,000
Materials	108,000	21,120
Labour	288,000	72,000
Production overheads	99,840	24,960
Production cost	495,840	118,080
add opening stock	8,264	5,904
less closing stock	90,904	5,904
Cost of sales	413,200	118,080
Profit	86,800	21,920

Working

Stock values = (production cost/units produced) x units of stock.

1   Opening stock of PS = (495,840/6,000) x 100 = £8,264
2   Closing stock of PS = (495,840/6,000) x 1,100 = £90,904
3   Opening stock of TG = (118,080/1,000) x 50 = £5,904
4   Closing stock of TG = (118,080/1,000) x 50 = £5,904

▷ ACTIVITY 2   ▷ ▷ ▷ ▷

Tiger plc

The managing director of Tiger plc is concerned that his company is not trading efficiently and is therefore losing profits. The company currently has no formal budgeting procedures. The financial accountant and production manager have produced the following information for the first six months of 20X5.

1   **Sales**

    The company has one product, the CAT. Sales are seasonal with sales in the months of March, April and May being twice the amount sold in other months of the year. Tiger plc expects to sell 45,000 CATs in the first half of 20X5.

    The current selling price is £25 per unit; there will be a price increase of 20% on 1 April 20X5.

2   **Production**

    Each CAT uses 10 kg of raw materials. Tiger plc has a contract with the raw material supplier for monthly deliveries at a fixed price of £60 per 100 kg. This contract expires at the end of April 20X5, when it is expected that the price will be increased by 25%.

Tiger has two categories of labour. Each CAT requires one hour's work by a skilled employee and two hours' work by an unskilled employee. The current wage rates are £5 per hour for skilled workers and £3 per hour for the unskilled.

3   **Stocks**

To keep the production line running smoothly, it is necessary for Tiger plc to hold enough raw material stocks to meet 80% of the following month's production quota.

To satisfy customer demand, the company holds enough stocks of finished goods to meet 50% of the next month's sales.

Expected stock levels

	1 January 20X5	30 June 20X5
Raw materials	40,000 kg	40,000 kg
Finished goods	2,500 units	2,500 units

Stocks of finished goods are valued at full production cost.

Required

(a) Prepare the functional budgets for the six-monthly period to 30 June 20X5 for:
  (i)   material usage (in kg only);
  (ii)   material purchases (in kg and £);
  (iii) labour utilisation, skilled and unskilled (in hours and £).

(b) Write notes for a meeting with the managing director where you will have to explain why Tiger plc should introduce a budgeting system.

[Answer on p. 263]

5   Practical aspects of functional budgets

5.1   Sales budgets

The sales income budget is uniquely difficult to prepare because it involves forecasting the actions of people outside the business (the potential customers).

The extent to which sales forecasting is necessary will depend on the period covered by the outstanding order book and on the consistency of the conversion rate from enquiries to orders. If there is a well-filled order book for some months ahead then less reliance will need to be placed on forecasting techniques.

Forecasts may be made in a variety of ways. The method used will depend on the nature of the business and the amount of information available, but a generalised formal procedure might be as follows:

· Review past years' sales for whatever period is appropriate to the company's business cycle.

· Analyse the time series to identify seasonal, cyclical and random fluctuations.

· Extrapolate from past years' figures, assuming no changes in products or prices.

· Adjust the extrapolation for proposed changes which are controllable by the company, such as price alterations, changes in marketing effort, the introduction of new products, and the discontinuance of existing products (depending on the products' life cycles).

· Adjust for market changes due to external factors, such as government controls, action of competitors or social changes affecting demand. In particular, appropriate adjustments should be made for changing price levels or seasonal trends.

· Check that the resultant quantities are compatible with the quantities that can be purchased or produced.

· Check acceptability of forecast to sectional sales managers. In addition, other personnel who might contribute towards making realistic forecasts of trends should be consulted.

· Check consistency of forecast with long-term corporate plans.

The forecasting method outlined above depends on the existence of a 'time series' of figures from which extrapolation can be made and is mainly applicable to items in continuous demand. For other types of business, the sales forecast will be based on some form of market survey or on subjective estimates by people familiar with the market concerned.

Whichever forecasting method is used, the forecast should take account of significant anticipated changes in circumstances which would affect the validity of any statistically derived calculations.

5.2 Cost budgets

Budgeting for costs, in the same way as budgeting for sales, begins with facts. What facts they are will depend on the nature of the business; but every business will employ people, and most businesses will use materials of some kind. A manufacturing business will use tools and probably machinery. Floor space will be needed, also office equipment and perhaps motor vehicles.

All these requirements will be related in some way to the output of the business – its sales and any changes in stocks or work in progress.

In practice there are a wide range of different ways to budget for costs, as follows:
· If standards for cost units are available, then there may be computer programs to identify the material and labour standards relative to a given output. It then remains for departmental managers to budget for material wastage or spoilage, labour efficiency and idle time.

· In a business carrying out long-term contracts, cost units (contracts) may be identical with cost centres (each contract having its own controller).

· In some businesses it may be sufficiently accurate for the budget for direct materials cost to be an extrapolation from past total figures, without any attempt at detailed justification or analysis.

5.3   Use of standards in budgeting

Budgeting will inevitably make use of standard costs, as in the worked example above, and you should ensure you are familiar with the techniques and principles involved in their determination.

However, budgeting will generally extend beyond the simple multiplication of planned production levels by the standard usages and costs for each product for the following reasons:

· Different ranges of output levels will often lead to changes in unit variable costs (e.g. materials discounts, learning effects, etc).
· Some variable costs will not vary neatly with production and will need to be estimated for each particular activity level (e.g. wastage, idle time, production set-up costs).
· Fixed costs are independent of production levels, although they may be stepped.
· A large proportion of a business's costs will not be directly involved in the production process (e.g. administration, marketing, capital expenditure, etc).

Idle time does not vary neatly with production

The following sections describe the common problems encountered in budgeting for the most common cost elements: labour, materials and overheads.

5.4   Budgeting for numbers and costs of employees

When budgeting for the number and costs of people to be employed, the starting point must be to assess the work to be done by people with various skills and this is equally necessary for manual, clerical and managerial activities.

Having defined what work is to be done, the establishment of budgets for the employment of people falls into two main stages:
· planning the number of people needed;
· calculating the relevant costs.

In defining the productive workload for the budget year it will be necessary to balance the requirements of the sales budget against the productive capacity available. If there is excess capacity over the year as a whole then a decision will be needed whether to operate below full capacity or to use the excess capacity in making goods for stock or getting ahead with work in progress for the following year.

If the sales budget does not provide a steady workload month by month, then in phasing the budgets it may be decided to keep productive output constant and to balance out the short-term differences by fluctuations in work-in-progress or finished stock.

The degree of precision possible in budgeting for numbers of people employed will depend on the type of work involved and the extent to which work measurement is possible.

5.5   Budgeting for the cost of materials

Considerable effort can be involved in preparing detailed budgets of quantities and purchase prices of materials. Whether this effort is justified will depend on the significance of materials in relation to total costs, and the extent to which effective control can be exercised.

The starting point for materials budgeting is the quantity of material to be used during the budget year, whether in retail sales or in production or for indirect use.

The form of the materials usage budget will depend on the nature of the business. Where repetitive operations are carried out it will be possible, and worth the effort, to set standards for the usage of the various items of material, and these standards can be associated with the production forecast to build up the total material requirements.

The purchase prices to be applied to the usage of the various items may be obtained from stock ledger records or recent purchase invoices, subject to adjustment for forecast price changes, using index numbers as necessary.

In budgeting for indirect materials (such as small tools, machine coolants and lubricants, fuel, cleaning materials and office stationery) the common practice is to budget merely for a total cost extrapolated from past experience. It will be important for control purposes, however, that the budget working papers contain as much detail as possible about anticipated usage, even though the individual items may not be evaluated separately.

5.6   Budgeting for overheads

The nature of overheads will depend on the type of business, but common categories are as follows:
(a)   Premises charges
(b)   Costs of plant, motor vehicles
        and other fixed assets
(c)   Communication expenses
(d)   Travelling and entertaining
(e)   Insurances
(f)   Discretionary costs
(g)   Financial policy costs
(h)   Random costs

5.7   Calculating budget and actual overheads

Earlier in the chapter we saw how budgeted overhead absorption rates (OARs) were calculated. The guidance notes to Unit 9 state that examinations might require you to use overhead absorption rates to deduce budgeted and actual activity levels.

5.8   Budgeted activity level

If we know the overhead absorption rate and the budgeted fixed overhead then the budgeted activity level can be found.

$$OAR = \frac{Budgeted\ fixed\ overhead}{Budgeted\ activity\ level}$$

Therefore:

$$Budgeted\ activity\ level = \frac{Budgeted\ fixed\ overhead}{OAR}$$

○ EXAMPLE   ○○○○

A business has an overhead absorption rate of £2 per unit produced. The budgeted fixed overhead was £400,000. What was the budgeted activity level?

Solution

Budgeted activity level	=	$\dfrac{Budgeted\ fixed\ overhead}{OAR}$
	=	$\dfrac{£400,000}{£2}$
	=	200,000 units

5.9   Actual activity level

When overheads are absorbed, this is done on the basis of the actual production level using the budgeted overhead absorption rate. Any under or over absorption is due to the difference between the overhead absorbed and the overhead actually incurred.

Under/over absorption = Overhead absorbed – overhead incurred

---

○ EXAMPLE   ○○○○

You are given the following information:

Budgeted fixed overhead	£250,000
Actual fixed overhead	£280,000
Budgeted activity level	100,000 units
Under absorption	£5,000

What was the actual activity level for the period?

Solution

OAR $\quad = \quad \dfrac{£250,000}{100,000}$

$\quad\quad\quad = \quad$ £2.50 per unit

Overhead absorbed $\quad = \quad$ £280,000 - £5,000

$\quad\quad\quad = \quad$ £275,000

Actual activity level $\quad = \quad \dfrac{\text{Fixed overhead absorbed}}{\text{OAR}}$

$\quad\quad\quad = \quad \dfrac{£275,000}{£2.50}$

$\quad\quad\quad = \quad$ 110,000 units

5.10 Permanent budget record

For every type of revenue or cost it is highly desirable that a permanent budget record be prepared, giving the detailed calculations from which the budgeted amount has been derived. In particular, the data relevant to projecting forecasts of income and expenditure must be identified. This will not only impose a discipline on the budget preparation but will also:

· facilitate the eventual explanation of any differences between budgeted and actual results;

· provide a starting point for budget revisions or for the preparation of budgets in future years.

The important features of such a record are as follows:

· details of the budget calculation;

· comparison with the actual figures for the previous year;

· basis of variability, noting how the amount is related to such factors as levels of output or numbers of people employed.

5.11 Capital expenditure budget

All short-term operating budgets are in effect abstracts from a continuously developing long-term plan. This, however, is particularly true of the capital expenditure budget because the major items included in it will not be completed within the bounds of any one budget year.

The main purpose of the capital expenditure budget, therefore, is to provide a forecast of the amount of cash likely to be needed for investment projects during the year ahead. It also indicates what items of plant, equipment, vehicles and so on will be needed for the purpose of implementing the profit and loss (or operating) budget; and therefore it must be submitted for approval at an early stage in the budgeting timetable.

KAPLAN PUBLISHING

Any capital expenditure budget would include the following:
- a brief descriptive title for the project;
- the total required expenditure;
- an analysis of the costs over various time periods;
- where appropriate, expenditure to date on the project;
- estimates of future benefits from the project;
- investment appraisal calculations including details of assumptions made.
- intangible benefits from the expenditure.

6   The master budget

6.1   Introduction

The master budget for approval by the board will take the form of a budgeted profit and loss account, a forecast balance sheet as at the year-end and a cash budget. These will be supported by such summaries of the various functional budgets as may be required, and by calculations of the key ratios which indicate conformity with the objectives for the year.

Cash budgets will not be assessed in Unit 9, though you should be aware of their existence.

6.2   The forecast balance sheet

In arriving at the forecast balance sheet, it will be necessary to take account of the following:
- The capital expenditure budget.
- Changes in stock levels and work in progress (as calculated in connection with the budgeting of material and labour costs). If work in progress and finished stocks are valued on a TAC basis, then it will be necessary to calculate overhead recovery rates.
- Changes in debtor balances. Subject to any special delays in collection, the closing debtor balances will be calculated by applying the company's normal credit terms to the phased budget of sales.
- Changes in creditor balances. In theory, the closing creditors will be calculated by applying a normal

Work in progress should be taken into account in arriving at the forecast balance sheet

credit period to the phased budgets of material purchases, subcontracted work and any other relevant items. In practice, it may be necessary to review the budgeted cash flow before finalising a decision on the credit to be taken.
- Changes in the cash balance. Initially, the closing cash balance may be taken as the balancing figure on the balance sheet, but at some stage this should be validated by building up a cash budget itemised from the other budgets. This is discussed in the following paragraph.

6.3 The cash budget

The purposes of the cash budget are as follows:

· To ensure that the various items of income and expenditure budgeted departmentally, and subject to the normal credit policy of the business, will result in cash flows which enable the company to pay its way at all times; in other words, to ensure that there is a practical plan.

· Where the cash flow over the year as a whole is satisfactory but there are intermediate periods of difficulty in financing operations, to give a basis from which the timing of particular items can be re-planned.

· Where cash proves inadequate to finance the plan as originally envisaged, to give the financial controller an opportunity to seek sources of additional capital. (If the budget cannot be financed as it stands, then a revised budget will have to be prepared.)

· Like any other budget, to provide a basis for control during the forth-coming year.

The preparation of cash budgets is not within the scope of the standards for Units 8 and 9.

▷ ACTIVITY 3

Product Q (AAT J95)

Product Q is a product which is manufactured and sold by Henry Limited. In the process of preparing budgetary plans for next year, the following information has been made available to you.

1 Forecast sales units of product Q for the year are 18,135 units.

2 Closing stocks of finished units of product Q at the end of next year will be increased by 15% from their opening level of 1,200 units.

3 All units are subject to a quality control check. The budget plans are to allow for 1% of all units checked to be rejected and scrapped at the end of the process. All closing stocks will have passed this quality control check.

4 Five direct labour hours are to be worked for each unit of product Q processed, including those which are scrapped after the quality control check. Of the total hours to be paid for, 7.5% are budgeted to be idle time.

5 The standard hourly rate of pay for direct employees is £6 per hour.

6 Material M is used in the manufacture of product Q. One finished unit of product Q contains 9 kg of M but there is a wastage of 10% of input of material M due to evaporation and spillage during the process.

7 By the end of next year, stocks of material M are to be increased by 12% from their opening level of 8,000 kg. During the year, a loss of 1,000 kg is expected due to deterioration of the material in store.

Required

(a) Prepare the following budgets for the forthcoming year.
   (i) Production budget for product Q, in units.

(ii)   Direct labour budget for product Q, in hours and in £.
(iii)   Material usage budget for material M, in kg.
(iv)   Material purchases budget for material M, in kg.

(b)   The supplier of material M has warned that available supplies will be below the amount indicated in your budget for part (a) (iv) above.

Explain the implications of this shortage and suggest four possible actions which could be taken to overcome the problem. For each suggestion, identify any problems which may arise.   [Answer on p. 266]

7 Test your knowledge

1   Name five purposes that a budget can fulfil.

2   What is the title given to the employee responsible for co-ordinating the construction of a budget?

3   Who ultimately approves a company's budget?

4   What is the master budget?   [Answers on p. 268]

8 Summary

The budget must be prepared in a logical and orderly manner, ensuring co-ordination and co-operation between departments and different levels of management. Final proposals must be fully understood and accepted by all involved via a clear set of instructions and detailed discussions where necessary.

You should be prepared to discuss the types of budgets that may be required for a particular business and how they might be prepared, probably with numerical illustrations.

Answers to chapter activities & 'test your knowledge' questions

△ ACTIVITY 1
Your organisation

MEMORANDUM

To: Marketing Manager

From: Assistant Management Accountant

Date: 12 December 20X4

Subject: Budgetary planning process

As requested, I provide below answers to your queries about the budgetary planning process.

(a) **The key factor**

Otherwise known as the principal budget factor or limiting factor, the key factor is the factor which limits the activity of an organisation. In our organisation it is sales volume, since there is a limit to how much we can sell. However, it is possible for other factors to be key factors, especially in the short term. Examples could be cash, machine capacity or skilled labour.

The determination of the key factor is important in the budgetary process because this is the budget which must be prepared first. Then all other budgets can be co-ordinated to this budget.

For example, once the sales budget has been determined, this will provide the basis for the production budget and for other budgets such as the purchasing budget and the cash budget.

(b) A number of steps can be taken to achieve co-ordination in the budgetary planning process, including the following:

(i) Set up a budget committee which consists of representatives from all parts of the organisation. Regular meetings of this committee should ensure that each part of the organisation is aware of what all other parts are doing.

(ii) Give one person the overall responsibility for ensuring that budgets are prepared on time and that they take into account all relevant factors. This person is often called the budget officer and will usually chair the budget committee.

(iii) Provide a timetable to all those involved in the budgetary process, detailing who is responsible for preparing each budget and when it must

Page 1 of 2

be prepared. This should reduce the risk of bottlenecks in the budgetary process and will co-ordinate the order of budget preparation.

(iv) Provide a budget manual to all those involved in the budgetary process. The contents of the budget manual would include the budget timetable mentioned above, instructions on completing the budget planning forms, details on key assumptions to be made in the planning process (such as the inflation rate and exchange rate), and so on.

(v) Provide regular feedback on the progress of budget preparation.

The key to co-ordinated budget preparation is communication.

Page 2 of 2

△ ACTIVITY 2   △ △ △ △

Tiger plc

(a) Although it is not specifically required by the question, a production budget is essential for material and labour budgets.

Information relating to production levels is therefore the first thing you must look for.

In this question, you are not given this information directly. You are, however, given information about sales quantities and stock levels, which can be used to derive production levels as follows:

$$\text{Production} = \text{Sales} + \begin{array}{c}\text{Closing stock}\\\text{(finished goods)}\end{array} - \begin{array}{c}\text{Opening stock}\\\text{(finished goods)}\end{array}$$

The monthly sales need a little computation, so this will be your first working. Note that you only need units for the production budget.

Your second working will then be the production budget, using the results from your sales working and the stock level requirements given in the question.

These and other workings should be done on a separate sheet of paper, to be included at the end of your answer, cross-referenced as appropriate.

These first two workings should enable you to complete the three parts of part (a).

(i)   *Material usage*

	Jan	Feb	Mar	Apr	May	Jun	Total
Production quantity (W2) @ 10 kg/unit	5,000	7,500	10,000	10,000	7,500	5,000	45,000
Kg used	50,000	75,000	100,000	100,000	75,000	50,000	450,000

(ii)   *Material purchases*

Remember the link between materials usage and purchases quantities:

Purchases = Usage   +   Closing stock   –   Opening stock
                                (raw materials)   (raw materials)

Usage is taken from your answer to (i) and stock information from the question - 'stocks to meet 80% of the following month's production quota' simply means 80% of the following month's usage.

	Jan	Feb	Mar	Apr	May	Jun	Total
Materials used (i)	50,000	75,000	100,000	100,000	75,000	50,000	450,000
Less: Opening stock	(40,000)	(60,000)	(80,000)	(80,000)	(60,000)	(40,000)	(40,000)
	10,000	15,000	20,000	20,000	15,000	10,000	410,000
Add: Closing stock	60,000	80,000	80,000	60,000	40,000	40,000	40,000
Purchases (kg)	70,000	95,000	100,000	80,000	55,000	50,000	450,000
@	60p	60p	60p	60p	75p	75p	
Purchases	£42,000	£57,000	£60,000	£48,000	£41,250	£37,500	£285,750

(iii)   *Skilled labour utilisation*

	Jan	Feb	Mar	Apr	May	Jun	Total
Units produced (W2)	5,000	7,500	10,000	10,000	7,500	5,000	45,000
Skilled labour cost (£5 per unit)	£25,000	£37,500	£50,000	£50,000	£37,500	£25,000	£225,000

Unskilled labour utilisation

	Jan	Feb	Mar	Apr	May	Jun	Total
Units produced (W2)	5,000	7,500	10,000	10,000	7,500	5,000	45,000
Unskilled labour cost (£6 per unit)	£30,000	£45,000	£60,000	£60,000	£45,000	£30,000	£270,000

(b) **Reasons for introducing a budgetary system**

The objectives of budgets are:
(i)   to plan and control income and expenditure in order to achieve maximum profitability;
(ii)   to ensure that sufficient working capital is available for the efficient operation of the company;
(iii)   to direct capital expenditure in the most profitable direction;
(iv)   to centralise control;
(v)   to decentralise responsibility;
(vi)   to provide a yardstick against which actual results may be compared;
(vii)   to show management when action is needed to remedy a situation;
(viii) to aid management in decision-making when unforeseen conditions affect the budget.

Workings

1   *Sales by month*

The easiest way to calculate these is to assign weights to each month – an 'ordinary' month having a weighting of 1, with the 'seasonal' months having twice this weighting. Thus, over the six-month period, there will be the equivalent of (3×1) plus $(3 \times 2) = 9$ 'ordinary' months worth of sales. As total sales are expected to be 45,000, this implies an 'ordinary' month's sales of $45,000/9 = 5,000$ units.

	Jan	Feb	Mar	Apr	May	Jun	Total
Weighting	1	1	2	2	2	1	9
Sales quantity	5,000	5,000	10,000	10,000	10,000	5,000	45,000

2   *Production budget (units)*

The opening and closing stocks for the period are given in the question (2,500 units). In between, the closing stock for each month (and the opening stock for the following month) represents 50% of the following month's sales units.

	Jan	Feb	Mar	Apr	May	Jun
Sales	5,000	5,000	10,000	10,000	10,000	5,000
Less: Opening stock	(2,500)	(2,500)	(5,000)	(5,000)	(5,000)	(2,500)
	2,500	2,500	5,000	5,000	5,000	2,500
Add: Closing stock	2,500	5,000	5,000	5,000	2,500	2,500
Production	5,000	7,500	10,000	10,000	7,500	5,000

Total production = 45,000 units

△ ACTIVITY 3   △ △ △ △
Product Q

(a)   (i)   *Production budget for product Q*

	Units
Forecast sales for year	18,135
Increase in stock (15% × 1,200)	180
Finished units required	18,315
Quality control loss (1/99)	185
Total units input to production	18,500

(ii)   *Direct labour budget for product Q*

	Hours
Active labour hours required (18,500 × 5)	92,500
Idle time allowance (7.5/92.5)	7,500
Total hours to be paid for	100,000
Standard hourly rate	£6
Budgeted labour cost	£600,000

(iii)   *Material usage budget for material M*

	Kg
Material required for processing (18,500 × 9 kg)	166,500
Wastage (10/90)	18,500
Material usage for year	185,000

(iv)   *Material purchases budget for material M*

	Kg
Material required for production input	185,000
Increase in material stocks (8,000 × 12%)	960
Expected loss in stores	1,000
Material purchases required	186,960

(b)   The implications of this shortage are that the budget plans cannot be achieved and the availability of material is a limiting factor. If the limiting factor cannot be alleviated, then the budgetary plans will need to be altered and raw material M will in fact become the principal budget factor. The material purchases budget would be prepared first and all other budgets would be co-ordinated to this one.

Four possible actions to overcome the problem could be as follows.

1   *Reduce the budgeted sales of product Q*

The problem with this course of action is that valued customers may be lost forever to competitors, who may be able to obtain the necessary material to take over Henry's customers permanently. Profits are likely to be reduced next year and possibly also in subsequent years.

2   *Reduce the rate of scrap due to quality control rejections of product Q at the end of the process*

This course of action should not cause problems if quality standards are not compromised and the reduction in scrapped units is achieved as part of a programme of total quality management throughout the organisation.

A problem could arise, however, if there is not a genuine reduction in poor quality work, but instead a relaxation in the quality control standards used. Customer dissatisfaction could have a permanent detrimental effect on sales, with consequent reductions in profit.

3   *Reduce the closing stock required of product Q and material M*

This could cause a problem of stock-outs, i.e. not having enough stock available when it is required, leading to disruptions in production and lost sales.

4   *Seek alternative suppliers for material M*

Possible problems that could arise are control over quality and reliability of supply. Any potential suppliers should be carefully vetted to ensure that their standards are acceptable.

Test your knowledge

1   A budget can:
    ·   authorise a particular level of expenditure;
    ·   assist in planning for the future;
    ·   assist in motivating managers to work hard;
    ·   assist in evaluating managers' performance;
    ·   assist in controlling the business.

2   The budget officer will co-ordinate the budget's construction.

3   The board of directors must ultimately approve a company's budget.

4   The master budget is the overall budget into which all the subsidiary budgets are consolidated. It will normally comprise a budgeted profit and loss account and a budgeted balance sheet (and possibly also a budgeted cash flow statement).

BUDGETARY CONTROL AND RESPONSIBILITY ACCOUNTING

INTRODUCTION
In order to be able to compare actual figures to budgeted figures to give a meaningful analysis, a flexible or flexed budget must be prepared. This will lead to budget variances and the broad principles are similar to those already studied in the chapters on variance analysis.

A further important aspect of budgeting that appears in examinations is the effect of the budgeting process and the final budget on the motivation of managers and employees.

KNOWLEDGE & UNDERSTANDING
· Budgets for control: flexible budgets, marginal costing (Elements 9.2 and 9.3)
· The effect of budgetary systems on the behaviour and motivation of managers and other employees (Element 9.2)
· Analysing the significance of budget variances and possible responses required by managers (Element 9.3)
· Presentation of budget data in a form that satisfies the differing needs of budget holders (Element 9.3)
· Relationship between budgets, forecasts and planning and product life cycles (Elements 9.1, 9.2 and 9.3)
· Responsibility centres: expense centres; profit centres; investment centres (Element 9.3)

CONTENTS
1 Budgeting and control
2 Flexible budgetary control
3 Flexing budgets with absorption and marginal costing
4 Zero-based budgeting (ZBB)
5 Budgets and control and motivation
6 Product life cycle

PERFORMANCE CRITERIA
· Review and revise the validity of forecasts in the light of any significant anticipated changes (Element 9.1)
· Verify that draft budget proposals are consistent with organisational objectives and include all relevant data and assumptions (Element 9.2)
· Communicate with budget holders in a manner which maintains goodwill and ensure budget proposals are agreed with budget holders (Element 9.2)
· Correctly code and allocate actual cost and revenue data to responsibility centres (Element 9.3)

1 Budgeting and control

1.1 Comparison of actual results to budget

So that managers can exercise control, the actual results of the business will be reported period by period to the managers responsible and will be compared with the budgeted allowance. Any discrepancies will be investigated and action will be taken either to modify the budget in line with current conditions or (in most cases more desirable) to adjust future performance so that the discrepancies will be eliminated in the longer run.

These deviations, in money value, between an item and the corresponding budget are variances, the computation of which was covered in Chapter 5.

1.2 Feedback

The reporting of actual results and of variances from plan is sometimes referred to as the feedback arising from the budgetary control system.

Feedback is the process of continuous self-adjustment of a system. It requires some predetermined standards against which to compare actual results. Any differences between the actual results and standard targets which are outside tolerance limits will indicate the need for action to be taken in an attempt to bring about consistency between actual and target.

Feedback is therefore a fundamental part of any system of control including financial control systems such as budgetary control.

1.3 Timing of feedback

Ideally feedback should take place with as little delay as possible from the occurrence of the event it reports. If there is undue delay then, in the intervening period, the underlying position itself may alter; there is then the danger that action correctly taken, given the information contained in the feedback report, will not be the action required by the time it takes place.

It is possible that delay in feedback may increase, rather than reduce, deviations from target.

1.4 Analysis of variances

The identification of variances from budget is only the first step in exercising control. So that effective action can be taken it will be necessary to identify:
· who was responsible for its occurrence – analysis by responsibility;
· why the variance has arisen – analysis by cause.

1.5 Analysis of variances by responsibility

With a well-designed budgetary control system the analysis of variances by responsibility is simple because the organisation will have been subdivided into budget centres which represent areas of responsibility (hence also known as responsibility centres) and separate operating statements will be prepared for each. For this to operate effectively, an integral part of the budgeting process will be to ensure that actual cost and revenue data are correctly coded and allocated to responsibility centres.

The general title for such a system is responsibility accounting; that is, a system which recognises various decision centres within a business and traces the results of those decisions to the individual managers who are primarily responsible for making them.

1.6 Analysis of variances by cause

In dealing with the analysis of variances by cause one will be dealing always with two aspects:
· a physical aspect – quantity of material used or hours worked, for example;
· a pricing aspect – the cost price per unit in the case of materials, labour and other expenses. (The cost of labour is, of course, the rate of pay.)

In some cases, it may not be possible to identify quantity changes without more effort than would be justified by any improvement in control, but in these cases it must be recognised that this weakness does exist in the control being exercised.

2 Flexible budgetary control

2.1 Variable and fixed costs

In connection with expense budgeting, the budget working sheets should include some indication of the 'basis of variability' of each item of cost.

The most common general bases of variability of costs are in line with sales or the volume of productive output. In some systems of budgetary control, therefore, costs are divided between those which tend to vary with the output or sales achieved, and those which tend to remain fixed regardless of sales or the volume of output over an expected range of volumes.

2.2 Flexed budgets

This distinction having been established then, for variable costs, it is possible to establish in any period an allowable level of cost appropriate to the output actually achieved. This new level is known as the budget allowance for that volume of output. This is also known as a flexed budget. The total variance from the original budget figure will then be divided into two parts:

· The difference between the original budget and the budget allowance, assumed to arise from the nature of the business. This is sometimes referred to as an 'activity variance' and may be excluded from sectional control reports.

· The difference between the budget allowance and the actual cost incurred. This, by definition, should not have occurred and might be thought of as the 'controllable variance' of the manager concerned.

A system incorporating budget allowances is referred to as flexible budgetary control.

This idea has been seized on by writers of textbooks and setters of examination questions and converted into the concept of 'flexible budgets'; in other words, at the beginning of the year there should be a schedule showing what the various cost allowances would be at various levels of output. With spreadsheet packages being used to assist budgeting, it is now becoming more common in practice.

○ EXAMPLE ○○○○

You are the budget officer of Majestic Limited, which produces a single product. The following forecasts have been prepared from the best information available for the production costs to be incurred at the highest and lowest production levels likely to be encountered in any particular period.

	Production level	
	10,000	20,000
	units	units
	£	£
Direct materials	2,000	4,000
Direct labour	15,000	30,000
Warehouse rental	8,000	13,000
Machine maintenance	2,400	3,000
Factory rent, rates, etc	4,000	4,000
Factory power	4,500	6,300

Machine maintenance is under contract with the machine supplier. The period cost is based upon the production level and is charged at £15 per 100 units, with a minimum charge payable of £2,400 per period.

Warehouse rent is fixed per warehouse per period. One warehouse is sufficient to cope with the storage demands up to 12,500 units. Should production exceed this level, a further warehouse will need to be rented for the period, at an additional cost of £5,000. This will give sufficient space to cover the highest production level.

All other variable costs and the variable part of semi-variable costs follow constant linear patterns.

Required

Prepare a set of flexible budgets which show the budget allowance for the period for the following activity levels: 10,000 units; 12,500 units; 15,000 units; 17,500 units; 20,000 units.

Solution

The following steps illustrate a good approach to such a question. You may like to try preparing your own answer as we go through before looking at our solution at the end.

1   **Draw up a proforma statement**

This will have the cost headings listed down the left-hand side and columns headed up with each production level; in this case, five columns will be needed. It is also a good idea to have an additional column next to the cost headings in which to insert references to workings (e.g. 'Note 2' etc).

The statement should also have a heading.

2   **Insert known figures**

You have already been given the costs for the lowest and highest production levels, so put these in.

3   **Deal with the particular costs you have further information about (in this case, machine maintenance and warehouse rental)**

Machine maintenance

This cost will be fixed up to a certain production level (to cover the minimum charge) and will then rise linearly (at £15 per 100 units or £0.15 per unit).

The level up to which the minimum charge is applicable is £2,400/£0.15 = 16,000 units. So the charge for the 12,500 and 15,000 unit levels will also be £2,400.

For 17,500 units the charge will be 17,500 × £0.15 = £2,625 and for 20,000 units it will reach 20,000 × £0.15 = £3,000 (as given).

These can now be inserted in your statement.

Warehouse rental

This is an example of a 'stepped' fixed cost. It will remain at £8,000 for all levels up to (and including) 12,500 units, and will rise to £13,000 for all levels above this.

These can now be inserted in your statement.

4   **Deal with remaining costs**

These will be strictly fixed, strictly variable or semi-variable.

Strictly fixed costs
These will be obvious – here, factory rent and rates must be fixed within the range, as the costs for the lowest and highest production levels are the same.

Insert this fixed cost across all levels on your statement.

Strictly variable costs
Usually direct materials and direct labour costs will be strictly variable. You can see here that, as the production level doubles, so does the cost. Use either level to determine the cost per unit.

Direct materials: £2,000/10,000   =   £0.20 per unit
Direct labour: £15,000/10,000   =   £1.50 per unit

Use these to calculate the appropriate cost for the other levels and insert them on the statement.

Semi-variable costs
These costs will not be the same for the two extreme levels, but they will not increase proportionately from one to the other either. If you are not sure, calculate a cost per unit at the two levels; these will not be the same, as they would be if the cost were strictly variable.

In this example, the power cost is semi-variable. It can be split between the fixed and variable elements by the 'high-low' method which we saw in Chapter 2.

	Production level (units)	Cost £
Highest	20,000	6,300
Lowest	10,000	4,500
Change	+10,000	+1,800

Variable cost = £1,800/10,000 = £0.18 per unit

Using the lowest level to determine the fixed cost element:

	£
Total cost	4,500
Less: Variable element (10,000 × £0.18)	(1,800)
Fixed element	2,700

So for each level, the total power cost can be calculated as follows.

£2,700 + £0.18 × Production level

For example, the cost for 15,000 units will be as follows.

£2,700 + £0.18 × 15,000 = £5,400

The remaining costs can be calculated in this way and the statement completed, as below.

	Production level				
	10,000 units	12,500 units	15,000 units	17,500 units	20,000 units
	£	£	£	£	£
Direct materials	2,000	2,500	3,000	3,500	4,000
Direct labour	15,000	18,750	22,500	26,250	30,000
Warehouse rental	8,000	8,000	13,000	13,000	13,000
Machine maintenance	2,400	2,400	2,400	2,625	3,000
Factory rent, rates	4,000	4,000	4,000	4,000	4,000
Factory power	4,500	4,950	5,400	5,850	6,300
Total	35,900	40,600	50,300	55,225	60,300

2.3 Budgetary control statement

A typical continuation to the above example would be the requirement to produce a budgetary control statement (or budget report) given some actual data for the period.

O EXAMPLE   ○ ○ ○ ○

In period 3 Majestic Limited produced 17,500 units and incurred the following costs.

	£
Direct materials	3,200
Direct labour	29,750
Warehouse rental	13,000
Machine maintenance	3,150
Factory rent, rates, etc	3,800
Factory power	4,720

Produce a budgetary control statement to compare these actual costs with the flexed costs that would be budgeted for.

Solution

The budgetary control statement will compare the actual costs with the relevant budget allowances from the flexible budget to highlight variances.

In this case, the relevant flexed budget is that for 17,500 units.

We have also included the original budget (for 20,000 units). This is good practice, as it is probable that a lot of managers who see the budgetary control statement will have had access to the original budget. If they don't see those figures on the statement, they will think they were given the wrong information before, or else they will think they are being given the wrong information now!

	20,000 units original budget (£)	17,500 units flexed budget (£)	17,500 units actual (£)	Flexed to actual variance (£)
Direct materials	4,000	3,500	3,200	300 F
Direct labour	30,000	26,250	29,750	3,500 A
Warehouse rental	13,000	13,000	13,000	-
Machine maintenance	3,000	2,625	3,150	525 A
Factory rent, rates, etc	4,000	4,000	3,800	200 F
Factory power	6,300	5,850	4,720	1,130 F
	60,300	55,225	57,620	2,395 A

You may then be asked to comment on the variances, suggesting any further investigations or action that might be required.

Note that if the actual costs for output of 17,500 units were compared to the original budget of 20,000 units of output, the resulting variances would be meaningless.

▷ ACTIVITY 1

Henry Limited (AAT J95)

Data

You work as the assistant to the management accountant for Henry Limited, a medium-sized manufacturing company. One of the company's products, product P, has been very successful in recent years showing a steadily increasing trend in sales volumes.

Sales volumes for the four quarters of last year were as follows.

	Quarter 1	Quarter 2	Quarter 3	Quarter 4
Actual sales volume (units)	420,000	450,000	475,000	475,000

A new assistant has recently joined the marketing department and she has asked you for help in understanding the terminology which is used in preparing sales forecasts and analysing sales trends.

She has said: 'My main problem is that I do not see why my boss is so enthusiastic about the growth in product P's sales volume. It looks to me as though the rate of growth is really slowing down and actually stopped in Quarter 4. I am told that I should be looking at the deseasonalised or seasonally adjusted sales data but I do not understand what is meant by this.'

You have found that product P's sales are subject to the following seasonal variations:

	Quarter 1	Quarter 2	Quarter 3	Quarter 4
Seasonal variation (units)	+ 25,000	+ 15,000	0	– 40,000

Required

(a) Adjust for the seasonal variations to calculate deseasonalised or seasonally adjusted sales volumes (i.e. the trend figures) for each quarter of last year.

(b) Assuming that the trend and seasonal variations will continue, forecast the sales volumes for each of the four quarters of next year.

(c) Prepare a memorandum to the marketing assistant which explains the following:

    (i) What is meant by seasonal variations and deseasonalised or seasonally adjusted data;

    (ii) How they can be useful in analysing a time series and preparing forecasts.

Use the figures for product P's sales to illustrate your explanations.

Further data
The marketing assistant has now approached you for more help in understanding the company's planning and control systems. She has been talking with the distribution manager who has tried to explain how flexible budgets are used to control distribution costs within Henry Limited. She makes the following comment:

'I thought that budgets were supposed to provide a target to plan our activities and against which to monitor our costs. How can we possibly plan and control our costs if we simply change the budgets when activity levels alter?'

Required

(d) Prepare a further memorandum to the marketing assistant which explains the following:

    (i) Why fixed budgets are useful for planning but flexible budgets may be more useful to enable management to exercise effective control over distribution costs;

    (ii) *Two* possible activity indicators which could be used as a basis for flexing the budget for distribution costs;

    (iii) How a flexible budget cost allowance is calculated and used for control purposes. Use your own examples and figures where appropriate to illustrate your explanations.   [Answer on p. 294]

3 Flexing budgets with absorption and marginal costing

3.1 Introduction

A particular problem occurs with situations where the budget has been prepared on a marginal costing basis (MC) and the actual results have been produced using total absorption costing (TAC). In this case, it is necessary to convert the actual results to the marginal costing basis.

Remember that the key difference between the two is that in total absorption costing, the fixed production overheads are absorbed into the production cost (the cost of sales) using an agreed basis of absorption (usually, but not always, labour or machine hours). In marginal costing, no fixed costs are absorbed into the product cost.

Note that it is only the fixed production overheads that are absorbed into the product cost (such things as supervisor's wages, depreciation of plant and even canteen costs spent on providing a canteen for the production worker). Non-production fixed costs are not absorbed into product cost.

3.2 Different profit with marginal and total absorption profit

The vital point to grasp is that profit will only be different with MC compared to TAC if there is a change in the level of stock during the period, i.e. if closing stock is different from opening stock.

If closing and opening stock are the same, the reported profit will be the same under both methods.

○ **EXAMPLE**   ○ ○ ○ ○

X Ltd has the following budget, prepared on the TAC basis.

For simplicity we are only including the production costs.

Sales (units)		10,000

		£
Sales revenue	10,000 × £2 =	20,000
Production costs		
Materials	10,000	
Labour	4,000	
Production overhead	4,000	
Cost of sales		18,000
Profit		2,000

You are required to produce the budget on a marginal cost basis.

Solution 1

	TAC (per question)		MC
Sales (units)	10,000		10,000
Sales revenue	20,000		20,000
Production costs			
Materials	10,000	10,000	
Labour	4,000	4,000	
Production overhead	4,000	–	
Cost of sales	(18,000)		(14,000)
Production overhead	–		(4,000)
Profit	£2,000		£2,000

Note: All that has happened from the accounting point of view is that the numbers appear in different parts of profit and loss account, but the profit is the same.

○ EXAMPLE ○○○○

We shall now consider a more complicated example where the budget is produced using marginal costing and the actual results indicate that production and sales were greater than budget.

Y Ltd has the following budget based on marginal costs.

Sales (units)		20,000
		£
Sales revenue	20,000 × £5 =	100,000
Production costs		
Materials	30,000	
Labour	40,000	
Cost of sales		70,000
Production overhead		20,000
Profit		10,000

There were no budgeted or actual opening or closing stocks.

The actual production and sales was 22,000 units.

The actual production overhead was £20,000 as per the budget.

You are required to produce the actual profit and loss account using both TAC and MC.

Solution

	TAC		MC	
Production (units)	22,000		22,000	
	£	£	£	£
Sales revenue (22,000 × £5)		110,000		110,000
Production costs				
Material (30,000 × $\frac{22}{20}$)	33,000		33,000	
Labour (40,000 × $\frac{22}{20}$)	44,000		44,000	
Production overhead	22,000 (W2)		–	
Cost of sales		(99,000)		(77,000)
Production overhead		–		(20,000) (W1)
Over-absorbed overhead		2,000 (W2)		–
		£13,000		£13,000

Working

1   The production overhead in the marginal cost statement is £20,000. This is the actual cost recorded for the period.

2   In the TAC statement, the situation is a little more complicated.

The overhead is budgeted as £20,000 for a budgeted production of 20,000 units, i.e. £1 per unit.

In the TAC statement therefore, where 22,000 units are produced, £22,000 will be the production overhead charged to product.

However, this is an over-absorption of £2,000 (the actual overhead was £20,000), and this £2,000 has to be added back to profit as a favourable variance.

○ EXAMPLE   ○ ○ ○ ○

We shall now consider an example where there is a change in stock over the period.

Z Ltd produces the following budget for March based on marginal costing.

	£	£
Sales (units)	10,000	
Sales revenue (10,000 × £4)		40,000
Production costs		
Material	10,000	
Labour	20,000	

Cost of sales	30,000
Production overhead	5,000
Profit	5,000

There was no budgeted opening or closing stock.

The actual results show the following:

1　　Closing stock of finished goods were 1,000 units.
2　　Production was 12,000 units and sales were 11,000 units.
3　　Overheads were £5,000 as per budget.
4　　The sales price of material and labour unit costs were as per the budget.

You are required to produce the actual results in both TAC and MC format.

Solution

		TAC		MC	
Production (units)		12,000		12,000	
Sales (units)		11,000		11,000	
	£	£		£	£
Sales revenue (11,000 × £4)		44,000			44,000
Production costs					
Material $(10,000 \times \frac{12}{10})$	12,000			12,000	
Labour $(20,000 \times \frac{12}{10})$	24,000			24,000	
Production overhead (12,000 × £0.50)	6,000 (W1)			–	
	42,000			36,000	
Closing stock $42,000 \times \frac{1,000}{12,000} =$	(3,500) (W2)		$36,000 \times \frac{1,000}{12,000} = (3,000)$		
Cost of sales		(38,500)			(33,000)
Production overhead		–			(5,000)
Over-absorbed overhead (2,000 × £0.50)		1,000 (W3)			–
Profit		6,500			6,000

Workings

Because there has been a change in the level of stock, the TAC and MC profits are different.

This is because with TAC, the overhead is absorbed into product at the rate of £0.50 per unit.

What therefore happens in the TAC statement can be explained as follows:

(W1) The production overhead absorbed is £6,000, i.e. £1,000 more than the actual overhead of £5,000.

(W3) The £1,000 over-absorbed per (W1) is added back as a favourable variance. This removes the over-absorption from the statement.

(W2) However (and this is the crucial point to grasp) the closing stock carries forward to the next period £500 of the actual £5,000 overhead (i.e. 1,000 units × £0.50). Thus, only £4,500 of the actual overhead is left as a charge to the period.

3.3 A very important note on presentation

In the examples 2 and 3, just covered, the TAC presentation of the operating statement has shown:

(a) the production overhead at the over-absorbed amount in the production costs, and

(b) the over-absorbed overhead as a reduction of cost after the cost of sales.

We have done this to emphasise the important points that with TAC:

(a) the production overhead is absorbed into production cost and will be over-absorbed if actual production exceeds budget, and

(b) if the production overhead is over-absorbed per (a), there will be a favourable variance to 'remove' the over-absorbed amount.

In the examination, the examiner may net these two figures off. Thus, in solution 3, in the TAC statement, we would have netted off the 6,000 production overhead and the £1,000 over-absorbed overhead to give a net figure of £5,000 in the production cost.

In many questions you are asked to prepare a revised statement showing actual results, (revised) budget and variances. A column approach is best here, but remember to label the columns clearly to distinguish between original budget, flexed budget and actual.

▷ ACTIVITY 2

You are employed as an accounting technician with a large firm of accountants and registered auditors. One of your firm's clients is Judith Myers. Judith is the major shareholder in Cheltenham Ltd. Last year she appointed a manager to run the company on her behalf.

The company makes a single product, the Zylo, and the manager has prepared the following operating statement for the year ended 31 May 2004.

Cheltenham Ltd: Budgeted and actual operating statement for the year ended 31 May 2004

	Budget	Actual
Sales volume, Zylos	9,000	8,800
Production volume, Zylos	9,000	10,000

	£	£
Turnover	630,000	616,000
Materials	45,000	52,000
Labour	55,800	65,000
Electricity	38,000	42,000
Depreciation	70,000	65,000
Rent and rates	24,000	25,000
Other fixed overheads	40,000	42,000
Cost of production	272,800	291,000
Less closing stock		34,920
Cost of sales	272,800	256,080
Operating profit	357,200	359,920

Judith cannot understand why the actual profit is greater than the budgeted profit despite selling less Zylos during the year. The manager gives you the following information.

· All Zylos are sold for the same price.
· Material and labour are variable costs.
· Electricity is a semi-variable cost. The budgeted fixed cost element was £20,000 and the actual fixed cost element was £21,000.
· All other costs are fixed costs.
· The actual closing stocks were valued at their actual variable cost plus an appropriate proportion of production overheads.
· Cheltenham did not buy or sell any fixed assets during the year.
· There were no stocks of work in progress at any time and no opening finished stocks.

Required

(a) Calculate the following data per Zylo:
    (i) budgeted selling price
    (ii) budgeted material cost
    (iii) budgeted labour cost
    (iv) budgeted variable cost of electricity
    (v) actual selling price
    (vi) actual material cost
    (vii) actual labour cost
    (viii) actual variable cost of electricity.

(b) Prepare a revised operating statement using marginal (or variable) costing to show the flexible budget, the actual results and any variances.

(c) Add a note to your statement to explain why your actual profit is different from the actual profit prepared by the manager.

[Answer on p. 297]

4 Zero-based budgeting (ZBB)

4.1 Introduction

ZBB (zero-based budgeting, also called priority-based budgeting) is a cost justification technique first developed by Texas Instruments, which is of particular use in controlling the costs of service departments and overheads. It does not simply look at last year's budget and add or subtract a little, but starts 'from scratch' each time a budget is prepared. It is particularly applicable for service cost centres, for non-product costs.

4.2 How ZBB works

ZBB involves the following:
· developing decision packages for each company activity;
· evaluating and ranking these packages;
· allocating resources to the various activities accordingly.

Decision packages include the following information:
· The function of the activity or department. This sets out the minimum goals that it must achieve;
· The goal of the department. This details the aim of the department – what it would like to achieve;
· The measure of the performance of the department.
· The costs and benefits associated with different ways of organising the department (at different levels of funding);
· The consequence of non-performance of the activity or department.

4.3 Advantages of ZBB

· It establishes minimum requirements for service departments; ranks departments; and allocates resources.
· It produces a plan to work to when more resources are available.
· It makes managers think about what they are doing.
· It can be done annually, quarterly, or when crises are envisaged.

4.4 Disadvantages of ZBB

· It takes up a good deal of management time and so may not be used every year.
· It generates a great deal of paper, requires education and training, and results may be initially disappointing.
· It is costly.

ZBB generates a great deal of paper

Most budgets are prepared on an incremental basis. In other words, the budget for next year is based on last time's figures plus/minus an incremental amount to cover inflation, etc. However, this technique has the obvious disadvantage of perpetuating poor spending control. As an alternative ZBB may be employed.

▷ ACTIVITY 3   ▷ ▷ ▷ ▷

Trygon Limited

Six months ago, Parmod plc established a new subsidiary, Trygon Limited. Trygon was formed to assemble and sell computers direct to the public. Its annual budget was drawn up by Mike Barratt, Parmod's Finance Director. Trygon's plant was capable of producing 150,000 computers per year although the budget for the first year was only 80% of this amount. Factory overheads – defined as all factory fixed costs other than labour – were to be charged to finished stocks at all times on the basis of this 80% activity, irrespective of actual activity.

Trygon had entered into an agreement with the employees whereby their wages were guaranteed provided the employees made themselves available to produce 120,000 computers per year. Because of this agreement, the labour element in finished stocks was always to be based on the production level of 120,000 computers. If output exceeded the 120,000 units, additional overtime equivalent to £70 per extra computer would be paid. Managers were also to be given a bonus of £15 per computer produced in excess of 120,000 units in the year.

At the beginning of the year, Mike had given all the managers a financial statement showing the annual budget (based on 80% activity) and the effect of operating at only half the planned activity level. This is reproduced below.

Trygon Limited budgeted profit for the year to 31 December 20X6

Activity	Annual budget (80%)	40%
	£	£
Direct materials	24,000,000	12,000,000
Direct labour	7,200,000	7,200,000
Light, heat and power	4,000,000	2,200,000
Production management salaries	1,500,000	1,500,000
Factory rent, rates and insurance	9,400,000	9,400,000
Depreciation of factory machinery	5,500,000	5,500,000
National advertising	20,000,000	20,000,000
Marketing and administration	2,300,000	2,300,000
Delivery costs	2,400,000	1,200,000
Total costs	76,300,000	61,300,000
Sales revenue	84,000,000	42,000,000
Operating profit/(loss)	7,700,000	(19,300,000)

In preparing the financial statement, Mike Barratt had made the following assumptions:

(a)   (i)   Unit selling prices were the same over the different activity levels.

      (ii)   No quantity discounts or other similar efficiencies had been assumed for purchases.

(b)   Production fixed overheads comprised the depreciation of the machinery, the rent, rates and insurance, the production management salaries (other than any possible bonus) and part of the cost of light, heat and power.

Six months after Mike Barratt had issued the statement, you are called to a meeting of the directors of Trygon Limited. Anne Darcy, the managing director, tells you that production and sales for the year are likely to be 112,500 computers.

Required

(a)   You are the Management Accountant to Trygon. Anne Darcy asks you to prepare a flexible budget for the year using the data given by Mike Barratt and assuming 112,500 computers are produced and sold. She also asks you to identity the budgeted profit.

Further data
On receiving your flexible budget, Anne Darcy reminds her fellow directors that Trygon plans a major marketing campaign at the beginning of the next financial year and this will require a building up of stocks in preparation for the campaign. The production director, Alan Williams believes it is feasible to increase production close to capacity without increasing any of the fixed costs. As a result, the Board agrees to budget for sales of 112,500 units by the year end but to produce at 95% capacity.

A discussion then followed about the role of budgeting in Trygon Limited *'I do not know why we should take up all this time discussing budgets'* said Anne Darcy. *'They are not my figures. I had no say in their preparation. Let Mike Barratt take responsibility for them – after all, it was his budget – and let us get on with the job of building up a business.'*

'I agree,' Alan Williams said. *'I wish Mike would make up his mind what we are supposed to be doing. Are we just concerned with making short-term profits or are we supposed to be building up a quality product? Just what are our objectives when budgeting? Besides, you can prove anything with figures. Just look at the budget prepared by the Management Accountant compared with the annual budget prepared by Mike Barratt.'*

Anne Darcy then turns to you. *'We need to resolve these issues. Will you please write a short report to the Board members giving us your advice.'*

Required

(b)   In response to Anne Darcy's request, you are required to write a short report drawing on the information given above. The report should:
  (i)   recalculate the flexible budget based on production at 95% capacity assuming fixed overheads in finished stock are based on 80% activity;
  (ii)   explain why the revised flexible budget may differ from the one prepared in (a);
  (iii)   answer the issues raised by Alan Williams regarding the two different budget statements, the uncertainty about budgetary objectives and the manipulation of budget data;
  (iv)   briefly discuss whether or not Anne Darcy should have been responsible for preparing the original budget.   [Answer on p. 298]

5 Budgets and control and motivation

5.1 Introduction

In addition to asking you to analyse and explain variances, examinations frequently require a discussion on whether the budgeting procedures used within an organisation are likely to achieve their aims.

These aims, and the methods used to achieve them, can be broadly categorised as follows:

· efficient management – management by exception;
· motivation of workforce – responsibility accounting.

5.2 Management by exception

The features of this method of reporting are that:

(a) attention is drawn only to areas where operations are seen to be 'out of control';

(b) this may be achieved by identifying those variances that are deemed to be 'exceptional';

(c) only these variances will be investigated and (where possible) corrected;

(d) management time and expertise are utilised where it can be most effective in improving the efficiency of future operations.

For it to be effective, it is important that:

· exceptional variances are correctly isolated;
· only such variances owing to factors capable of correction be considered for investigation;
· costs and benefits of investigation are assessed.

5.3 Responsibility accounting

The aim of a responsibility accounting system is to motivate management at all levels to work towards the company's objectives with the minimum of direction.

What is involved?

(a) The use of budgets as 'targets' against which management performance may be measured and (often) rewarded.

(b) The presentation of 'performance reports' relating to particular responsibility centres. These centres fall into three categories as follows.

    (i) **Cost centre** or **expense centre** where a manager is held responsible for control of expenditure.

    (ii) **Profit centre** where a manager is held responsible for control of sales revenue and expenditure.

    (iii) **Investment centre** where a manager is held responsible for investment decisions as well as the control of sales revenue and expenditure.

(c) The requirement that the person deemed responsible for that area should give explanations of significant variances shown therein.

Examinations on this subject tend to concentrate on a practical application of the principles necessary for a system of responsibility accounting to work effectively, and often require the preparation of a draft performance report, or the criticism of such a report. An in-depth theoretical knowledge of the work carried out in this field is not needed; a commonsense approach to a practical problem suffices.

5.4 Budgets and motivation

Three main areas need to be examined in relation to the use of budgets in responsibility accounting:
(a) participation in budget setting;
(b) budgets as motivational targets;
(c) performance evaluation and reward.

The conclusions under each of these headings are largely common sense – you should try to think up practical examples in relation to your own position in study or at work to help you remember them.

5.5 Participation in budget setting

Conventional wisdom suggests that managers should be encouraged to participate in the budget setting process and that the budget should be built up from the lower rungs of management ('bottom up' budgeting) rather than imposed from above ('top down' budgeting). These are the advantages:
· Managers will then feel that they 'own' the budget and will therefore be more committed to the targets and motivated to achieve them.
· Operating managers are often the only people with sufficient detailed knowledge to develop a meaningful budget.

5.6 Disadvantages of participation

However, there are disadvantages to participation.
· The objectives of the managers and the objectives of the organisation may not be the same. 'Goal congruence' does not automatically result from empowering managers to develop their own budgets.
· Operating management may use their knowledge to manipulate the budget. They may deliberately set targets that they cannot fail to achieve, particularly if bonuses are awarded for meeting the budget.
· Managers may not wish to participate in the budget setting process. This may be because:
(i) they simply want to know what their targets are;
(ii) they do not have the technical expertise to participate in bugdet setting;
(iii) they do not have the necessary commitment to the organisation;
(iv) they feel that the budget will be 'used against them'.

5.7 Budgets as motivational targets

In general, it is accepted that corporate objectives are more likely to be met if they are expressed as quantified targets, often in the form of budgets.

If a target is to have any influence on performance:
· the recipient must be aware of its existence and feel committed to achieving it;
· it must be set at the right level of difficulty to act as a motivator; both unrealistic and over-generous targets will be demotivational.

In theory, there may be a need for two budgets to be prepared for the same area.
· One should be a challenging (aspirations) budget to motivate the manager.
· The second should be a lower, and more realistic, expectations budget for planning and decision purposes.

Care should be taken to reward success as well as penalising failure, in order that a benefit is perceived in bettering rather than just achieving the target.

Budgets become stronger motivators as they become tighter up to a point, but thereafter motivation declines. The optimal degree of tightness depends on both the situation and the personality of the individuals concerned.

5.8 Performance evaluation and reward

Managers should only be held accountable for items over which they have control, and measures of performance should be devised that promote decisions in line with corporate objectives.

Thus a manager of a profit centre may be judged by variances affecting sales and direct costs (before allocated fixed costs); the performance of the centre itself will be measured by direct controllable contribution (having accounted for costs that are directly attributable to that centre, but not necessarily all controlled by the manager).

There are three main styles of management in the use of budget performance reports:

(a)   The budget-constrained style, which lays particular emphasis on results being closely in accordance with the budget plan;
(b)   The profit-conscious style, which is less concerned with current deviations from budget than with a manager's ability to achieve a trend of results which is acceptable in relation to changing conditions;
(c)   The non-accounting style, which tends to disregard accounting reports as a means of measuring management performance and instead looks at factors such as:
· the number of customer complaints or substandard items produced;
· staff turnover;
· morale in the department;
· other qualitative measures.

The non-accounting style looks at factors such as the morale in the department

Of the three styles, the middle is probably the most successful in achieving the company's long-term goals. The first creates good cost consciousness but also a great deal of tension between a manager and his subordinates, and manipulation of accounting information. The last promotes general good morale, but managers have a low involvement with costs.

▷ ACTIVITY 4 ▷ ▷ ▷

World History Museum (AAT CA J94)

The World History Museum has an Education Department which specialises in running courses in various subjects. The courses are run on premises which the museum rents for the purpose and they are presented by free-lance expert speakers. Each course is of standard type and format and can therefore be treated alike for budgetary control purposes.

The museum currently uses fixed budgets to control expenditure. The following data shows the actual costs of the Education Department for the month of April compared with the budgeted figures.

Education Department - April

	Actual	Budget	Variance
Number of courses run	5	6	(1)
	£	£	£
Expenditure			
Speakers' fees	2,500	3,180	680
Hire of premises	1,500	1,500	–
Depreciation of equipment	200	180	(20)
Stationery	530	600	70
Catering	1,500	1,750	250
Insurance	700	820	120
Administration	1,650	1,620	(30)
	8,580	9,650	1,070

You have recently started work as the assistant management accountant for the museum. During a discussion with Chris Brooks, the general manager, she expresses to you some doubt about the usefulness of the above statement in providing control information for the Education Department manager.

Chris is interested in the possibility of using flexible budgets to control the activities of the Education Department. You therefore spend some time analysing the behaviour patterns of the costs incurred in the Education Department. Your findings can be summarised as follows:

1   Depreciation of equipment is a fixed cost.

2   Administration is a fixed cost.

3   The budget figures for the catering costs and insurance costs include a fixed element as follows:

| Catering | £250 |
| Insurance | £100 |

The remaining elements of the catering and insurance costs follow linear variable patterns.

4   All other costs follow linear variable patterns.

Required

(a)   Use the above information to produce a budgetary control statement for April, based on a flexible budget for the actual number of courses run.

(b)   Calculate the revised variances based on your flexible budget.

(c)   Chris Brooks's interest in the control aspects of budgeting has been sparked by her attendance on a course entitled 'Budgetary control for managers'. She has shown you the following extract from the course notes she was given:

'A system of participative budgeting involves managers in the process of setting their own budgets. Participative systems are likely to be more successful in planning and controlling the activities of an organisation.'

Write a brief memo to Chris Brooks which explains the advantages and disadvantages of participative budgeting as a part of the budgetary planning and control process.   [Answer on p. 302]

6   Product life cycle

6.1   Sales forecasts

When using time series analysis to forecast sales figures, consideration should be given to the position of the product within its life cycle. Most products have a limited life and there are generally thought to be five stages of the product life cycle, each of which will have different characteristics:
·   Development
·   Launch
·   Growth
·   Maturity
·   Decline.

6.2   Development stage

During this time of the product's life there is likely to be large amounts of cost incurred but no sales income yet.

6.3 Launch stage

In the early stages of the product's life, immediately after its launch, sales levels are likely to be quite low. However, some eagerly awaited products, for example the PlayStation 3 games console, have had incredibly high sales in the launch stage.

6.4 Growth stage

If the product is successfully launched then the product is likely to show fairly large increases in sales indicated by a steep upward trend. However, such large sales increases are unlikely to continue indefinitely.

6.5 Maturity stage

During this stage the demand for the product is likely to start to slow or at least become more constant. The trend line in this stage will not show such a steep curve.

6.6 Decline stage

Most products will eventually reach the end of their life and sales will begin to decline with the trend line, therefore now also declining.

6.7 Time series analysis and product life cycle

Due to the changes in sales demand throughout the life cycle of a product, care should be taken when using time series analysis to estimate the trend of future sales. If the time series figures are based upon the growth stage then the trend line in this stage is unlikely to continue but will be likely to become less steep.

6.8 Life cycle costing

Life cycle costing is the maintenance of cost records for assets over their entire life, so that decisions concerning the acquisition, use or disposal of the assets can be made in a way that achieves the optimum asset usage at the lowest possible cost to the entity.

For example, when buying a machine, a business might be offered either a poor quality machine for £20,000 or a high quality machine for £50,000. If the poor quality machine is expected to continually break down and need to be repaired all the time, while the high quality machine is expected never to break down, then life cycle costing might argue that the high quality machine should be bought, despite it being more expensive, since its total cost of ownership over its entire life will be less than the poor quality alternative.

7 Test your knowledge ▷ ▷ ▷

1 Which is more appropriate for planning – a fixed budget or a flexed budget?

2 Which is more appropriate for control – a fixed budget or a flexed budget?

3 Maintenance is a semi-variable cost. For activity levels of 10,000 and 12,000 units respectively, maintenance costs are budgeted to be £50,000 and £55,000. What maintenance cost would be budgeted for an activity level of 13,000 units?

4 What is meant by 'management by exception'?

5 Is participative budgeting likely to motivate managers to achieve the budget?

[Answers on p. 304]

8 Summary

One of the purposes of the budgetary system is to help management control operations. This is done in part by comparing actual results to budgeted figures on a regular basis. However, where the actual level of activity is different from the budgeted level of activity comparison of the actual results to the original budget will give largely meaningless results. Therefore, the budget should be flexed to reflect the actual activity level.

If set appropriately, budgets can also be used as motivation for managers and employees to reach budget targets. However, in order to achieve this the budget level must be carefully considered as budgets which are too easy to achieve or too hard to achieve will tend to be demotivational.

Answers to chapter activities & 'test your knowledge' questions

△ ACTIVITY 1   △ △ △ △

Henry Limited

(a)

	Quarter 1 units	Quarter 2 units	Quarter 3 units	Quarter 4 units
Actual sales volume	420,000	450,000	475,000	475,000
Seasonal variation	+25,000	+15,000	–	-40,000
Deseasonalised sales volumes	395,000	435,000	475,000	515,000

(b)   The trend is for sales volume to increase by 40,000 units each quarter.

Forecast for next year:	Quarter 1 units	Quarter 2 units	Quarter 3 units	Quarter 4 units
Trend projection	555,000	595,000	635,000	675,000
Seasonal variation	+25,000	+15,000	–	-40,000
Forecast sales volumes	580,000	610,000	635,000	635,000

(c)

MEMORANDUM

To: Marketing Assistant

From: Assistant to the Management Accountant

Date: 21 June X5

Subject: Deseasonalised sales data

I am writing in response to your request for an explanation of deseasonalised or seasonally adjusted data.

What is meant by deseasonalised data and seasonal variations?

Seasonal variations are consistent patterns in sales volumes which arise during each year. For example, for Product P, the seasonal variation for quarter 1 is +25,000 units. This means that sales volumes in quarter 1 tend to be 25,000 units higher than the underlying trend in sales. In contrast, the seasonal variation for quarter 4 is minus 40,000 units. This means that sales volumes in quarter 4 are generally 40,000 units below the underlying trend.

Page 1 of 2

Deseasonalised data is data from which these seasonal variations have been removed. Apart from any random variations, the remaining figures show the trend in the data. It is then possible to see the general direction of movement of the time series.

In the case of Product P, the underlying trend is upwards, at a rate of increase of 40,000 units each quarter. This upward trend was masked in the actual data because of the distorting effect of the seasonal variations. These variations meant that, when one year's actual sales volumes were viewed in isolation, the rate of increase in sales appeared to be slowing.

How can deseasonalised data and seasonal variations be used in preparing forecasts?

If the trend revealed by deseasonalised data can be assumed to continue, then it can be projected to forecast the trend for future quarters. These trend values can then be adjusted, i.e. increased or decreased, to allow for the seasonal variations in each quarter. The resulting figure represents the forecast for each quarter's sales volumes.

If I can help with providing any further information or explanations, please let me know.

Page 2 of 2

(d)

MEMORANDUM

To: Marketing Assistant

From: Assistant to the Management Accountant

Date: 21 June X5

Subject: Fixed and flexible budgets

In response to your query, I hope that the following explanations will help you to understand the use of fixed and flexible budgets.

(i)   *Fixed budgets and flexible budgets*

A fixed budget is one which is designed to remain unaltered regardless of changes in activity levels. It is useful for planning because it provides a single activity level for planning and co-ordinating the activities of all parts of the organisation. An expected activity level has to be determined initially in order to ensure that all departments plan to provide the appropriate capacity.

Page 1 of 2

However, if activity levels alter, then a fixed budget may not be very useful for exercising control over distribution costs. For example, if activity increases, then certain costs (such as petrol and wages costs) may increase above the level planned in the original budget. A comparison with a fixed budget would reveal adverse cost variances and it would not be possible to tell whether these variances were a result of overspending or whether they were due to the increased activity.

A flexible budget identifies the fixed and variable costs. It is designed to increase to provide a higher expenditure allowance for variable costs if activity levels increase. The budget cost allowance can correspondingly be decreased if activity levels fall. The resulting variances are more meaningful for cost control because the effect of the change in activity levels has been eliminated.

(ii)   *Possible activity indicators*

Possible activity indicators for flexing the budget for distribution costs include the following:
   ·   Miles travelled
   ·   Journeys made
   ·   Tonnes carried
   ·   Tonne-miles achieved
   ·   Deliveries made

(iii)   *How a flexible budget cost allowance is calculated and used*

A flexible budget cost allowance is calculated by giving a fixed allowance for the budgeted fixed costs and then adding an amount for variable costs based on the actual activity level achieved:

Flexible budget cost allowance = Budgeted fixed costs + (Standard variable cost per unit × Number of units activity)

For example, if 'miles travelled' is to be used as the activity indicator, the budgeted fixed cost is £10,000, the standard variable cost per mile is £5 and 3,000 miles are travelled:

Flexible budget cost allowance = £10,000 + (£5 × 3,000) = £25,000

This allowance would then be compared with the actual cost and the resulting variance would indicate whether management attention was needed.

Page 2 of 2

△ ACTIVITY 2 △ △ △ △

(a) (i)   Budgeted selling price: £630,000/9,000   £70.00
     (ii) Budgeted material cost per Zylo: £45,000/9,000   £5.00
     (iii) Budgeted labour cost per Zylo: £55,800/9,000   £6.20
     (iv) Budgeted variable cost of electricity per Zylo: £2.00
           (£38,000 – £20,000)/9,000
     (v)   Actual selling price per Zylo: £616,000/8,800   £70.00
     (vi) Actual material cost per Zylo: £52,000/10,000   £5.20
     (vii) Actual labour cost per Zylo: £65,000/10,000   £6.50
     (viii) Actual variable cost of electricity per Zylo: £2.10
           £(42,000 – £21,000)/10,000

(b) **Statement of budgeted and actual profit year to 31 May 2004 using marginal costing**

Sales volume		Flexed budget 8,800	Actual 8,800	Variance
		£	£	£
Turnover	(W1)	616,000	616,000	0
Variable costs				
Materials	(W2)	44,000	45,760	1,760 (A)
Labour	(W3)	54,560	57,200	2,640 (A)
Electricity	(W4)	17,600	18,480	880 (A)
		116,160	121,440	5,280 (A)
Contribution		499,840	494,560	5,280 (A)
Fixed costs				
Electricity		20,000	21,000	1,000 (A)
Depreciation		70,000	65,000	5,000 (F)
Rent and rates		24,000	25,000	1,000 (A)
Other fixed overheads		40,000	42,000	2,000 (A)
		154,000	153,000	1,000 (F)
Profit		345,840	341,560	4,280 (A)

Workings

(W1) Budgeted turnover: £70 × 8,800 = £616,000
      Actual turnover (given) = £616,000

(W2) Budgeted material cost: £5 × 8,800 = £44,000
      Actual material cost: £5.2 × 8,800 = £45,760

(W3) Budgeted labour cost: £6.2 × 8,800 = £54,560
      Actual labour cost: £6.5 × 8,800 = £57,200

(W4) Budgeted variable cost of electricity: £2 × 8,800 = £17,600
      Actual variable cost of electricity: £2.1 × 8,800 = £18,480

(c) **Reason for the different actual profits**

The difference between the two actual profits (£359,920 – £341,560 = £18,360) is entirely due to the treatment of fixed overheads. The manager's statement is based on absorption costing whereby the actual fixed overheads are included in the production cost and therefore in the cost of stock. Some part of this cost is therefore carried forward in stock to the next period, thereby increasing profit in the current period.

The statement based on marginal costing writes off all the fixed costs in the current period, therefore causing the profit to be reduced. The calculations are as follows.

Fixed costs included in product cost

	£
Electricity	21,000
Depreciation	65,000
Rent and rates	25,000
Other	42,000
	153,000

Fixed costs included in stock: $£153,000 \times \dfrac{1,200}{10,000} = £18,360$

△ ACTIVITY 3

Trygon Limited

(a) *Trygon Limited: Flexible budget at 75% activity*

	(80%) 120,000	(40%) 60,000	Variable cost/ revenue per unit	(75%) 112,500
Sales and production (units)	£	£	£	£
Direct materials	24,000,000	12,000,000	200	22,500,000
Direct labour	7,200,000	7,200,000		7,200,000
Light, heat and power*	4,000,000	2,200,000	30	3,775,000
Production management salaries	1,500,000	1,500,000		1,500,000
Factory rent, rates and insurance	9,400,000	9,400,000		9,400,000
Depreciation of factory machinery	5,500,000	5,500,000		5,500,000
National advertising	20,000,000	20,000,000		20,000,000
Marketing and administration	2,300,000	2,300,000		2,300,000
Delivery costs	2,400,000	1,200,000	20	2,250,000
Total costs	76,300,000	61,300,000		74,425,000
Sales revenue	84,000,000	42,000,000	700	78,750,000
Operating profit				4,325,000

*Variable cost for 120,000 units = £3,600,000 to give fixed costs of £400,000.

(b)

REPORT

To: The Board of Directors

From: The Management Accountant

Date: X June 20X6

Subject: Budgeting within Trygon Limited

Following the instructions from the Group Finance Director, finished stocks are to be valued as material and labour plus an appropriate proportion of factory overheads based on normal activity. Each unsold computer will therefore be valued at £430 and comprise the following costs:

Valuation of closing stock

Fixed overheads	£
Production management salaries	1,500,000
Factory rent, rates and insurance	9,400,000
Depreciation of factory machinery	5,500,000
Fixed element of light, heat and power	400,000
Total fixed overheads	16,800,000
Unit fixed cost based on normal activity – £16,800,000/120,000	140

Unit direct costs	
Light, heat and power	30
Direct materials	200
Direct labour £7,200,000/120,000	60
Unit cost for stock valuation	430

Closing stock = (150,000 x 0.95) – 112,500

= 142,500 – 112,500 = 30,000 units

With each unit of closing stock valued at £430, the total closing stock will be valued at £12,900,000 to give an operating profit of £8.4 million. The revised budget is reproduced below.

Page 1 of 3

(i),(ii) *Trygon Limited: flexible budget at 75% sales activity but 95% production activity*

	£
Direct material – 142,500 × £200	28,500,000
Direct labour – £7,200,000 + (£70 × 22,500)	8,775,000
Light, heat and power – £400,000 + (£30 × 142,500)	4,675,000
Production management salaries – £1,500,000 + (£15 × 22,500)	1,837,500
Factory rent, rates and insurance	9,400,000
Depreciation of factory machinery	5,500,000
Factory cost of production	58,687,500
Less closing stock – 30,000 × £430	12,900,000
Factory cost of sales	45,787,500
Marketing, administration and distribution expenses	
National advertising	20,000,000
Marketing and administration	2,300,000
Delivery costs – 112,500 × £20	2,250,000
Total expenses	70,337,500
Sales turnover – 112,500 × £700	78,750,000
Operating profit	8,412,500

The reason for this increase in budgeted profit from £4,325,000 to £8,412,500 despite the additional costs of overtime and bonus payments is mainly due to the treatment of overheads. Fixed costs are essentially time-based but by using absorption costing some of these are carried forward in the value of unsold stocks. With no opening stocks and production equalling sales, all overheads are charged to the current period, even under an absorption costing system. With production being greater than sales volume and with overheads being based on normal activity, the difference in profit can be explained in terms of the treatment of fixed costs and the additional payments resulting from production being greater than the budgeted activity.

(iii) *Fixed and flexible budgets*

The original budget prepared by the group director was a fixed budget. Fixed budgets are designed to remain unaltered. Their primary uses are for planning and co-ordinating. Prior to commencing sales and production activity, the enterprise needs to know what is possible and what is achievable. The co-ordination role of budgeting helps to identify possible bottlenecks and to resolve them before production and selling commences. The planning role is concerned with where the enterprise wants to be at the end of the budget period and provides a target and a commitment to that target.

The flexible budgets I prepared serve two purposes. First, they help to show likely outcomes as conditions change. Secondly, they help managers to control the business by identifying what expenses and turnover should be at different levels of activity. The flexible budget can then be compared with the actual results which enables meaningful variances to be produced. This a flexible budget does by recognising (i) that fixed costs are unlikely to change as a matter of course over a range of activity levels and (ii) that variable costs, by their nature, will increase in proportion to increases in volume.

Budgetary objectives

For a budget to have meaning, there has to be a clear, unambiguous objective. Traditionally, this has involved the key or principal budget factor being identified, that is the factor which will limit the possible achievements for the period. Normally, this is sales although it could be production if there is a shortage of inputs or limited capacity. Being asked to both maximise sales and develop a long-term market position may not be compatible.

Confusion about the company's objectives or how those objectives can be achieved can lead to difficulties for the managers of Trygon. This might lead you to attempt to achieve the budget – but not in the way anticipated. For Trygon, it is clear that we are unlikely to achieve the budget target set at the beginning of the year. However, if Parmod plc is only concerned with profits, the directors of Trygon are more than able to meet the original profit target, not by actually selling more but by manipulating the results. This we can do by simply producing more. As a consequence, some of the fixed costs are carried forward to another period. The outcome is that we will have appeared to have achieved the target. The reality is we will have caused an increase in costs such as storekeeping costs which do not directly appear in the budget or the actual results.

(iv) *Participation in budgets*

Turning to the issue raised by Anne Darcy, conventional wisdom suggests that managers should be encouraged to participate in the budget process and that the budget should be built up from the lower rungs of management rather than imposed from the top. The belief is that managers will then feel they have ownership of the budget and this will encourage commitment and motivation. More than that it is argued that the operating managers are the only ones with sufficient detailed knowledge to develop a meaningful budget.

Unfortunately, the budget process is not always as simple as that. First, the objectives of the managers and the objectives of the organisation may not be the same. There is a need for a similarity of goals – goal congruence – and this does not automatically result from empowering managers to develop their own budgets. Secondly, the operating management may have detailed knowledge but they might use this to their own benefits – as with the current plan to build up stocks and so manipulate the budget. Thirdly the managers may not wish to participate in the budget setting process. This may be because of some psychological fear resulting in managers simply wanting to be told what their targets are; it might be because they do not have the technical knowledge to participate in budget setting; or it might be that they either do not have the necessary degree of commitment to the organisation or they feel that the budgetary control system will be used against them. Because of this, it is not self-evident that participation will always help managers and the organisation.

Page 3 of 3

△ ACTIVITY 4

World History Museum

(a)/(b) Analysis of budgeted costs

	Fixed cost	Variable cost	Variable cost per course
	£	£	£
Speakers' fees	–	3,180	530
Hire of premises	–	1,500	250
Depreciation of equipment	180	–	–
Stationery	–	600	100
Catering	250	1,500	250
Insurance	100	720	120
Administration	1,620	–	–

Flexible budget control statement for April – 5 courses

Expenditure	Fixed cost budget	Variable cost budget	Total cost budget	Actual cost	Variance
	£	£	£	£	£
Speakers' fees	–	2,650	2,650	2,500	150
Hire of premises	–	1,250	1,250	1,500	(250)
Depreciation of equipment	180	–	180	200	(20)
Stationery	–	500	500	530	(30)
Catering	250	1,250	1,500	1,500	–
Insurance	100	600	700	700	–
Administration	1,620	–	1,620	1,650	(30)
	2,150	6,250	8,400	8,580	(180)

(c)

MEMORANDUM

To: Chris Brooks

From: Assistant Management Accountant

Date: 13 June 20X4

Subject: Participative budgeting

As requested, I enclose brief explanations of the advantages and disadvantages of participative budgeting.

Page 1 of 2

Advantages

(i) Managers are likely to be demotivated if budgets are imposed on them without any prior consultation. If they are consulted, they are more likely to accept the budgets as realistic targets.

(ii) If managers are consulted, then the budgets are more likely to take account of their own aspiration levels. Aspiration levels are personal targets which individuals or departments set for themselves. If budget targets exceed aspiration levels, then the budgets can have a negative motivational impact because they will be perceived as unachievable. However, if the targets fall too far below aspiration levels, then the performance of the individuals or departments may be lower than might otherwise have been achieved.

(iii) Managers who are consulted may be motivated by the feeling that their views are valuable to senior management.

(iv) Managers who are closely involved with the day to day running of operations may be able to give very valuable input to the forecasting and planning process.

Disadvantages

(i) If too many people are involved in budgetary planning, it can make the process very slow and difficult to manage.

(ii) Senior managers may need to overrule decisions made by local managers. This can be demotivating if it is not dealt with correctly.

(iii) The participative process may not be genuine. Managers must feel that their participation is really valued by senior management. A false attempt to appear to be interested in their views can be even more demotivating than a system of imposed budgets.

(iv) Managers may attempt to include excess expenditure in their budgets, due to 'empire-building' or to a desire to guard against unforeseen circumstances.

Page 2 of 2

Test your knowledge △ △ △

1 A fixed budget is appropriate for planning purposes.

2 A flexed budget is appropriate for control purposes.

3

	Maintenance cost £	Activity level (units)
High	55,000	12,000
Low	50,000	10,000
Difference	5,000	2,000

Variable cost $= \dfrac{£5,000}{2,000} = £2.50$ per unit

Fixed cost $=$ £25,000

At activity of 13,000 units, maintenance would be budgeted to cost £25,000 + £32,500 = £57,500.

4 Management by exception is the practice of focusing on activities that require attention and ignoring those that appear to be conforming to expectations.

5 It is impossible to be 100% sure, since different managers with different personalities will react in different ways, but generally managers will be more motivated if they have been involved in establishing the budget.

KEY TECHNIQUES QUESTIONS

Chapter 2
Collection of cost information

QUESTION 1

You work as an accounting technician for Eastoft Feeds and Fertilisers Ltd.

You use a computer model for forecasting the quarterly costs on your various product lines. The software includes a regression analysis program which builds a simple linear cost model. After inputting data for product 'EF 3', values for the quarterly fixed cost and marginal cost per unit are determined and the cost model is $y = 25,000 + 35x$, where x is the quarterly production volume (in tonnes) and y is the total quarterly cost (in £).

The following is the estimated volume of output for the quarters ended March, June, September and December 2002.

Product 'EF3'

Quarter ended	Volume (tonnes)
March	15,000
June	12,000
September	16,000
December	14,000

Task

Estimate the fixed cost, variable cost and total cost for each quarter of 2002 and complete the table below.

Product 'EF3'

Quarter ended	Volume (tonnes)	Fixed cost £	Variable cost £	Total cost £
March	15,000			
June	12,000			
September	16,000			
December	14,000			

Draw a graph to show the total cost against output and estimate from the graph the total cost for an output volume of 20,000 tonnes.

QUESTION 2 (June 1999)

Data

Margaret Brown is the financial director of Wilmslow Ltd. She is not convinced that the use of linear regression, even when adjusted for seasonal variations, is the best way of forecasting sales volumes for Wilmslow Ltd.

The quality of sales forecasting is an agenda item for the next meeting of the Board of Directors and she asks for your advice.

Task

Write a *brief* memo to Margaret Brown. Your memo should:
(a) Identify TWO limitations of the use of linear regression as a forecasting technique.
(b) Suggest TWO other ways of sales forecasting.

Chapter 3
Accounting for overheads

QUESTION 3

Sandsend Engineers Ltd specialise in agricultural engineering. The business is divided into three cost centres: machining, fabrication and outside contract work.

The budgeted overhead for the quarter ended 31 March 2003 shows:

Cost centre	Machining	Fabrication	Outside contracts	Total
	£	£	£	£
Allocated overhead	21,000	25,500	19,500	66,000
Apportioned overhead	15,000	16,100	9,100	40,200
	36,000	41,600	28,600	106,200
Budgeted machine hours	4,000	5,200		
Budgeted labour hours			1,950	

In early January, the company receives an order for a replacement door on a grain silo for a local farmer. The specification of costs includes:
Direct material   £3,100
Direct labour rate per hour   £7.50

Machine hours and labour hours per cost centre:

Machining	12 hours
Fabrication	8 hours
Outside contracts	6 hours

The business has a pricing policy based on full absorption costing principles. It adds 10% to production costs to cover for administration, selling and distribution. It then plans for profit based on 25% of the selling price or contract price.

Task

Determine, using absorption costing principles, the contract price of the replacement grain silo door. (Calculate to the nearest '£'.)

QUESTION 4

Roberts and Ranson are partners trading as licensed accounting technicians. They employ one other fully qualified technician and two trainees, together with a general administration assistant.

The budgeted salaries for the year comprise:

	£
Roberts	30,000
Ranson	30,000
Qualified senior	18,500
Trainee (1)	10,500
Trainee (2)	12,000
Administrator	14,500*
	115,500

*The administrator's salary is to be treated as overhead.

The budgeted overheads include:

	£
Building occupancy costs	9,100
Telephone, postage, stationery	4,700
Other overheads	11,200
	25,000

The total forecast labour hours for the year include:

	Hours
Partners	3,760
Qualified senior	1,880
Trainees (split equally)	3,760
	9,400

Clients' work is priced on full absorption costing principles. Overhead is recovered on labour hours. The labour charge-out rates for partners, the qualified senior and the trainees are based on their budgeted salaries divided by their labour hours.

The business accepts a new client, the White Rose Hotel, and the senior partner estimates, having met with the client, that the hours required on the work will be:

	Hours	
Partners	5	
Qualified senior	12	
Trainees	6	(3 hours each)
	23	

The pricing policy is based on adding an element for profit which will yield a 30% profit margin on the price charged to the client.

Task

Determine the estimated fees chargeable to the White Rose Hotel based on the partner's notes.

QUESTION 5

Refer again to the scenario in Question 3, Sandsend Engineers Ltd.

The actual overhead incurred during the quarter ended 31 March 2003 was:

	£
Machining	37,800
Fabrication	42,000
Outside work	29,100
	108,900

Overhead is recovered on machine hours in machining and fabrication, and labour hours on outside work.

The actual level of activity in the quarter was:

Machining	4,250	machine hours
Fabrication	5,300	machine hours
Outside work	1,975	labour hours

Task

(a) Calculate the overhead recovered in each cost centre for the period.
(b) Post both the actual overhead incurred and the overhead recovered to the overhead control ledger account for the period, showing the under or over recovery transferred to the profit and loss account.

QUESTION 6

Blidworth Loam Ltd manufacture a single product 'Cricketloam' and supply this product to cricket clubs for grounds at professional level through to village greens.

Its cost specification includes the following budgeted details per tonne of product, together with budgeted data for the current year:

Direct labour hours	4.5
Labour rate per hour	£8.50
Direct material	1.1 tonnes per tonne of good output
Material cost	£25 per tonne
Variable production overheads (total)	£378,000
Fixed production overheads (total)	£250,000
Selling price per tonne	£132
Production volume	12,000 tonnes
Sales volume	11,500 tonnes

Task

Considering the above information, what is the budgeted marginal cost per tonne of product?

A £65.75
B £59.00
C £97.25
D £118.08

QUESTION 7

Task

Using the information in Question 6, what is the contribution per tonne of product?

A £66.25
B £73.00
C £13.92
D £34.75

QUESTION 8

Task

Using the information in Question 6:
(a) Prepare a budgeted operating statement for the company in both marginal costing and full absorption costing format.
(b) Explain clearly the reason for the difference in reported profit shown in your two statements produced in part (a).

QUESTION 9

As with other management accounting methods and techniques, activity-based costing (ABC) has its own specific terminology.

Task

Define the following terms associated with the ABC method of dealing with overhead cost:
· activity;
· cost driver;
· cost pool;
· cost driver rate;

QUESTION 10

The application of activity based costing involves a set procedure.

Task

Outline the steps required from accounting for overhead to the recovery of overhead using this method.

QUESTION 11

Refer again to the scenario outlined in Question 6 under marginal costing, Blidworth Loam Ltd.

The accounting technician and the planning engineer have recently analysed the value adding processes and identified various activities, cost drivers within those activities and current volumes of production and decide to apply the ABC methodology.

Budgeted plans 2003

	Activity	Cost pool £	Cost driver volume
(1)	Process set up	260,000	200 set ups
(2)	Material procurement	74,000	50 purchase orders
(3)	Maintenance	64,000	12 maintenance plans
(4)	Material handling	120,000	2,500 material movements
(5)	Quality costs	80,000	200 inspections
(6)	Order processing	30,000	1,000 customers
		628,000	

The company plan to produce 1,000 tonnes per month which will require the following approximate activity demand:

17 set ups
4 purchase orders
1 maintenance plan
210 material movements
16 inspections
80 customers

Task

(a)   Calculate the cost driver rates.

(b)   Determine the amount of overhead to be recovered per tonne of product.

QUESTION 12 (June 2002)

Data

Drampton plc has recently taken over Little Ltd, a small company making mainframe and desktop computers. Little appears to make all of its profits from mainframe computers. Drampton's finance director tells you that Little's fixed overheads are currently charged to production using standard labour hours and gives you their standard cost of making mainframe and desktop computers. These are shown below.

Little Ltd : Standard cost per computer

Model	Mainframe	Desktop
Annual budgeted volume	5	5,000
Unit standard cost	£	£
Material and labour	50,000	500
Fixed overhead	4,000	40
Standard cost per computer	54,000	540

The finance director asks for your help and suggests you reclassify the fixed overheads between the two models using activity-based costing. You are given the following information:

· Budgeted total annual fixed overheads

	£
Set-up costs	10,000
Rent and power – production time	120,000
Rent – stores area	50,000
Salaries of store issue staff	40,000
Total	220,000

· Every time Little makes a mainframe computer, it has to stop making desktop computers and rearrange the factory layout. The cost of this is shown as set-up costs. If the company did not make any mainframe computers, these costs would be eliminated.

· Cost drivers

	Mainframe	Desktop	Total
Number of set-ups	5	0	5
Number of weeks of production	10	40	50
Floor area of stores (square metres)	400	400	800
Number of issues of stock	2,000	8,000	10,000

Task

Prepare a note for Drampton's finance director. In the note you should use the cost drivers to:

(a)   reallocate Little's budgeted total fixed annual overheads between mainframe and desktop production;

(b)   show the revised *unit* fixed overheads for each of the two types of computers.

Chapter 4
Time series analysis, sampling and index numbers

QUESTION 13

Eastoft Feeds and Fertilisers use a system of standard costing as a basis for their monthly management reporting.

Standards are revised on a quarterly basis to account for changes in price based on an index for specific categories of cost. The following information relates to current standards.

Category of cost	Standard
Direct labour rate per hour	£7.00
Raw material cost per tonne	£55.00
Fixed overhead recovery rate per hour	£12.50

The current price index for these categories and the index for each quarter were:

	Current	Q1	Q2	Q3	Q4
Direct labour	105.00	108.15	108.15	108.15	108.15
Raw material	110.00	112.75	113.87	114.45	114.45
Fixed overhead	108.00	109.08	109.62	110.17	110.50

Task

Revise the standards for each quarter on the basis of the changes highlighted in the index for each category of cost shown above.

QUESTION 14 (June 2004)

Sam Thomas is concerned about the rise in prices of direct materials used to make desks and has asked you to investigate.

The prices per kg of direct materials charged by suppliers for the period January 2004 to May 2004 are as follows.

	£
January	5.05
February	5.02
March	5.08
April	5.11
May	5.20

Task

(a) Calculate the moving average of monthly direct material prices over a period of three months.

(b)   Write a memo to Sam Thomas to:

    (i)   explain what the trend in direct material prices, based on the moving average series, shows

    (ii)   suggest ONE possible use of the trend in setting the standard cost of direct materials for 2004

    (iii)   give TWO more pieces of information needed to set the standard cost of direct materials for 2004.

QUESTION 15

Eastoft Feeds and Fertilisers Ltd uses a number of standard raw materials for its product range. Product F4's main raw material is 'EF1'. The average price per tonne for this material, which is subject to seasonal change, for each quarter during 2001 was as below. The material is in short supply.

2001	Q1	Q2	Q3	Q4
Average price per tonne	£40	£44	£64	£76
Seasonal variation	–£4	–£8	+£4	+£8

Task

(a)   Determine the seasonally adjusted price per tonne for raw material 'EF1' for each of the four quarters of 2001.

(b)   If a similar pattern of price movements were to continue, determine the likely purchase price per tonne for each of the four quarters of 2002.

QUESTION 16 (June 2000)

Data

Garden Care is a division of Alton Products plc. The sales director of Garden Care, Hazel Brown, has noticed a distinct trend and pattern of seasonal variations for one of Garden Care's products since the product was introduced in the third quarter of 1997. She provides you with the following sales volumes for the product.

UNITS SOLD BY QUARTER

Year	Quarter 1	Quarter 2	Quarter 3	Quarter 4
1997			142	142
1998	150	150	142	158
1999	150	166	142	174
2000	150	182*		

*Estimate

Task

Hazel Brown asks you to:

(a)   Calculate the *Centred Four-Point Moving Average Trend* figures.

(b)   Calculate the seasonal variations on the assumption that the seasonal variations are additive.

(c)   Use your results in (a) and (b) to forecast the sales volume for quarter 2 of year 2000.

(d)   Suggest TWO reasons why there might be a difference between the forecast figure calculated in (c) and the result given in the data.

QUESTION 17 (December 2003)

Data

Telford plc has a subsidiary, Ironbridge Ltd. This was formed on 1 January 1999. Ironbridge makes a single product, the Delta. The directors of Ironbridge are considering using time series to improve sales forecasting.

The company has collected quarterly turnover data for its first 19 quarters of trading. Quarter 1 was the first three months of 1999; quarter 2 the second three months of 1999; quarter 5 the first three months of 2000; and quarter 19 the three months ended 30 September 2003.

Two models have been suggested.

Model A

This uses the linear regression formula of $y = a + bx$ to describe the trend. The term y represents the forecast trend (or seasonally adjusted) turnover, a is a constant and x represents the quarter number being forecast. Applying the 19 quarters' data resulted in the development of the following formula:

$$y = £200,000 + £58,000x$$

For quarter 19, the three months ended 30 September 2003, x would be 19. The effect of this formula is for the forecast trend to increase by a constant £58,000 per quarter.

Model B

The formula for model B is $y = a + z(1+g)^x$. In this model, a is a constant, x is the quarter number being forecast and g is a constant growth percentage. Applying the 19 quarters' data produced the following formula:

$$y = £1,000,000 + £60,000(1.1)^x$$

Barry Jones explained how the formula for model B worked. The first term, the £1,000,000, is a constant. However, the value of the second term, $£60,000(1.1)^x$, increases quarterly by 10% over the previous quarter's figure.

To demonstrate this, Barry explained that the value of the second term for quarter 16 was £275,698, and so the value for quarter 17 would be 10% more, £303,268. Similarly, the value of the second term for quarter 18 would be 10% more than the value for quarter 17, a total of £333,595.

Barry gives you the actual seasonally adjusted data for the first three quarters of 2003.

Seasonally adjusted actual data	Quarter 17	Quarter 18	Quarter 19
Three months ended	31 March 2003	30 June 2003	30 September 2003
	£1,300,000	£1,350,000	£1,390,000

Task

(a)   Calculate the forecast turnover for quarters 17, 18 and 19 using both models.

(b)   Identify the model that gives the better estimate of the seasonal adjusted actual data. Give ONE reason for your answer.

(c)   Write a memo to Barry Jones. In your memo, you should:

(i)   use the model that gives the better estimate to forecast the seasonally adjusted turnover for quarter 20, the three months ending 31 December 2003;

(ii)   identify TWO limitations to using that model as a forecasting technique.

Chapters 5 and 6
Standard costing and variance analysis

QUESTION 18

Malik Brothers run a taxi and courier service both locally and a specific service to Manchester Airport for holiday makers and business personnel.

On the Manchester Airport run the 'round trip' is benchmarked as 5 standard hours.

In the quarter ended 31 March 2002, 182 standard trips are planned.

The fixed costs incurred by the business, including the drivers' salary, are budgeted to be £11,500 for the period.

The actual fixed costs for the period were £12,400 and 175 standard trips were made. The actual hours worked were 940.

Task

Calculate:

(a)   The standard hours in the budget.

(b)   The fixed overhead recovery rate per standard hour.

(c)   The fixed overhead recovered in the quarter ended 31 March 2002.

(d)   The fixed overhead total variance.

(e)   The fixed overhead expenditure variance.

(f)   The fixed overhead volume variance.

(g)   The fixed overhead capacity variance.

(h)   The fixed overhead efficiency variance.

(i)   Briefly explain how such an analysis can be of use to the owners of the business in controlling costs.

QUESTION 19 (December 2001)

Data

You are employed as a trainee Accounting Technician with Gransden, Yelling and Co, a firm of accountants and registered auditors. One of your clients is CD Products Ltd.

CD Products uses expensive equipment to make compact discs for customers in other companies. It has two manufacturing departments: the CD pressing department and the finishing department. The CD pressing department uses one machine to write digital data from a master disc to blank discs. The finishing department then prints information on the front of the discs, packages them and sends the completed discs to the customers.

CD Products uses standard costs to help prepare quotations for customers but does not yet use them for reporting purposes. Details of the standard costs used in the pressing department are shown below.

STANDARD COST PER MACHINE HOUR - CD PRESSING DEPARTMENT	
Blank compact discs: 800 × £0.20 each	£160.00
Labour: 8 labour hours × £7.00	£56.00
Fixed overheads	£200.00
Standard cost of pressing 800 compact discs per machine hour	£416.00

CD Products has prepared the following financial and operating information for the week ended 30 November 2001.

CD Pressing Department information:
- Budgeted labour hours   880 hours
- Actual number of compact discs manufactured   96,000 CDs
- Actual cost of blank compact discs issued to production   £20,790
- Actual price paid for each blank compact disc   £0.21
- Actual labour hours worked   980 hours
- Actual cost of labour   £7,252
- Factory information:
- Budgeted total factory fixed costs   £33,000
- Actual total factory fixed costs   £34,500
- Budgeted total factory labour hours   1,320 hours
- Both budgeted and actual fixed overheads are apportioned between the pressing and finishing departments on the basis of budgeted labour hours.

The Chief Executive of CD Products is Jamil Baharundin. He tells you that the weekly financial and operating information does not help him manage the business. You suggest a standard costing statement might be more helpful. Jamil asks you to prepare a standard costing statement for the CD Pressing Department, using the information for the week ended 30 November 2001.

Task 19.1

(a) Calculate the following information for the CD Pressing Department for the week ended 30 November 2001:
    (i)   Standard number of compact discs produced per *labour* hour.
    (ii)   The budgeted *machine* hours of the department.
    (iii)   Budgeted fixed overheads of the department.

(iv) Actual fixed overheads of the department.
(v) Standard fixed overhead rate per *labour* hour.
(vi) Standard labour hours produced.
(vii) Actual number of blank compact discs issued to production.
(viii) Actual cost of actual production, including fixed overheads.
(ix) Standard cost of actual production, including fixed overheads.

(b) Calculate the following variances for the CD Pressing Department:
(i) Material price variance.
(ii) Material usage variance.
(iii) Labour rate variance.
(iv) Labour efficiency variance.
(v) Fixed overhead expenditure variance.
(vi) Fixed overhead volume variance.
(vii) Fixed overhead capacity variance.
(viii) Fixed overhead efficiency variance.

(c) Prepare a statement for the CD Pressing Department reconciling the standard absorption cost of actual production to the actual absorption cost of actual production.

Data

In a letter to you, Jamil tells you that your standard costing statement helped explain why CD Products' profits have recently been falling. He plans to use similar statements in the future but, before doing so, he raises the following issues:

· He is not certain if all variances should be investigated. As an example, he explains that for every 100 fault-free compact discs produced in the week ended 30 November 2001, two had to be scrapped. As the unit cost of a blank CD is so small, he feels it is not worth investigating the other reasons for the material usage variance.

· The standard costs for quotation purposes assumed customers would want their discs to be both pressed and finished. The demand for disc pressing is so high that it exceeds the capacity of the CD Pressing Department but most customers then take the pressed compact discs elsewhere for finishing.

· The CD Pressing Department requires a dust-free, air-conditioned environment using an expensive machine but the Finishing Department does not use any expensive resources.

An analysis of the budgeted factory fixed overheads showing their usage by department was included in the letter and is reproduced below.

	CD Pressing	Finishing	Total
Rent, rates and insurance	£8,600	£1,300	£9,900
Air conditioning, heat, light and power	£9,600	£900	£10,500
Depreciation and maintenance	£12,600		£12,600
	£30,800	£2,200	£33,000

Task 19.2

Write a letter to Jamil Baharundin. In your letter you should:
(a)   Identify FOUR issues to consider before deciding to investigate a variance.
(b)   Sub-divide the material usage variance into that part due to discs being scrapped and that part due to other reasons.
(c)   *Briefly* explain, with reasons, why there might be excess demand for the CD Pressing Department but much less demand for the Finishing Department.

QUESTION 20 (December 2000)

Data

You are employed as a management accountant in the head office of Travel Holdings plc. Travel Holdings owns a number of transport businesses. One of them is Travel Ferries Ltd. Travel Ferries operates ferries which carry passengers and vehicles across a large river. Each year, standard costs are used to develop the budget for Travel Ferries Ltd. The latest budgeted and actual operating results are shown below.

Travel Ferries Ltd					
Budgeted and actual operating results for the year to 30 November 2000					
Operating data:	*Budget*			*Actual*	
Number of ferry crossings		6,480			5,760
Operating hours of ferries		7,776			7,488
Cost data:		£			£
Fuel	1,244,160 litres	497,664	1,232,800 litres		567,088
Labour	93,312 hours	466,560	89,856 hours		471,744
Fixed overheads		466,560			472,440
Cost of operations		1,430,784			1,511,272

Other accounting information:
·   Fuel and labour are variable costs.
·   Fixed overheads are absorbed on the basis of budgeted operating hours.

One of your duties is to prepare costing information and a standard costing reconciliation statement for the Chief Executive of Travel Holdings.

Task 20.1

(a)   Calculate the following information:
    (i)   The standard price of fuel per litre.
    (ii)   The standard litres of fuel for 5,760 ferry crossings.
    (iii)   The standard labour rate per hour.
    (iv)   The standard labour hours for 5,760 ferry crossings.
    (v)   The standard fixed overhead cost per budgeted operating hour.
    (vi)   The standard operating hours for 5,760 crossings.
    (vii)   The standard fixed overhead cost absorbed by the actual 5,760 ferry crossings.

(b)   Using the data provided in the operating results and your answers to part (a), calculate the following variances:

(i)   The material price variance for the fuel.

(ii)   The material usage variance for the fuel.

(iii)   The labour rate variance.

(iv)   The labour efficiency variance.

(v)   The fixed overhead expenditure variance.

(vi)   The fixed overhead volume variance.

(vii) The fixed overhead capacity variance.

(viii) The fixed overhead efficiency variance.

(c)   Prepare a statement reconciling the actual cost of operations to the standard cost of operations for the year to 30 November 2000.

Data

On receiving your reconciliation statement, the Chief Executive is concerned about the large number of adverse variances. She is particularly concerned about the excessive cost of fuel used during the year. A colleague informs you that:

·   the actual market price of fuel per litre during the year was 20% higher than the standard price;

·   fuel used directly varies with the number of operating hours;

·   the difference between the standard and actual operating hours for the 5,760 ferry crossings arose entirely because of weather conditions.

Task 20.2

Write a memo to the Chief Executive. Your memo should:

(a)   Sub-divide the material price variance into:

(i)   that part arising from the standard price being different from the actual market price of fuel, and

(ii)   that part due to other reasons.

(b)   Identify ONE variance which is not controllable and give ONE reason why the variance is not controllable.

(c)   Identify TWO variances which are controllable and which should be investigated. For each variance, give ONE reason why it is controllable.

QUESTION 21 (June 2000)

Data

NGJ Ltd is a furniture manufacturer. It makes 3 products: the Basic, the Grand and the Super. You are the management accountant reporting to the product line manager for the Basic. Reproduced below is NGJ's unit standard material and labour cost data and budgeted production for the year to 31 May 2000 together with details of the budgeted and actual factory fixed overheads for the year.

Unit standard material and labour cost data by product for the year to 31 May 2000

Product	Basic	Grand	Super
Material at £12 per metre	6 metres	8 metres	10 metres
Labour at £5.00 per hour	6 hours	1 hour	1 hour
Budgeted production	10,000 units	70,000 units	70,000 units

Total budgeted and actual factory fixed overheads for the year to 31 May 2000

	Budgeted £	Actual £
Rent and rates	100,000	100,000
Depreciation	200,000	200,000
Light, heat and power	60,000	70,000
Indirect labour	240,000	260,000
Total factory fixed overheads	600,000	630,000

Apportionment policy:
As all products are made in the same factory, budgeted and actual total factory fixed overheads are apportioned to each product on the basis of budgeted total labour hours per product.

During the year 11,500 *Basics* were made. The actual amount of material used, labour hours worked and costs incurred were as follows:

Actual material and labour cost of producing 11,500 Basics for the year to 31 May 2000

	Units	Total cost
Material	69,230 metres	£872,298
Labour	70,150 hours	£343,735

Task 21.1

(a) Calculate the following information:
  (i) The total budgeted labour hours of production for NGJ Ltd.
  (ii) The standard factory fixed overhead rate per labour hour.
  (iii) The budgeted and actual factory fixed overhead apportioned to *Basic* production.
  (iv) The actual cost of material per metre and the actual labour hourly rate for *Basic* production.
  (v) The total standard absorption cost of actual *Basic* production.
  (vi) The actual absorption cost of actual *Basic* production.

(b) Calculate the following variances for *Basic* production:
  (i) The material price variance.
  (ii) The material usage variance.
  (iii) The labour rate variance.
  (iv) The labour efficiency variance.
  (v) The fixed overhead expenditure variance.
  (vi) The fixed overhead volume variance.

(vii)   The fixed overhead capacity variance.

(viii) The fixed overhead efficiency variance.

(c)   Prepare a statement reconciling the actual absorption cost of actual *Basic* production with the standard absorption cost of actual *Basic* production.

Data

The product line manager for the *Basic* is of the opinion that the standard costs and variances do not fairly reflect the effort put in by staff. The manager made the following points:

· Because of a shortage of materials for the *Basic*, the purchasing manager had entered into a contract for the year with a single supplier in order to guarantee supplies.

· The actual price paid for the material per metre was 10% less than the market price throughout the year.

· The *Basic* is a hand-made product made in a small, separate part of the factory and uses none of the expensive machines shared by the *Grand* and the *Super*.

· *Grand* and *Super* production uses the same highly mechanised manufacturing facilities and only one of those products can be made at any one time. A change in production from one product to another involves halting production in order to set up the necessary tools and production line.

In response to a request from the *Basic* product line manager, a colleague has re-analysed the budgeted and actual factory fixed overheads by function. The revised analysis is reproduced below.

Functional analysis of factory fixed overheads for the year ended 31 May 2000		
	Budget £	Actual £
Setting up of tools and production lines	202,000	228,000
Depreciation attributable to production	170,000	170,000
Stores	60,000	59,000
Maintenance	40,000	48,000
Light, heat and power directly attributable to production	48,000	45,000
Rent and rates directly attributable to production	80,000	80,000
Total factory fixed overheads	600,000	630,000

Task 21.2

Write a memo to the *Basic* product line manager. Your memo should:

(a)   Identify the market price of the material used in the *Basic*.

(b)   Sub-divide the material price variance into that part due to the contracted price being different from the market price and that due to other reasons.

(c)   Identify ONE benefit to NGJ Ltd, which is not reflected in the variances, arising from the purchasing manager's decision to enter into a contract for the supply of materials.

(d)   *Briefly* explain what is meant by activity-based costing.

(e)   Refer to the task data, where appropriate, to *briefly* discuss whether or not activity-based costing would have reduced the budgeted and actual fixed overheads of *Basic* production.

QUESTION 22 (December 1999)

Data

You are the assistant management accountant at the Bare Foot Hotel complex on the tropical island of St Nicolas. The hotel complex is a luxury development. All meals and entertainment are included in the price of the holidays and guests only have to pay for drinks.

The Bare Foot complex aims to create a relaxing atmosphere. Because of this, meals are available throughout the day and guests can eat as many times as they wish.

The draft performance report for the hotel for the seven days ended 27 November 1999 is reproduced below.

Bare Foot Hotel Complex					
Draft performance report for seven days ended 27 November 1999					
	Notes	Budget		Actual	
Guests		[540]		[648]	
		$	$	$	$
Variable costs					
Meal costs	1		34,020		49,896
Catering staff costs	2, 3		3,780		5,280
Total variable costs			37,800		55,176
Fixed overhead costs					
Salaries of other staff		5,840		6,000	
Local taxes		4,500		4,200	
Light, heat and power		2,500		2,600	
Depreciation of buildings and equipment		5,000		4,000	
Entertainment		20,500		21,000	
Total fixed overheads			38,340		37,800
Total cost of providing for guests			76,140		92,976

Notes

1   Budgeted cost of meals: number of guests × 3 meals per day × 7 days × $3 per meal.

2   Budgeted cost of catering staff: each member of the catering staff is to prepare and serve 12 meals per hour. Cost = (number of guests × 3 meals per day × 7 days ÷ 12 meals per hour) × $4 per hour.

3   Actual hours worked by catering staff = 1,200 hours.

> *Other notes*
> The amount of food per meal has been kept under strict portion control. Since
> preparing the draft performance report, however, it has been discovered that
> guests have eaten, on average, four meals per day.

You report to Alice Groves, the general manager of the hotel, who feels that the
format of the draft performance report could be improved to provide her with
more meaningful management information. She suggests that the budgeted
and actual data given in the existing draft performance report is rearranged in
the form of a standard costing report.

Task 22.1

(a) Use the budget data, the actual data and the notes to the performance report to calculate the following for the seven days ended
27 November 1999:
  (i) The actual number of meals served;
  (ii) The standard number of meals which should have been served for
  the actual number of guests;
  (iii) The actual hourly rate paid to catering staff;
  (iv) The standard hours allowed for catering staff to serve three meals
  per day for the actual number of guests;
  (v) The standard fixed overhead per guest;
  (vi) The total standard cost for the actual number of guests.

(b) Use the data given earlier and your answers to part (a) to calculate the
following variances for the seven days ended 27 November 1999:
  (i) The material price variance for meals served;
  (ii) The material usage variance for meals served;
  (iii) The labour rate variance for catering staff;
  (iv) The labour efficiency variance for catering staff, based on a standard of three meals served per guest per day;
  (v) The fixed overhead expenditure variance.
  (vi) The fixed overhead volume variance on the assumption that the
  fixed overhead absorption rate is based on the budgeted number
  of guests per seven days.

(c) Prepare a statement reconciling the standard cost for the actual number
of guests to the actual cost for the actual number of guests for the seven
days ended 27 November 1999.

Data

On receiving your reconciliation statement, Alice Groves asks the following
questions:
· How much of the labour efficiency variance is due to guests taking, on average, four meals per day rather than the three provided for in the budget
and how much is due to other reasons?
· Would it be feasible to sub-divide the fixed overhead volume variance into
a capacity and efficiency variance?

Task 22.2

Write a memo to Alice Groves. Your memo should:
(a)   Divide the labour efficiency variance into that part due to guests taking more meals than planned and that part due to other efficiency reasons.
(b)   Explain the meaning of the fixed overhead capacity and efficiency variances.
(c)   *Briefly* discuss whether or not it is feasible to calculate the fixed overhead capacity and efficiency variances for the Bare Foot Hotel Complex.

QUESTION 23 (June 1999)

Data

You are the management accountant at Brighter Chemicals Ltd. Brighter Chemicals makes a single product, Zed, which is sold in 5-litre tins.

One of your responsibilities is to prepare a report each month for the management team comparing the actual cost of Zed production with its standard cost of production. This involves taking data from a computer printout, preparing standard cost variances and reconciling the standard cost of actual production to the actual cost of actual production. After the data is analysed, you attend a management meeting where the performance of the company is discussed. The printout for May 1999 is reproduced below.

Brighter Chemicals Ltd – Production report for May 1999						
Number of tins of Zed	Budgeted production 1,750				Actual production 1,700	
Inputs	Units of input	Standard cost per unit of input	Standard cost per tin of Zed	Standard cost of budgeted production	Actual cost per unit of input	Actual cost of actual production
Material	5 litres	£40.00	£200.00	£350,000	£40.20	£338,283
Labour	10 hrs	£6.00	£60.00	£105,000	£5.90	£110,330
Fixed overheads	10 hrs	£24.00	£240.00	£420,000		£410,000
			£500.00	£875,000		£858,613

Task 23.1

In preparation for the management meeting:
(a)   Calculate the:
   (i)   Actual litres of material used in producing the 1,700 tins of Zed;
   (ii)   Actual hours worked in May;
   (iii) Standard litres of material which should have been used to produce 1,700 tins of Zed;
   (iv)   Standard number of labour hours that should have been incurred in producing 1,700 tins of Zed;
   (v)   Standard hours of fixed overheads charged to the *budgeted* production of 1,750 tins;
   (vi)   Standard hours of fixed overheads charged to the *actual* production of 1,700 tins;

    (b)   Calculate the following variances, making use of the answers in Task 23.1 (a):
          (i)   Material price variance.
          (ii)   Material usage variance.
          (iii)   Labour rate variance.
          (iv)   Labour efficiency variance.
          (v)   Fixed overhead expenditure variance.
          (vi)   Fixed overhead volume variance.
          (vii) Fixed overhead capacity variance.
          (viii) Fixed overhead efficiency variance.

    (c)   Prepare a report reconciling the standard cost of *actual* production to the actual cost of *actual* production.

Data

On receiving your report, the production director makes the following comments:

- The material used in Zed production is purchased in drums. A notice on each drum states that the minimum content per drum is 50 litres.
- Finished production of Zed is automatically poured into tins by a machine which also measures the contents. An error of 0.5% either way in the accuracy of measurement is acceptable.
- The reported material price variance does not truly reflect the efficiency of the purchasing department. An index of raw material prices stood at 124.00 when the standard price was set but stood at 125.86 in May.
- It seems unnecessary to investigate favourable variances. Favourable variances improve profitability and should be encouraged. Only adverse variances should be investigated.

Task 23.2

Write a *short* memo to the production director. Your memo should:

    (a)   Sub-divide the material price variance calculated in Task 20.1 into that part caused by the change in the standard cost as measured by the material price index and that part caused by the efficiency or inefficiency of the purchasing department.
    (b)   Give THREE separate reasons why Zed production might result in a favourable material usage variance.
    (c)   *Briefly* discuss whether or not a favourable material usage variance should be investigated.

QUESTION 24 (June 2002)

Data

You are employed as a financial analyst at Drampton plc, a computer retailer. One of your duties is to prepare a standard costing reconciliation statement for the finance director.

KEY TECHNIQUES : **QUESTIONS**

The company sells two types of computer, desktop computers for individual use and mainframe computers for large organisations. Desktop computers are sold by advertising in newspapers. Customers telephone Drampton to place an order and the telephone call is answered by trained operators. Drampton pays the cost of the telephone call. The total standard cost of one telephone call is shown below.

STANDARD COST OF ONE CALL			
Expense	*Quantity*	*Cost*	*Cost per call*
Telephone cost	1 unit	£0.07 per unit	£0.07
Operators' wages	6 minutes	£3.50 per hour	£0.35
Fixed overheads[1]	6 minutes	£6.50 per hour	£0.65
Standard cost of one telephone call			£1.07

[1] Fixed overheads are based on budgeted operator hours.

Drampton's finance director gives you the following information for the three months ended 31 May 2002.

· Budgeted number of calls		900,000 calls
· Actual number of calls		1,000,000 calls
· Actual expenses	*Quantity*	*Cost*
Telephone cost	1,200,000 units	£79,200
Operators' wages	114,000 hours	£478,800
Fixed overheads		£540,400
Actual cost of actual operations		£1,098,400

Task

(a) Calculate the following information:
   (i)   Actual cost of a telephone unit.
   (ii) Actual hourly wage rate of operators.
   (iii) Standard number of operator hours for 1,000,000 calls.
   (iv) Budgeted cost of fixed overheads for the three months ended 31 May 2002.
   (v)   Budgeted number of operator hours for the three months ended 31 May 2002.
   (vi) Standard cost of actual operations.

(b) Using the data given and your answers to part (a), calculate the following variances:
   (i)   Price variance for telephone calls.
   (ii)   Usage variance for telephone calls.
   (iii) Labour rate variance for the telephone operators.
   (iv)   Labour efficiency variance for the telephone operators.
   (v)   Fixed overhead expenditure variance.
   (vi)   Fixed overhead volume variance.
   (vii) Fixed overhead capacity variance.
   (viii) Fixed overhead efficiency variance.

(c)   Prepare a statement for the three months ended 31 May 2002 reconciling the standard cost of actual operations to the actual cost of actual operations.

QUESTION 25 (December 2002)

Data

You are a newly appointed trainee accounting technician with Primary Chemicals plc. One of your responsibilities is to prepare and monitor standard costing variances for the distillation department. The distillation department prepares barrels of a refined chemical using a continuous process.

Fixed overheads are charged to production on the basis of machine hours. This is because the machine hours required determines the speed of production.

The budgeted and actual results of the distillation department for the week ended 30 November 2002 are shown below.

Distillation Department – Operating results – week ended 30 November 2002					
		Budget			*Actual*
Production		2,500 barrels			2,400 barrels
		Standard cost			*Actual cost*
Material	12,500 litres	£106,250	11,520	litres	£99,072
Labour	10,000 labour hrs	£60,000	10,080	labour hrs	£61,488
Fixed overheads	20,000 machine hrs	£200,000	18,960	machine hrs	£185,808
Total cost		£366,250			£346,368

Task 25.1

(a)   Calculate the following information:
   (i)   Standard price of material per litre.
   (ii)   Actual price of material per litre.
   (iii)   Standard litres of material per barrel.
   (iv)   Standard labour rate per hour.
   (v)   Standard labour hours per barrel.
   (vi)   Standard machine hours per barrel.
   (vii) Budgeted fixed overheads per budgeted machine hour.
   (viii) Standard absorption cost per barrel.

(b)   Using the data provided in the operating results and your answers to part (a), calculate the following variances:
   (i)   Material price variance.
   (ii)   Material usage variance.
   (iii)   Labour rate variance.
   (iv)   Labour efficiency variance.
   (v)   Fixed overhead expenditure variance.
   (vi)   Fixed overhead volume variance.
   (vii) Fixed overhead capacity variance.
   (viii) Fixed overhead efficiency variance.

(c)   Prepare a statement reconciling the standard absorption cost of actual operations to the actual absorption cost of actual operations.

Data

Anthony Bush is the Financial Controller of Primary Chemicals. Shortly after you prepare the reconciliation statement, he tells you how he calculates the material standard cost per litre.

·   He forecasts a trend price per litre for each of the four quarters of the year. He then divides the total by four. This forecast average trend price then becomes the standard cost per litre for the year.
·   He ignores seasonal variations in the price of materials.

Anthony tells you that he ignores the seasonal variations as, on average, they equal zero and that, by taking the average trend figure, the standard cost per litre is still accurate. He also tells you that production volume varies according to demand throughout the year.

The data used by Anthony for the year to 31 December 2002 is shown below.

	Quarter 1 1/1 – 31/3	Quarter 2 1/4 – 30/6	Quarter 3 1/7 – 30/9	Quarter 4 1/10 – 31/12
Forecast quarterly trend	£7.00	£8.00	£9.00	£10.00
Seasonal variations	– 10%	– 20%	+ 10%	+ 20%

Task 25.2

Write a memo to Anthony Bush. In your memo you should:
(a)   Briefly explain whether or not:
        (i)   his way of calculating the forecast average trend price produced a valid forecast of the average trend price for the year
        (ii)   it was valid to ignore seasonal variations when calculating variances.
(b)   Use the data provided to calculate a revised standard cost of material per litre for the week ended 30 November 2002.
(c)   Sub-divide the material price variance into that part due to the revised standard cost per litre being different from the original standard cost and that part due to other reasons.

QUESTION 26 (December 2003)

Data

You are an accounting technician employed by Garforth Cookridge and Co, a firm of accountants and registered auditors. A new client is Econair Ltd. Econair is a small airline that operates two routes from its home airport.

One of your tasks is to prepare standard costing variances for Econair. To help you, the airline provides you with the following information for the 28 days ended 30 November 2003 for the route between the home airport and Alpha City.

Budgeted and actual operating results 28 days ended 30 November 2003				
		Budget		*Actual*
Operating data				
Number of flights		168		160
Number of flying hours		672		768

Expenses	*Quantity*	£	*Quantity*	£
Fuel	33,600 gallons	50,400	38,400 gallons	61,440
Pilots' remuneration	1,344 pilot hours	67,200	1,536 pilot hours	79,872
Aircraft fixed overheads	672 flying hours	75,600	768 flying hours	76,200
Cost of operations		193,200		217,512

Other information

· Pilot hours are the same as labour hours for a manufacturer.
· Flying hours are the same as machine hours for a manufacturer.
· The number of flights is the same as production volume for a manufacturer.
· Fuel and pilots' remuneration are treated as variable costs.
· Fixed overheads are charged to operations on the basis of flying hours.

Task 26.1

(a)   Use the budgeted data to calculate the following information:
  (i)   Standard price of fuel per gallon.
  (ii)   Standard fuel usage for 160 flights.
  (iii)   Standard hourly rate for pilots.
  (iv)   Standard pilot hours per flight.
  (v)   Standard pilot hours for 160 flights.
  (vi)   Standard fixed overhead cost per budgeted flying hour.
  (vii)   Standard flying hours per flight.
  (viii)   Standard flying hours for 160 flights.
  (ix)   Standard fixed overhead absorbed by the 160 flights.
  (x)   Standard cost of actual operations.

(b)   Using the data given and your answers to part (a), calculate the following variances:
  (i)   Fuel price variance.
  (ii)   Fuel usage variance.
  (iii)   Pilots' labour rate variance.
  (iv)   Pilots' labour efficiency variance.
  (v)   Fixed overhead expenditure variance.
  (vi)   Fixed overhead volume variance.
  (vii)   Fixed overhead capacity variance.
  (viii)   Fixed overhead efficiency variance.

(c)   Prepare a statement for the 28 days ended 30 November 2003 reconciling the standard cost of actual operations to the actual cost of actual operations.

Data

The Chief Executive of Econair, Lisa Margoli, is given a copy of the standard costing reconciliation statement you prepared. Lisa tells you she is concerned about the fixed overhead variances and gives you the following information.

· **Flight and passenger data:** During the 28 days to 30 November 2003, the actual number of flights to Alpha City was 8 less than budgeted. Although the budget assumed 70 passengers per flight, the actual number of passengers per flight was 80.

· **Current policy for apportioning and charging fixed overheads:** The second route operated by Econair is from the home airport to another country, Betaland. Econair's current practice is to apportion budgeted and actual fixed overheads between the two routes based on the number of aircraft. The apportioned fixed overheads are then charged to operations using flying hours.

· **Budgeted operating data for the 28 days to 30 November 2003**

Route	Alpha City	Betaland	Total
Number of aircraft	2	4	6
Number of flights per 28 days	168	448	616
Number of flying hours per 28 days	672	2,240	2912
Insurance value of each aircraft	£10m	£20m	
Total aircraft insurance value per route	£20m	£80m	£100m

· **Analysis of total budgeted fixed overhead expenses for both routes for the 28 days to 30 November 2003**

Aircraft maintenance	£116,480
Insurance	£98,020
Luggage handling and in-flight facilities *	£12,300
Budgeted fixed overheads	£226,800

* Luggage handling and in-flight facilities only apply to the route to Betaland.

Budgeted fixed overhead per aircraft   (£226,800/6 aircraft)   £37,800

Budgeted fixed overheads apportioned to Alpha City route
                                             (£37,800 × 2 aircraft)   £75,600

Task 26.2

Write a memo to Lisa Margoli. In your memo you should:
(a)   identify a more appropriate method than flying hours for charging standard fixed overheads;
(b)   briefly explain why your chosen method for charging standard fixed overheads would give different fixed overhead capacity and efficiency variances to those calculated in Task 23.1;
(c)   use the analysis of budgeted fixed overhead expenses and the operating data to reallocate the budgeted fixed overheads apportioned to the Alpha City route.

QUESTION 27 (June 2004)

Data

Brown Ltd manufactures and sells office furniture. The company operates an integrated standard cost system in which:

·   purchases of materials are recorded at standard cost;
·   finished goods are recorded at standard cost;
·   direct materials and direct labour costs are both variable costs;
·   fixed production overheads are absorbed using direct labour hours.

You are an accounting technician at Brown Ltd. You report to Sam Thomas, the Finance Director.

The company's most popular product is an executive desk. Its standard cost is as follows:

Product: Executive desk

Inputs	Quantity	Unit price £	Total cost £
Direct materials	30 kgs	5.00	150.00
Direct labour	5 hours	6.00	30.00
Fixed production overheads	5 hours	4.00	20.00
Standard cost			200.00

Actual and budgeted data for the manufacture of executive desks for May 2004 are shown below:

·   27,500 kgs of direct materials were purchased for £143,000.
·   Issues from stores to production totalled 27,500 kgs.
·   The actual output for the month was 900 desks.
·   The budgeted output for the month was 1,000 desks.
·   4,200 direct labour hours were worked at a cost of £26,040.
·   Actual fixed production overheads were £23,000.

Task

(a)   Calculate the following information for May:
   (i)   Actual price of materials per kg.
   (ii)   Standard usage of materials for actual production.
   (iii) Actual labour rate per hour.
   (iv)   Standard labour hours for actual production.
   (v)   Budgeted production overheads.

(b)   Calculate the following variances for the production of executive desks for May:
   (i)   The material price variance.
   (ii)   The material usage variance.
   (iii) The labour rate variance.
   (iv)   The labour efficiency variance.
   (v)   The fixed overhead expenditure variance.

(vi)   The fixed overhead volume variance.

(vii) The fixed overhead capacity variance.

(viii) The fixed overhead efficiency variance.

(c)   Prepare an operating statement for May which reconciles the standard absorption cost of total actual production with the actual absorption cost of total actual production.

(d)   Write a memo for Sam Thomas to present to the Board of Directors. Your memo should comment on the usefulness, or otherwise, of the statement you have prepared in your answer to (c) above.

Chapter 7
Performance indicators

QUESTION 28

Having implemented a policy of TQM, management need to be aware of the costs of quality which include:
·   appraisal costs;
·   prevention costs;
·   internal failure costs;
·   external failure costs.

Task

Explain clearly the characteristics of each of the above categories. You may assume that you work as an accounting technician for a group of hotels, if you wish to give examples of costs that may be incurred.

QUESTION 29

Task

Distinguish between the terms 'cost reduction' and 'cost control', and outline the process of a cost reduction programme.

QUESTION 30

Task

Value analysis is a technique widely used in cost reduction programmes. Outline the process involved in this technique.

QUESTION 31

Stonehill Quarries Ltd
You work as an accounting technician for Moran and Geoff, a firm of licensed accounting technicians.

One of your clients, Stonehill Quarries Ltd, has experienced an increase in turnover but a downturn in their overall financial performance in recent times. The company is owner managed by Ernie Heyes and a small management team.

The following is a summary of the Quarrying Trade Association's performance for the sector as a whole for the year 20X3.

Performance indicators

Return on capital employed	24%
Asset turnover	1.6
Net profit before interest and tax to sales	15%
Current ratio	1.5 : 1
Liquidity ratio (acid test)	1.03 : 1
Debtors collection period	60 days
Creditors payment period	70 days
Finished goods stock in days	38 days
Labour costs as % of turnover	18.1%
Operating costs as % of turnover	85.01%
Distribution costs as % of turnover	9.5%
Administrative costs as % of turnover	4.5%
Value added per '£' of employee costs	£1.95

An extract from the company's financial statements for the years 20X2 and 20X3 shows the following:

Profit and loss accounts

	20X2 £m	20X3 £m
Turnover	5.38	6.68
*Operating costs	4.43	5.82
	0.95	0.86
Interest	0.08	0.08
	0.87	0.78
Taxation	0.30	0.27
Profit after tax	0.57	0.51
Dividends	0.16	0.16
Retained profit	0.41	0.35

*Operating costs comprise:

	£m	£m
Wages, salaries and other employee costs	0.98	1.25
Bought in materials and services	3.21	4.32
Depreciation	0.24	0.25
	4.43	5.82

Operating costs include the following:

	£m	£m
Distribution	0.49	0.61
Administration	0.22	0.27

Balance sheets

		20X2	20X3
		£m	£m
Fixed assets		3.77	3.88
Current assets:			
Stocks	Raw materials	0.12	0.15
	Finished goods	0.43	0.45
Debtors		0.88	1.19
Bank		0.04	0.05
		1.47	1.84
Less current liabilities:			
Creditors		0.66	0.82
Taxation		0.30	0.27
Dividends		0.16	0.16
		1.12	1.25
Net current assets		0.35	0.59
Total assets less current liabilities		4.12	4.47
Less liabilities due after one year:			
Debentures		1.00	1.00
		3.12	3.47
Financed by:			
Capital and reserves		3.12	3.47

Task

(a) Calculate the ratios listed in the trade association statistics for Stonehill Quarries based on the accounts for the years 20X2 and 20X3.

(b) Comment on the performance of Stonehill Quarries compared with the sector as a whole.

QUESTION 32

Task

(a) Define the term 'value added'.

(b) From the following information, draft the value added statement for the years 20X2 and 20X3.

Sandsend Engineering Ltd
Extract from profit and loss accounts for the years ended 31 December 20X2 and 20X3

	20X2	20X3
	£m	£m
Turnover	6.1	6.5
*Costs	4.2	4.5
Profit before interest and tax	1.9	2.0
Interest	0.6	0.6
	1.3	1.4
Taxation	0.3	0.3
	1.0	1.1
Dividends	0.2	0.2
Retained profit	0.8	0.9

*Costs comprise:

	£m	£m
Wages and salaries	1.8	1.9
Depreciation	0.4	0.5
Other bought in items	2.0	2.1

(c) Calculate for both years the value added per '£' of employee costs, and state why this measure is considered an indicator of labour productivity.

(d) Outline at least two other measures of labour productivity.

QUESTION 33

Kaplan and Norton's concept of the 'balanced scorecard' is a way of viewing performance from four perspectives, namely:
· the financial perspective;
· the customer perspective;
· the internal perspective;
· the innovation and learning perspective.

Task

(a) Explain what is meant by each of these perspectives.

(b) You work as an accounting technician in the business planning unit of a large company which has a number of subsidiaries. You use the balanced scorecard concept in appraising performance.

The following information relates to subsidiary A for the year ended 31 December 20X3.

	£m
Turnover	6.85
Cost of sales	5.71
Operating profit	1.14
Number of employees	75

Cost of sales includes training costs of £40,000 and quality assurance costs of £350,000. Assets employed by the subsidiary total £6.30m.

Analysis of turnover by products:

	£m
Existing products	4.85
New products	2.00

Analysis of turnover by customer:

	£m
Existing established customers	4.90
New customers	1.95

Identify a performance indicator for each of the four perspectives for subsidiary A for the year ended 31 December 20X3.

QUESTION 34 (June 2001)

Data

Smithex Ltd makes a single product, the Alpha, which is sold directly to domestic customers. Smithex is able to sell as many Alphas as it can produce.

Each Alpha contains a specialist part, the A10, which is in short supply. Smithex operates a just-in-time stock policy for the other material plus bought in services but not for the A10.

Smithex does not offer credit facilities to customers or hold any stock of Alphas.

The internal accounts of Smithex for the year to 31 May 2001 are shown below.

OPERATING STATEMENT FOR THE YEAR ENDED 31 MAY 2001

	Units	£	£
Turnover			6,480,000
Purchases A10	12,000	1,200,000	
Less returns	1,200	120,000	
Net purchases	10,800	1,080,000	
Add opening stocks	1,200	120,000	
Less closing stocks	(1,200)	(120,000)	
A10 issued to production	10,800	1,080,000	
Other material plus bought in services		108,000	
Production wages		1,296,000	
Variable cost of production and sales			2,484,000
Contribution			3,996,000
Production overhead		3,024,000	
Inspection cost of A10 goods received		69,600	
Cost of A10 returns		48,000	
Cost of remedial work		120,000	
Customer support for faulty products		194,400	
Administrative and distribution expenses		216,000	
Total fixed overheads			3,672,000
Net operating profit			324,000

BALANCE SHEET AT 31 MAY 2001

	£	£
Net fixed assets		1,600,000
Stock	120,000	
Cash	80,000	
Creditors	(180,000)	
Net current assets		20,000
Net assets		1,620,000
Financed by:		
Shareholders' funds		800,000
Loans		820,000
		1,620,000

Other data

- Number of production employees — 140
- Maximum production capacity per year — 12,000
- Closing stock only consists of units of A10
- Creditors only arise from purchases of A10

You are employed by Smithex as its management accountant. One of your duties is to prepare management accounting information for Janet Noble, the Managing Director of Smithex.

Task 34.1

Janet Noble asks you to prepare the following performance indicators for Smithex:
(a) Sales (or net profit) margin.
(b) Return on capital employed.
(c) Asset turnover.
(d) Average age of stock in months.
(e) Average age of creditors in months.
(f) Added value per production employee.
(g) Wages per production employee.
(h) Capacity ratio (defined as actual production as a percentage of maximum production).
(i) Contribution per Alpha.

Data

At a board meeting to consider the performance indicators, the directors express concern about the high *cost of quality*. This is defined as the total of all costs incurred in preventing faults plus those costs involved in correcting faults once they have occurred. It is a single figure measuring all the explicit costs of quality – that is, those costs collected within the accounting system.

The directors have also asked the supplier of the A10 to implement a Total Quality Management (TQM) programme to avoid faulty units of A10 being purchased and to also operate a Just-in-Time (JIT) policy to eliminate the need for Smithex to carry stocks.

Janet Noble tells you that:

· All costs making up the cost of quality are caused by the faulty units of A10.
· The supplier would agree to the TQM and JIT proposals but:
  - the cost per A10 would increase by £10;
  - supplies of the A10 would be limited to the 12,000 currently provided but each A10 would be guaranteed fault-free;
  - supplies of the A10 would have to be paid for in the month received and no credit would be allowed.
· Smithex's cost of quality would be saved and stocks eliminated if the supplier implemented the TQM and JIT proposals.
· Smithex would want to keep its cash balance at £80,000.
· Any surplus cash arising from the proposals would be used to reduce the £820,000 of loans.

Janet Noble is interested in knowing what the results of Smithex would have been if the TQM and JIT proposals had been applied to the results for the year ended 31 May 2001.

Task 34.2

Janet Noble asks you to calculate the following:
(a) Cost of quality for Smithex Ltd.
(b) Revised operating profit if the supplier's conditions were accepted.
(c) Increase in cash balance before reducing the amount of the loans.
(d) Revised capital employed if there were no stocks or creditors and if any surplus cash had been used to reduce the amount of the loans.
(e) Revised return on capital employed.

QUESTION 35 (December 2000)

Data

Travel Bus Ltd is a company owned by Travel Holdings plc. It operates in the town of Camford. Camford is an old town with few parking facilities for motorists. Several years ago the Town Council built a car park on the edge of the town and awarded Travel Bus the contract to carry motorists and their passengers between the car park and the centre of the town.

Originally, the Council charged motorists £4.00 per day for the use of the car park but, to encourage motorists not to take their cars into the town centre, parking has been free since 1 December 1999.

The journey between the car park and the town centre is the only service operated by Travel Bus Ltd in Camford. A summary of the results for the first two years of operations, together with the net assets associated with the route and other operating data, is reproduced below.

Operating statement year ended 30 November			Extract from balance sheet at 30 November		
	1999	*2000*		*1999*	*2000*
	£	£		£	£
Turnover	432,000	633,600	Buses	240,000	240,000
Fuel	129,600	185,328	Accumulated depreciation	168,000	180,000
Wages	112,000	142,000	Net book value	72,000	60,000
Other variable costs	86,720	84,512	Net current assets	14,400	35,040
Gross profit	103,680	221,760		86,400	95,040
Bus road tax and insurance	22,000	24,000			
Depreciation of buses	12,000	12,000			
Maintenance of buses	32,400	28,512			
Fixed garaging costs	29,840	32,140			
Administration	42,000	49,076			
Net profit/(loss)	(34,560)	76,032			

Other operating data	*1999*	*2000*
Fare per passenger per journey	£0.80	£1.00
Miles per year	324,000	356,400
Miles per journey	18.0	18.0
Days per year	360	360
Wages per driver	£14,000	£14,200

Throughout the two years the drivers were paid a basic wage per week, no bonuses were paid and no overtime was incurred.

In two weeks there will be a meeting between officials of the Town Council and the Chief Executive of Travel Holdings to discuss the performance of Travel Bus for the year to 30 November 2000. The previous year's performance indicators were as follows:

Gross profit margin	24%
Net profit margin	–8%
Return on capital employed	–40%
Asset turnover	5 times
Number of passengers in the year	540,000
Total cost per mile	£1.44
Number of journeys per day	50
Maintenance cost per mile	£0.10
Passengers per day	1,500
Passengers per journey	30
Number of drivers	8

Task 35.1

In preparation for the meeting, you have been asked to calculate the following performance indicators for the year to 30 November 2000:
(a) Gross profit margin.
(b) Net profit margin.
(c) Return on capital employed.
(d) Asset turnover.
(e) Number of passengers in the year.
(f) Total cost per mile.
(g) Number of journeys per day.
(h) Maintenance cost per mile.
(i) Passengers per day.
(j) Passengers per journey.
(k) Number of drivers.

Data

On receiving your performance indicators, the Chief Executive of Travel Holdings raises the following issues with you:
·   The drivers are claiming that the improved profitability of Travel Bus reflects their increased productivity.
·   The managers believe that the change in performance is due to improved motivation arising from the introduction of performance related pay for managers during the year to 30 November 2000.
·   The officials from the Town Council are concerned that Travel Bus is paying insufficient attention to satisfying passenger needs and safety.

The Chief Executive asks for your advice.

Task 35.2

Write a memo to the Chief Executive of Travel Holdings plc. Where relevant, you should make use of the data and answers to Task 32.1 to:
(a) *Briefly* discuss whether or not increased productivity always leads to increased profitability.
(b) Develop ONE possible measure of driver productivity and suggest whether or not the drivers' claim is valid.

(c) Suggest ONE reason, other than improved motivation, why the profitability of Travel Bus might have improved.

(d) Suggest:
  (i) ONE *existing* performance indicator which might measure the satisfaction of passenger needs; and
  (ii) ONE other possible performance indicator of passenger needs which cannot be measured from the existing performance data collected by Travel Bus.

(e) Suggest:
  (i) ONE *existing* performance indicator which might measure the safety aspect of Travel Bus's operations; and
  (ii) ONE other possible safety performance indicator which cannot be measured from the existing performance data collected by Travel Bus.

QUESTION 36 (June 2000)

Data

LandAir and SeaAir are two small airlines operating flights to Waltonville. LandAir operates from an airport based at a town on the same island as Waltonville but SeaAir operates from an airport based on another island. In both cases, the flight to Waltonville is 150 air-miles. Each airline owns a single aircraft, an 80-seat commuter jet and both airlines operate flights for 360 days per year.

You are employed as the management accountant at SeaAir and report to Carol Jones, SeaAir's chief executive. Recently both airlines agreed to share each other's financial and operating data as a way of improving efficiency. The data for the year to 31 May 2000 for both airlines is reproduced below. The performance indicators for LandAir are reproduced further below.

Operating statement year ended 31 May 2000

	LandAir $000	SeaAir $000
Revenue	51,840	29,700
Fuel and aircraft maintenance	29,160	14,580
Take-off and landing fees at Waltonville	4,320	2,160
Aircraft parking at Waltonville	720	2,880
Depreciation of aircraft	500	400
Salaries of flight crew	380	380
Home airport costs	15,464	8,112
Net profit	1,296	1,188

Extract from balance sheet at 31 May 2000

	LandAir	SeaAir
	$000	$000
Fixed assets		
Aircraft	10,000	10,000
Accumulated depreciation	2,500	4,000
Net book value	7,500	6,000
Net current assets	3,300	5,880
	10,800	11,880

Other operating data

	LandAir	SeaAir
Number of seats on aircraft	80	80
Return flights per day	12	6
Return fare	$200	$275
Air-miles per return flight	300	300

Performance indicators

	LandAir
Return on capital employed	12.00%
Asset turnover per year	4.80
Sales (or net profit) margin	2.50%
Actual number of return flights per year	4,320
Actual number of return passengers per year	259,200
Average seat occupancy[1]	75.00%
Actual number of passenger-miles[2]	77,760,000
Cost per passenger mile	$0.65

Notes:

[1] Actual number of return passengers ÷ maximum possible number of return passengers from existing flights.

[2] Actual number of passengers carried × number of miles flown.

Task 36.1

Carol Jones asks you to prepare the following performance indicators for SeaAir:
(a) Return on capital employed.
(b) Asset turnover.
(c) Sales (or net profit) margin.
(d) Actual number of return flights per year.
(e) Actual number of return passengers per year.
(f) Average seat occupancy.
(g) Actual number of passenger-miles.
(h) Cost per passenger mile.

Data

Carol Jones is concerned that the overall performance of SeaAir is below that of LandAir, despite both airlines operating to the same destination and over a similar distance. She finds it all the more difficult to understand as LandAir has

to compete with road and rail transport. Carol Jones has recently attended a seminar on maintaining competitive advantage and is eager to apply the concepts to SeaAir. She explains that there are two ways to gain a competitive advantage:
· by being the lowest cost business; or
· by having a unique aspect to the product or service allowing a higher price to be charged.

This involves managers attempting to eliminate costs which do not enhance value, that is, costs for which customers are not prepared to pay either in the form of a higher price or increased demand.

She makes the following proposals for next year, the year ending 31 May 2001:
· The number of return flights is increased to 9 per day.
· The estimated average seat occupancy will change to 55%.
· The price of a return fare will remain the same.

As a result of the proposals, there will be some changes in operating costs:
· Fuel and aircraft maintenance, and take-off and landing fees at Waltonville airport, will increase in proportion with the increase in flights.
· Aircraft parking at Waltonville will be halved.
· Aircraft depreciation will increase to $600,000 for the forthcoming year.
· Additional flight crew will cost an extra $58,000.
· There will be no other changes in costs.

Task 36.2

Carol Jones is interested in forecasting the performance of SeaAir for next year, the year to 31 May 2001. Write a memo to Carol Jones. In your memo you should:
(a) Calculate the forecast number of passengers next year for SeaAir.
(b) Calculate SeaAir's forecast net profit for next year.
(c) Show SeaAir's forecast return on capital employed for next year assuming no change in its net assets other than any additional depreciation.
(d) Identify ONE competitive advantage SeaAir has over LandAir.
(e) Identify ONE expense in SeaAir's operating statement which does not add value.

QUESTION 37 (December 1999)

Data

You are employed as a financial analyst with Denton Management Consultants and report to James Alexander, a local partner. Denton Management Consultants has recently been awarded the contract to implement accrual accounting in the St Nicolas Police Force and will shortly have to make a presentation to the Head of the Police Force. The presentation is concerned with showing how performance indicators are developed in 'for profit' organisations and how these can be adapted to help 'not for profit' organisations.

James Alexander has asked for your help in preparing a draft of the presentation that Denton Management Consultants will make to the Head of the Police

Force. He suggests that a useful framework would be the balanced scorecard and examples of how this is used by private sector organisations.

The balanced scorecard views performance measurement in a 'for profit' organisation from four perspectives.

The financial perspective
This is concerned with satisfying shareholders and measures used include the return on capital employed and the sales margin.

The customer perspective
This attempts to measure how customers view the organisation and how they measure customer satisfaction. Examples include the speed of delivery and customer loyalty.

The internal perspective
This measures the quality of the organisation's output in terms of technical excellence and consumer needs. Examples include unit cost and total quality measurement.

The innovation and learning perspective
This emphasises the need for continual improvement of existing products and the ability to develop new products to meet customers' changing needs. In a 'for profit' organisation, this might be measured by the percentage of turnover attributable to new products.

To help you demonstrate how performance indicators are developed in 'for profit' organisations, he gives you the following financial data relating to a manufacturing client of Denton Management Consultants.

Profit and loss account 12 months ended 30 November 1999	£000	£000
Turnover		240.0
Material	18.0	
Labour	26.0	
Production overheads	9.0	
Cost of production	53.0	
Opening finished stock	12.0	
Closing finished stock	(13.0)	
Cost of sales		52.0
Gross profit		188.0
Research & development	15.9	
Training	5.2	
Administration	118.9	
		140.0
Net profit		48.0

Extract from balance sheet at 30 November 1999	Opening balance £000	Additions £000	Deletions £000	Closing balance £000
Fixed assets				
Cost	200.0	40.0	10.0	230.0
Dep'n	80.0	8.0	8.0	80.0
Net book value				150.0
Net current assets				
Stock of finished goods				13.0
Debtors				40.0
Cash				6.0
Creditors				(9.0)
				50.0
Net assets				200.0

Task 37.1

James Alexander asks you to calculate the following performance indicators and, for each indicator, to identify ONE balanced scorecard perspective being measured:
(a)   The return on capital employed.
(b)   The sales margin (or net profit) percentage.
(c)   The asset turnover.
(d)   Research and development as a percentage of production.
(e)   Training as a percentage of labour cost.
(f)   Average age of finished stock in months.

Data

On receiving your calculations, James Alexander tells you that he has recently received details of the current performance measures used by the St Nicolas Police Force. Four indicators are used:
· the percentage of cash expenditure to allocated funds for the year;
· the average police hours spent per crime investigated;
· the average police hours spent per crime solved;
· the clear-up rate (defined as number of crimes solved ÷ number of crimes investigated).

He also provides you with data for the current year used in developing the current indicators as follows:

· Funds allocated for the year:	$3,000,000
· Cash expenditure during the year:	$2,910,000
· Number of reported crimes in the last year:	8,000 crimes
· Number of crimes investigated in the year:	5,000 crimes
· Number of crimes solved in the year:	2,000 crimes
· Number of police hours spent on investigating and solving crimes:	40,000 hours
· Number of police hours spent on crime prevention:	500 hours

Task 37.2

James Alexander asks you to prepare short notes for him. Your notes should:
(a)   Calculate the four indicators currently used by the St Nicolas Police Force.
(b)   Identify ONE limitation in the calculation of the clear-up rate.
(c)   Briefly suggest:
(i)   ONE reason why the percentage of cash expenditure to allocated funds may be an inadequate measure of the financial perspective.
(ii)   ONE reason why the clear-up rate might be an inadequate measure of the customer perspective other than because of the limitation identified in part (b).
(iii)   ONE reason why the hours spent per crime investigated might be an inadequate measure of the internal perspective.
(iv)   ONE measure which might focus on the innovation and learning perspective.

QUESTION 38 (June 1999)

Data

You are employed by ALV Ltd as an accounting technician. Two companies owned by ALV Ltd are ALV (East) Ltd and ALV (West) Ltd. These two companies are located in the same town and make an identical electrical product which sells for £84.

Financial data relating to the two companies is reproduced below. In addition, performance indicators for ALV (East) Ltd are also enclosed. Both companies use the same straight-line depreciation policy and assume no residual value.

ALV (East) Ltd					
Extract from balance sheet at 31 May 1999				**Income statement - year to 31 May 1999**	
	Cost	Accumulated depreciation	Net book value		
	£000	£000	£000		£000
Fixed assets				Turnover	840
Buildings	1,000	700	300	Material and	
Plant & machinery	300	240	60	bought-in services	340
	1,300	940	360	Production labour	180
				Other production expenses	52
Net current assets				Depreciation – buildings	20
Stock		45		Dep'n – plant and machinery	30
Debtors		30		Admin and other expenses	50
Cash		5		Operating profit	168
Creditors		(40)	40		
			400		
Other data					
Number of employees		18		Units produced	10,000
Performance indicatorsfor ALV (East) Ltd					
Asset turnover		2.1 times		Production labour cost per unit	£18.00
Net profit margin		20.00%		Output per employee	556
Return on capital employed		42.00%		Added value per employee	£27,778
Wages per employee		£10,000		Profit per employee	£9,333

ALV (West) Ltd					
Extract from balance sheet at 31 May 1999				**Income statement – year to 31 May 1999**	
	Cost	Accumulated depreciation	Net book value		£000
	£000	£000	£000		
Fixed assets				Turnover	2,520
Buildings	1,500	120	1,380	Material and bought-in services	1,020
Plant & machinery	900	180	720	Production labour	260
	2,400	300	2,100	Other production expenses	630
Net current assets				Depreciation – buildings	30
Stock		20		Dep'n – plant and machinery	90
Debtors		30		Admin and other expenses	112
Cash		5		Operating profit	378
Creditors		(55)	Nil		
			2,100		
Other data					
Number of employees		20		Units produced	30,000

ALV Ltd is considering closing one of the companies over the next two years. As a first step, the board of directors wish to hold a meeting to consider which is the more efficient and productive company.

Task 38.1

In preparation for the board meeting, calculate the following performance indicators for ALV (West) Ltd:
(a)   Asset turnover.
(b)   Net profit margin.
(c)   Return on capital employed.
(d)   Wages per employee.
(e)   Production labour cost per unit.
(f)   Output per employee.
(g)   Added value per employee.
(h)   Profit per employee.

Data

Shortly after preparing the performance indicators for ALV (West) Ltd, the chief executive of ALV Ltd, Jill Morgan, issued a statement to a local newspaper. In that statement she said that the workforce at ALV (East) was far less productive than at the other company despite both companies making an identical product. She concluded that it was up to the workforce to improve productivity. In response, the employees stated that the normal way of measuring efficiency is profit and, therefore, ALV (East) was more efficient than ALV (West).

Jill Morgan asks you to prepare a report for the next board meeting to explain the issues involved so that all board members can be properly briefed.

Task 38.2

Write a report to Jill Morgan for distribution to the board of directors. Your report should:
(a)   Explain what is meant by:
    (i)   productivity;
    (ii)   efficiency.
(b)   Identify the best TWO performance indicators used by ALV to measure efficiency and use those indicators to identify which of the two companies is the more efficient.
(c)   Identify the best TWO performance measures used by ALV to measure productivity and use those indicators to identify which of the two companies has the higher productivity.
(d)   Use the NET FIXED ASSETS to derive a different measure of productivity for both companies.
(e)   Use the data in Task 35.1 and your answer to Task 35.2 (d) to explain ONE reason why the productivity and efficiency measures might give different rankings.

QUESTION 39 (December 1999)

Data

On completing the budget for quarter 1, the production director of Northern Products Ltd tells you that the company is likely to introduce a third product, the Zed, in the near future. Because of this, he suggests that future budgets should be prepared using a spreadsheet. He explains that the use of spreadsheets to prepare budgets not only saves time but also provides flexibility by allowing the results of changes in the budget to be readily shown. The sales director is not convinced.

The production director suggests you demonstrate the advantages of budgets prepared on spreadsheets by using a template of a spreadsheet and sales data for the planned third product.

He gives you the following sales data he has received from the sales director:
·   estimated annual volume for Zed: 20,000 units – sales are spread evenly over the year.
·   planned unit selling price: £90.00;
·   seasonal variations:

Quarter	Seasonal variation percentage change
1	+ 20%
2	+ 30%
3	– 10%
4	– 40%

Task

(a) Calculate the budgeted volume of Zed for each quarter.

(b) Using the information provided by the sales director and a copy of the suggested spreadsheet template reproduced below, express the data provided by the sales director as formulae which would enable revised sales budgets to be calculated with the minimum of effort if sales price and annual volume were to change. (You may amend the template if desired to suit any spreadsheet with which you are familiar.)

A	B	C	D	E	F
1	Unit selling price	£90			
2	Annual volume (units)	20,000			
3	Seasonal variations	20%	30%	– 10%	– 40%
4		Quarter 1	Quarter 2	Quarter 3	Quarter 4
5	Seasonal variations (units)				
6	Quarterly volume				
7	Quarterly turnover				

QUESTION 40 (June 2002)

Data

Drampton plc is considering purchasing Hand Power Systems Ltd. Hand Power Systems makes a hand-held computer and has provided Drampton with its latest operating statement and balance sheet. These are shown below together with details of the orders received during the year and information about the sales returns.

Hand Power Systems Ltd: Operating statement for the year ended 31 May 2002

	Volume	£000	£000
Gross sales	21,000		6,300
Less sales returns	1,000		300
Turnover	20,000		6,000
Material		3,360	
Labour		960	
Production fixed overheads		480	
Cost of production	24,000	4,800	
Add opening finished stock	1,000	300	
Less closing finished stock	(5,000)	(1,350)	
Cost of sales	20,000		3,750
Gross profit			2,250
Research and development		768	
Training		576	
Customer support		240	
Marketing		200	
Administration		226	2,010
Net operating profit			240

Extract from balance sheet at 31 May 2002

	£000	£000
Fixed assets		
Machinery and equipment		
Cost		5,000
Accumulated depreciation		4,000
Net book value		1,000
Net current assets		
Stock of finished goods	1,350	
Debtors	1,500	
Cash	(426)	
Creditors	(424)	2,000
Net assets		3,000

Additional information

· Orders for 26,000 hand-held computers were received during the year ended 31 May 2002.

· Sales returns represent hand-held computers found to be faulty by customers. Customers had these replaced by fault-free computers.

Task 40.1

Prepare the following performance indicators for Drampton's finance director:

(a) Gross profit margin.

(b) Net profit (or sales) margin.

(c) Return on capital employed.

(d) Asset turnover.

(e) Average age of debtors in months.

(f) Research and development as a percentage of the cost of production.

(g) Training as a percentage of the cost of production.

(h) Customer support as a percentage of turnover.

(i) Returns as a percentage of turnover.

(j) Average delay in months between placing an order and receiving a fault-free, hand-held computer.

Data

The finance director believes that a balanced scorecard will help in the analysis of Hand Power Systems' performance and gives you the following information.

The balanced scorecard views performance measurement from four perspectives:
- the financial perspective: this is concerned with satisfying shareholders and measures used include the return on capital employed;
- the customer perspective: this attempts to measure how customers view the organisation and with measuring customer satisfaction. Examples include the speed of delivery and customer loyalty;
- the internal perspective: this measures the quality of the organisation's output in terms of technical excellence and consumer needs. Examples include unit cost and total quality measurement;
- the innovation and learning perspective: this emphasises the need for continual improvement of existing products and developing new products to meet customers' changing needs. In a 'for profit' organisation, this might be measured by the percentage of turnover attributable to new products.

Task 40.2

Name ONE balanced scorecard perspective being measured for each of the performance indicators in Task 40.1.

Data

The finance director gives you the following additional information relating to Hand Power Systems for the year to 31 May 2003.

Accounting policies

- Stocks: the closing stock of finished goods is valued on a last-in, first-out basis and material prices have been falling throughout the year ended 31 May 2002.

  There are no raw material or work in progress stocks at any time.

- Depreciation: this is calculated on a straight-line basis assuming no residual value.

  The depreciation charge for the year was £1,000,000.

  Similar fixed assets in other companies have an average life of 10 years.

Other information

	Selling prices	Material costs	Sales volume
Indices for this year and next year			
Index year ended 31 May 2002	120	175	100
Forecast index year ended 31 May 2003	100	140	130

- Total quality management will be introduced. As a result, there will no longer be any sales returns.

· The hand-held computers will be made to order and so there will be no closing stocks.
· As a result of this year's research and development, new machinery and equipment will be introduced from 1 June 2002. This will result in a 25% saving in the labour cost per hand-held computer.
· The new machinery and equipment will also result in savings of £160,000 in the production fixed overheads.

Task 40.3

Write a memo to the finance director. In your memo you should:
(a) briefly state and explain the effect of the following accounting policies on Hand Power Systems' profit for the year ended 31 May 2002:
　　(i)　stock valuation
　　(ii)　depreciation

(b) calculate the following FORECAST data for the year ending 31 May 2003:
　　(i)　Selling price per hand-held computer.
　　(ii)　Sales volume.
　　(iii)　Sales turnover.
　　(iv)　Material cost per hand-held computer.
　　(v)　Labour cost per hand-held computer.
　　(vi)　Production volume.
　　(vii)　Cost of production.
　　(viii)　Cost of sales.
　　(ix)　Gross profit.

QUESTION 41 (December 2002)

Data

You are the Management Accountant of Care4, a registered charity. You report to Carol Jones, the Chief Executive. Care4 owns Highstone School, a residential school for children with special needs. One of your duties is to prepare performance indicators for Highstone School. The accounts for the year to 31 August 2002 are shown below.

Operating statement – year to 31 August 2002		
	£	£
Fee income		1,760,000
Teacher salaries	600,000	
Nursing and support staff salaries	480,000	
Administrative expenses	120,000	
Power	128,000	
Housekeeping	160,000	
Depreciation	236,800	
Total expenses		1,724,800
Operating surplus		35,200

Balance sheet extract at 31 August 2002			
	Land	Buildings and equipment	Total
	£	£	£
Fixed assets			
Cost	4,502,800	11,840,000	16,342,800
Depreciation to date		9,708,800	9,708,800
Net book value	4,502,800	2,131,200	6,634,000
Net current assets			
Debtors	440,000		
Cash	62,000		
Creditors	(96,000)		406,000
Net assets			7,040,000

Local authorities refer children with special needs to the school and pay the school fees. There is a standard contract that states the number of children per teacher and the number of nursing and support staff required.

You are provided with the following additional information:

· The school fee per child for the year ended 31 August 2002 was £22,000.
· The contracts state there must be:
  – one teacher for every four children (The average salary per teacher is £30,000;)
  – one member of the nursing and support staff for every two children. (The average salary per member of the nursing and support staff is £12,000).
· The school can accommodate a maximum of 100 children.
· The buildings and equipment are depreciated by equal amounts each year and are assumed to have no residual value.
· Creditors entirely relate to power and housekeeping.

Task 41.1

Prepare the following school performance indicators for Carol Jones:
(a)   Operating surplus as a percentage of fee income.
(b)   Return on net assets.
(c)   Average age of debtors in months.
(d)   Average age of creditors in months.
(e)   Number of children in the school.
(f)   Occupancy rate of the school.
(g)   Number of teachers in the school.
(h)   Number of nursing and support staff in the school.
(i)   Total of cash-based expenses.
(j)   Number of months that cash-based expenses could be paid from the cash balance.

Data

On receiving your performance indicators, Carol Jones tells you she is worried about the financial viability of the school. Some creditors are objecting to the late payment of their invoices and the cash balance is insufficient to pay expenses when due. She also tells you that the school wants to purchase new equipment costing £400,000 in September 2003.

Carol Jones feels that the productivity and efficiency of the school must be improved and sets the following targets for the year to 31 August 2003:
· Operating surplus as a percentage of fee income should double.
· Return on net assets should double.
· The school should generate sufficient cash to be able to:
  – pay for the new equipment; and
  – have a cash balance equivalent to one month's cash-based expenses.

She proposes the following action plan for the year to 31 August 2003.

> **Action plan – year to 31 August 2003**
> · The number of children will increase by 10%.
> · The school fee per child will not change.
> · The number of teachers and the number of nursing and support staff will increase according to the contract.
> · There will be no change in the average salaries of either teachers or nursing and support staff.
> · No other expenses will change.
> · Debtors will only be allowed 1½ months to pay.
> · The average age of creditors will be 2 months.
> · There will be no additional funding by Care4 nor will the school make any payments to Care4.

Task 41.2

Prepare the following forecast information for the year to 31 August 2003 using the assumptions of the action plan and before the purchase of the new equipment:
(a)   Operating statement.
(b)   Year end debtors.
(c)   Year end creditors.
(d)   Year end net book value of fixed assets.
(e)   Year end cash balance.
(f)   Year end net assets.

Task 41.3

Write a memo to Carol Jones. In your memo you should:
(a)   Calculate the following forecast information for the year ended 31 August 2003:
  (i)   operating surplus as a percentage of fee income;
  (ii)   return on net assets;
  (iii)   cash available after allowing for buying the new equipment;
  (iv)   number of months that cash-based expenses could be paid from the cash balance after allowing for buying the new equipment.
(b)   State if the action plan achieves all of the proposed targets.
(c)   Explain the difference between productivity and efficiency.
(d)   Give ONE example of increased productivity as a result of implementing the action plan.

QUESTION 42 (December 2003)

Data

You are employed as an accounting technician by Aspex Technologies Ltd. One of your duties is to prepare performance indicators and other information for Stuart Morgan, the Financial Director.

Aspex Technologies make a single product, the Zeta. In the year to 30 November 2003, the company has had problems with the quality of the material used to make Zetas and Stuart would like to know what the cost of quality has been for the year.

The cost of quality is defined as the total of all costs incurred in preventing faults plus those costs involved in correcting faults once they have occurred. It is a single figure measuring all the explicit costs of quality – that is, those costs collected within the accounting system.

Stuart provides you with the following financial statements and data.

Operating statement – year ended 30 November 2003			
	Units	£000	£000
Turnover	360,000		14,400
Purchases	400,000	6,400	
Less returns	(40,000)	(640)	
Net purchases	360,000	5,760	
Add opening stocks	90,000	1,440	
Less closing stocks	(90,000)	(1,440)	
Material issued to production	360,000	5,760	
Production labour		3,600	
Variable cost of production and sales			9,360
Contribution			5,040
Heat, light and power		720	
Depreciation		1,000	
Inspection cost		80	
Production overhead		2,000	
Reworking of faulty production		40	
Customer support		200	
Marketing and administrative expenses		424	
Total fixed overheads			4,464
Operating profit			576

Balance sheet at 30 November 2003

	£000	£000
Fixed assets at cost		8,000
Cumulative depreciation		2,000
Net book value		6,000
Stock of materials	1,440	
Debtors	2,400	
Cash	960	
Creditors	(1,200)	
Net current assets		3,600
		9,600
Financed by		
Debt		6,000
Equity		3,600
		9,600

- The number of production employees in the company is 180.
- Production labour is a variable expense.
- The demand for Zetas in the year to 30 November 2003 was 390,000 but not all could be produced and sold due to poor quality materials. Any orders not completed this year can be completed next year.
- The only reason for the reworking of faulty production and customer support expenses was the poor quality of the materials.
- Material and heat, light and power are the only bought-in expenses.
- Creditors relate entirely to material purchases.
- There are no stocks of finished goods or work in progress.
- Depreciation is based on the straight-line method.

Task 42.1

Prepare the following information for Stuart Morgan:
(a)   Selling price per Zeta.
(b)   Material cost per Zeta.
(c)   Labour cost per Zeta.
(d)   Contribution per Zeta.
(e)   Contribution percentage.
(f)   Net profit (or sales) margin.
(g)   Return on capital employed.
(h)   Asset turnover.
(i)   Average age of debtors in months.
(j)   Average age of stock in months.
(k)   Average age of creditors in months
(l)   Added value per employee.
(m)   Average delay in completing an order in months.
(n)   Cost of quality.

Data

Stuart Morgan tells you that the Directors of Aspex Technologies have agreed an action plan for the year to 30 November 2004. The plan involves:

- using market research to forecast likely sales volume and prices;
- implementing total quality management and just-in-time stock control;
- greater working capital control.

Stuart provides you with the following information.

Market research
- Indices for this year and next year

	Selling Price Index	Sales Volume Index
Indices for year ended 30 November 2003	180	70
Forecast indices for year ending 30 November 2004	171	84

- The total forecast sales volume for the year ending 30 November 2004 is made up of two elements:
  - a revised volume from applying the sales volume indices to the 360,000 Zetas sold in the year to 30 November 2003;
  - an additional volume from completing orders placed in the year to 30 November 2003 but not made in that year because of the poor quality materials.
- The forecast selling price applies to the total forecast sales volume using the selling price indices.

Total quality management and just-in-time stock control
- The material supplier has agreed to take back the existing closing stock and replace it with fault-free materials.
- The supplier has also agreed to guarantee all material will be fault-free next year and improve the speed and reliability of deliveries. In exchange, Aspex has agreed that the unit cost of material will remain the same as last year.
- Aspex will no longer keep stocks of material.
- The costs making up the cost of quality will be saved.

Working capital control and other matters
- The unit cost of production labour will remain the same and there will be no change in the remaining fixed overheads.
- The average age of debtors will be 2 months.
- Aspex has agreed that the average age of creditors will be 1 month.
- The cash balance will remain the same. Any surplus cash will be used to pay off the existing loans.
- No fixed assets will be bought or sold during the year to 30 November 2004.

Task 42.2

Prepare the following estimates for the year to 30 November 2004 for Stuart Morgan:
- (a) Sales volume.
- (b) Purchases.
- (c) Cost of purchases.
- (d) Selling price per Zeta.
- (e) Turnover.
- (f) Total contribution.

(g)   Fixed costs.
(h)   Operating profit.
(i)   Net assets at 30 November 2004.
(j)   Net profit (or sales) margin.
(k)   Return on capital employed.

QUESTION 43 (June 2004)

Data

The actual and budgeted operating results for the sale and production of executive desks for the year to May 2004 are set out below.

	Actual £	Budget £
Sales	2,750,000	3,000,000
Cost of sales		
Opening finished goods stock	200,000	200,000
Cost of production	2,329,600	2,400,000
Closing finished goods stock	(240,000)	(200,000)
Cost of sales	2,289,600	2,400,000
Gross profit	460,400	600,000
Distribution and administration costs	345,000	360,000
Operating profit	115,400	240,000

Other data for the production and sale of executive desks for the year to May 2004 is as follows:

	Actual	Budget
Number of desks sold	11,000	12,000
Number of desks produced	11,200	12,000
Direct labour hours	58,200	60,000
Net assets employed	£1,075,400	£1,200,000

Task 43.1

(a)   Calculate the following actual and budgeted performance indicators:
   (i)   Gross profit margin.
   (ii)   Operating profit margin.
   (iii) Return on capital employed.
   (iv)   Stock turnover in months.
   (v)   Labour capacity ratio.
   (vi)   Labour efficiency ratio.

   Note: All performance indicators – except (iv) – should be expressed as percentages.

(b)   Write a memo to Sam Thomas. Your memo should include ONE course of action the company could take to improve EACH performance indicator.

Data

Sam Thomas has been on a course on product management. He was particularly interested in the concept of value engineering or value analysis. This was explained to be a process which involves different specialists to evaluate a product's design. The objective of the process is to identify how a product may be redesigned to improve its value.

Task 43.2

Write a brief memo to Sam Thomas. Your memo should describe how value engineering or value analysis may be used to reduce the production cost of an item such as an executive desk.

Chapter 8
Budget preparation

QUESTION 44 (December 2001)

Data

You are employed as the assistant management accountant at Wimpole Ltd where one of your duties is the preparation of budgets every four weeks. You report to Ann Jones, the senior management accountant.

Wimpole Ltd makes several products, two of which are the Alpha and the Beta. Budget data for the two products for the four weeks ending 1 February 2002 is shown below.

Production and sales data	Alpha	Beta
Budgeted sales volume	2,000 units	3,000 units
Opening finished stocks	300 units	297 units
Closing finished stocks	500 units	595 units
Material per unit	10.00 metres	12.00 metres
Labour per unit	1.150 hours	1.380 hours

Note: Production takes place evenly over the four weeks.

Material data	
Cost of material per metre	£17.00
Opening material stock	8,750 metres
Closing material stock	15,530 metres
Wastage rate of material	3% of material issued to production

Labour data

46 employees work a guaranteed 35-hour week. The guaranteed wage for each employee is £210.00 per week.

Any overtime necessary is paid at a rate of £8.00 per hour.

Since collecting the original budget data, you have discovered that:

· The maximum amount of material available from the supplier for the four weeks ending 1 February 2002 will be 61,580 metres.

· The wastage is material left over after lengths have been cut to make Alphas and Betas but before any labour cost has been incurred. The wastage has no scrap value.

· Betas are sold to a large furniture retailer under a long-term contract that cannot be broken. The budgeted sales volume of 3,000 Betas for the four weeks ending 1 February 2002 must be provided under the contract.

· It is not possible to reduce the level of any of the opening or closing stocks.

Task 44.1

Prepare the following information for Ann Jones for the four weeks ended 1 February 2002:

(a)   The production budget in units for Alpha and Beta assuming there was no shortage of materials.

(b)   A statement taking into account the shortage of material and showing the:
   (i)   Metres of material available for production before any wastage.
   (ii)   Metres of material required for Beta production (including any wastage).
   (iii)   Metres of material available for Alpha production.
   (iv)   Number of Alphas to be produced.
   (v)   Labour hours to be worked.
   (vi)   Cost of labour budget.

(c)   The revised budgeted sales volumes for Alpha and Beta.

Data

Ann Jones is preparing the budgeted operating statement for a third product, the Delta, using a computer spreadsheet. Although she has entered selling price and cost data, these are uncertain and may be changed before the budget is agreed.

She asks you to complete the spreadsheet for the Delta using formulae that will allow a revised budgeted operating profit to be calculated automatically if price, cost and volume data change.

Task 44.2

Using the template provided below, enter formulae for:

(a)   Turnover
(b)   Total variable cost
(c)   Contribution
(d)   Fixed costs
(e)   Operating profit

in cells B6 to B10 of the spreadsheet.

	A	B
1	Selling price per unit	£140
2	Variable cost per unit	£70
3	Fixed costs per 4-week period	£40,000
4	Volume per period	1,000
5	4 weeks ending	1 February 2002
6		
7		
8		
9		
10		

QUESTION 45 (December 2000)

Data

You are a management accountant employed by Aspen Ltd and you report to Adrian Jones, the managing director. One of your responsibilities is the production of budgets. Aspen Ltd only has one customer, Advanced Industries plc, for whom it makes the Omega, a specialist product. Advanced Industries demands that Aspen keeps a minimum closing stock of Omegas in case there is an error in the forecast requirements. There is no work-in-progress at any time.

· Both companies divide the year into four-week periods. Each week consists of five days and each day comprises eight hours.
· Advanced Industries plc has recently informed Aspen Ltd of its Omega requirements for the five periods ending Friday 25 May 2001. The details are reproduced below.

Forecast demand for Omegas					
Four weeks ending:	2 February Period 1	2 March Period 2	30 March Period 3	27 April Period 4	25 May Period 5
Number of Omegas required	5,700	5,700	6,840	6,460	6,080
Closing stock of Omegas					
Closing stocks are to equal 3 days of the next period's demand for Omegas.					

The production director gives you the following information:
· The actual opening stocks for period 1, the four weeks ending 2 February, will be 1,330 Omegas.
· Each Omega requires 6 litres of material.
· The material is currently supplied under a long-term contract at a cost of £8.00 per litre and is made exclusively for Aspen by Contrax plc.
· Contrax only has sufficient production capacity to make a maximum of 34,000 litres in any four-week period. Aspen normally purchases the material in the same four-week period it is used.
· Should Aspen require more than 34,000 litres in a four-week period, Contrax would be willing to supply additional material in the preceding period, providing it had spare capacity.
· There is a readily available alternative source for the material but the cost is £12.00 per litre.
· Before buying from the alternative source, any shortage of material in a period should be overcome, where possible, by first purchasing extra material from Contrax in the immediately preceding period.
· There are 78 production employees who are paid a guaranteed basic wage of £160 per 40-hour week.
· Each Omega should take 2 labour hours to make but, due to temporary technical difficulties, the workforce is only able to operate at 95% efficiency in periods 1 to 4.
· Any overtime incurred is payable at a rate of £6.00 per hour.

Task 45.1

Adrian Jones asks you to prepare the following budgets for each of the periods 1 to 4:
(a) The production budget in Omegas using the stock levels given in the data.
(b) The material purchases budget in litres.
(c) The cost of the material purchases.
(d) The labour budget in hours including any overtime hours.
(e) The cost of the labour budget including the cost of any overtime.

Data

On receiving your budgets, Adrian Jones, the managing director, tells you that:
· He is concerned about the cost of the planned overtime and the extra cost of purchasing materials from the alternative supplier.
· The minimum demand in any four week period is forecast to be 5,700 Omegas.
· It is not possible to reduce costs by Advanced Industries plc improving its current method of forecasting.

However, he believes that some immediate and longer-term cost savings are possible.

Task 45.2

Write a memo to Adrian Jones. In your memo you should:

(a) Use the budget information prepared in Task 45.1 to identify ONE immediate possible cost saving proposal other than renegotiating the conditions imposed by Advanced Industries plc.

(b) Calculate the value of the cost savings in the proposal identified in part (a).

(c) Use the forecast minimum demand for Omegas to show whether or not:
   (i) the need to obtain material supplies from the alternative source is a short-term problem, and
   (ii) the need for overtime payments is also a short-term problem.

(d) Suggest TWO cost savings which may be possible in the longer term.

QUESTION 46 (June 2000)

Data

You are employed as a management accountant in the head office of Alton Products plc. One of your tasks involves helping to prepare quarterly budgets for the divisional companies of Alton Products. Each quarter consists of 12 five-day weeks for both production and sales purposes.

One division, Safety Care, makes two chemicals, Delta and Omega. These are sold in standard boxes. Both products use the same material and labour but in different proportions. You have been provided with the following information relating to the two products for quarter 3, the 12 weeks ending 29 September 2000.

	Delta	Omega
Budgeted sales		
Quarter 3: 12 weeks to 29 September 2000	3,000 boxes	2,400 boxes
Quarter 4: 12 weeks to 22 December 2000	3,300 boxes	2,640 boxes
Finished stocks for quarter 3		
Opening stock	630 boxes	502 boxes
Closing stock (days sales in quarter 4)	6 days	8 days
Production inputs		
Material per box	12 kilograms	15 kilograms
Labour per box	3 hours	6 hours
Material stocks and costs for quarter 3		
Opening stock (kilograms)	13,560	
Closing stock (kilograms)	21,340	
Budgeted purchase price per kilogram	£7.00	
Labour costs for quarter 3		
52 production employees work a 36 hour week and are each paid £180 per week. Any overtime is payable at £7.50 per hour.		

> · **Faulty production**
> 10% of production is found to be faulty on completion. Faulty production has to be scrapped and has no scrap value.

Task

The production director of Safety Care asks you to prepare the following for quarter 3:
(a)   The number of boxes of *Delta* and *Omega* planned to be in closing stock.
(b)   The number of labour hours available for production before incurring overtime.
(c)   The production budget for *Deltas* and *Omegas* required to meet the budgeted sales.
(d)   The material purchases budget in kilograms and cost.
(e)   The labour budget in hours and cost.

QUESTION 47 (December 1999)

Data

You have recently been promoted to the post of management accountant with Northern Products Ltd, a company formed four years ago. The company has always used budgets to help plan its production of two products, the Exe and the Wye. Both products use the same material and labour but in different proportions.

You have been asked to prepare the budget for quarter 1, the 12 weeks ending 24 March 2000. In previous budgets the closing stocks of both raw materials and finished products were the same as opening stocks. You questioned whether or not this was the most efficient policy for the company.

As a result, you have carried out an investigation into the stock levels required to meet the maximum likely sales demand for finished goods and production demand for raw materials. You conclude that closing stocks of finished goods should be expressed in terms of days sales for the next quarter and closing stocks of raw materials in terms of days production for the next quarter.

Your findings are included in the data below which also shows data provided by the sales and production directors of Northern Products Ltd.

Product data

	Exe	Wye
· Budgeted sales in units, quarter 1	930 units	1,320 units
· Budgeted sales in units, quarter 2	930 units	1,320 units
· Budgeted material per unit (litres)	6 litres	9 litres
· Budgeted labour hours per unit	12 hours	7 hours
· Opening units of finished stock	172 units	257 units
· Closing units of finished stocks (days sales next quarter)	8 days	9 days

	Exe	Wye
· Failure rate of finished production*	2%	3%
· Finance and other costs of keeping a unit in stock per quarter	£4.00	£5.00

* Failed products are only discovered on completion of production and have no residual value.

Other accounting data

· Weeks in accounting period	12 weeks
· Days per week for production and sales	5 days
· Hours per week	35 hours
· Number of employees	46 employees
· Budgeted labour rate per hour	£6.00
· Overtime premium for hours worked in excess of 35 hours per week	30%
· Budgeted cost of material per litre	£15.00
· Opening raw material stocks (litres)	1,878 litres
· Closing raw material stocks (days production next quarter)	5 days
· Financing and other costs of keeping a litre of raw material in stock per quarter	£1.00

Task

(a) Calculate the following information for *quarter* 1, the 12 weeks ending 24 March 2000:
 (i) The number of production days.
 (ii) The closing finished stock for Exe and Wye in units.
 (iii) The labour hours available before overtime has to be paid.

(b) Prepare the following budgets for quarter 1, the 12 weeks ending 24 March 2000:
 (i) The production budget in units for Exe and Wye including any faulty production.
 (ii) The material purchases budget in litres and value.
 (iii) The production labour budget in hours and value including any overtime payments.

(c) Calculate the savings arising from the change in the required stock levels for the 12 weeks ending 24 March 2000.

QUESTION 48 (June 1999)

Data

Wilmslow Ltd makes two products, the Alpha and the Beta. Both products use the same material and labour but in different amounts. The company divides its year into four quarters, each of 12 weeks. Each week consists of five days and each day comprises seven hours.

You are employed as the management accountant to Wilmslow Ltd and you originally prepared a budget for quarter 3, the 12 weeks to 17 September 1999. The basic data for that budget is reproduced below.

**Original budgetary data: quarter 3
12 weeks to 17 September 1999**

Product	Alpha	Beta
Estimated demand	1,800 units	2,100 units
Material per unit	8 kilograms	12 kilograms
Labour per unit	3 hours	6 hours

Since the budget was prepared, three developments have taken place:

1   The company has begun to use linear regression and seasonal variations to forecast sales demand. Because of this, the estimated demand for quarter 3 has been revised to 2,000 Alphas and 2,400 Betas.

2   As a result of the revised sales forecasting, you have developed more precise estimates of sales and closing stock levels:

·   The sales volume of both the Alpha and Beta in quarter 4 (the 12 weeks ending 10 December 1999) will be 20% more than in the revised budget for quarter 3 as a result of seasonal variations.

·   The closing stock of finished Alphas at the end of quarter 3 should represent five days' sales for quarter 4.

·   The closing stock of finished Betas at the end of quarter 3 should represent 10 days' sales for quarter 4.

·   Production in quarter 4 of both Alpha and Beta is planned to be 20% more than in the revised budget for quarter 3. The closing stock of materials at the end of quarter 3 should be sufficient for 20 days production in quarter 4.

3   New equipment has been installed. The workforce is not familiar with the equipment. Because of this, for quarter 3, they will only be working at 80% of the efficiency assumed in the original budgetary data.

Other data from your original budget which has not changed is reproduced below:

·   50 production employees work a 35-hour week and are each paid £210 per week.

·   Overtime is paid for at £9 per hour.

·   The cost of material is £10 per kilogram.

·   Opening stocks at the beginning of quarter 3 are as follows:

    – Finished Alphas   500 units
    – Finished Betas   600 units
    – Material   12,000 kilograms

·   There will not be any work in progress at any time.

Task

The production director of Wilmslow Ltd wants to schedule production for quarter 3 (the 12 weeks ending 17 September 1999) and asks you to use the revised information to prepare the following:

(a)   The revised production budget for Alphas and Betas.

(b)   The material purchases budget in kilograms.

(c)   A statement showing the cost of the material purchases.

(d)   The labour budget in hours.

(e)   A statement showing the cost of labour.

QUESTION 49 (June 2002)

Data

You are employed as an Accounting Technician by Guildshot Ltd, a company that makes statues. Statues are made in batches. A special powdered rock is added to water and poured into moulds. These moulds are then placed in ovens. Afterwards, the statues are removed from their moulds and inspected before being sold. At this inspection stage, some of the statues are found to be faulty and have to be destroyed. The faulty statues have no residual value.

Guildshot makes two types of statues, the Antelope and the Bear. Both use the same type of material and labour but in different amounts.

One of your duties is to prepare the production, material purchases and labour budgets for each four-week period. You are given the following information for period 8, the four weeks ending 26 July 2002.

Forecast sales	Antelope	Bear
· Sales volume, period 8, four weeks ending 26 July 2002	141,120 units	95,000 units

Product information		
· Opening finished stocks	30,576 units	25,175 units
· Kilograms of powdered rock per statue	0.75 kg	0.50 kg
· Production labour hours per statue	0.10 hrs	0.05 hrs
· Faulty production	2%	5%

Material information	
· Material: opening stock of powdered rock	30,000 kg
· Material: closing stock of powdered rock	40,000 kg
· Price per kilogram of powdered rock	£8.00

Labour information	
· Number of production employees	140 employees
· Days per week	5 days
· Weeks per period	4 weeks
· Hours per production employee per week	38 hours
· Guaranteed weekly wage*	£228.00

*The guaranteed weekly wage is paid even if hours produced are less than hours worked.

Closing finished stocks

The closing finished stocks are based on the forecast sales volume for period 9, the four weeks ending 23 August 2002.

·   Demand for the Antelope in period 9 is forecast to be 50% more than in period 8. The closing finished stock of Antelope statues for period 8 must

be equal to four days' sales in period 9.
· Demand for the Bear in period 9 is forecast to be 30% more than in period 8. The closing finished stock of Bear statues for period 8 must be equal to five days' sales in period 9.

Other information
· The faulty production is only discovered after the statues have been made.
· For technical reasons, the company can only operate the ovens for five days per week.

Task 49.1

Prepare the following information for period 8, the four weeks ending 26 July 2002:
(a) Production budget in units for Antelopes and Bears.
(b) Material purchases budget in kilograms.
(c) Cost of the materials purchases budget.
(d) Labour budget in hours.
(e) Cost of the labour budget.

Data

Hilary Green is the production director of Guildshot. She tells you that there are likely to be material and labour shortages in period 9. For commercial reasons, the company must fully meet the demand for Bear statues. As a result, it will not be able to meet all the demand for Antelope statues.

Hilary suggests it might be possible to meet the demand by producing extra Antelope statues in period 8. She gives you the following information:
· Because of the technology involved, Guildshot cannot increase the number of production employees and the existing employees cannot work any overtime. The maximum hours are limited to the 38 hours per week for each production employee.
· It would be possible to buy up to a maximum 3,000 extra kilograms of powdered rock in period 8.

Task 49.2

(a) Calculate the maximum number of extra fault-free Antelope statues that could be made in period 8.
(b) Prepare a revised purchases budget in kilograms to include the production of the extra fault-free statues.

QUESTION 50 (December 2002)

Data

You are employed by JDJ plc as a management accountant where you help prepare budgets for all of the company's divisions. One division makes a single product, the Zeta, and its sales forecast for the five accounting periods to Friday 1 August 2003 is shown below.

Sales forecast for Zetas to 1 August 2003					
Accounting period ending	14 February Period 1	28 March Period 2	9 May Period 3	20 June Period 4	1 August Period 5
Sales volume (Zetas)	14,400	15,000	15,600	16,800	16,800

The Production Director gives you the following information.

Production
· The division works a five-day week for both production and sales.
· There are six weeks in each accounting period.
· The opening finished stock for period 1 will be 5,760 Zetas.
· The current policy of the division is that finished stocks in each period must equal 12 working days sales volume of the next period.

Material
· Raw material has to be purchased in the period it is used and so there are no stocks.
· There is a 4% wastage of material due to evaporation before being issued to production.
· The division can purchase up to 130,000 litres of material in any six-week accounting period under an existing contract at a price of £7.00 per litre. Any extra purchases of material have to be bought on the open market at a cost of £12.00 per litre.
· Each Zeta requires 8 litres of material.

Labour
· Employees work a guaranteed 40-hour, five-day week.
· The guaranteed weekly wage is £240.00.
· There are 130 production employees in the division.
· It takes two labour hours to produce one Zeta.
· Any overtime required is payable at £7.00 per labour hour.

Task 50.1

Prepare the following budgets for EACH of the four periods 1 to 4 in accordance with the division's policy on finished stocks:
(a) Production budget in Zetas.
(b) Purchases budget in litres.
(c) Cost of purchases budget.
(d) Labour hours required for budgeted production.
(e) Cost of labour budget.

Data

After presenting your budgets to the Production Director, she tells you that budgeted profits are less than planned because of:
· the large amount of overtime; and
· purchasing materials on the open market.

She tells you that the policy on finished stocks is to be amended. There must always be sufficient stocks to meet customer needs. Closing stocks cannot, therefore, be less than 12 working days, but can be more than 12 working days if this results in cost savings. This would involve producing more Zetas than required in some periods in order to make savings in later periods.

The Production Director asks you to revise your budgets to take account of the revised stock policy.

Task 50.2

(a)   Prepare the following REVISED budgets for each of the periods 1 to 4 to maximise any possible cost savings:
(i)   Purchases budget in litres.
(ii)   Cost of purchases budget.
(iii) Production budget in Zetas.
(iv) Labour hours required for the revised budgeted production.
(v)   Cost of labour budget.

(b)   Write a memo to the Production Director. In the memo you should:
(i)   calculate the total cost savings possible;
(ii)   identify TWO possible costs that might be necessary to achieve the savings.

QUESTION 51 (December 2003)

Data

Tipton Ltd makes two types of container for the chemical industry, the Exe and the Wye. Both containers use the same type of material and labour but in different amounts. You are the Management Accountant and you are responsible for preparing the production and resource budgets for both products. The company operates a five-day week for both production and sales and prepares production and resource budgets every 20 working days.

You are given the following information relating to period 1, the 20 working days ending 30 January 2004.

Forecast sales volumes	*Exe*	*Wye*
Period 1: 20 days to 30 January 2004	8,820 units	5,800 units
Period 2: percentage increase over period 1	20%	30%

Finished stocks
·   At the beginning of period 1, there will be 4,410 Exes and 2,320 Wyes in finished stock.
·   The finished stock of Exes at the end of period 1 must be equal to ten working days sales of Exes in period 2.
·   The finished stock of Wyes at the end of period 1 must be equal to eight working days sales of Wyes in period 2.

Materials
- Each Exe requires 5 square metres and each Wye requires 7 square metres of materials.
- The cost of material is £2.00 per square metre. There has been no change in the price of materials for several months.
- 2% of material issued to production is lost through wastage.
- At the beginning of period 1, the opening material stock will be 16,950 square metres.
- At the end of period 1, the closing material stock will be 18,000 square metres.

Labour
- Tipton produces six Exes per labour hour and four Wyes per labour hour.
- The company employs 22 production employees who work a 35-hour, five-day week.
- The labour rate per hour is £8.00 and any overtime is at a premium of 50% per hour.
- Any overtime premium is charged to the production overhead account and not directly to production.

Production overheads
- Overheads are charged to production at the rate of £12.00 per labour hour.

Task 51.1

Prepare the following information for period 1, the 20 working days ending 30 January 2004:
(a)   production budgets in units for the Exe and the Wye;
(b)   material purchase budget in square metres;
(c)   cost of materials purchases budget;
(d)   budgeted labour hours to be worked, including any overtime;
(e)   cost of labour budget;
(f)   cost of production budgets for the Exe and the Wye.

Data

Susan Fellows is the Production Director of Tipton Ltd. She tells you that there will not be sufficient factory capacity in period 2 to meet the likely demand for the Exe and the Wye. One way of overcoming the capacity constraint in period 2 is to increase production of Exe in period 1 as Exe requires less material and labour than Wye. She tells you that:
- the surplus capacity of the factory in period 1 is equivalent to 88 labour hours and the production employees would be willing to work these extra hours;
- Tipton can obtain up to 2,000 square metres of extra material for period 1.

Task 51.2

Write a memo to Susan Fellows. In your memo you should:
(a)   identify whether it is the material or labour constraints that limit extra Exe production;

(b)   prepare a revised production budget in units after allowing for the increased production of Exes;

(c)   briefly identify TWO other short-term ways of overcoming the capacity constraint in period 2.

QUESTION 52 (June 2004)

You are employed as a management accountant by Newmarket Ltd. Newmarket makes two similar products, the Alpha and the Beta, and operates a five-day week for both production and sales. Both products use the same material and labour, but the Beta requires more labour and materials than the Alpha.

The company divides its year into five-week periods for budgetary purposes. One of your responsibilities is to prepare budgets for the Alpha and the Beta.

You are given the following information to help you prepare the production and resource budgets for period 8, the five weeks ending 30 July 2004.

Forecast sales volumes (units)	*Days in period*	*Alpha*	*Beta*
· Period 8: 5 weeks to 30 July 2004	25	8,460	9,025
· Period 9: 5 weeks to 3 September 2004	25	10,575	12,635

Finished stocks
·   There will be 1,692 Alphas and 3,610 Betas in finished stock at the beginning of period 8.
·   The closing stock of both Alphas and Betas depends on the forecast sales in period 9.
    -   Period 8's closing finished stocks of Alphas must equal 5 days sales of Alphas in period 9.
    -   Period 8's closing finished stocks of Betas must equal 10 days sales of Betas in period 9.
    -   The first-in-first-out stock valuation method is used to value closing finished stocks.

Production failure rates
·   10% of Alpha finished production and 5% of Beta finished production is faulty and has to be destroyed. This faulty production has no value.
·   The faulty production arises from the production technology and is only discovered on completion. The cost of the faulty production is part of the cost of producing fault-free Alphas and Betas.

Materials
·   Each Alpha produced requires 20 kilograms of materials and each Beta produced requires 40 kilograms of materials.
·   The opening stock of materials at the beginning of period 8 is 64,800 kilograms.
·   The closing stock of materials at the end of period 8 is 52,600 kilograms.
·   The material costs 50p per kilogram.

Labour

· Each Alpha produced requires two labour hours and each Beta produced requires three labour hours.
· Newmarket employs 300 production employees who work 35 hours per-five-day week.
· The hourly rate per employee is £5 and if any overtime is required the over-time premium is £3 per employee per hour of overtime.
· Any overtime premium is charged to factory overheads and not to the cost of production.

Factory overheads

· Budgeted factory overheads are charged to production on the basis of labour hours.
· For Alpha, the budgeted factory overheads are £62 per labour hour. For Beta, they are £58 per labour hour.

Task 52.1

Prepare the following information for period 8, the 25 working days ending 30 July 2004:
(a)   Production budgets in units for Alpha and Beta.
(b)   Material purchases budget in kilograms.
(c)   Cost of materials budget.
(d)   Budgeted labour hours to be worked, including any overtime.
(e)   Cost of labour budget.
(f)   Total absorption cost of production budget for Alpha and Beta.
(g)   Absorption cost of good production per unit for Alpha and Beta.
(h)   Value of closing finished stocks of Alpha and Beta using the unit absorption costs calculated in (g).

Data

The Chief Executive of Newmarket Ltd is Bob Scott. He developed the sales forecasts used in your budget statements without consulting Newmarket's sales staff. The sales staff have now told Bob that Alpha sales in period 8 will be 2,000 more than he originally forecast. Bob gives you the following information.

· Newmarket's production employees can work up to a maximum of 5,000 overtime hours in any five-week period.
· The material used in Alpha and Beta production can only be made by one company and Newmarket is the only user of the material. Currently, there is a shortage of the material and the maximum additional material the company can produce in period 8 is 34,000 kilograms.
· The demand for the Beta in period 8 will remain at 9,025 units.
· There will be no change in the level of finished stocks or the failure rate.

Task 52.2

Write a memo to Bob Scott. In your memo you should:
(a)   (i)   prepare calculations to show whether it is the material or labour hours that limits extra production of Alphas in period 8;

    (ii)   prepare a revised production budget in units for Alphas in period 8;

    (iii)   calculate any shortfall in the planned extra sales of 2,000 Alphas arising from the limit to extra production;

    (iv)   suggest ONE way to overcome any shortfall;

(b)   give TWO reasons why a budget might be imposed on staff without consultation.

Chapter 9
Budgetary control and responsibility accounting

QUESTION 53 (June 2001)

Data

You are employed by Sparrow and Co, a firm of accountants and registered auditors. Eagle Ltd, a small company making a single product, is a client of Sparrow and Co. Just over a year ago, you helped prepare Eagle's budget for the year to 31 May 2001. Shortly afterwards you prepared a revised budget to take account of a change in the forecast demand for the product. The original and revised budgets are shown below, together with the actual results for the year.

Eagle Ltd - Budgeted and actual operating results for the year to 31 May 2001						
	Original budget		*Revised budget*		*Actual results*	
	Units	£000	Units	£000	Units	£000
Turnover	20,000	700	22,000	770	23,000	782
Material		160		176		225
Labour		300		330		350
Production overhead		74		74		75
Cost of production	20,000	534	22,000	580	25,000	650
Less closing stock	Nil	Nil	Nil	Nil	2,000	52
Cost of sales	20,000	534	22,000	580	23,000	598
Gross profit		166		190		184
General expenses		110		114		125
Operating profit		56		76		59

From your working papers, you note that:

·   the only change in costs and revenues between the two budgets arose from the forecast change in volume;

·   both budgets assumed there would be no opening and no closing stocks.

Kate Smith is the new managing director of Eagle Ltd. She gives you the following information about the actual results:

·   The actual results have been prepared using absorption costing.

·   The closing stock valuation includes a proportion of production overhead.

· General expenses include £71,000 which do not vary with changes in either sales or production volumes.
· The balance of general expenses are selling expenses and vary with units sold.
· The actual unit cost of material and labour has remained the same through-out the year.

Kate Smith is concerned that the actual profit for the year is less than the revised budgeted profit. She asks you to prepare an analysis showing why the two profit figures are different.

Task 53.1

Prepare an analysis for Kate Smith. In your analysis you should:
(a) Calculate the following BUDGETED data:
   (i)   Selling price per unit.
   (ii)   Material cost per unit.
   (iii) Labour cost per unit.
   (iv)   Variable (or marginal) cost of general expenses per unit.
   (v)   Fixed cost of general expenses.

(b) Identify the actual production fixed costs incurred during the year.

(c) Redraft the actual results for the year on a marginal costing basis.

(d) Prepare a statement showing the following for the year:
   (i)   The actual results on a marginal costing basis.
   (ii)   The appropriate flexible budget.
   (iii) Any variances.

Data

After receiving your statement comparing the actual marginal costing results with the flexible budget, Kate Smith tells you that:
· She does not understand why the budget in your statement is different from the agreed revised budget nor why some costs have changed but others have remained the same.
· She does not understand why the actual results are different from the original actual results for the year to 31 May 2001.
· She is considering changing the bonus scheme currently payable to the General Manager responsible for day-to-day operations. In order to encourage him to increase sales, this year's bonus was based on sales volume. For next year she is planning to base the bonus on profits made. The General Manager has suggested that the bonus should be based on an absorption costing profit.

Task 53.2

Write a letter to Kate Smith. In your letter you should BRIEFLY:
(a) Give ONE reason why the budget in your statement answering Task 53.1 (d) is different from the revised budget.
(b) Explain why the actual results in your statement are different from the original actual results.

(c)   Discuss whether or not profit calculated using absorption costing rather than marginal costing is a better measure of management performance.

QUESTION 54 (December 2000)

Data

You have recently been appointed as the management accountant of Parkside Manufacturing Ltd. Parkside Manufacturing makes a single product, the Delta. The previous management accountant has already prepared an analysis of budgeted and actual results for the year to 30 November 2000. These are reproduced below.

Parkside Manufacturing Ltd Operating statement for year ended 30 November 2000					
Volume (number of Deltas)	Budget 100,000		Actual 125,000		Variance
	£000	£000	£000	£000	£000
Turnover		2,000		2,250	250 (F)
Material	600		800		200 (A)
Light, heat and power	200		265		65 (A)
Production labour	120		156		36 (A)
Rent, rates and depreciation	140		175		35 (A)
Administrative expenses	110		110		Nil
		1,170		1,506	
Profit		830		744	86 (A)

Key: (F) = favourable
      (A) = adverse

Judith Green, the production director, tells you that the following assumptions were made when the budget was originally prepared:
· Material is entirely a variable cost.
· Light, heat and power is a semi-variable cost. The fixed element included in the budgeted figure was £40,000.
· Production labour is a stepped cost. Each production employee can make up to 10,000 Deltas. Each production employee was budgeted to receive a basic wage of £12,000 per year with no overtime and no bonuses.
· There are no part-time employees.
· Rent, rates and depreciation, and administrative expenses are fixed costs.

Task 54.1

(a)   In preparation for the next Board meeting of Parkside Manufacturing Ltd, calculate the:
      (i)   budgeted cost of material per Delta;
      (ii)   budgeted variable cost per Delta of light, heat and power;
      (iii)   number of production employees assumed in the budget.

(b)   Prepare a statement which compares the actual results of Parkside Manufacturing with the flexible budget and identify any variances.

Data

On receiving your flexible budget and variances, Judith Green tells you that:

· She does not understand why there is a need for the two types of budget, the one prepared by the previous management accountant and the flexible budget prepared by yourself.

· She does not know if it is necessary to investigate all variances.

· She is concerned that the original budgeted sales volume was so different from the actual sales volume and is considering the use of linear regression to improve sales forecasting of Deltas.

Task 54.2

Judith Green asks you to write a brief report in preparation for the Board meeting. In your report you should:

(a)   Briefly explain the different purposes of the two types of budget and explain which one should be used to compare with the actual results.

(b)   Suggest THREE general factors that need to be taken into account in deciding whether or not to investigate variances.

(c)   Briefly explain THREE limitations to the use of linear regression in sales forecasting.

QUESTION 55 (June 2000)

Visiguard Ltd is a division of Alton Products plc. It makes a single product, the Raider. Just over a year ago, the chief executive of Alton Products, Mike Green, was concerned to find that Visiguard was budgeting to make only £20,000 profit in the year to 31 May 2000. As a result, he imposed his own budget on the division. His revised budget assumed:

· increased sales volume of the Raider;

· increased selling prices; and

· that suppliers would agree to reduce the cost of the material used in the Raider by 10%.

The only other changes to the original budget arose solely as a result of the increased volume in the revised budget.

The original budget and the revised budget imposed by Mike Green are reproduced below, together with the actual results for the year to 31 May 2000.

Visiguard Limited
Budgeted and actual operating statements for one year ended 31 May 2000

	Original budget	Revised budget	Actual results
Sales and production volume	10,000	11,000	11,600
	£	£	£
Turnover	1,400,000	1,760,000	1,844,400

Variable materials	400,000	396,000	440,800
Production and administrative labour	580,000	630,000	677,600
Light, heat and power	160,000	164,000	136,400
Fixed overheads	240,000	240,000	259,600
Budgeted profit	20,000	330,000	330,000

Task 55.1

Using the information provided in the two budgets, calculate the following:
(a) The unit selling price of the Raider in the revised budget.
(b) The material cost per Raider in the revised budget.
(c) The variable cost of production and administrative labour per Raider.
(d) The fixed cost of production and administrative labour.
(e) The variable cost of light, heat and power per Raider.
(f) The fixed cost of light, heat and power.

Data

On receiving the actual results for the year, Mike Green states that they prove that his revised budget motivated managers to produce better results.

Task 55.2

Write a memo to Mike Green. Your memo should:
(a) Use the information calculated in Task 55.1 to prepare a flexible budget statement for Visiguard including any variances.
(b) Identify TWO situations where an imposed budget might be preferable to one prepared with the participation of managers.
(c) Briefly discuss whether or not his requirement that material costs be reduced would have motivated the managers of Visiguard.
(d) Identify TWO ways in which profit could have increased without additional effort by the managers of Visiguard.

QUESTION 56 (December 1999)

Data

HFD plc opened a new division on 1 December 1998. The division, HFD Processes Ltd, produces a special paint finish. Because of the technology, there can never be any work in progress. The original budget was developed on the assumption that there would be a loss in the initial year of operation and that there would be no closing stock of finished goods.

One year later, HFD Processes Ltd prepared its results for its first year of operations. The chief executive of HFD plc was pleased to see that, despite budgeting for an initial loss, the division had actually returned a profit of £74,400. As a result, the directors of HFD Processes were entitled to a substantial bonus. Details of the budget and actual results are reproduced below.

HFD Processes Ltd operating results - year ended 30 November 1999

	Budget		Actual	
Volume (units)		20,000		22,000
	£	£	£	£
Turnover		960,000		1,012,000
Direct costs				
Material	240,000		261,800	
Production labour	260,000		240,240	
Light, heat and power	68,000		65,560	
	568,000		567,600	
Fixed overheads	400,000		370,000	
Cost of sales		968,000		937,600
Operating profit/(loss)		(8,000)		74,400

You are employed as a management accountant in the head office of HFD plc and have been asked to comment on the performance of HFD Processes Ltd. Attached to the budgeted and actual results were the relevant working papers. A summary of the contents of the working papers is reproduced below.

· The budget assumed no closing finishing stocks. Actual production was 25,000 units and actual sales 22,000 units.

· Because of the technology involved, production employees are paid per week, irrespective of production levels. The employees assumed in the budget are capable of producing up to 26,000 units.

· The cost of material varies directly with production.

· The cost of light, heat and power includes a fixed standing charge. In the budget this fixed charge was calculated to be £20,000 per year. However, competition resulted in the supplier reducing the actual charge to £12,000 for the year.

· During the year HFD Processes Ltd produced 25,000 units. The 3,000 units of closing finished stock were valued on the basis of direct cost plus 'normal' fixed overheads:

   – the number of units was used to apportion direct costs between the cost of sales and closing finished stocks;

   – the budgeted fixed overhead of £20 per unit was used to calculate the fixed overheads in closing finished stocks;

   – The detailed composition of the cost of sales and closing stocks using these policies was:

	Closing finished stocks	Cost of sales	Cost of production
Units	3,000	22,000	25,000
	£	£	£
Material	35,700	261,800	297,500
Production labour	32,760	240,240	273,000
Light, heat and power	8,940	65,560	74,500
Fixed overheads	60,000	370,000	430,000
	137,400	937,600	1,075,000

Task 56.1

(a)   Calculate the following:
(i)   The budgeted unit selling price.
(ii)   The budgeted material cost per unit.
(iii) The budgeted marginal cost of light, heat and power per unit.
(iv) The actual marginal cost of light, heat and power per unit.

(b)   Prepare a flexible budget statement for the operating results of HFD Processes Ltd using a *marginal costing* approach, identifying fixed costs for the year and showing any variances.

Data

You present your flexible budget statement to the chief executive of HFD plc who is concerned that your findings appear different to those in the original operating results.

Task 56.2

You are asked to write a *brief* memo to the chief executive. In your memo you should:
(a)   Give TWO reasons why the flexible budget operating statement shows different results from the original operating results.
(b)   Give ONE reason why the flexible budget operating statement might be a better measure of management performance than the original operating results.

QUESTION 57 (June 1999)

Data

Rivermede Ltd makes a single product called the Fasta. Last year, Steven Jones, the managing director of Rivermede Ltd, attended a course on budgetary control. As a result, he agreed to revise the way budgets were prepared in the company. Rather than imposing targets for managers, he encouraged participation by senior managers in the preparation of budgets.

An initial budget was prepared but Mike Fisher, the sales director, felt that the budgeted sales volume was set too high. He explained that setting too high a budgeted sales volume would mean his sales staff would be demotivated because they would not be able to achieve that sales volume. Steven Jones agreed to use the revised sales volume suggested by Mike Fisher.

Both the initial and revised budgets are reproduced below complete with the actual results for the year ended 31 May 1999.

Rivermede Ltd – Budgeted and actual costs for the year ended 31 May 1999

	Original budget	Revised budget	Actual results	Variances from revised budget
Fasta production and sales (units)	24,000	20,000	22,000	2,000 (F)
	£	£	£	£
Variable costs				
Material	216,000	180,000	206,800	26,800 (A)
Labour	288,000	240,000	255,200	15,200 (A)
Semi-variable costs				
Heat, light and power	31,000	27,000	33,400	6,400 (A)
Fixed costs				
Rent, rates				
and depreciation	40,000	40,000	38,000	2,000 (F)
	575,000	487,000	533,400	46,400 (A)

Assumptions in the two budgets
1. No change in input prices.
2. No change in the quantity of variable inputs per Fasta.

As the management accountant at Rivermede Ltd, one of your tasks is to check that invoices have been properly coded. On checking the actual invoices for heat, light and power for the year to 31 May 1999, you find that one invoice for £7,520 had been incorrectly coded. The invoice should have been coded to materials.

Task 57.1

(a) Using the information in the original and revised budgets, identify:
· the variable cost of material and labour per Fasta;
· the fixed and unit variable cost within heat, light and power.

(b) Prepare a flexible budget, including variances, for Rivermede Ltd after correcting for the miscoding of the invoice.

Data

On receiving your flexible budget statement, Steven Jones states that the total adverse variance is much less than the £46,400 shown in the original statement. He also draws your attention to the actual sales volume being greater than in the revised budget. He believes these results show that a participative approach to budgeting is better for the company and wants to discuss this belief at the next board meeting. Before doing so, Steven Jones asks for your comments.

Task 57.2

Write a memo to Steven Jones. Your memo should:
(a) *Briefly* explain why the flexible budgeting variances differ from those in the original statement given in the data to Task 57.1.
(b) Give TWO reasons why a favourable cost variance may have arisen other than through the introduction of participative budgeting.

(c) Give TWO reasons why the actual sales volume compared with the revised budget's sales volume may not be a measure of improved motivation following the introduction of participative budgeting.

QUESTION 58 (June 2002)

Data

Just over a year ago, Guildshot formed a subsidiary, Alderford Ltd, to make a new type of chemical. The chemical is sold in drums to the building industry where it is used to dry out new buildings.

You have been asked to help James Alexander, Alderford's managing director, prepare a report on the first 12 months of Alderford's operations.

James gives you a copy of the company's operating statement for the first 12 months of operations. This is shown below.

Alderford Ltd : Operating statement – 12 months ended 31 May 2002		
	Budget	*Actual*
Number of drums produced and sold	80,000	125,000
	£000	£000
Turnover	2,400	4,000
Variable costs		
Material A	240	425
Material B	480	680
Material C	320	500
Semi-variable costs		
Power	270	440
Water	122	200
Stepped costs		
Supervisors	160	258
Fixed costs		
Rent and rates	250	250
Lighting and heating	120	118
Administrative expenses	200	240
Operating profit	238	889

James also tells you that:
- the budgeted fixed cost element of power was £110,000;
- the budgeted fixed cost element of water was £90,000;
- each supervisor can supervise the production of up to 10,000 drums of the chemical;
- all other expenses are either totally fixed or vary directly with production and sales;
- there are no opening or closing stocks of any sort.

Task 58.1

(a) Calculate the budgeted variable cost per drum of the following inputs:
   (i)   Material A.
   (ii) Material B.
   (iii) Material C.
   (iv) Power.
   (v)   Water.

(b) Prepare a statement showing Alderford's actual results, the flexible budget and any variances.

Data

James Alexander notices that there is a significant difference between the budgeted and actual number of drums sold during Alderford's first 12 months of trading.

He tells you that he has three strategies to increase the number of drums sold. These are:
·   more sales to existing customers;
·   sales to new customers in the building industry;
·   the development of new markets.

James wants to increase the accuracy of forecasting for the year to 31 May 2003 and asks for your advice.

Task 58.2

Write a memo to James Alexander. In your memo, you should explain:
(a) FOUR forecasting techniques that Alderford could currently use;
(b) ONE forecasting technique that Alderford is currently unable to use;
(c) the most appropriate forecasting technique available for EACH of the three strategies to increase the number of drums sold.

QUESTION 59 (December 2002)

Data

JDJ plc has a division that makes a single product, the Omicron. Just over a year ago the senior managers of the Omicron division prepared a budget for the year ended 30 November 2002. The Managing Director of the division, Robert Maxton, rejected their budget. In its place, he imposed a budget of his own that assumed a 10% increase in sales volume. The original budget prepared by the senior managers, the revised budget prepared by Robert Maxton and the actual results for the year are shown below.

Budgeted and actual operating results year ended 30 November 2002

	Original budget Vol 000	Revised budget Vol 000	Actual results Vol 000
Sales volume (Omicrons)	400	440	450
Production volume (Omicrons)	400	440	600
	£000	£000	£000
Turnover	6,400	7,040	6,840
Expenditure type			
Material	1,600	1,760	2,520
Labour	2,000	2,200	3,180
Electricity	880	960	1,200
Depreciation	500	500	300
Maintenance	300	300	200
Other fixed costs	700	700	800
Cost of production	5,980	6,420	8,200
Less:Closing finished stock	Nil	Nil	2,050
Cost of sales	5,980	6,420	6,150
Operating profit	420	620	690

You are provided with the following information.

Budget data

· The difference between the original and revised budgets arose entirely from the change in volume. Both budgets used the same selling price and the same prices for all of the expenses.

· Material and labour are variable (or marginal) costs and electricity is a semi-variable cost. All other costs are fixed costs.

Actual data

· There was no opening finished stock and no opening or closing work in progress.

· The closing finished stock of 150,000 Omicrons included an appropriate proportion of overheads. The value of this closing stock was based on the absorption cost of production.

· From 1 November 2001, the electricity supplier no longer imposed a fixed charge for electricity.

Task 59.1

(a) Calculate the following budgeted data:
   (i)   Selling price per Omicron.
   (ii)   Variable cost of material per Omicron.
   (iii) Variable cost of labour per Omicron.
   (iv)   Variable cost of electricity per Omicron.
   (v)   Fixed cost of electricity.

(b) Calculate the following actual data:
   (i) Variable cost of material per Omicron.
   (ii) Variable cost of labour per Omicron.
   (iii) Variable cost of electricity per Omicron.

(c) Prepare a variable (or marginal) costing statement showing the *actual expenses* by *expenditure type* for the actual 450,000 Omicron sales volume.

(d) Using the task data and your answer to part (c), prepare a variable (or marginal) costing flexible budget statement for the sales volume of 450,000 Omicrons. Your statement should show the budgeted and actual results and any variances.

Data

Robert Maxton believes that the improved actual operating profit of £690,000 over the original budgeted profit of £420,000 is evidence that his imposed budget motivated managers.

Task 59.2

Write a memo to Robert Maxton. In your memo you should:
(a) identify TWO situations where an imposed budget might be preferable to one prepared with the participation of senior managers;
(b) identify THREE reasons, other than increased sales, why the original operating profit of £690,000 was greater than the revised budget's operating profit of £620,000;
(c) briefly explain why the actual operating profit used in the flexible budget statement prepared in Task 59.1 (d) is different from the £690,000 actual operating profit originally shown.

QUESTION 60 (December 2003)

Data

You are an accounting technician employed by Telford plc. Telford has a subsidiary, Shifnal Ltd that makes one product, the Omega. Barry Jones, the Finance Director of Telford, has asked you to prepare a statement analysing the performance of Shifnal Ltd. He gives you a copy of the company's latest operating statement and tells you the assumptions made about costs when preparing the statement.

Shifnal Ltd: operating statement – 12 months ended 30 November 2003	Budget	Actual
Number of Omegas produced and sold	120,000	95,000
	£000	£000
Turnover	4,800	3,990

Variable expenses		
Material A	480	456
Material B	840	665
Material C	360	266
Semi-variable expenses		
Light, heat and power	290	249
Water	212	182
Stepped expenses		
Labour	200	168
Maintenance	60	54
Fixed expenses		
Rent and rates	360	355
Distribution expenses	600	620
Administrative expenses	300	280
Operating profit	1,098	695

Assumptions made

· Budgeted semi-variable expenses
   – The variable cost of light, heat and power was £2.00 per Omega.
   – The fixed cost of water was £20,000 per year.
· Budgeted stepped expenses
   – For every £5,000 spent on labour, Shifnal could produce up to 3,000 Omegas.
   – For every £10,000 spent on maintenance, Shifnal could produce up to 20,000 Omegas.
· The budgeted selling price per Omega was the same throughout the year.
· There were no stocks of any kind.

Task 60.1

(a)   Calculate the budgeted selling price per Omega.

(b)   Calculate the budgeted variable cost per Omega of:
   (i)   material A;
   (ii)   material B;
   (iii)   material C.

(c)   Calculate the:
   (i)   budgeted fixed cost of light, heat and power;
   (ii)   budgeted variable cost of water per Omega.

(d)   Prepare a statement showing Shifnal's actual results, the flexible budget and any variances.

QUESTION 61 (June 2004)

Data

The Oxbridge District Council has recently asked your firm to investigate possible improvements to the Council's financial reports.

You report to Mike Town, the partner carrying out the investigation. He gives you a copy of a monthly report prepared for the General Manager of Oxbridge's leisure centre.

The leisure centre has a swimming pool, a gymnasium, a sauna and a sports hall. Mike tells you that the leisure centre's financial year starts on 1 March and that each month managers receive a similar report. A copy of the monthly report is shown below.

Oxbridge District Council Management Report

Cost centre: Leisure complex			Period: three months to 31 May 2004		
	Total budget for the year £000	Budget to date £000	Cash expenditure to date £000	Under/ over spend £000	Budget remaining £000
Management staff	240	90	60	30 Cr	150
Operations staff	680	150	170	20 Dr	530
Administrative staff	40	12	10	2 Cr	28
Cleaning staff	28	5	7	2 Dr	23
Repairs and maintenance	44	2	11	9 Dr	42
Lighting and heating	36	3	9	6 Dr	33
Fixed assets	240	0	60	60 Dr	240
Sundry expenses	12	5	3	2 Cr	7
Central services recharge	120	120	30	90 Cr	0
Total	1,440	387	360	27 Cr	1,053

Task

Prepare notes for Mike Town. Your notes should identify SIX weaknesses of the current report.

MOCK EXAMINATION – UNIT 8
QUESTIONS

This examination is in TWO sections.

You have to show competence in BOTH sections.

You should therefore attempt and aim to complete EVERY task in BOTH sections.

You should spend about 100 minutes on Section 1 and 80 minutes on Section 2.

All essential workings should be included within your answers, where appropriate.

Section 1

Data

Holden plc manufactures several chemicals at its main factory. One chemical, X40, has proven so popular that Holden has recently opened a new factory in another town to meet the increased demand.

The X40 is produced in tins and its standard cost is as follows:

STANDARD COST CARD for X40			
Expense	Units	Unit cost	Cost per tin
Material	7 litres	£8.00	£56.00
Labour	4 hours	£5.00	£20.00
Fixed overheads	4 hours	£6.00	£24.00
Standard cost per tin			£100.00

The new factory's actual results for the first four weeks of operations are shown below.

OPERATING RESULTS OF NEW FACTORY 4 WEEKS ENDED 1 JUNE 2001		
Production (tins)		16,000
Material	113,600 litres	£920,160
Labour	68,640 hours	£336,336
Fixed overheads		£410,000
Cost of production		**£1,666,496**

Other information relating to the new factory:
· The X40 is the only product made.
· Budgeted fixed overheads total £5,040,000 per year.
· Fixed overheads are charged to production on the basis of labour hours.
· There are 50 operating weeks in the year.
· Production is budgeted to take place evenly throughout the 50 operating weeks.

You are employed in the Central Accounts Department of Holden. One of your responsibilities is to prepare and monitor standard costing variances at the new factory.

Task 1.1

(a)   Calculate the following information relating to the new factory:
   (i)   Actual price of material per litre.
   (ii)   Actual labour rate per hour.
   (iii)   Actual labour hours per tin.
   (iv)   Budgeted production of tins for the year.
   (v)   Budgeted production of tins for the 4 weeks ended 1 June 2001.
   (vi)   Budgeted fixed overheads for the 4 weeks ended 1 June 2001.

(b)   Calculate the following variances for X40 production at the new factory:
   (i)   Material price variance.
   (ii)   Material usage variance.
   (iii)   Labour rate variance.
   (iv)   Labour efficiency variance.
   (v)   Fixed overhead expenditure variance.
   (vi)   Fixed overhead volume variance.
   (vii)   Fixed overhead capacity variance.
   (viii) Fixed overhead efficiency variance.

(c)   Prepare a statement reconciling the standard cost of actual production to the actual cost of actual production for the four weeks ended 1 June 2001.

Data

At a meeting called to discuss the performance of the new factory, the general manager tells you that:
·   The material and labour standard costs were based on the standards at the main factory.
·   The cost of material per litre at the new factory will always be 1.25% more than at the main factory due to additional transport costs.
·   Production workers are currently taking 10% longer to make a tin of X40 than they will when fully trained.
·   The standard fixed overhead was based on estimated costs at the new factory alone.
·   The machinery at the new factory is more modern than the machinery at the main factory.

Task 1.2

Write a memo to the general manager. Your memo should:
(a)   Identify a revised standard price of material per litre for the new factory.
(b)   Estimate the labour hours per tin of X40 after the production workers are fully trained.
(c)   Sub-divide the labour efficiency variance into:
   (i)   that part due to the production workers being not yet fully trained, and
   (ii)   that part due to other reasons.

(d)   Suggest TWO possible explanations for the labour efficiency variance due to other reasons.

Section 2

You should spend about 80 minutes on this section.

Data

The Bon Repose hotel group is a French company. It builds and operates economy class hotels close to major roads to provide overnight accommodation for motorists. Each bedroom is a standard size and the only food provided for guests is breakfast.

Recently, Bon Repose formed a UK subsidiary and shortly afterwards you were appointed its management accountant. You report to Helene de la Tour, the chief executive of the UK subsidiary, who provides you with the following information:

·   All Bon Repose hotels have 80 bedrooms and operate for 365 days per year.
·   Sales volume is measured in room-nights. Customers are charged for the use of the room per night whether it is used for either single or double occupancy. A customer staying three nights will, therefore, be charged for three room-nights.
·   Creditors relate only to the variable costs incurred by the hotel.
·   The company does not provide for depreciation.

The first Bon Repose UK hotel was opened one year ago. Its financial and operating information is shown below.

Operating statement year ended 30 November 2001			Net assets at 30 November 2001		
	£	£		£	£
Turnover		560,640			
Variable costs			Fixed assets		669,556
Breakfasts and laundry		175,200	Net current assets		
Contribution		385,440	Debtors	35,040	
Fixed costs			Cash	10,804	
Labour	133,865			45,844	
Light and heat	89,045		Creditors	(14,600)	31,244
Rates, insurance, maintenance	120,482	343,392	Net assets		700,800
Net profit		42,048			
Actual number of room-nights sold – 17,520					

Task 2.1

Helene de la Tour asks you to prepare the following performance indicators for the hotel:
(a)   Gross (or contribution) margin.
(b)   Net profit (or sales) margin.
(c)   Return on capital employed.
(d)   Asset turnover.
(e)   Average age of debtors in months.
(f)   Average age of creditors in months.
(g)   The number of months that expenses could be paid from the cash balance.
(h)   Maximum capacity of the hotel in room-nights.
(i)   The percentage room-night occupancy rate of the hotel.

Data

On receiving your performance indicators, Helene de la Tour tells you that similar hotels in France are more profitable. She believes one of the reasons for the poor profits at the UK hotel is because the manager has been giving discounts. She tells you of the following company policies:
·   The price of each room is £40.00 per night but the manager can reduce this to £20 where necessary.
·   The average age of debtors should be 0.5 months.
·   The company should take twice as many months to pay its creditors as it currently does.
·   The cash balance at the hotel should only be £3,000. Any surplus cash should be transferred to the head office bank account.

You agree to investigate the reasons for the poor profits.

Task 2.2

Write a memo to Helene de la Tour. In your memo you should:
(a)   Calculate:
        (i)   what the turnover would have been had there been no discounts;
        (ii)   the total discount;
        (iii)   the number of discounted room-nights;
        (iv)   the percentage of room-nights discounted.

(b)   Prepare a revised operating statement and statement of net assets assuming that the company's policies had been met but no discounts offered.

(c)   Calculate the revised:
        (i)   gross (or contribution) margin;
        (ii)   net profit (or sales) margin;
        (iii)   return on capital employed.

(d)   *Briefly* discuss whether or not the discounting of prices would have been the reason for the reduced profits.

Task 2.1

Helena de la Tour asks you to prepare the following performance indicators for the hotel.

(a) Gross (or contribution) margin.
(b) Net profit (or sales) margin.
(c) Return on capital employed.
(d) Asset turnover.
(e) Average age of debtors in months.
(f) Average age of creditors in months.
(g) The number of months that expenses could be paid from the cash balance.
(h) Maximum capacity of the hotel in room-nights.
(i) The percentage room-night occupancy rate of the hotel.

Data

On receiving your performance indicators Helena de la Tour tells you that similar hotels in France are more profitable. She believes some of the reasons for the poor profits at the hotel is because the manager has been giving discounts. She tells you of the following company policies:

- The price of each room is £80.00 per night but the manager can reduce this to £70 where necessary.
- the average age of debtors should be 0.5 months.
- The company should take as many months to pay its creditors as it currently does.
- The cash balance at the hotel should be only £5000. Any surplus cash should be transferred to the head office bank account.

You agree to investigate the reasons for the poor profits.

Task 2.2

Write a memo to Helena de la Tour. In your memo you should
(a) Calculate:
(i) what the turnover would have been had there been no discounts
(ii) the total discount
(iii) the number of discounted room-nights
(iv) the percentage of room-nights discounted.

(b) Prepare a revised operating statement and state if net of net a statement (ing) that the company's policies had been met but no discounts offered.

(c) Calculate the revised:
(i) gross (or contribution) margin
(ii) net profit (or sales) margin
(iii) return on capital employed.

(d) Briefly discuss whether or not the discounting of prices would have been the reason for the reduced profits.

MOCK EXAMINATION – UNIT 9
QUESTIONS

This examination is in TWO sections.

You have to show competence in BOTH sections.

You should therefore attempt and aim to complete EVERY task in BOTH sections.

You should spend about 80 minutes on Section 1 and 100 minutes on Section 2.

Include all essential workings within your answers, where appropriate.

Section 1

Data

Sandwell Ltd makes a single product, the Gamma. You are Sandwell's management accountant and you are responsible for preparing its operating budgets. The accounting year is divided into 13 four-week periods. There are five days in each week.

The sales director of Sandwell has recently completed the following forecast sales volume for the next five periods.

Sales forecast five periods to 18 November 2001					
Period number	1	2	3	4	5
Four weeks ending	29 Jul	26 Aug	23 Sep	21 Oct	18 Nov
Number of Gammas	19,400	21,340	23,280	22,310	22,310

The production director provides you with the following information:
· On completion of production, 3% of the Gammas are found to be faulty and have to be scrapped. The faulty Gammas have no scrap value.
· Opening stocks: period 1, four weeks ending 29 July:
  - finished stock 3,880 Gammas
  - raw materials 16,500 litres.
· Closing stocks at the end of each period:
  - finished stock must equal four days' sales volume of Gammas in the next period
  - raw materials must equal five days' gross production in the next period.
· Each Gamma requires 3 litres of material costing £8 per litre.
· Each Gamma requires 0.5 hours of labour.
· Sandwell employs 70 production workers who each work a 40-hour week. Each employee is paid a guaranteed wage of £240 per week.
· The cost of any overtime is £9 per hour.

Task 1.1

Prepare the following budgets for the production director:
(a) Gross production budget in Gammas (including faulty production) for each of the first four periods.
(b) Material purchases budget in litres for each of the first three periods.

(c)   Cost of the material purchases for each of the first three periods.
(d)   Labour budget in hours for each of the first three periods including any overtime required in each period.
(e)   Cost of the labour budget for each of the first three periods including the cost of any overtime.

Data

After receiving your budgets, Sandwell's production director raises the following points:
·   Overtime payments should only be made if absolutely necessary.
·   The faulty Gammas are thought to be caused by poor work practices by some of the production workers although this is not known for certain.
·   The 70 production workers work independently of one another in making Gammas.

Task 1.2

Write a memo to the production director. In your memo, you should:
(a)   Explain and quantify the value of any possible overtime savings.
(b)   Suggest ONE extra cost which might be necessary to achieve the overtime savings.
(c)   Identify TWO advantages of sampling as a way of discovering reasons for the faulty Gammas.
(d)   Briefly explain the difference between true (or simple) random sampling, systematic sampling and stratified sampling.
(e)   State which form of sampling Sandwell should use.

Section 2

You should spend about 100 minutes on this section.

Data

Wimpole Ltd owns a subsidiary, Hall Ltd, which makes a single product, the Omega. The budgeted and actual results for the year ended 30 November 2001 are shown below.

Hall Ltd
Budgeted and actual operating statement
Year ended 30 November 2001

	Budget	Actual
Sales volume (units)	36,000	35,000
	£	£
Turnover	1,440,000	1,365,000
Direct costs		
Material	432,000	500,000
Labour	216,000	232,000
Light, heat and power	92,000	96,000
Fixed overheads		
Depreciation	100,000	70,000
Other fixed overheads	400,000	420,000
Cost of production	1,240,000	1,318,000
Less closing stock	–	164,750
Cost of sales	1,240,000	1,153,250
Operating profit	200,000	211,750

Ann Jones, the senior management accountant, tells you:

· Material and labour are variable costs.
· The budgeted total cost of light, heat and power includes a fixed element of £20,000.
· The actual cost of light, heat and power includes a fixed element of £12,000.
· There were no budgeted or actual opening stocks.
· During the year, *actual* production was 40,000 Omegas, of which 5,000 were unsold at the year end.
· The closing stock of 5,000 Omegas were valued at their actual direct cost plus an appropriate proportion of fixed overheads.
· The company did not purchase or sell any fixed assets during the year.
· There was no work in progress at any time.

Task 2.1

(a) Calculate the following:
    (i)   Budgeted selling price per Omega.
    (ii)   Budgeted material cost per Omega.

(iii)   Budgeted labour cost per Omega.

(iv)   Budgeted variable cost of light, heat and power per Omega.

(v)   The percentage of cost of production carried forward in closing stock.

(vi)   Total actual variable cost of sales by expenditure type.

(vii)   Total actual fixed costs.

(b)   Prepare a flexible budget statement using variable (or marginal) costing, showing the budgeted and actual results and any variances.

Data

The Chief Executive of Wimpole Ltd is Harry Easton. On receiving the original budgeted and actual operating statement, he had been very pleased with the performance of Hall Ltd. After reading your revised statement, however, he is concerned about the changes in both the budgeted profits and actual profits and is considering investigating whether or not the managers of Hall Ltd were responsible for the differences. Ann Jones suggests you write a memo to the Chief Executive.

Task 2.2

Write a short memo to Harry Easton, the Chief Executive. In your memo you should:

(a)   Briefly explain the main reason for:

(i)   the difference between the original budget and the budget you prepared in Task 2.1;

(ii)   the difference between the original operating profit and the operating profit you prepared in Task 2.1.

(b)   Give TWO possible reasons why the original actual operating profit shown was greater than the budgeted operating profit despite a lower sales volume.

KEY TECHNIQUES
ANSWERS

Chapter 2
Collection of cost information

QUESTION 1

Product 'EF3'

Quarter ended	Volume tonnes	Fixed cost £	Variable cost £	Total cost £
March	15,000	25,000	525,000	550,000
June	12,000	25,000	420,000	445,000
September	16,000	25,000	560,000	585,000
December	14,000	25,000	490,000	515,000

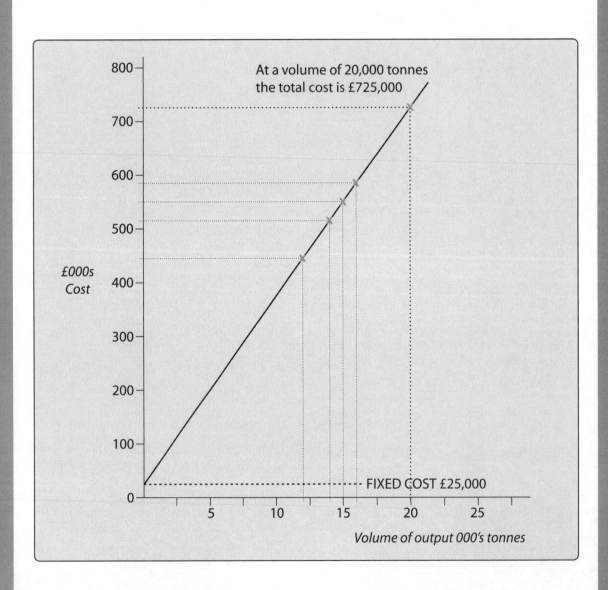

QUESTION 2 (June 1999)

MEMO

To: Margaret Brown

From: Management Accountant

Date: 16 June 1999

Subject: Sales forecasting

I refer to your observations and concerns regarding the accuracy of the sales forecasting.

(a) Limitations of linear regression as a forecasting technique

The technique uses data from a sample of previous performance to establish a trend. Where the sample size is small then the result may be inaccurate.

It assumes that there is always a linear relationship and that the change in sales volume from period to period is constant.

Historical data is used to establish the trend and it is assumed that the trend will continue. However, with the introduction of new products to the market, demand for existing products can change significantly.

Seasonal variations assumed in the forecast may change if there are abnormal conditions affecting a season.

(b) Other ways of forecasting

Depending on the size of the customer base and the relationship with the customer, it may be possible to ask them about their planned requirements.

The company could consider market research including both primary and secondary research methods. It may also be possible to identify leading indicators which can influence demand.

Chapter 3
Accounting for overheads

QUESTION 3

Overhead recovery rates for each cost centre:

Machining $\dfrac{£36,000}{4,000 \text{ machine hours}}$ = £9.00 per machine hour

Fabrication $\dfrac{£41,600}{5,200 \text{ machine hours}}$ = £8.00 per machine hour

Outside contract work $\dfrac{£28,600}{1,950 \text{ labour hours}}$ = £14.67 per direct labour hour

Production cost of contract:

		£
Direct material		3,100
Direct labour:		
Machining	12 hours	
Fabrication	8 hours	
Outside work	6 hours	
	26 hours × £7.50	195
Overheads:		
Machining	12 hours × £9.00	108
Fabrication	8 hours × £8.00	64
Outside work	6 hours × £14.67	88
Production cost		3,555
Add 10% for admin, selling and distribution		356
		£3,911
Selling price/contract price (£3,911/75) ×100 =		£5,215

Check:

	£
Contract price/selling price	5,215
Cost	3,911
Profit	£1,304

Profit = 25% of selling price as required.

QUESTION 4

Overhead recovery rate:

	£
Overheads	
Building occupancy	9,100
Telephone, postage and stationery	4,700
Other overheads	11,200
Administrator's salary	14,500
	£39,500

Labour hours		9,400
Overhead rate per labour hour	£39,500/9,400 =	£4.20

Partners' labour charge-out rate	£30,000/1,880 =	£15.96	per hour
Qualified senior	£18,500/1,880 =	£9.84	per hour
Trainee (1)	£10,500/1,880 =	£5.59	per hour
Trainee (2)	£12,000/1,880 =	£6.38	per hour

White Rose Hotel estimated fees:

		£
Direct labour:		
Partners	5 hours × £15.96 =	79.80
Qualified senior	12 hours × £9.84 =	118.08
Trainee (1)	3 hours × £5.59 =	16.77
Trainee (2)	3 hours × £6.38 =	19.14
		233.79
Overheads:		
23 hours × £4.20		96.60
Total cost		330.39
Thus charge to client	(£330.39/70) × 100 =	£471.99

QUESTION 5

Task

(a) **Sandsend Engineers Ltd overhead recovered:**

		£
Machining	4,250 machine hours × £9.00	38,250
Fabrication	5,300 machine hours × £8.00	42,400
Outside work	1,975 labour hours × £14.67	28,973
		£109,623

(b)

Overhead control account

	£		£
Actual:		*Recovered in work-in-progress*	
Machining	37,800	Machining	38,250
Fabrication	42,000	Fabrication	42,400
Outside work	29,100	Outside work	28,973
Over-recovered P/L account (bal)	723		
	£109,623		£109,623

QUESTION 6

Answer is C.

		£
Direct labour	4.5 hours × £8.50	38.25
Direct material	1.1 tonnes × £25	27.50
Variable overhead	£378,000/12,000 tonnes	31.50
Marginal cost = Total variable costs per tonne		£97.25

QUESTION 7

Answer is D.

Contribution per tonne	=	Selling price – Variable cost
	=	£132 – £97.25
	=	£34.75

QUESTION 8

(a)   **Blidworth Loam Ltd**

Budgeted operating statement for the year

	Marginal costing format	Absorption costing format
Production (tonnes)	12,000	12,000
Sales (tonnes)	11,500	11,500
	£	£
Sales	1,518,000	1,518,000
Variable costs		
Direct labour (12,000 x 38.25)	459,000	459,000
Direct material (12,000 x 27.50)	330,000	330,000
Variable overhead (12,000 x 31.50)	378,000	378,000
Closing stock for marginal costing (W1)	(48,625)	
	1,118,375	
Contribution	399,625	
Fixed costs	250,000	250,000
Closing stock for absorption costing (W2)		(59,042)
Operating profit	£149,625	£160,042

(b)   The difference in reported profit is due to the basis on which the closing stock is valued.

In the case of the marginal cost approach, the stock is valued at total variable or marginal cost whereas in the full absorption cost approach the closing stock includes an element of fixed costs carried forward.

The marginal cost format simply treats fixed costs as period costs, written off in the period to which they relate.

The difference in profit can be proved as 500 tonnes × £20.833 = £10,417.

Workings
(W1) 500 tonnes × £97.25 = £48,625
(W2) Fixed production overheads are absorbed at £250,000 ÷ 12,000 = £20.833 per tonne
Stock adjustment = 500 tonnes × (£97.25 + £20.833) = £59,042

QUESTION 9

Definitions:
· *Activity* – a value adding process which consumes resources.
· *Cost driver* – an activity or factor which generates cost. For example, in a hospital the number of images taken in the X-ray department would be a cost driver.
· *Cost pool* – the pooling of overhead cost relating to a specific activity.
· *Cost driver rate* – this is the result of dividing the cost pool for the activity by the cost driver volume.

QUESTION 10

The application of ABC involves the following set procedure:
· Accounting for and collection of overhead for each activity.
· Allocation of the overhead to form cost pools associated with 'value adding' activities.
· Identification of cost drivers.
· Determination of cost driver rates.
· Recovery and charging of overhead to each product/service based on the demand for the activity.

QUESTION 11

(a) **Cost driver rates:**

Activity	Cost pool £	Cost driver volume		Cost driver rate
Process set up	260,000	200	set ups	£1,300 / set up
Material procurement	74,000	50	purchase orders	£1,480 per purchase order
Maintenance	64,000	12	maintenance plans	£5,333 per plan
Material handling	120,000	2,500	material movements	£48 per movement
Quality costs	80,000	200	inspections	£400 per inspection
Order processing	30,000	1,000	customers	£30 per customer

(b) Using the ABC method, the following overhead would be recovered for each 1,000 tonnes of output:

			£
17 set ups	×	£1,300	22,100
4 purchase orders	×	£1,480	5,920
1 maintenance plan	×	£5,333	5,333
210 material movements	×	£48	10,080
16 inspections	×	£400	6,400
80 customers	×	£30	2,400
			£52,233

Thus the overhead cost per tonne of product would be:
£52,233/1,000 = £52.23 per tonne

QUESTION 12 (June 2002)

Note to the Finance Director

From: Financial Analyst

Date: X-X-XX

Subject: **ABC apportionment of fixed overheads**

(a) **Allocation of overheads**

		Mainframe £		Desktop £
Set up costs		10,000		Nil
Rent and power – production	120,000 × 10/50	24,000	120,000 × 40/50	96,000
Rent – stores	50,000 × 400/800	25,000	50,000 × 400/800	25,000
Salaries – store issue staff	40,000 × 2,000/10,000	8,000	40,000 × 8,000/10,000	32,000
Total		67,000		153,000

(b) **Fixed overheads per unit**

		Mainframe		Desktop
Number of computers		5		5,000
Fixed overhead per computer	£67,000/5	£13,400	£153,000/5,000	£30.60

Chapter 4
Time series, sampling and index numbers

QUESTION 13

Revision of standards based on changes in the index

Category of cost	Current standard		Revised standards		
		Q1	Q2	Q3	Q4
Direct labour hour rate	£7.00	£7.21 (W1)	£7.21	£7.21	£7.21
Raw material cost/tonne	£55.00	£56.38	£56.94	£57.23	£57.23
Fixed overhead recovery rate per hour	£12.50	£12.70	£12.69	£12.75	£12.79

Working

(W1) $£7 \times \dfrac{108.15}{105.00} = £7.21$

The other numbers are obtained in a similar manner.

QUESTION 14 (June 2004)

Task

(a)

Average prices in the period January to March were:

$$\frac{5.05 + 5.02 + 5.08}{3} = \frac{15.15}{3} = £5.05$$

Average prices in the period February to April were:

$$\frac{5.02 + 5.08 + 5.11}{3} = \frac{15.21}{3} = £5.07$$

Average prices in the period March to May were:

$$\frac{5.08 + 5.11 + 5.20}{3} = \frac{15.39}{3} = £5.13$$

(b)

MEMO	
To:	Sam Thomas
From:	Accounting Technician
Date:	June 2004
Subject:	Material prices

Trend in material prices

The trend shows an upward movement in prices over the period. By smoothing the individual prices, the trend is more apparent than in the original data where the upward and downward monthly prices show a less clear picture.

Use of trend in setting standards

The trend can be extrapolated to indicate what future prices are likely to be in the remainder of 2004. This may cause the organisation to alter the standard for material prices if the expected prices are going to diverge significantly from the current standard.

Other information

Two other pieces of information are as follows:
(i)   The amount of materials used to make a desk. This may be unchanged but it is possible that the desk could be re-engineered to simplify its construction, possibly using less material.
(ii)   The overall demand for desks – if demand were to increase significantly, the greater demand for desks would generate an increased demand for materials. The company may be able to buy these materials cheaper by obtaining quantity discounts.

QUESTION 15

(a) **2001**

	Q1	Q2	Q3	Q4
Actual price per tonne	£40	£44	£64	£76
Seasonal variation	– £4	– £8	+ £4	+ £8
Trend	£44	£52	£60	£68

(b) **2002**

	Q1	Q2	Q3	Q4
Trend (+ £8 per quarter)	£76	£84	£92	£100
Seasonal variation	– £4	– £8	+ £4	+ £8
Forecast price per tonne	£72	£76	£96	£108

QUESTION 16 (June 2000)

(a) **Trend and seasonal variations**

Year	Quarter	Actual	4 quarter total	4 quarter average	Centred trend	Seasonal variation
1997	3	142				
	4	142				
			584	146		
1998	1	150			146	4
			584	146		
	2	150			148	2
			600	150		
	3	142			150	− 8
			600	150		
	4	158			152	6
			616	154		
1999	1	150			154	− 4
			616	154		
	2	166			156	10
			632	158		
	3	142			158	− 16
			632	158		
	4	174			160	14
			648	162		
2000	1	150				
	2	182				

(b) **Analysis of seasonal variations**

	Quarter 1	Quarter 2	Quarter 3	Quarter 4	Residual
1998	4	2	− 8	6	
1999	− 4	10	− 16	14	
Total	0	12	− 24	20	
Average	0	6	− 12	10	4
Adjustment for residual	− 1	− 1	− 1	− 1	− 4
Seasonal variations	− 1	5	− 13	9	0

(c)   **Forecast demand – quarter 2**

Trend (160 + 2 + 2)	164
Seasonal variation	5
Forecast	169
Actual (estimate)	182
Residual	13

The forecast demand for quarter 2 of 2000 is 169 units.

(d)   **Reasons why there might be a difference**
·   Possibility of random errors.
·   Seasonal variations might not be additive.
·   The original actual data was only an estimate.
·   The sales volume data ignores some factors which might influence demand, e.g. price changes.

QUESTION 17

(a)   **Model A: a + bx = y**

Quarter 17:	£200,000 + (£58,000 × 17)	£1,186,000
Quarter 18:	£200,000 + (£58,000 × 18)	£1,244,000
Quarter 19:	£200,000 + (£58,000 × 19)	£1,302,000

Model B: a + z(1+g)^x = y

Quarter 17:	£1,000,000 + £303,268	£1,303,268
Quarter 18:	£1,000,000 + £333,595	£1,333,595
Quarter 19:	£1,000,000 + £366,955 (W)	£1,366,955

Working
£333,595 × 1.1 = £366,955

(b)   **Model A**

y Actual	Difference
£1,186,000 – £1,300,000 =	– £114,000
£1,244,000 – £1,350,000 =	– £106,000
£1,302,000 – £1,390,000 =	– £88,000

Model B

y Actual	Difference
£1,303,268 – £1,300,000	£3,268
£1,333,595 – £1,350,000	– £16,405
£1,366,955 – £1,390,000	– £23,045

The better fit is model B as the difference between the actual results and the forecast results are smaller than with model A.

(c)

> **MEMO**
>
> **To:**   Barry Jones
>
> **From:**   Accounting
>
> **Date:**   4 December 2003
>
> **Subject:** Forecasting
>
> (i)   Model B provides the more accurate forecast. It assumes a constant percentage rate of growth which is more in line with the results analysed.
>
> For period 19, the second term of the equation was £366,955, and so for period 20 the second term will be £366,955 × 1.1 = 403,650. This gives a total forecast of £1,403,650.
>
> (ii) The limitations of using model B are as follows.
>
> It assumes that time is the only variable. This may not be the case and in the longer term such things as income, tastes and interest rates may be important.
>
> It is unlikely that a constant rate of growth will be sustained over even a fairly short period of time. Seasonal variations will upset this trend as will some of the other factors referred to above, particularly interest rates.
>
> The sample of 19 is very small and the figures should be kept under review until a stable pattern emerges.

Chapters 5 and 6
Standard costing and variance analysis

QUESTION 18

Revision of standards based on changes in the index

(a)   **Standard hours in the budget**
182 trips × 5 standard hours
=   910 standard hours

(b)   **Fixed overhead recovery rate per standard hour**
£11,500/910   =   £12.637 per standard hour

(c)   **Fixed overhead recovered**
175 x 5 standard hours
=   875 standard hours × £12.637
=   £11,058

(d) **Fixed overhead total variance**

	£
Fixed overhead recovered	11,058
Actual fixed cost	12,400
	£1,342 Adverse

(e) **Fixed overhead expenditure variance**

	£
Budgeted fixed costs	11,500
Actual fixed costs	12,400
	£900 Overspend Adverse

(f) **Fixed overhead volume variance**
(Standard hours produced – Budgeted hours) × FORR
(875 – 910) × £12.637
= £442 Adverse

(g) **Fixed overhead capacity variance**
(Budgeted hours – Actual hours worked) × FORR
(910 – 940) × £12.637
= £379 Favourable

(h) **Fixed overhead efficiency variance**
(Standard hours produced – Actual hours worked) × FORR
(875– 940) × £12.637
= £821 Adverse

(i) Fixed costs in the short run need to be recovered so that the business can operate profitably.

The fixed overhead total variance informs the owners whether or not the fixed overhead for the period has been under or over-recovered. They would need to know what part of this is due to either expenditure or volume factors.

In the period under review, there has been an under-recovery of £1,342. Much of this is revealed as an overspend of £900, by the expenditure variance.

The owners need to analyse fully the fixed costs to identify where the overspend occurred.

The £442 balance of the under-recovery was due to poor volume. The planned volume was 182 trips whereas, for some reason, only 175 were achieved.

Although more hours were worked than planned, driver efficiency was down and this reflected in the volume. Conditions may have been, at times, more adverse in this period than anticipated.

For control purposes, the owner managers need to focus on keeping fixed costs in the short run within budget and striving to increase, wherever possible, volume.

QUESTION 19 (December 2001)

Task 19.1

(a) (i) Standard number of compact discs produced per labour hour:
  800 CDs/8 labour hours   =   100

    (ii) Budgeted machine hours of the department:
  880 budgeted labour hours/8 labour hours
  per machine hour   =   110 hours

    (iii) Budgeted departmental fixed overheads:
  £33,000 × 880 labour hours/1,320 labour hours   =   £22,000

    (iv) Actual fixed overheads:
  £34,500 × 880 labour hours/1,320 labour hours   =   £23,000

    (v) Standard fixed overhead rate per labour hour:
  £33,000/1,320 labour hours*   =   £25.00
  *or £22,000/880 labour hours or £200/8 labour hours

    (vi) Standard labour hours produced:
  96,000 CDs/100 per labour hour   =   960 hours

    (vii) Actual number of blank CDs issued to production:
  £20,790/£0.21   =   99,000 blank CDs

    (viii) Actual cost of actual production including fixed overheads:

Labour	£7,252
Material	£20,790
Fixed overhead	£23,000
	£51,042

    (ix) Standard cost of actual production:
  £416/800 × 96,000   =   £49,920

(b) (i) Material price variance:
  (Standard price – Actual price) × Actual usage
  (£0.20 – £0.21) × 99,000   =   £(990)A

    (ii) Material usage variance:
  (Standard usage – Actual usage) × Standard price
  (96,000 – 99,000) × £0.20   =   £(600)A

    (iii) Labour rate variance:
  (Standard rate – Actual rate) × Actual hours
  (£7 – £7.40) × 980   =   £(392)A

    (iv) Labour efficiency variance:
  (Standard hours produced – Actual hours worked) × Standard rate
  (960 – 980) × £7   =   £(140)A

    (v) Fixed overhead expenditure variance:

	£
Budgeted fixed cost	22,000
Actual fixed cost	23,000
	£(1,000)A

    (vi) Fixed overhead volume variance:
  (Standard hours produced – Budgeted hours) × FORR
  (960 – 880) × £25   =   £2,000 F

    (vii) Fixed overhead capacity variance:
  (Budgeted hours – Actual hours worked) × FORR
  (880 – 980) × £25   =   £2,500 F

(viii)   Fixed overhead efficiency variance:
(Standard hours produced – Actual hours worked) × FORR
(960 – 980) × £25   =   £(500) A

(c)   **Standard costing reconciliation statement – week ended 30 November 2001**

	£
Standard cost of actual production	49,920

Summary of variances:

Material price	(990) A
Material usage	(600) A
Labour rate	(392) A
Labour efficiency	(140) A
Fixed overhead expenditure	(1,000) A
Fixed overhead volume	2,000 F
	(1,122) A
Actual cost of production	51,042

Task 19.2

LETTER

Gransden, Yelling and Co
Accountants and Registered Auditors

5 December 2001

Jamil Baharundin
CD Products Ltd
Anytown

Dear Mr Baharundin

Thank you for your letter and observations regarding the introduction of the new reporting format based on the standing costing technique.

I list my response to your questions below:

(a)   **Issues to consider before investigating a variance**
There are two principal factors to consider here:
· Cost v benefit.
· Is the variance a 'one off' or an early warning of a longer term problem?

A variance may thus be investigated if it:
· exceeds a minimum absolute amount
· exceeds a minimum percentage amount
· constitutes an element of a continuing trend
· is totally unexpected
· is considered to be a sign of a longer term problem.

You may decide not to investigate a variance if:
· the cause is already known and considered out of management's span of control.
· it is considered as 'one off' and will correct itself in the short-run.

(b) **Sub-division of the material usage variance**

For the week ended 30 November 2001, 96,000 CDs were pressed although 99,000 blank CDs were used. Of the 3,000 difference, 1,920 (96,000 × 2%) could be accounted for as scrapped production, leaving 1,080 unaccounted for. The sub-division of the material usage variance is:

Variance arising from scrapped discs (1,920 × £0.20)	£384 A
Variance arising from other reasons (1,080 × £0.20)	£216 A
Material usage variance	£600 A

(c) **Demand for pressing and finishing**

Fixed overheads have simply been apportioned to cost centres on the basis of labour hours and a recovery rate based on labour hours has been pre-determined.

An analysis of the activities reveals that a large proportion of the fixed costs relate to the CD Pressing Department.

As a result the standard costs of the pressing activity have been understated while finishing costs are overstated. If this has been built into selling prices for these activities then it may explain why there is excess demand in the CD Pressing Department.

Budgeted fixed overheads of £30,800 are attributable to pressing and thus the fixed overhead recovery rate for this activity should be £35 (£30,800 ÷ 880) per labour hour and not £25 as the 'blanket rate' suggests.

Yours sincerely
AAT Student

QUESTION 20 (December 2000)

Task 20.1

(a)
(i)	Standard price of fuel per litre:			
	£497,664/1,244,160		=	£0.40
(ii)	Standard litres of fuel for 5,760 ferry crossings:			
	1,244,160 × (5,760/6,480)		=	1,105,920 litres
(iii)	Standard labour rate per hour:			
	£466,560/93,312		=	£5.00
(iv)	Standard labour hours for 5,760 ferry crossings:			
	93,312 × (5,760/6,480)		=	82,944 hours
(v)	Standard fixed overhead per budgeted operating hour:			
	£466,560/7,776		=	£60.00
(vi)	Standard operating hours for 5,760 crossings:			
	5,760 × (7,776/6,480)		=	6,912 hours
(vii)	Standard fixed overhead cost absorbed by the actual 5,760 ferry crossings:			
	6,912 hours × £60.00		=	£414,720

(b) (i) Material price variance:
(Standard price – Actual price) × Actual usage
(£0.40 – £0.46) × 1,232,800   =   £(73,968) A

(ii) Material usage variance:
(Standard usage – Actual usage) × Standard price
(1,105,920 – 1,232,800) × £0.40   =   £(50,752) A

(iii) Labour rate variance:
(Standard rate – Actual rate) × Actual hours
(£5.00 – £5.25) × 89,856   =   £(22,464) A

(iv) Labour efficiency variance:
(Standard hours produced – Actual hours worked) × Standard rate
(82,944 – 89,856) × £5   =   £(34,560) A

(v) Fixed overhead expenditure variance:

	£
Budgeted fixed overhead	466,560
Actual fixed overhead	472,440
Variance	£(5,880) A

(vi) Fixed overhead volume variance:
(Standard operating hours produced – Budgeted operating hours) × FORR
(6,912 – 7,776) × £60   =   £(51,840) A

(vii) Fixed overhead capacity variance:
(Budgeted operating hours – Actual operating hours) × FORR
(7,776 – 7,488) × £60   =   £(17,280) A

(viii) Fixed overhead efficiency variance:
(Standard operating hours produced – Actual operating hours) × FORR
(6,912 – 7,488) × £60   =   £(34,560) A

(c) **Travel Ferries Ltd – Reconciliation statement for the year ended 30 November 2000**

F = Favourable
A = Adverse

	£
Standard cost of actual operations (W)	1,271,808
Summary of variances:	
Material price	(73,968) A
Material usage	(50,752) A
Labour rate	(22,464) A
Labour efficiency	(34,560) A
Fixed overhead expenditure	(5,880) A
Fixed overhead volume	(51,840) A
	(239,464)
Actual cost	1,511,272

Working

£1,430,784 x 5,760/6,480 = £1,271,808

Task 20.2

MEMO

To: Chief Executive

From: Management Accountant

Date: 6 December 2000

Subject: Explanation of variances

I refer to the concern you have expressed recently regarding the adverse variances in the report on Travel Ferries' operations for the year ended 30 November.

In reply to your comments, I wish to make the following observations concerning:
· further analysis of the material price variance.
· identification of uncontrollable variances.
· controllable variances and their investigation.

(a) **Material price variance (fuel)**
Actual market price was £0.40 × 1.2 = £0.48 per litre.
Actual price paid was £0.46 per litre.
The variance due to an invalid standard was:

(£0.40 − £0.48) × 1,232,800 litres	=	£(98,624) A
Variance due to other reasons:		
(£0.48 − £0.46) × 1,232,800 litres	=	£24,656 F
Price variance reported		£(73,968) A

(b) The labour efficiency variance is due to the extra time worked due to adverse weather conditions. The additional operating hours resulted in an extra 6,912 labour hours being worked.

This adverse efficiency is not controllable by management since management cannot control the weather.

(c) Controllable variances would include the labour rate variance and the fixed overhead capacity variance. Neither of these can be attributed to adverse conditions.

The capacity variance is adverse as the number of ferry crossings made was well below budget.

QUESTION 21 (June 2000)

Task 21.1

(a) (i) Budgeted labour hours of production for NGJ Ltd:

Labour hours	Budgeted hours per unit	Budgeted production	Budgeted hours
Basic	6	10,000	60,000
Grand	1	70,000	70,000
Super	1	70,000	70,000
Total budgeted labour hours			200,000

(ii) Standard factory fixed overhead rate per labour hour:
(£600,000/200,000 hours)   £3.00

(iii) *Basic* budgeted factory fixed overhead:
(£600,000 × [60,000/200,000])   £180,000
Basic actual factory fixed overhead:
(£630,000 × [60,000/200,000])   £189,000

(iv) Actual material cost per metre:
(£872,298/69,230)   £12.60
Actual labour hourly rate:
(£343,735/70,150)   £4.90

(v) Standard absorption cost of actual *Basic* production:
Material (£12 × 6 metres × 11,500 *Basics*)   £828,000
Labour (£5 × 6 hours × 11,500 *Basics*)   £345,000
Factory fixed overheads (£3 × 6 hours × 11,500 *Basics*)   £207,000

                                                            £1,380,000

(vi) Actual absorption cost of actual *Basic* production:
Material   £872,298
Labour   £343,735
Factory fixed overheads   £189,000

                                                            £1,405,033

(b) (i) Material price variance:
(Standard price – Actual price) × Actual usage
(£12 – £12.60) × 69,230   =   £(41,538) A

(ii) Material usage variance:
(Standard usage – Actual usage) × Standard price
(69,000 – 69,230) × £12   =   £(2,760) A

(iii) Labour rate variance:
(Standard rate – Actual rate) × Actual hours
(£5 – £4.90) × 70,150   =   £7,015   F

(iv) Labour efficiency variance:
(Standard hours produced – Actual hours worked) × Standard rate
(69,000 – 70,150) × £5   =   £(5,750) A

(v) Fixed overhead expenditure variance:

	£
Budgeted fixed cost	180,000
Actual fixed cost	189,000
Variance	£(9,000) A

(vi)   Fixed overhead volume variance:
       (Standard hours produced – Budgeted hours) × FORR
       (69,000 – 60,000) × £3   =   £27,000 F

(vii) Fixed overhead capacity variance:
       (Budgeted hours – Actual hours) × FORR
       (60,000 – 70,150) × £3   =   £30,450 F

(viii) Fixed overhead efficiency variance:
       (Standard hours produced – Actual hours worked) × FORR
       (69,000 – 70,150) × £3   =   £(3,450) A

(c)   **Standard costing reconciliation statement – year ended 31 May 2000**

			£
Standard cost of actual production			1,380,000
Summary of variances:			
Material price	(41,538)	A	
Material usage	(2,760)	A	
Labour rate	7,015	F	
Labour efficiency	(5,750)	A	
Fixed overhead expenditure	(9,000)	A	
Fixed overhead volume	27,000	F	
			(25,033) A
Actual cost of production			1,405,033

F = Favourable
(A) = Adverse

Task 21.2

> **MEMO**
>
> **To:**   *Basic* Product Line Manager
>
> **From:**   Management Accountant
>
> **Date:**   21 June 2000
>
> **Subject:** Variances
>
> Further to your comments on the variances relating to *Basic* production, I wish to make the following observations.
>
> (a)   Market price of material per metre during the year was:
>   £12.60 × (100/90) = £14.00
>
> (b)   The sub-division of the price variance on further analysis shows a variance arising due to the contracted price being different from the actual price, amounting to:
>   (£14.00 – £12.60) × 69,230   =   £96,922 F
>
>   Variance arising from other reasons:
>   (£12.00 – £14.00) × 69,230   £(138,460) A
>   £(41,538) A

(c) A value adding benefit from the purchasing manager's action not shown in the variances is the continuous supply of material supporting production as a result of the contract.

(d) Overhead recovery based on traditional absorption costing concepts focuses on charging overheads to production rather than seeking to control these overheads.

Activity based costing, however, firstly identifies activities which consume cost and recognises the reason why overheads are incurred.

The technique analyses the fixed costs and identifies cost drivers, the factors which generate cost, together with seeking to control these overheads.

Overhead is then recovered to products using cost driver rates, thus charging overhead to products which cause them to be incurred.

(e) It is clear that £202,000 of the budgeted overhead arose because of the mechanised production of *Grand* and *Super* products.

It may also be the case that most of the depreciation charge also relates to machinery used on those products.

As the *Basic* production only uses a small area of the production facility, much of the rent and rates relate to production driven by the needs of *Grand* and *Super*.

It is highly likely that the ABC method would have reduced the overhead attributed to *Basic* production.

QUESTION 22 (December 1999)

Task 22.1

(a) **Budget and actual data**

   (i)   Actual number of meals:
          4 meals × 7 days × 648 guests   =   18,144

   (ii)   Standard number of meals:
          3 meals × 7 days × 648 guests   =   13,608

   (iii) Actual hourly rate for catering staff:
          $5,280 cost ÷ 1,200 hours   = $4.40

   (iv) Standard hours allowed to serve three meals:
          (648 × 3 meals × 7 days) ÷ 12   =   1,134

   (v)   Standard overhead per guest:
          $38,340 budgeted overheads ÷ 540 budgeted guests   = $71.00

   (vi) Standard cost of providing for 648 guests:
          Meals: $3.00 × 13,608 meals   = $40,824
          Catering staff: $4.00 × 1,134 hours   = $4,536
          Fixed overheads:
          $71.00 standard overhead per guest × 648 guests   = $46,008
                                                $91,368

(b) **Variances**

(i) Material price variance:
(Standard price – Actual price) × Actual usage
($3.00 – $2.75) × 18,144 = $4,536 F

(ii) Material usage variance:
(Standard usage – Actual usage) × Standard price
(13,608 – 18,144) × $3.00 = $(13,608) A

(iii) Labour rate variance:
(Standard rate – Actual rate) × Actual hours
($4.00 – $4.40) × 1,200 = $(480) A

(iv) Labour efficiency variance:
(Standard hours produced – Actual hours worked) × Standard rate
(1,134 – 1,200) × $4.00 = $(264) A

(v) Fixed overhead expenditure variance:

	$
Budgeted fixed costs	38,340
Actual fixed costs	37,800
Variance	540 F

(vi) Fixed overhead volume variance:
(Actual guests – Budgeted guests) × Overhead per guest
(648 – 540) × $71 = $7,668 F

(c) **Bare Foot Hotel Complex**
Standard costing reconciliation statement – week ended 27 November 1999

	$	
Standard cost of providing for guests	91,368	
Summary of variances:		
Material price variance	4,536	F
Material usage variance	(13,608)	A
Labour rate variance	(480)	A
Labour efficiency variance	(264)	A
Fixed overhead expenditure variance	540	F
Fixed overhead volume variance	7,668	F
	(1,608)	A
Actual cost of providing for guests	92,976	

Task 22.2

MEMO

To: Alice Groves

From: Assistant Management Accountant

Date: 1 December 1999

Subject: Standard costing reconciliation statement

(a) The labour efficiency variance can be sub-divided into that part due to guests taking, on average, four meals per day and that part due to other underlying efficiency reasons. The detailed analysis is reproduced below:

Standard cost of standard hours – 3 meals per guest (1,134 × $4): $4,536

Standard cost of standard hours – 4 meals per guest:

[(648 ÷ 12) × 4 meals × 7 days] × $4 $6,048

Variance due to guests taking more meals than planned $(1,512) A

Standard cost of standard hours – 4 meals per guest $6,048

Standard cost of actual hours (1,200 × $4) $4,800

Other efficiency variances $1,248 F

(b) **Fixed overhead capacity and efficiency variances**

Both the capacity and efficiency variances are sub-divisions of the fixed overhead volume variance.

The volume variance measures the amount of under or over-recovery of fixed overhead due to either an increase or decrease in volume; in this case meals served and/or guest days.

The capacity element of this variance considers the increase or decrease in hours worked compared with the hours budgeted or planned and its effect on volume.

The efficiency variance measures the effect of the efficiency of labour on the volume achieved.

In the situation under review the capacity was favourable although the efficiency was adverse. The additional volume was achieved by increasing the hours worked.

(c) The fixed overhead relates to a number of hotel activities, not just catering, and therefore a sub-division of the volume variance would not 'add value' to the reporting of the variances; as such an analysis would be of no use to management.

QUESTION 23 (June 1999)

Task 23.1

(a) **Calculation of quantities**

   (i)   Actual litres used:

      £338,283 / £40.20   8,415

   (ii)   Actual hours worked:

      £110,330 / £5.90   18,700

   (iii) Standard litres for 1,700 tins of Zed:

      1,700 × 5 litres   8,500

   (iv) Standard labour hours for 1,700 tins of Zed:

      1,700 × 10 hours   17,000

   (v)   Standard hours of fixed overheads charged to budgeted production:

      1,750 × 10 hours   17,500

   (vi) Standard hours of fixed overheads charged to actual production:

      1,700 × 10 hours   17,000

(b) (i) Material price variance:
(Standard price – Actual price) × Actual usage
(£40.00 – £40.20) × 8,415 = £(1,683) A
(ii) Material usage variance:
(Standard usage – Actual usage) × Standard price
(8,500 – 8,415) × £40 = £3,400 F
(iii) Labour rate variance:
(Standard rate – Actual rate) × Actual hours
(£6.00 – £5.90) × 18,700 = £1,870 F
(iv) Labour efficiency variance:
(Standard hours produced – Actual hours worked) × Standard rate
(17,000 – 18,700) × £6.00 = £(10,200) A
(v) Fixed overhead expenditure variance:

	£
Budgeted fixed cost	420,000
Actual fixed cost	410,000
Variance	£10,000 F

(vi) Fixed overhead volume variance:
(Standard hours produced – Budgeted hours) × FORR
(17,000 – 17,500) × £24 = £(12,000) A
(vii) Fixed overhead capacity variance:
(Budgeted hours – Actual hours) × FORR
(17,500 – 18,700) × £24 = £28,800 F
(viii) Fixed overhead efficiency variance:
(Standard hours produced – Actual hours worked) × FORR
(17,000 – 18,700) × £24 = £(40,800) A

(c) **Standard costing reconciliation statement; standard to actual cost – May 1999**

	£
Standard cost of actual production (1,700 tins @ £500)	850,000
Summary of variances:	
Material price	(1,683) A
Material usage	3,400 F
Labour rate	1,870 F
Labour efficiency	(10,200) A
Fixed overhead expenditure	10,000 F
Fixed overhead volume	(12,000) A
	(8,613) A
Actual cost of production	858,613

Task 23.2

MEMO

To:	Production Director
From:	Management Accountant
Date:	16 June 1999
Subject:	Material variances

I refer to your observations regarding the material variances shown on my recent standard costing reconciliation statement.

If the standard price of material had been revised to incorporate the index then the price would have been:

£40 × (125.86/124.00) = £40.60 per litre

(a) It is possible, using this additional information, to sub-divide the price variance to that element due to the price increase highlighted in the index and that attributed to the efficiency of the purchasing department:

Revised standard price £40.60		Revised standard price	£40.60
Original standard price £40.00		Actual price	£40.20
Difference	£0.60 (A)	Difference	£0.40 (F)
Actual quantity (litres) 8,415		Actual quantity (litres)	8,415
Price variance due to revised price	£5,049 (A)	Price variance due to purchasing	£3,366 (F)

(b) There can be a number of factors which influence the reporting of a favourable usage variance; these include:

  (i) incorrect setting of the standard usage
  (ii) data errors as when a clerk misreads a figure
  (iii) some drums of material containing more than 50 litres resulting in more material being used than recorded as being used
  (iv) errors in the automatic weighing system. In May, 8,415 litres of material were used to produce 1,700 tins of Zed. This is equivalent to 4.95 litres per tin. The lowest acceptable error is only 0.5% or 4.975 litres per tin. This suggests that there might be a problem with the settings of the measuring machine.

(c) As it is possible for variances to be reported because of the errors outlined above, it is essential to investigate such variances fully.

QUESTION 24 (June 2002)

(a) (i) Actual cost of a telephone unit:
£79,200/1,200,000 units = £0.066

  (ii) Actual hourly wage rate of operators:
£478,800/114,000 hours = £4.20

  (iii) Standard number of operator hours for 1,000,000 calls:
1,000,000 × 6/60 = 100,000

  (iv) Budgeted cost of fixed overheads:
900,000 × £0.65 = £585,000

  (v) Budgeted number of operator hours:
900,000 × 6/60 = 90,000

  (vi) Standard cost of actual operations:
1,000,000 × £1.07 = £1,070,000

(b) (i) Price variance for telephone calls:
(£0.070 – £0.066) × 1,200,000 = £4,800 (F)

(ii) Usage variance for telephone calls:
(1,000,000 – 1,200,000) × £0.07 = £14,000 (A)

(iii) Labour rate variance:
(£3.50 – £4.20) × 114,000 = £79,800 (A)

(iv) Labour efficiency variance:
(100,000 – 114,000) × £3.50 = £49,000 (A)

(v) Fixed overhead expenditure variance:
£585,000 – £540,400 = £44,600 (F)

(vi) Fixed overhead volume variance:
(100,000 – 90,000) × £6.50 = £65,000 (F)

(vii) Fixed overhead capacity variance:
(114,000 – 90,000) × £6.50 = £156,000 (F)

(viii) Fixed overhead efficiency variance
(100,000 – 114,000) × £6.50 = £91,000 (A)

(c)

Standard costing reconciliation statement – 3 months ended 31 May 2002		
	£	£
Standard cost of actual operations		1,070,000
Price variance, telephone calls	4,800 (F)	
Usage variance, telephone calls	(14,000) (A)	
Labour rate variance	(79,800) (A)	
Labour efficiency variance	(49,000) (A)	
Fixed overhead expenditure variance	44,600 (F)	
Fixed overhead capacity variance	156,000 (F)	
Fixed overhead efficiency variance	(91,000) (A)	28,400 (A)
Actual cost of actual operations		1,098,400

QUESTION 25 (December 2002)

Task 25.1

(a)
(i)	Standard price of material per litre	(£106,250/12,500)	£8.50
(ii)	Actual price of material per litre	(£99,072/11,520)	£8.60
(iii)	Standard litres of material per barrel	(12,500/2,500)	5.00
(iv)	Standard labour rate per hour	(£60,000/10,000)	£6.00
(v)	Standard labour hours per barrel	(10,000/2,500)	4.00
(vi)	Standard machine hours per barrel	(20,000/2,500)	8.00
(vii)	Fixed overheads per budgeted machine hour	(£200,000/20,000)	£10.00
(viii)	Standard absorption cost per barrel	(£366,250/2,500)	£146.50

(b) (i) **Material price variance**

Standard price × actual quantity	(£8.50 × 11,520)	£97,920
Actual price × actual quantity (given)		£99,072
		£1,152 (A)

(ii) **Material usage variance**

Standard price × standard quantity		
(£8.50 × 5 litres × 2,400)		£102,000
Standard price × actual quantity		
(£8.50 × 11,520)		£97,920
		£4,080 (F)

(iii) **Labour rate variance**

Standard rate × actual hours		
(£6.00 × 10,080)		£60,480
Actual rate × actual hours (given)		£61,488
		(£1,008) (A)

(iv) **Labour efficiency variance**

Standard rate × standard hours		
(£6.00 × 4 × 2,400)		£57,600
Standard rate × actual hours		
(£6.00 × 10,080)		£60,480
		(£2,880) (A)

(v) **Fixed overhead expenditure variance**

Budgeted fixed overheads		£200,000
Actual fixed overheads		£185,808
		£14,192 (F)

(vi) **Fixed overhead volume variance**

Standard rate × budgeted machine hours		
(£10.00 × 8 × 2,500)		£200,000
Std rate × actual machine hours produced		
(£10.00 × 8 × 2,400)		£192,000
		(£8,000) (A)

(vii) **Fixed overhead capacity variance**

Standard rate × budgeted machine hours		
(£10.00 × 8 × 2,500)		£200,000
Standard rate × actual machine hours worked		
(£10.00 × 18,960)		£189,600
		(£10,400) (A)

(viii) **Fixed overhead efficiency variance**

Standard rate × actual machine hours worked		
(£10.00 × 18,960)		£189,600
Std rate × actual machine hours produced		
(£10.00 × 8 × 2,400)		£192,000
		£2,400 (F)

(c)

Standard costing reconciliation statement week ended 30 November 2002		
Standard cost of actual production (£146.50 × 2,400)		£351,600
Material price variance	(£1,152) (A)	
Material usage variance	£4,080 (F)	
Labour rate variance	(£1,008) (A)	
Labour efficiency variance	£2,880 (A)	
Fixed overhead expenditure variance	(£14,192) (F)	
Fixed overhead capacity variance	(£10,400) (A)	
Fixed overhead efficiency variance	£2,400 (F)	£5,232 (F)
Actual cost of actual production		£346,368

Task 25.2

MEMO

To: Anthony Bush

From: Accounting Technician

Date: 4 December 2002

Subject: Standard costs

Thank you for explaining how you currently develop the material standard costs per litre. My observations are shown below.

(a) **Validity of current calculations**

(i) In taking the average of the four trend figures by totalling them and dividing by 4, you are calculating a simple average trend price. This will give a valid average trend price for the year if the volumes are the same in each quarter. In the case of Primary Chemicals, however, the volume of production varies throughout the year and so to develop a valid average trend price, you need to weight each trend price by the volume per quarter.

(ii) If all the seasonal variations occurred in the same accounting period, there would be little benefit in taking account of seasonal variations. In the case of Primary Chemicals, however, this is not so. If variances are to give correct signals, the standard needs to be as accurate as possible. If not, an adverse variance could be reported not because of inefficiencies but because the standard was out-of-date. This suggests that standards should include seasonal variations – and hence vary from quarter to quarter – if variances are to show both the correct direction and correct magnitude of a deviation from standard.

(b) During quarter 4, the trend price was £10.00 per litre. To this must be added the 20% seasonal variation and so the most up-to-date standard would have been £12.00.

(c) This enables the original material price variance of £1,152 (A) to be sub-divided.

Forecast price 4th quarter	£12.00
Standard price	£8.50
Difference per litre	(£3.50) (A)

Variance due to difference in standard price
(£3.50 × 11,520)   (£40,320) (A)

Forecast price 4th quarter	£12.00
Actual price paid	£8.60
Difference per litre	£3.40 (F)

Variance due to other reason
(£3.40 × 11,520)   £39,168 (F)

Total material price variance   (£1,152) (A)

QUESTION 26 (December 2003)

Task 26.1

(a)	(i)	Standard price of fuel per gallon: £50,400 / 33,600	£1.50
	(ii)	Standard fuel usage for 160 flights: 33,600 × 160 / 168	32,000 gallons
	(iii)	Standard hourly rate for pilots: £67,200 / 1,344	£50.00
	(iv)	Standard pilot hours per flight: 1,344 / 168	8 hrs
	(v)	Standard pilot hours for 160 flights: 1,344 × 160 / 168 Alternative answer: 160 × 8 = 1,280 hrs	1,280 hrs
	(vi)	Standard fixed overhead cost per budgeted flying hour: 75,600 / 672	£112.50
	(vii)	Standard flying hours per flight: 672/168	4 hrs
	(viii)	Standard flying hours for 160 flights: 672 × 160 / 168 Alternative answer: 160 × 4 = 640 hrs	640 hrs
	(ix)	Standard fixed overhead absorbed by the 160 flights: 640 × £112.5	£72,000
	(x)	Standard cost of actual operations: £193,200 × 160 / 168	£184,000

(b)   (i)   Fuel price variance:
             (£1.50 × 38,400) – £61,440   £3,840 (A)
      (ii) Fuel usage variance:
             (32,000 – 38,400) × £1.50   £9,600 (A)
      (iii) Rate variance for pilots:
             (£50.00 × 1,536) – £79,872   £3,072 (A)
      (iv) Efficiency variance for pilots:
             (1,280 – 1,536) × £50.00   £12,800 (A)
      (v)   Fixed overhead expenditure variance:
             £75,600 – £76,200   £600 (A)
      (vi) Fixed overhead volume variance:
             (640 – 672) × £112.50 = £3,600 (A) (W1)   £3,600 (A)
      (vii) Fixed overhead capacity variance:
             (768 – 672) × £112.50 (W1)   £10,800 (F)
      (viii) Fixed overhead efficiency variance:
             (640 – 768) × £112.50 (W1)   £14,400 (A)

Working 1
Budgeted absorption
168 × 4 hrs = 672 hrs × £112.50 = £75,600
(Budget flights × Standard hours)

Actual absorption
160 × 4 hrs = 640 hrs × £112.50 = £72,000
(Actual flights × Standard hours)

Actual hours = 768 × £112.50   = £86,400

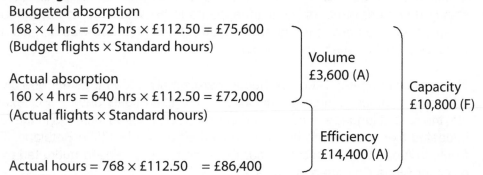

Volume
£3,600 (A)

Efficiency
£14,400 (A)

Capacity
£10,800 (F)

(c)   Standard Costing Reconciliation Statement - 28 days ended 30 November 2003

	£	£
Standard cost of actual operations		184,000
Fuel price variance	(3,840) (A)	
Fuel usage variance	(9,600) (A)	
Rate variance for pilots	(3,072) (A)	
Efficiency variance for pilots	(12,800) (A)	
Fixed overhead expenditure variance	(600) (A)	
Fixed overhead capacity variance	10,800 (F)	
Fixed overhead efficiency variance	(14,400) (A)	
	(33,512) (A)	
Actual cost of operations		217,512

Task 26.2

MEMO

To:	Lisa Margoli
From:	Accounting Technician
Date:	3 December 2003
Subject:	Fixed overheads

Thank you for raising your concerns with me about the fixed overheads for the Alpha City route.

(a)   The use of flying hours to absorb the fixed overheads is justified because in the traditional absorption system of selecting a single driver to absorb costs, it is preferable to choose a driver that the fixed costs depend on. In this example, flying hours does influence the level of fixed costs. However, an alternative would be to use the number of passenger journeys as this is the actual product that Econair is selling.

(b)   Using flying hours to absorb the fixed overheads results in an apparently illogical capacity variance; the number of flights are below budget (160 rather than 168) and yet the number of flying hours are above budget. This results in a favourable capacity variance. However, if passenger journeys were used to absorb the fixed overheads, the capacity variance will be favourable because more passengers are flown on each journey.

It should be noted that the main cause of the illogical variances is that the standard number of hours per flight appears to be set incorrectly at 4 hours, whereas each journey takes nearly 5 hours. If the standard was revised, the variances would appear more logical.

(c)   The original budgeted fixed overheads were simply added together and divided by the number of aircraft. This ignores the fixed costs drivers. For example, the cost of luggage handling and in-flight facilities was included in the total budgeted fixed overheads but only consumed by the flights to Betaland. The flights to Alpha City should not bear these costs. The revised budgeted fixed costs for Alpha City are as follows:

Fixed overhead	Driver	Apportionment	Total
Aircraft maintenance	Flying hours	£116,480 × 672/2912	£26,880
Insurance	Insurance value	£98,020 × 20/100	£19,604
			£46,484

QUESTION 27 (June 2004)

Task

(a)   (i)   Actual price of materials per kg $\dfrac{£143,000}{27,500}$ =   £5.20

(ii)   Standard usage of materials for actual production
900 units × 30 kg   =   27,000 kgs

(iii)   Actual labour rate per hour $\dfrac{£26,040}{4,200}$ =   £6.20

(iv)   Standard labour time for actual production
900 units × 5 hours   =   4,500 hours

(v)   Budgeted production overheads
1,000 units × £20   =   £20,000

(b)   (i)   The material price variance
              (£5.20 – £5.00) × 27,500 = £5,500 (A)
              OR

Actual price paid for 27,500 kg	= £143,000
Standard price 27,500 kg × £5	= £137,500
	£5,500 (A)

       (ii)   The material usage variance
              (27,500 kgs – 27,000 kgs) × £5 = £2,500 (A)
              OR

Actual material used for 900 desks	= 27,500 kg
Standard usage for 900 desks = 900 × 30	= 27,000 kg
Variance	500 kg × £5 = £2,500 (A)

       (iii) The labour rate variance
              (£6.20 – £6.00) × 4,200 = £840 (A)
              OR

Actual price paid for 4,200 hours	= £26,040
Standard price for 4,200 hours × £6	= £25,200
Variance	840 (A)

       (iv)   The labour efficiency variance
              (4,500 – 4,200) × £6 = £1,800 (F)
              OR

Actual hours producing 900 desks	= 4,200 hours
Standard hours = 900 × 5 hours	= 4,500 hours
Variance	300 hrs × £6 = £1,800 (F)

       (v)   The fixed overhead expenditure variance
              £23,000 – £20,000 = £3,000 (A)

       (vi)   The fixed overhead volume variance
              (5,000 – 4,500) × £4 = £2,000 (A) (W1)

       (vii) The fixed overhead capacity variance
              (5,000 – 4,200) × £4 = £3,200 (A) (W1)

       (viii) The fixed overhead efficiency variance
              (4,500 – 4,200) × £4 = £1,200 (F) (W1)

Working 1
Budgeted absorption
1,000 units × 5 hrs = 5,000 hrs × £4 = £20,000 ⎫
(Budget units × Standard hours)   ⎬ Volume
                                                            £2,000 (A)
Actual absorption
   900 units × 5 hrs = 4,500 hrs × £4 = £18,000 ⎭   ⎫ Capacity
(Actual flights × Standard hours)   £3,200 (A)
                                                            ⎬ Efficiency
                                                            £1,200 (F)
Actual hours   = 4,200 hrs × £4 = £16,800 ⎭

(c)   Operating statement for May 2004

	£	£	£
Standard absorption cost of actual production (900 × £200)			180,000
	Favourable	Adverse	
Material price variance		5,500	
Material usage variance		2,500	
Labour rate variance		840	
Labour efficiency variance	1,800		
Fixed overhead expenditure variance		3,000	
Fixed overhead capacity variance		3,200	
Fixed overhead efficiency variance	1,200		
	3,000	15,040	12,040
Actual absorption cost of actual production			192,040

(d)

MEMO

To: Sam Thomas

From: Accounting Technician

Date: June 2004

Subject: Operating statement

The operating statement shows the variances that cause the difference between the standard and actual cost of production.

The report would be improved if the variances were reviewed and the cause of the variances identified. In particular, significant adverse variances should receive particular attention. It may be that the standards are out-of-date and should be changed. On the other hand, the variances may reflect inefficiencies that need to be addressed.

The statement should also consider the responsibility of the managers of the departments where the major variances are found. The idea of controllable and uncontrollable costs are relevant here. It may be that some cost variances are not under the control of the managers and the responsibility for these costs needs to be identified.

Chapter 7
Performance indicators

QUESTION 28

Appraisal costs are those associated with determining if goods or services meet the required standard specifications. In a hotel would include costs related to goods inward inspection, ie food and consumables for the restaurant, bar and housekeeping; in-house inspection of room cleaning standards and quality of food served. Also checks of customer service in the reception area.

Prevention costs are costs associated with any action taken to investigate or reduce poor quality service. Quality can only be achieved by making sure that all personnel are trained to the standard required to perform their tasks efficiently. Training is thus classed as a prevention cost.

Internal failure costs arise before the customer receives the goods or service. In a hotel they may include having to re-visit rooms once they had been set up and cleaned or having to prepare more food when some has been ill-prepared and wasted. Failing to re-stock the drinks bar in guests' rooms could also be considered as an internal failure cost.

External failure costs arise after the customer receives the goods or service. In a hotel they would include those which are associated with a loss of the customer base because of a poor reputation caused by customer complaints. Dealing with complaints adds to cost.

QUESTION 29

Cost reduction is the reduction in unit cost of goods or services without impairing suitability for the use intended, whereas cost control involves the use of control methods, such as budgetary control and standard costing.

Cost reduction is a technique which has the objective of reducing costs from some predetermined accepted norm or standard, but at the same time maintaining the desired quality of the product or service.

It is a concept which attempts to extract more 'value added' from the resources without loss of effectiveness.

Cost reduction programmes require the support of the senior management team and should embrace the full range of the firm's value adding activities and products.

Focus on a number of issues should be considered:
· reduction of waste
· streamlining activities
· product improvement.

Cost reduction compels planning and good practice and benchmarks for achievement may be set.

Some formal management techniques can be used to implement cost reduction programmes, including:
· variety reduction
· value analysis
· work study
· organisation and method study.

All members of the management team should have a clear perception of cost reduction and its benefits in contributing, other things being equal, to improved profitability.

QUESTION 30

Value analysis is an assessment process underpinning the cost reduction technique. It is usually undertaken by a quality team during the design stages of the product or delivery of a service. The team would comprise a number of managers including technical and production personnel together with finance staff.

The task the team undertakes is to design the product, or plan the service, at minimum cost, but meeting the quality standard required.

The assessment is a systematic attempt to eliminate unnecessary cost on every aspect of the product's functions, methods of production and components.

The process involves asking a series of questions which may include:
· Can the function of the product be achieved in an alternative way?
· Are all the product functions essential?
· Can the product be made more compact and from alternative, cheaper material?
· Can we standardise components, eg some components on the Mercedes 'C' class are also on the 'S' class?
· Can the design or process be modified so that the product or service can be supplied more easily and at less cost?

This is an ongoing process where each of the company's products or services should come under regular scrutiny.

QUESTION 31

Stonehill Quarries Ltd

(a) **Return on capital employed**

$$\frac{\text{Net profit before interest and tax}}{\text{Total assets} - \text{Current liabilities}} \times 100\%$$

20X2	*20X3*
$\frac{0.95}{4.12} \times 100\%$	$\frac{0.86}{4.47} \times 100\%$
= 23.06%	= 19.24%

Asset turnover

$$\frac{\text{Turnover}}{\text{Total assets} - \text{Current liabilities}}$$

20X2	*20X3*
$\frac{5.38}{4.12}$	$\frac{6.68}{4.47}$
= 1.31 times	= 1.49 times

Net profit before interest and tax as a % of sales

$$\frac{\text{Net profit before interest and tax}}{\text{Turnover}} \times 100\%$$

20X2

$$\frac{0.95}{5.38} \times 100\%$$

= 17.66%

20X3

$$\frac{0.86}{6.68} \times 100\%$$

= 12.87%

Current ratio

Current assets : Current liabilities

20X2
1.47 : 1.12
= 1.31 : 1

20X3
1.84 : 1.25
= 1.47 : 1

Acid test

(Current assets – Stocks) : Current liabilities

20X2
(1.47 - 0.55) : 1.12
= 0.82 : 1

20X3
(1.84 - 0.60) : 1.25
= 0.99 : 1

Debtors collection period

$$\frac{\text{Debtors}}{\text{Turnover}} \times 365 \text{ days}$$

20X2

$$\frac{0.88}{5.38} \times 365 \text{ days}$$

= 60 days

20X3

$$\frac{1.19}{6.68} \times 365 \text{ days}$$

= 65 days

Creditors payment period

$$\frac{\text{Trade creditors}}{\text{Purchases*}}$$

*In this case bought in materials and services.

20X2

$$\frac{0.66}{3.21} \times 365 \text{ days}$$

= 75 days

20X3

$$\frac{0.82}{4.32} \times 365 \text{ days}$$

= 69 days

Finished goods stock in days

$$\frac{\text{Stocks (finished goods)}}{\text{Cost of sales}} \times 365 \text{ days}$$

20X2

$$\frac{0.43}{4.43} \times 365 \text{ days}$$

$$= \quad \underline{35 \text{ days}}$$

20X3

$$\frac{0.45}{5.82} \times 365 \text{ days}$$

$$= \quad \underline{28 \text{ days}}$$

Labour cost % of turnover

20X2

$$\frac{0.98}{5.38} \times 100\%$$

$$= \quad \underline{18.22\%}$$

20X3

$$\frac{1.25}{6.68} \times 100\%$$

$$= \quad \underline{18.71\%}$$

Operating costs % of turnover

20X2

$$\frac{4.43}{5.38} \times 100\%$$

$$= \quad \underline{82.34\%}$$

20X3

$$\frac{5.82}{6.68} \times 100\%$$

$$= \quad \underline{87.13\%}$$

Distribution costs % of turnover

20X2

$$\frac{0.49}{5.38} \times 100\%$$

$$= \quad \underline{9.11\%}$$

20X3

$$\frac{0.61}{6.68} \times 100\%$$

$$= \quad \underline{9.13\%}$$

Admin costs % of turnover

20X2

$$\frac{0.22}{5.38} \times 100\%$$

$$= \quad \underline{4.09\%}$$

20X3

$$\frac{0.27}{6.68} \times 100\%$$

$$= \quad \underline{4.04\%}$$

Value added per '£' of employee costs

Value added:

	20X2	20X3
	£m	£m
Turnover	5.38	6.68
Bought in materials and services	3.21	4.32
Value added	2.17	2.36

Value added per '£' of employee costs

20X2	20X3
$\dfrac{2.17}{0.98}$	$\dfrac{2.36}{1.25}$
= £2.21	= £1.89

(b) **Return on capital employed**

The company has experienced a significant decline in profitability in 20X3 to a level below that for the sector as a whole. However, a return of 19% may be considered a good level of performance but a further decline may be the sign of longer term problems.

Asset turnover

The company has increased its volume of sales to net assets ratio, but is not generating the volume experienced by the sector.

Profit margin

One reason for the reduction in the primary ratio (the ROCE) is highlighted here. There has been a significant fall in the profit margin, so although sales volume has increased there has been a reduction in the margin.

The return to sales is now approximately 13% compared with 15% for the sector.

Current ratio and acid test

The company's liquidity is still relatively sound, with the acid test only marginally less than the desired level of 1 : 1 and also the average for the sector.

Liquidity has strengthened in 20X3.

Debtors collection period

The debtor day period has increased and is currently 65 days compared with 60 days average for the sector.

Tighter controls are required here and if the trend continues upward the company may be exposing itself to the incidence of bad debts.

Creditors payment period

The company's period is typical of the sector as a whole. There has been a fall in creditor days as the company has utilised some of its excess cash flow in this area.

Finished goods stock in days

The company is holding less than one month's supply of finished stock. It is not sacrificing liquidity by tying up excess working capital in the form of stocks.

The company's inventory management controls are tighter than those for the sector.

Labour costs % of sales

There has been a marginal increase here but the ratio is still at an acceptable level of control.

Operating costs % of sales

There has been a significant increase here which indicates that operating overheads and some other direct costs need tighter controls. It may be that the company has an ageing plant and maintenance charges are on an upward trend.

If these assumptions are not the case, there may have been a significant shift in product mix which can influence product profitability.

An analysis of the above factors needs to be carried out to assess fully the change in this measure of efficiency.

Distribution and admin costs to sales

These measures are well in line with the sector average and indicate good sound controls in these areas of cost.

Value added per '£' of employee costs

The effectiveness and efficiency of the human asset resource has been offset by the adverse factors highlighted above.

The productivity of labour is now some 3% less than the sector average.

QUESTION 32

(a)   Value added is defined as turnover less bought in materials and services.

It constitutes that 'pool of wealth' from which a company applies to:
·   pay employees
·   pay providers of capital
·   pay government taxation
·   maintain and expand assets.

(b)   **Value added statements**

	20X2 £m	20X3 £m
Turnover	6.1	6.5
Less bought in materials and services	2.0	2.1
Value added	4.1	4.4

Applied as follows:

	20X2	20X3
To pay employees wages, salaries and other benefits	1.8	1.9
To pay providers of capital		
Interest	0.6	0.6
Dividends	0.2	0.2
To pay government taxation	0.3	0.3
To maintenance and expansion of assets		
Depreciation	0.4	0.5
Retained profit	0.8	0.9
Value added	4.1	4.4

(c)   **Value added per £ of employee costs**

	20X2 £m	20X3 £m
Value added	4.1	4.4
Employee costs	1.8	1.9
Value added per '£' of employee costs	£2.28	£2.32

Bought in materials and services are consumed by value adding activities which are driven by labour and other resources to produce finished goods or services rendered. These outputs have a value in the form of turnover and when offset by the bought in items create a pool of wealth we know as value added.

Labour is a major resource which contributes to this wealth and therefore we can measure labour's productivity as:

$$\frac{\text{Value added}}{\text{Labour cost}}$$

If the productivity of labour increases then this ratio will increase.

In the case of the company above, the ratio has improved from £2.28 to £2.32 – showing an increase in labour productivity.

(d)   Other measures of labour productivity may include:
   · Output per employee (physical output, ie units, tonnage).
   · Efficiency ratio expressed as:

$$\frac{\text{Standard hours produced}}{\text{Actual hours worked}} \times 100\%$$

   · Output per shift.

QUESTION 33

(a)   The four perspectives within the 'balanced scorecard' view of performance are:
·   *The financial perspective*
    This is concerned with satisfying shareholders and measures used include the return on capital employed and the sales margin.

·   *The customer perspective*
    This attempts to measure how customers view the organisation and how they measure customer satisfaction. Examples include the speed of delivery and customer loyalty.

·   *The internal perspective*
    This measures the quality of the organisation's output in terms of technical excellence and consumer needs. Examples include unit cost and total quality measurement.

·   *The innovation and learning perspective*
    This emphasises the need for continual improvement of existing products and the ability to develop new products to meet customers' changing needs. In a 'for profit' organisation, this might be measured by the percentage of turnover attributable to new products.

(b)   **Financial perspective:**
Shareholder satisfaction
Return on capital employed

$$\frac{\text{Operating profit}}{\text{Assets employed}} \times 100\%$$

$$\frac{1.14}{6.30} \times 100\% \quad = \quad \underline{18.1\%}$$

Customer perspective:
Customer satisfaction
% of turnover to established and existing customers

$$\frac{4.90}{6.85} \times 100\% \quad = \quad \underline{71.5\%}$$

Internal perspective:
Quality assurance costs as a % of total cost

$$\frac{0.35}{5.71} \times 100\% \quad = \quad \underline{6.1\%}$$

Innovation and learning perspective:
Turnover on new products as a % of total turnover

$$\frac{2.00}{6.85} \times 100\% \quad = \quad \underline{29.2\%}$$

QUESTION 34 (June 2001)

Task 34.1

(a) **Sales margin**
(£324,000/£6,480,000) × 100   =   5%

(b) **Return on capital employed**
(£324,000/£1,620,000) × 100   =   20%

(c) **Asset turnover**
(£6,480,000/£1,620,000)   =   4 times

(d) **Average age of stock**
(£120,000/£1,080,000) × 12   =   1.33 months

(e) **Average age of creditors**
(£180,000/£1,080,000) × 12   =   2 months

(f) **Added value per employee**

Turnover		£6,480,000
Less: Material A10	£1,080,000	
Less: Other material and bought in services	£108,000	£1,188,000
Added value		£5,292,000
Added value per employee (£5,292,000/140)	=	£37,800

(g) **Wages per production employee**
(£1,296,000/140)   =   £9,257

(h) **Capacity ratio**
(10,800 Alphas/12,000 Alphas) × 100   =   90%

(i) **Contribution per Alpha**

Selling price per unit (£6,480,000/10,800) =	£600	
Marginal cost per unit (£2,484,000/10,800) =	£230	
Contribution per Alpha =		£370

Task 34.2

(a) **Cost of quality**

Cost of remedial work	£120,000
Inspection costs of A10 goods received	£69,600
Cost of A10 returns	£48,000
Customer support for faulty products	£194,400
Cost of quality	£432,000

(b) **Revised profit**

Revised unit contribution (£370 – £10)		£360
Revised volume		12,000
Revised total contribution (£360 × 12,000)		£4,320,000
Revised fixed costs:		
Existing	£3,672,000	
Less: Saving in cost of quality	£432,000	£3,240,000
Revised profit		£1,080,000

(c) **Increase in cash**

Increase in profit (£1,080,000 – £324,000)	£756,000
Add: Decrease in stocks	£120,000
Less: Decrease in creditors	(£180,000)
Increase in cash	£696,000

(d) **Revised capital employed***

Net fixed assets	£1,600,000
Cash	£80,000
	£1,680,000

(e) **Revised return on capital employed**

(£1,080,000/£1,680,000) × 100 =	64%

Alternative answer to (d):

Shareholders funds (£800,000 + £756,000)	£1,556,000
Loans (£820,000 – £696,000)	£124,000
Revised capital employed	£1,680,000

QUESTION 35 (December 2000)

Task 35.1

(a) Gross profit margin:
£221,760/£633,600 × 100%   35%

(b) Net profit margin:
£76,032/£633,600 × 100%   12%

(c) Return on capital employed:
£76,032/£95,040 × 100%   80%

(d) Asset turnover:
£633,600/£95,040   6.67 times

(e) Number of passengers in the year:
£633,600/£1   633,600 passengers

(f) Total cost per mile:
(£633,600 – £76,032)/356,400   £1.56

(g) Number of journeys per day:
356,400/(18 miles × 360 days)   55 journeys

(h) Maintenance cost per mile:
£28,512/356,400   £0.08

(i) Passengers per day:
633,600/360   1,760 passengers

(j) Passengers per journey:
1,760/55   32 passengers

(k) Number of drivers:
£142,000/£14,200   10

Task 35.2

MEMO

To: Chief Executive

From: Management Accountant

Date: 6 December 2000

Subject: Performance of Travel Bus Ltd

I refer to your observations relating to the performance of Travel Bus Ltd and detail my comments below.

(a) Relationship between productivity and profitability

Productivity is the measure of outputs against inputs and is usually a non-financial measure.

An example of productivity is output per employee. Increases in productivity do not always lead to an increase in profitability. Profits may fall if finished goods or services rendered are sold at a market price less than previously charged. Cost increases not passed on in increased prices may also adversely affect profitability, even though productivity may have risen.

(b) Driver productivity

One measure of driver productivity is miles driven per driver. There has been a reduction in this measure from 40,500 miles per driver in 1999 to 35,640 in 2000. These results do not support the drivers' claims.

(NB: An alternative measure could have been passengers per driver.)

(c) Reasons for improved profitability

Both volume and price have increased, passengers per day and per journey have increased together with fare per passenger journey.

These factors have resulted in fixed costs being recovered faster by an increase in contribution.

Volume has increased and may be the effect of the free parking supported by council policy.

(d) **Indicator of passenger satisfaction**

The number of journeys per day has increased from 50 to 55. This indicates that there was a decrease in waiting time between journeys.

The figures provided do not indicate any measure of the punctuality of the service.

(NB: Other comments could include the number of passengers having to stand throughout the journey and the catering for disabled passengers.)

(e) **Possible safety indicators**

Maintenance cost per mile is an indicator of safety issues. The maintenance cost per mile has fallen from £0.10 to £0.08 and as the fleet is a further year older the question of safety needs to be reviewed.

One additional safety indicator is the provision of security facilities at both the car park and the bus terminal.

(NB: Accidents per year would also be a useful measure.)

QUESTION 36 (June 2000)

Task 36.1

(a) Return on capital employed:
($1,188,000/$11,880,000) × 100%   10.00%

(b) Asset turnover:
$29,700,000/$11,880,000   2.50 times

(c) Sales (or net profit) margin:
$1,188,000/$29,700,000 × 100%   4.00%

(d) Actual number of return flights per year:
6 × 360   2,160

(e) Actual number of return passengers per year:
$29,700,000/$275   108,000

(f) Average seat occupancy:
108,000/(2,160 × 80) × 100%   62.50%

(g)   Actual number of passenger-miles:
      $108,000 \times 300$ 32,400,000

(h)   Cost per passenger mile:
      $28,512,000/32,400,000$ miles $0.88
      (Total cost = turnover − profit = $29,700,000 − $1,188,000 = $28,512,000)

Task 36.2

MEMO

To:	Carol Jones
From:	Management Accountant
Date:	21 June 2000
Subject:	Competitive advantage

I outline below the forecast performance for SeaAir for the year to 31 May 2001.

(a)   Forecast number of passengers:
      9 flights × 80 seats × 55.00% occupancy × 360 days =   142,560

(b)   Forecast net profit for the year to 31 May 2001:

	$000
Revenue: 142,560 flights × $275	39,204
Fuel and aircraft maintenance: $14,580,000 × 9/6	21,870
Take off and landing fees at Waltonville: $2,160,000 × 9/6	3,240
Aircraft parking at Waltonville: $2,880,000 × 50%	1,440
Depreciation of aircraft	600
Salaries of flight crew: $380,000 + $58,000	438
Home airport costs	8,112
Net profit	3,504

(c)   Revised return on capital employed:
      ($3,504,000/$11,280,000) × 100%   31%
      (Net assets: $11,880,000 − $600,000 extra depreciation = $11,280,000)

(d)   SeaAir has a competitive advantage as its route to Waltonville is over the sea
      and therefore cannot be threatened by other rail or road transport. This allows
      SeaAir to charge an economic fare. Also, with a lower seat occupancy, SeaAir
      customers may have a better choice of flights.

(e)   One major expense which does not add value in the eyes of a customer is the
      cost of aircraft parking at Waltonville.

QUESTION 37 (December 1999)

Task 37.1

(a) Return on capital employed:
(£48,000 ÷ £200,000) × 100%   = 24%
Scorecard: financial perspective.

(b) Sales margin percentage:
(£48,000 ÷ £240,000) × 100%   = 20%
Scorecard: financial perspective (and possibly internal perspective as partly measuring unit cost).

(c) Asset turnover:
£240,000 ÷ £200,000   = 1.2 times
Scorecard: internal perspective, demonstrating intensive use of assets and, hence, unit cost.

(d) Research and development as percentage of production:
(£15,900 ÷ £53,000) × 100%   = 30%
Scorecard: innovation and learning perspective.

(e) Training as percentage of labour costs:
(£5,200 ÷ £26,000) × 100%   = 20%
Scorecard: innovation and learning perspective or possibly the internal perspective (TQM).

(f) Average age of finished stocks:
(£13,000 ÷ £52,000) × 12   = 3 months
Scorecard: customer perspective as the greater the amount of finished stock, the less time customers have to wait for delivery.

Task 37.2

NOTES ON PERFORMANCE INDICATORS FOR THE ST NICOLAS POLICE FORCE

To: James Alexander

Prepared by: Financial Analyst

Date: 1 December 1999

The following are my observations on the issues you raised on the performance indicators.

(a) **Calculation of the four indicators currently used by the St Nicolas Police Force**
- Percentage of cash expenditure to allocated funds for the year:
($2,910 ÷ $3,000) × 100% = 97%
- Average police hours spent per crime investigated:
[40,000 ÷ 5,000] = 8 police hours
- Average police hours per crime solved:
[40,000 ÷ 2,000] = 20 police hours

· Clear-up rate:
[(2,000 ÷ 5,000) × 100%] = 40%

(b) **Limitations to the clear-up rate**

There may be an element of timing differences. Some crimes solved this year may have been investigated in the previous year.

Not all crimes are investigated.

There is no particular definition of a crime. For example, if a criminal burgles 30 homes, is that one crime or a series of crimes?

(c) **Performance indicators and the balanced scorecard**

(i) The percentage of cash expenditure to allocated funds may be considered inadequate in terms of the financial perspective as it ignores the investment in resources used. It also focuses on only one aspect of performance – keeping within spending limits.

(ii) The clear-up rate may be considered inadequate from the customer perspective as it takes no account of investment in crime prevention. Crime prevented does not feature in the statistics and the public may feel that they are receiving 'added value' from the force if there was less crime with high clear-up rates.

(iii) Hours spent on investigating crime may be a measure of energy invested by the force in attempting to solve crime. It may also be a pointer to inefficient investigatory work.

(iv) Innovation and learning perspective may be satisfied by a number of measures. The force's objectives would include making St Nicolas a safer environment.

Hours invested in crime prevention measured against crime reduction may be considered under this perspective.

The police training and continuing professional development programmes are also relevant here.

QUESTION 38 (June 1999)

Task 38.1

Performance indicators for ALV (West) Ltd

(a) Asset turnover:
£2,520/£2,100   =   1.2 times

(b)   Net profit margin:
      (£378/£2,520) × 100   =   15%

(c)   Return on capital employed:
      £378/£2,100 × 100   =   18%

(d)   Wages per employee:
      £260,000/20   =   £13,000

(e)   Production labour cost per unit:
      £260,000/30,000   =   £8.67

(f)   Output per employee:
      30,000/20   =   1,500 units

(g)   Added value:
      £2,520,000 – £1,020,000 = £1,500,000
      Added value per employee:
      £1,500,000/20   =   £75,000

(h)   Profit per employee:
      £378,000/20   =   £18,900

Task 38.2

**REPORT ON THE EFFICIENCY AND PRODUCTIVITY
OF ALV (EAST) AND ALV (WEST)**

Prepared for: Jill Morgan, Chief Executive

Prepared by: Accounting Technician

Date: 16 June 1999

Introduction

The objective of this report is to define the terms 'productivity' and 'efficiency' and relate these concepts to the divisions within the company.

It then considers performance indicators for these concepts and compares divisional performance, finally deriving further measures of productivity relevant to both divisions.

(a)   **The meaning of productivity and efficiency**

      These terms are often used to mean the same measure of performance. Both relate to volume of output from a given input, for example, in the quarry industry, output in tonnage per labour hour or employee.

      ·   Productivity is a measure of outputs related to inputs – usually in physical terms.

· Efficiency is usually measured using financial values for inputs and out-puts. The value of outputs less value of inputs when measured against resources used is a measure of efficiency.

(b) **Two performance indicators to measure efficiency**

In 'for-profit' organisations, the ultimate tests of efficiency are return on invest-ment and the net return to sales.

Comparing the two divisions using these measures:

Indicator	East	West
Return on investment (ROCE)	42%	18%
Net profit margin	20%	15%

East is more efficient than West.

(c) **Two performance indicators to measure productivity**
· Output per employee.
· Value added per employee.

Comparing divisional performance using these measures of productivity, it is clear that West is the division with the higher productivity.

Indicator	East	West
Output/employee	556 units	1,500 units
Value added/employee	£27,778	£75,000

(d) **An alternative measure of productivity**

Indicator	East	West
Net fixed assets	£360,000	£2,100,000
Output	10,000 units	30,000 units
Net fixed assets/unit output	£36.00	£70.00

(e) **Why productivity and efficiency measures may give different rankings**

There are two main factors here which cause these differences in ranking:
· West division has a greater investment in fixed assets and, as the produc-tivity measures indicate, it is relatively new investment.
· East has much older plant; balance sheet figures indicate that the plant is 8 years old compared with 2 years in the case of West. The buildings are also of a similar pattern, much older for East than West.

This relatively new investment in West reflects in the higher productivity. Much more up-to-date plant, probably hi-tech, and better plant layout would 'add value' to productive capability.

Likewise, as East's assets are almost written off, their return looks much more favourable. The older capital equipment has a lower depreciation charge which also affects profitability.

QUESTION 39 (December 1999)

(a) **Sales per quarter**

Demand per quarter before seasonal variations = 20,000 ÷ 4 = 5,000 units

	Quarter 1	Quarter 2	Quarter 3	Quarter 4
Quarterly demand before seasonal variations	5,000	5,000	5,000	5,000
Seasonal variations	+ 1,000	+ 1,500	− 500	− 2,000
Budgeted volume (units)	6,000	6,500	4,500	3,000

(b) **Spreadsheet formulae**

A	B	C	D	E	F
1	Unit selling price	£90			
2	Annual volume (units)	20,000			
3	Seasonal variations	20%	30%	− 10%	− 40%
4		Quarter 1	Quarter 2	Quarter 3	Quarter 4
5	Seasonal variations (units)	= (C2/4)*C3	= (C2/4)*D3	= (C2/4)*E3	= (C2/4)*F3
6	Quarterly volume	= (C2/4) + C5	= (C2/4) + D5	= (C2/4) + E5	= (C2/4) + F5
7	Quarterly turnover	= C1*C6	= C1*D6	= C1*E6	= C1*F6

QUESTION 40 (June 2002)

Task 40.1

(a) Gross profit margin: £2,250,000/£6,000,000 × 100% =   37.5%
(b) Net profit (or sales) margin: £240,000/£6,000,000 × 100% =   4%
(c) Return on capital employed: £240,000/£3,000,000 × 100% =   8%
(d) Asset turnover: £6,000,000/£3,000,000 =   2 times
(e) Average age of debtors: £1,500,000/£6,000,000 × 12 =   3 months
(f) Research and development/Production: £768,000/£4,800,000 × 100% =   16%
(g) Training/Production: £576,000/£4,800,000 × 100% =   12%
(h) Customer support/Turnover: £240,000/£6,000,000 × 100% =   4%
(i) Returns/Turnover: £300,000/£6,000,000 × 100% =   5%
(j) Average delay in supplying customers: 6,000/20,000 × 12 =   3.6 months
(= annual shortfall ÷ annual production) x 12

Task 40.2

(a) **Gross profit margin:**
Internal (since measuring unit cost); financial
(b) **Net profit (or sales) margin:**
Internal (since measuring unit cost); financial
(c) **Return on capital employed:**
Financial

(d)　**Asset turnover:**
　　Internal (since measuring the intensive use of assets and, hence, unit cost)

(e)　**Average age of debtors:**
　　Customer (since offering an extra service); financial

(f)　**Research and development/Production:**
　　Innovation and learning

(g)　**Training/Production:**
　　Innovation and learning

(h)　**Customer support/Turnover:**
　　Customer

(i)　**Returns/Turnover:**
　　Internal (since measuring quality); customer

(j)　**Average delay in supplying customers:**
　　Internal; customer

Task 40.3

MEMO

To:　　　　Finance Director

From:　　　Financial Analyst

Date:　　　19 June 2002

Subject:　　Profitability of Hand Power Systems Ltd

(a)　**Accounting policies**

　　(i)　**Stock valuation:** the stock has been valued on a last-in, first-out basis. This means that the cost of sales is found by using the latest cost of purchases first and then working backwards through earlier purchases. As a result, the closing stock will relate to the cost of even earlier purchases. With decreasing prices, this means that the cost of sales might be understated and, hence, profit overstated.

　　(ii)　**Depreciation:** the fixed assets originally cost £5,000,000. Assuming straight line depreciation and no residual value, if the annual depreciation is £1,000,000 then the fixed assets are being depreciated over 5 years. If the normal life is 10 years then the effect of this over prudent policy will be to reduce profits.

(b)　**Forecast data for the year to 31 May 2003**

　　(i)　Selling price per computer: £6,000,000/20,000 × (100/120) =　£250
　　(ii)　Sales volume: 20,000 × 130% =　26,000
　　(iii)　Sales turnover: £250 × 26,000 =　£6,500,000
　　(iv)　Unit material cost: £3,360,000/24,000 × (140/175) =　£112
　　(v)　Unit labour cost: £960,000/24,000 × 75% =　£30

(vi) Production volume:

Sales volume	26,000
Less opening stock	5,000
Production	21,000

(vii) Forecast cost of production:

Materials (21,000 × £112)	£2,352,000
Labour (21,000 × £30)	£630,000
Fixed overhead (£480,000 – £160,000)	£320,000
Cost of production	£3,302,000

(viii) Forecast cost of sales:

Cost of production	£3,302,000
Add opening stock	£1,350,000
Cost of sales	£4,652,000

(ix) Forecast gross profit (£6,500,000 – £4,652,000) £1,848,000

QUESTION 41 (December 2002)

Task 41.1

(a)	Operating surplus/fee income	(£35,200/£1,760,000 × 100%)	2%
(b)	Return on net assets	(£35,200/£7,040,000 × 100%)	0.50%
(c)	Average age of debtors	(£440,000/£1,760,000 × 12)	3 months
(d)	Average age of creditors	(£96,000/(£128,000 + £160,000) × 12)	4 months
(e)	Number of children in school	(£1,760,000/£22,000)	80
(f)	Occupancy rate of school	(80/100 × 100%)	80%
(g)	Number of teachers	(80 children/4 children per teacher)*	20
(h)	Number of nursing and support staff	(80 children/2 children per member of staff)*	40
(i)	Total cash-based expenses = total expenses – depreciation	= £1,724,800 – £236,800	£1,488,000
(j)	Number of months cash-based expenditure payable	(£62,000/£1,488,000 × 12)	0.5 months

*Alternative answers:

Total teachers' salaries/average salary	(£600,000/£30,000)	20
Total nursing and support staff salaries/average salary	(£480,000/£12,000)	40

Task 41.2

(a)

Forecast operating statement – year to 31 August 2003			
Fee income	(88 × £22,000)		£1,936,000
Teacher salaries	(22 × £30,000)	£660,000	
Nursing salaries	(44 × £12,000)	£528,000	
Administrative costs (no change)		£120,000	
Power (no change)		£128,000	
Housekeeping (no change)		£160,000	
Depreciation (no change)		£236,800	£1,832,800
Surplus			£103,200

(b)	Debtors	(£1,936,000 × 1½/12)	£242,000
(c)	Creditors	([£128,000 + £160,000] × 2/12)	£48,000

(d) Revised net book value of fixed assets:

Net book value 31 August 2002	£6,634,000
Depreciation year to 31 August 2003	£236,800
Net book value 31 August 2003	£6,397,200

(e)

Cash balance 31 August 2002		£62,000
Add: Operating surplus		£103,200
Non-cash items (depreciation)		£236,800
Change in debtors	(£440,000 – £242,000)	£198,000
Less: Change in creditors	(£96,000 – £48,000)	(£48,000)
Cash balance 31 August 2003		£552,000

(f) Capital employed:

Net book value of fixed assets 31 August 2003	£6,397,200
Debtors	£242,000
Cash	£552,000
Less: Creditors	(£48,000)
Net assets 31 August 2003	£7,143,200

MEMO

To: Carol Jones

From: Management Accountant

Date: 4 December 2002

Subject: Action plan and targets

(a)   If the action plan is achieved, the target results will be as follows:

   (i)   Operating surplus as a percentage of fee income
          (£103,200/£1,936,000 × 100%)   5.33%

   (ii)   Return on net assets
          (£103,200/£7,143,200 × 100%)   1.44%

   (iii) Cash available after buying new equipment:
          Forecast cash balance before buying equipment   £552,000
          Less: Cost of new equipment   £400,000
          _____
          Forecast cash balance after buying equipment   £152,000
          _____

   (iv)   Number of months cash-based expenses can be paid
          from the cash balance:

          Cash expenses
          (£1,832,800 – £236,800 = £1,596,000)

          Number of months cash
          (£152,000/£1,596,000 × 12)   1.14 months

(b)   In all cases, the action plan exceeds the proposed targets.

(c)   Productivity measures output from a given input, generally in physical terms. Productivity, however, does not measure the value of that output, efficiency does. Efficiency measures the value of the output from the value of the input.

(d)   An example of improved productivity in the current action plan is the more intensive use of the school's land and buildings by increasing the number of children. In financial terms, there has also been an increase in efficiency as both the operating surplus and the return on net assets have improved. Had the extra child places been provided free of charge, productivity would still have increased, but financial efficiency would have fallen.

QUESTION 42 (December 2003)

Task 42.1

(a)	Selling price per Zeta: £14,400,000/360,000	£40
(b)	Material cost per Zeta: £5,760,000/360,000	£16
(c)	Labour cost per Zeta: £3,600,000/360,000	£10
(d)	Contribution per Zeta: £5,040,000/360,000	£14
(e)	Contribution percentage: £5,040,000/£14,400,000 × 100%	35%
(f)	Net profit (or sales) margin: £576,000/£14,400,000 × 100	4%
(g)	Return on capital employed: £576,000/£9,600,000 × 100	6%
(h)	Asset turnover: £14,400,000/£9,600,000	1.5 times
(i)	Average age of debtors in months: £2,400,000/£14,400,000 × 12	2 months
(j)	Average age of stock in months: £1,440,000/£5,760,000 × 12	3 months
(k)	Average age of creditors in months: £1,200,000/£5,760,000 × 12	2.5 months

(l) Added value per employee

Turnover:	£14,400,000	
Material:	(£5,760,000)	
Heat, light and power:	(£720,000)	
Added value:	£7,920,000	
Added value per employee: £7,920,000/180		£44,000

(m) Average delay in completing an order months

Order volume:	390,000	
Sales volume:	360,000	
Backlog:	30,000	
Average delay: 30,000/360,000 × 12		1 month

(n) Cost of quality

Inspection:	£80,000	
Reworking:	£40,000	
Customer support:	£200,000	£320,000

Task 42.2

(a)

Forecast demand: 360,000 × 84/70		432,000
Add backlog		30,000
Sales volume (units)		462,000

(b) Planned sales volume: 462,000
     less available stock of material   90,000
     Purchases (units)   372,000

(c) Cost of purchases: 372,000 × £16   5,952,000

(d) Selling price per Zeta: £40 × 171/180   £38

(e) Turnover: £38 × 462,000   £17,556,000

(f) Total contribution. As the cost of material remains the same, the contribution is only affected by the selling price.
     Reduction in selling price: £40 – £38 = £2
     Revised unit contribution: £14 – £2 = £12
     Total contribution: £12 × 462,000   £5,544,000

(g) Fixed costs
     Existing fixed costs: £4,464,000
     less cost of quality (80 + 40 + 200) (000s)   £320,000
                                        £4,144,000

(h) Profit: £5,544,000 – £4,144,000   £1,400,000

(i) Net assets
     Net fixed assets last year: £6,000,000
     less extra year's depreciation   £1,000,000
     Net book value   £5,000,000
     Debtors: £17,556,000 × 2/12 (turnover × 2 mths)   £2,926,000
     Cash (given)   £960,000
     Creditors: £5,952 × 1/12 (purchases × 1 mth)   (£496,000)
     Net assets   £8,390,000

(j) Revised NP (or sales) margin: £1,400/£17,556 × 100 $\left(\dfrac{\text{Net profit}}{\text{Turnover}}\right)$ 7.9745%

(k) Revised return on capital employed: £1,400/£8,390 × 100 $\left(\dfrac{\text{Net profit}}{\text{Net assets}}\right)$ 16.687%

QUESTION 43

Task 43.1

(a)

	Actual	Budget
Gross profit margin (W1)	16.7%	20.0%
Operating profit margin (W2)	4.2%	8.0%
Return on capital employed (W3)	10.7%	20.0%
Stock turnover (in months) (W4)	1.3	1.0
Labour capacity ratio (W5)	97.0%	100.0%
Labour efficiency ratio (W6)	96.2%	100.0%

Workings – note that the workings only show the calculation of the actual figure. The budget is calculated in the same way.

1 $\dfrac{\text{Gross profit}}{\text{Sales}}$ = $\dfrac{460,400}{2,750,000}$ = 16.7%

2 $\dfrac{\text{Operating profit}}{\text{Sales}}$ = $\dfrac{115,400}{2,750,000}$ = 0.0419 = 4.2%

3 $\dfrac{\text{Operating profit}}{\text{Net assets}}$ = $\dfrac{115,400}{1,075,400}$ = 0.1073 = 10.7%

4 Stock turnover (also called 'stock holding period')

$\dfrac{\text{Closing stock}}{\text{Cost of sales}} \times 12$ = $\dfrac{240,000}{2,289,600} \times 12$ = 1.257 = 1.3

5 Labour capacity ratio

$\dfrac{\text{Actual hours worked}}{\text{Budget hours}}$ = $\dfrac{58,200}{60,000}$ = 0.97 = 97%

6 Labour efficiency ratio

$\dfrac{\text{Actual output in standard hours}}{\text{Actual production hours}}$ = $\dfrac{11,200 \times 5(W)}{58,200}$ = 0.96 = 96%

Working

Standard hours per desk = $\dfrac{60,000}{12,000}$ = 5 hours

(b)

> **MEMO**
>
> **To:** Sam Thomas
>
> **From:** Accounting Technician
>
> **Date:** June 2004
>
> **Subject:** Performance indicators
>
> **(i) Gross profit margin**
>
> An increase in the selling price or a reduction in the cost of a desk will result in an increase in the gross margin. At present, however, the company is achieving the budgeted price of £250 per desk and it may not be possible to increase the price. If this is the case, efforts should be made to reduce the cost of production.
>
> **(ii) Operating profit margin**
>
> The operating profit margin will increase if the company can reduce its distribution and administration costs. The actual results are £15,000 below budget, so it may be difficult to make further savings in this area.

(iii)   Return on capital employed

The return on capital employed will improve if operating profits improve with no increase in capital employed. The measures detailed above will, therefore, have the effect of improving the return.

One could also examine whether an asset disposal programme could be implemented and the proceeds distributed to shareholders. This would have the effect of reducing capital employed and improving the return on capital employed.

(iv)   Stock turnover

The current stock of desks represents 1.2 months' production. An increase in sales volumes may lead to a reduction in the number of desks held in stock and will consequently improve this indicator. Alternatively, the company should examine whether stock levels can be reduced.

(v)   Labour capacity ratio

The labour capacity ratio is below budget and probably results from a lower than anticipated demand for desks. Increased sales will again improve this ratio.

(vi)   Labour efficiency ratio

The efficiency ratio is below budget and indicates inefficiencies within the production department. This may be caused by machine breakdowns or poor quality materials that are difficult to work. Workplace training and increased supervision are also likely to lead to improvements in this indicator.

Task 43.2

MEMO

To: Sam Thomas

From: Accounting Technician

Date: June 2004

Subject: Value Engineering

Production cost of an executive desk

It is clear from the actual results for November that, although the budgeted sales price has been achieved, the gross margin has not. Value engineering may be employed to examine ways in which production costs may be reduced.

Value engineering is the process of reducing costs by:
·   simplifying the product design
·   eliminating unnecessary functions in the production process.

Value engineering requires the use of functional analysis which involves the identi-fication of the attributes of the executive desk. Once these are established, a price can be determined for each attribute.

Functional analysis may lead to a change in design and a reduction in the materi-als required for production. Also, if the product design is simplified, assembly time may be reduced and this will lead to lower labour costs.

Chapter 8
Budget preparation

QUESTION 44 (December 2001)

Task 44.1

(a) **Production budget – no shortage**

	Alpha units	Beta units
Sales volume	2,000	3,000
Add closing stock	500	595
Less opening stock	(300)	(297)
Production	2,200	3,298

(b) (i) **Material available for production**

	Metres
Maximum purchases possible	61,580
Add opening stock	8,750
Less closing stock	(15,530)
Material available for production	54,800

(ii) **Material required for Beta production**

	Metres
Net material required for Beta production (3,298 × 12)	39,576
Faulty (3/97 × 39,576)	1,224
Gross material required for Beta production	40,800

(iii) **Material available for Alpha production**

	Metres
Material available for production	54,800
Gross material required for Beta production	40,800
Gross material available for Alpha production	14,000

(iv) Production of Alphas

	Metres
Gross material available for Alpha production	14,000
Wastage (3/100 × 14,000)	420
Net material available for Alpha production	13,580
Alphas produced (13,580/10)	1,358 units

(v) Labour hours to be worked

	Hours
Alpha production (1,358 units × 1.15 hours)	1,561.70
Beta production (3,298 units × 1.38 hours)	4,551.24
Total hours to be worked	6,112.94

(vi) Cost of labour budget

Labour hours available (46 employees × 35 hours × 4 weeks)	6,440.00
Cost of labour (46 employees × £210 per week × 4 weeks)*	£38,640

*As employees are guaranteed a 35-hour week, the labour cost will be based on the contracted amount and not the hours worked.

(c) Revised budgeted sales volumes

	Units
Production of Alphas	1,358
Add opening stock	300
Less closing stock	(500)
Sales volume – Alphas	1,158
Sales volume – Betas (contracted volume)	3,000

Task 44.2

	A	B
1	Selling price per unit	£140
2	Variable cost per unit	£70
3	Fixed costs per 4 week period	£40,000
4	Volume per period	1,000
5	4 weeks ending	1 February 2002
6	Turnover	= B1 × B4
7	Total variable cost	= B2 × B4
8	Contribution	= B6 – B7
9	Fixed costs	= B3
10	Operating profit	= B8 – B9

QUESTION 45 (December 2000)

Task 45.1

(a) **Production budget in units**

	Period 1	Period 2	Period 3	Period 4	Period 5
Demand	5,700	5,700	6,840	6,460	6,080
Less Opening stock	(1,330)	(855)	(1,026)	(969)	(912)
Add Closing stock	855	1,026	969	912	
Production	5,225	5,871	6,783	6,403	

(b) **Material purchases budget (litres)**

		Period 1	Period 2	Period 3	Period 4
Production (units)		5,225	5,871	6,783	6,403
Material required					
(production x 6 litres)	(i)	31,350	35,226	40,698	38,418
Maximum material available	(ii)		34,000	34,000	34,000
Shortfall of material					
available (i − ii)			1,226	6,698	4,418
Reschedule purchases		1,226	−1,226		
Material purchases from					
Contrax plc	(iii)	32,576	34,000	34,000	34,000
Material purchases from					
outside supplier	(iv)			6,698	4,418

(c) **Material purchases budget (£)**

	Period 1 £	Period 2 £	Period 3 £	Period 4 £
Material purchases from				
Contrax plc (c) × £8	260,608	272,000	272,000	272,000
Material purchases from				
outside supplier (d) × £12			80,376	53,016
	260,608	272,000	352,376	325,016

(d) **Labour hours budget**

	Period 1	Period 2	Period 3	Period 4
Production (units of Omega)	5,225	5,871	6,783	6,403
Standard hours required				
(units × 2 hours)	10,450	11,742	13,566	12,806
Inefficiency				
$(5/95 \times \text{standard hours})$	550	618	714	674
Total labour hours required	11,000	12,360	14,280	13,480
Basic hours				
(78 employees × 4 weeks × 40 hours)	12,480	12,480	12,480	12,480
Overtime	Nil	Nil	1,800	1,000

(e) **Labour budget (£)**

	Period 1	Period 2	Period 3	Period 4
Basic wage (£160 × 78 employees × 4 weeks)	49,920	49,920	49,920	49,920
Overtime (Overtime hours × £6)			10,800	6,000
	49,920	49,920	60,720	55,920

Task 45.2

MEMO

To: Adrian Jones

From: Management Accountant

Date: X-X-XX

Subject: Cost savings

Following our recent discussions and your observations regarding the level of over-time and the material supplier, I list my comments below.

(a) **Immediate cost savings**

The material available in period 1 is 34,000 litres, whereas our requirement is 32,576 litres. A further 1,424 litres is available from Contrax and could result in a saving in one of two ways.

(b) By bringing production forward to period 1, there would be a saving of £5,696 because of the reduction in purchases, at a later date, from the alternative supplier – 1,424 litres × £4 = £5,696.

The same saving is possible by simply buying the 1,424 litres in advance to be used in a later period.

(c) **Continuing difficulties**

If minimum demand for the product continues at 5,700 per four-week period, the material requirements will be 34,200 litres per period, which suggests that the material constraint is a longer term problem.

The planned labour hours for minimum demand would be 12,000 per period, even if the inefficiency problem continues. However, with 12,480 hours available each period, this constraint is considered short-term.

(d) **Possible long-term cost savings**

In the longer term it may be possible to renegotiate the stock requirements with Advanced Industries. This would allow a lower investment in finished stocks.

However, we would need to satisfy them that we could supply them on time if their forecast requirement were inaccurate. One way of dealing with this would be flexible working, whereby excess demand was met by working unpaid overtime and allowing time off, paid in lieu, when demand was low.

QUESTION 46 (June 2000)

(a)   **Closing stocks quarter 3**
Delta   3,300 boxes × (6/60)   330 boxes
Omega   2,640 boxes × (8/60)   352 boxes

(b)   **Labour hours available**
52 employees × 36 hours × 12 weeks   22,464 hours

(c)   **Production budget**

	Delta	Omega
Sales demand quarter 3	3,000	2,400
Add Closing stocks	330	352
Less Opening stocks (given)	(630)	(502)
Good production	2,700	2,250
Add Scrap (1/9)	300	250
Total production (boxes)	3,000	2,500

(d)   **Material purchases budget**

		kg
Material for Delta production	12 kg × 3,000 boxes	36,000
Material for Omega production	15 kg × 2,500 boxes	37,500
Material used in production		73,500
Add Closing stock		21,340
Less Opening stock		(13,560)
Material purchases		81,280
Cost of purchases	£7 × 81,280	£568,960

(e)   **Labour budget**

		Hours
Labour hours for Delta production	3 hours × 3,000 boxes	9,000
Labour hours for Omega production	6 hours × 2,500 boxes	15,000
Labour hours required		24,000
Labour hours before overtime		22,464
Overtime hours		1,536
Cost of labour		
Wages	£180 × 52 employees × 12 weeks	£112,320
Overtime	£7.50 × 1,536 hours	£11,520
		£123,840

QUESTION 47 (December 1999)

(a)   (i)   Number of production days in quarter 1:
12 weeks x 5 days   =   60 days

(ii)   Units of closing finished stock:

Exe $930 \times \dfrac{8}{60}$ =   124 units

Wye $1,320 \times \dfrac{9}{60}$ =   198 units

(iii)   Labour hours in the period before overtime:
        12 weeks × 35 hours × 46 employees   =   19,320 hours

(b) (i)   **Production budget for the 12 weeks ending 24 March 2000**

	Exe	Wye
Budgeted sales (units)	930	1,320
Add Closing stocks	124	198
Less Opening stocks	(172)	(257)
Production of good units	882	1,261
Faulty production (Exe = 2/98 × 882, Wye = 3/97 × 1,261)	18	39
Gross production before faults	900	1,300

(ii)   **Material purchases budget for the 12 weeks ending 24 March 2000**

	Litres
Material requirement for Exe production (6 litres × 900 Exe)	5,400
Material requirement for Wye production (9 litres × 1,300 Wye)	11,700
Total material required for production	17,100
Add Closing raw material stock (5 days/60 days × 17,100 litres)	1,425
Less Opening raw material stock	(1,878)
Material purchases (litres)	16,647
Total material cost (16,647 × £15)	£249,705

(iii) **Production labour budget for the 12 weeks ending 24 March 2000**

		Hours
Budgeted hours required for Exe production (12 hours × 900)		10,800
Budgeted hours required for Wye production (7 hours × 1,300)		9,100
Total planned labour hours		19,900
Hours available before overtime		19,320
Overtime hours		580
Cost of normal hours	(19,320 × £6)	£115,920
Cost of overtime	(580 × £6 × 130%)	£4,524
Total labour cost		£120,444

(c) **Finance and other savings per quarter**

Exe	([172 – 124] × £4)	£192
Wye	([257 – 198] × £5)	£295
Raw material	([1,878 – 1,425] × £1)	£453
		£940

QUESTION 48 (June 1999)

(a) **Production budget – quarter ended 17 September 1999**

	Alphas (units)	Betas (units)
Budgeted sales	2,000	2,400
Add: Closing stock (see Note 1)	200	480
Less: Opening stock	(500)	(600)
Production (finished units)	1,700	2,280

Note 1

	Alphas	Betas
Sales this quarter 3	2,000	2,400
Add 20% seasonal variation	400	480
Budgeted sales next quarter 4	2,400	2,880
Closing stock (5/60 × 2,400 = 200) (10/60 × 2,880 = 480)	200	480

(b) **Material purchases budget – quarter ended 17 September 1999**

	Kilograms
Usage – Alpha production (8 kg × 1,700)	13,600
Usage – Beta production (12 kg × 2,280)	27,360
	40,960
Add Closing material stock (see Note 2)	16,384
Less Opening material stock	(12,000)
Purchases of material	45,344

Note 2
Closing stock of materials:

Usage this period	40,960
Add 20%	8,192
Material required for production next period	49,152
Stock required (20/60 × 49,152)	16,384

(c) **Cost of purchases**
(45,344 kg × £10)   £453,440

(d) **Labour budget – quarter ended 17 September 1999**

	Hours
Labour hours required for Alpha production (3 hours × 1,700)	5,100
Labour hours required for Beta production (6 hours × 2,280)	13,680
Total hours required before efficiency adjustment	18,780
Efficiency adjustment (20% / 80%)	4,695
Gross labour hours	23,475
Normal hours (50 employees × 35 hours × 12 weeks)	21,000
Overtime hours required	2,475

(e)   Normal hours (50 employees × 12 weeks × £210)   £126,000
       Overtime (2,475 hours × £9)   £22,275

       Direct labour cost   £148,275

QUESTION 49 (June 2002)

Task 49.1

(a)   **Production budget, period 8**

	Antelope	Bear
Planned sales volume (units)	141,120	95,000
Add closing finished stock[1]	42,336	30,875
Less opening finished stock	(30,576)	(25,175)
Net production required	152,880	100,700
Faulty production[2]	3,120	5,300
Gross production required	156,000	106,000

Notes:
[1] Antelope: 141,120 × 150% × 4/20. Bear: 95,000 × 130% × 5/20
[2] Antelope: 152,880 × 2/98. Bear: 100,700 × 5/95

(b)   **Material purchases budget in kilograms, period 8**

		Kilograms
Antelope production:	156,000 statues × 0.75 kilograms	117,000
Bear production:	106,000 statues × 0.50 kilograms	53,000
		170,000
Add closing stock of powdered rock		40,000
Less opening stock of powdered rock		(30,000)
Purchases of powdered rock		180,000

(c)   **Budgeted cost of purchases, period 8**
       180,000 kilograms × £8.00   £1,440,000

(d)   **Labour budget in hours, period 8**

		Hours
Antelope production:	156,000 statues × 0.10 hours	15,600
Bear production:	106,000 statues × 0.05 hours	5,300
Total hours required		20,900

(e)   **Budgeted cost of labour, period 8**

       140 production employees × 4 weeks × £228 per week   £127,680

Note: Guaranteed week (= 140 x 4 x 38 = 21,280 hrs) and so hours planned to be worked are not relevant.

Task 49.2

(a) **Maximum number of extra Antelope statues possible in period 8**

Extra production possible with surplus labour

	Hours
Total labour hours available: 140 employees × 4 weeks × 38 hours	21,280
Labour hours used [see Task 29.1 (d)]	20,900
Surplus labour hours	380

	Statues
Gross extra production possible: 380 hours/0.1 hours	3,800
Number of fault-free statues possible: 3,800 × 98%	3,724

Extra production possible with extra material

Kilograms of powdered rock available [given in task data]	3,000

	Statues
Gross extra production possible: 3,000 kg/0.75 kg	4,000
Number of fault-free statues possible: 4,000 × 98%	3,920

Extra production is restricted by the labour constraint. Extra production will, therefore, be a maximum of 3,724 statues.

(b) **Revised purchases budget for period 8**

	Kilograms
Original purchases of powdered rock	180,000
Additional purchases: 3,800 × 0.75 kilogram	2,850
Revised purchases of powdered rock	182,850

QUESTION 50 (December 2002)

Task 50.1

(a)

Production budget	Period 1	Period 2	Period 3	Period 4
Sales volume (units)	14,400	15,000	15,600	16,800
Add: Closing stock[1]	6,000	6,240	6,720	6,720
Less: Opening stock	(5,760)	(6,000)	(6,240)	(6,720)
Production	14,640	15,240	16,080	16,800

[1] 12/30 × next period's sales volume

(b)

Purchases budget	Period 1	Period 2	Period 3	Period 4
Production (units)	14,640	15,240	16,080	16,800
Material used in production[2] (litres)	117,120	121,920	128,640	134,400
Add: Wastage[3]	4,880	5,080	5,360	5,600
Material required	122,000	127,000	134,000	140,000
Contracted purchases	122,000	127,000	130,000	130,000
Outside purchases	Nil	Nil	4,000	10,000

[2] Production × 8 litres
[3] 4/96 × material used in production

(c) **Cost of purchases budget**

	Period 1 £	Period 2 £	Period 3 £	Period 4 £
Contracted purchases @ £7	854,000	889,000	910,000	910,000
Outside purchases @ £12			48,000	120,000
	854,000	889,000	958,000	1,030,000

(d) **Labour budget**

	Period 1	Period 2	Period 3	Period 4
Production (units)	14,640	15,240	16,080	16,800
Labour hours required[4]	29,280	30,480	32,160	33,600
Guaranteed hours[5]	31,200	31,200	31,200	31,200
Overtime	Nil	Nil	960	2,400

[4] Production × 2 hours
[5] 40 hours × 6 weeks × 130 employees

(e) **Cost of labour budget**

	Period 1 £	Period 2 £	Period 3 £	Period 4 £
Guaranteed wage[6]	187,200	187,200	187,200	187,200
Overtime @ £7			6,720	16,800
	187,200	187,200	193,920	204,000

[6] £240 × 6 weeks × 130 employees

Task 50.2

(a) (i) **Revised purchases budget**

	Period 1	Period 2	Period 3	Period 4
Material requirements (litres)	122,000	127,000	134,000	140,000
Contract availability	130,000	130,000	130,000	130,000
Surplus/(shortfall)	8,000	3,000	(4,000)	(10,000)
Cumulative surplus/(shortfall) to meet cumulative production targets if excess finished stocks carried forward	8,000	11,000	7,000	(3,000)
Revised material required	130,000	130,000	130,000	133,000
Contracted purchases	130,000	130,000	130,000	130,000
Outside purchases	Nil	Nil	Nil	3,000

(ii) **Revised cost of purchases**

	Period 1 £	Period 2 £	Period 3 £	Period 4 £
Contracted purchases @ £7	910,000	910,000	910,000	910,000
Outside purchases @ £12				36,000
	910,000	910,000	910,000	946,000

(iii) | **Revised production budget** | *Period 1* | *Period 2* | *Period 3* | *Period 4* |
|---|---|---|---|---|
| Revised material required (litres) | 130,000 | 130,000 | 130,000 | 133,000 |
| Less: Wastage[1] | 5,200 | 5,200 | 5,200 | 5,320 |
| Material available for production | 124,800 | 124,800 | 124,800 | 127,680 |
| Production[2] (units) | 15,600 | 15,600 | 15,600 | 15,960 |

[1] Material required $\times$ 4%
[2] Material available for production/8 litres

(iv) | **Revised labour budget** | *Period 1* | *Period 2* | *Period 3* | *Period 4* |
|---|---|---|---|---|
| Revised production (units) | 15,600 | 15,600 | 15,600 | 15,960 |
| Revised labour hours[3] | 31,200 | 31,200 | 31,200 | 31,920 |
| Guaranteed hours | 31,200 | 31,200 | 31,200 | 31,200 |
| Overtime hours | Nil | Nil | Nil | 720 |

[3] Revised production $\times$ 2 hours

(v) | **Revised cost of labour budget** | *Period 1* £ | *Period 2* £ | *Period 3* £ | *Period 4* £ |
|---|---|---|---|---|
| Guaranteed wage | 187,200 | 187,200 | 187,200 | 187,200 |
| Overtime @ £7 | | | | 5,040 |
| | 187,200 | 187,200 | 187,200 | 192,240 |

(b)

> **MEMO**
>
> **To:** Production Director
>
> **From:** Management Accountant
>
> **Date:** 5 December 2002
>
> **Subject:** Revised budgets
>
> I have prepared revised budgets for Zeta production. As a result of producing more Zetas in earlier periods, there will be savings in both material cost and labour. The material savings arise because there is less need to buy the material at the more expensive open market price. The labour savings arise because there is greater production in periods when the employees are not working the full hours implied in the guaranteed week. As a result, there is a saving in overtime.
>
> (i) The detailed savings are shown below.
>
> **Cost of purchases budget**
>
> | | *Period 1* £ | *Period 2* £ | *Period 3* £ | *Period 4* £ | *Total* £ |
> |---|---|---|---|---|---|
> | Original | 854,000 | 889,000 | 958,000 | 1,030,000 | 3,731,000 |
> | Revised | 910,000 | 910,000 | 910,000 | 946,000 | 3,676,000 |
> | Savings | | | | | 55,000 |

Cost of labour budget

	Period 1 £	Period 2 £	Period 3 £	Period 4 £	Total £
Original	187,200	187,200	193,920	204,000	772,320
Revised	187,200	187,200	187,200	192,240	753,840
Savings					18,480
Total savings (£55,000 + £18,480)					£73,480

(ii) There are two possible extra costs that might be incurred. The revised budgets involve producing more Zetas than required in the first two periods and less in the subsequent two periods. As a result, the division may incur extra costs of storage. There may also be extra finance costs.

QUESTION 51

Task 51.1

(a) **Production budget (units)**

	Exe	Wye
Sales volume	8,820	5,800
Add closing finished stocks (W)	5,292	3,016
Less opening finished stocks	(4,410)	(2,320)
Planned production	9,702	6,496

Working

Closing stocks

	Exe	Wye
Sales in period 1	8,820	5,800
Sales in period 2 (20% / 30% higher)	8,820 × 1.20	5,800 × 1.30
Closing stock = 10/8 days sales	$8,820 \times 1.2 \times \dfrac{10}{20}$	$5,800 \times 1.3 \times \dfrac{8}{20}$

(b) **Materials purchase budget (square metres)**

	sq metres
Production – Exe: 9,702 × 5 sq m	48,510
Production – Wye: 6,496 × 7 sq m	45,472
	93,982
Wastage (W)	1,918
Gross material issued to production	95,900
Add closing material stock	18,000
Less opening material stock	(16,950)
Purchase (square metres)	96,950

Working

The percentage of waste is calculated as follows:

Good production	98	93,982
Waste	2	?
Input material	100	?

Therefore waste = $\dfrac{93,982}{98} \times 2 = 1,918$

(c) **Cost of purchases budget**

96,950 × £2.00	£193,900

(d) **Labour hours worked budget**

Exe: 9,702/6	1,617
Wye: 6,496/4	1,624
	3,241
Basic hours available:	
22 × 35 × 4	3,080
Overtime	161

(e) **Cost of labour budget**

Basic hours: 3,080 × £8.00	£24,640
Overtime: 161 × £12.00	£1,932
	£26,572

(f) **Cost of production budget by product**

	Exe £	Wye £
Materials issued to production (W1)	99,000	92,800
Labour (W2)	12,936	12,992
Production overhead (W3)	19,404	19,488
	131,340	125,280

Workings

1 Materials

     Exe: 48,510 × 100/98 × £2.00 = £99,000
     Wye: 45,472 × 100/98 × £2.00 = £92,800

2 Labour

     Exe: 1,617 × £8.00 = £12,936
     Wye: 1,624 × £8.00 = £12,992

3 Production overhead

     Exe: 1,617 × £12.00 = £19,404
     Wye: 1,624 × £12.00 = £19,488

Note that it is a coincidence that the production overhead rate of £12 per hour equals the overtime rate. 161 hours of overtime at £4 per hour (£644) is charged to the production overhead account, along with the other (unspecified) overheads. These are all then charged to production at £12 per hour.

Task 51.2

MEMO

To: Susan Fellows

From: Management Accountant

Date: 4 December 2003

Subject: Production constraints period 2

(a) **Extra possible productionof Exe**

The calculations to determine whether materials or labour are the constraint are as follows:

	Material	Labour
Available resource	2,000 sq m	88 hours
Waste (2,000 × 2%) =	40 sq m	–
	1,960 sq m	88 hours
Possible production	1,960 ÷ 5 = 392	88 × 6 = 528

Material is, therefore, the effective constraint in period 1 if extra production is required, and 392 extra units of Exe can be produced.

(b) **Revised production budget for period 1**

With no extra production of Wye, the revised production budget will be as follows:

	Exe	Wye
Original production budget	9,702	6,496
Add additional production	392	
Revised Production budget	10,094	6,496

(c) **Other ways of overcoming the constraint in period 2**

There are several possible short-term solutions. The company should consider:
· holding less raw material stock: this will reduce the material constraint identified above
· holding less finished stock, which would release Exes and Wyes for sale
· sub-contracting out extra production

QUESTION 52

Task 52.1

(a) **Production budget**

	Alpha Units	Beta Units
Sales	8,460	9,025
Add closing stocks (W1)	2,115	5,054
Less opening stocks	(1,692)	(3,610)
Good production	8,883	10,469
Add faulty production (W2)	987	551
Gross production	9,870	11,020

Workings

1   Alpha: 10,575 × 5/25 = 2,115 units
    Beta: 12,635 × 10/25 = 5,054 units

2   **Faulty production**

	Alpha	Beta	Alpha	Beta
Gross production	100	100		
Faulty	10	5	987	551
Good production	90	95	8,883	10,469

    Alpha: 8,883 × 10%/90% = 987 units
    Beta: 10,469 × 5%/95% = 551 units

(b) **Material purchases budget**

Alpha production: 9,870 × 20kg	197,400
Beta production: 11,020 × 40kg	440,800
Material issued to production	638,200
Add closing stocks	52,600
Less opening stocks	(64,800)
Purchases (kg)	626,000

(c) **Cost of materials budget**

Cost of materials purchased 626,000 × 50p	£313,000

(d) **Labour hours budget**

Alpha production: 9,870 × 2	19,740
Beta production: 11,020 × 3	33,060
Total labour hours required	52,800
Total labour hours available before overtime (300 × 35 × 5)	52,500
Overtime	300

(e) **Cost of labour budget**

Normal hours: 52,500 × £ 5	£262,500
Overtime: 300 × £8	£2,400
	£264,900

OR

Labour hours at normal rate: 52,800 × £5	£264,000
Overtime premium: 300 × £3	£900
	£264,900

(f) **Total absorption cost of production budget**

	Alpha £	Beta £
Materials (W1)	98,700	220,400
Labour (W2)	98,700	165,300
Factory overheads (W3)	1,223,880	1,917,480
	1,421,280	2,303,180

Workings

1. Cost of materials – Alpha: 197,400 × 50p = £98,700
   Cost of materials – Beta: 440,800 × 50p = £220,400
2. Cost of labour – Alpha: 19,740 × £5.00 = £98,700
   Cost of labour – Beta: 33,060 × £5.00 = £165,300
3. Factory overheads – Alpha : 19,740 × £62 = £1,223,880
   Factory overheads – Beta: 33,060 × £58 = £1,917,480

(g) **Unit cost of good production**

	Alpha	Beta
Cost of production	£1,421,280	£2,303,180
Good production	8,883	10,469
Unit cost	£160	£220

(h) **Budgeted value of closing stock**

	Alpha	Beta
Closing stock (units)	2,115	5,054
Unit cost	£160	£220
Value of closing stock	£338,400	£1,111,880

Task 52.2

MEMO

To:	Bob Scott
From:	Management Accountant
Date:	17 June 2004
Subject:	Budgetary constraints

(a) (i) **Possible extra gross production of Alphas**

Extra production required to meet demand 2,000 × 100/90 = 2,222
Material

Material required 2,222 × 20kg	44,440
Material available (given)	34,000
Shortfall	10,440

Labour

Labour hours required 2,222 × 2 hours	4,444
Labour hours available 5,000 – 300 current overtime hours	4,700
Surplus hours	256

Therefore, material limits production in period 8.

(ii) **Revised production budget**

Original gross production	9,870
Add maximum additional production 34,000kg/20kg	1,700
Revised gross production	11,570

(iii) **Shortfall in Alpha production/sales**

Gross extra production of Alphas	1,700
Less faulty production 10%	170
Net additional production/sales	1,530
Additional sales volume required	2,000
Shortfall	470

(iv) **Overcoming the shortfall**
  · Subcontracting is not possible as Newmarket is currently taking up all available material in period 8.
  · The level of finished stocks cannot be changed. Nor can the failure rate.
  · The only option available to Newmarket is to change the stock levels of the raw materials.

(b) **Reasons why a budget might be imposed (any two of the following)**
· Urgency and lack of time for participation.
· Managers preferring to have budgets set for them.
· Managers lacking the technical/marketing knowledge to set budgets.

I hope you find these observations helpful. Please do contact me if you have any queries or require any additional information.

Chapter 9
Budgetary control and responsibility accounting

QUESTION 53 (June 2001)

Task 53.1

(a) **Budgeted data**

(i)	Selling price (£700,000/20,000)	=	£35
(ii)	Material cost per unit (£160,000/20,000)	=	£8
(iii)	Labour cost per unit (£300,000/20,000)	=	£15
(iv)	Variable cost of general expenses per unit (£4,000/2,000)	=	£2
(v)	Fixed cost of general expenses:		

Total cost for 20,000 units	£110,000
Total variable cost (£2 × 20,000)	£40,000
Fixed costs	£70,000

(b) **Actual production fixed costs incurred during the year**
£75,000

(c) **Actual marginal costing operating results for the year to 31 May 2001**

	£000
Turnover	782
Material (23,000/25,000 × £225,000)	207
Labour (23,000/25,000 × £350,000)	322
Variable general expenses (£125,000 − £71,000)	54
Contribution	199
Fixed costs:	
Production overhead	75
General expenses	71
Operating profit	53

(d) **Flexible budget statement for the year to 31 May 2001**

	Budget workings	Budget £000	Actual £000	Variance £000
Volume		23,000	23,000	
Turnover	(23,000 × £35)	805	782	23 (A)
Material	(23,000 × £8)	184	207	23 (A)
Labour	(23,000 × £15)	345	322	23 (F)
Variable general expenses	(23,000 × £2)	46	54	8 (A)
Contribution		230	199	
Fixed costs:				
Production overhead		74	75	1 (A)
General expenses		70	71	1 (A)
Operating profit		86	53	33 (A)

Key: (A) = adverse; (F) = favourable

Task 53.2

LETTER

Sparrow and Co
Accountants and Registered Auditors
2 The High Street, Anytown

21 June 2001

Kate Smith
Eagle Ltd
4 The Mall, Anytown

Dear Ms Smith

Thank you for your letter and observations regarding the flexible budgetary control statement recently prepared for Eagle Ltd.

(a) **Differences in the structure of the two budget statements**

The revised budget represented a fixed budget or plan to which the management were committed. This was based on a revision to a value of 22,000 units for the year.

The flexible budget however has a different perspective, one of control. As the actual sales volume was 23,000 units, the flexed budget shows revenue and costs budgeted for that level of activity.

This enables a 'like with like' comparison and the variances reported are more meaningful for control purposes.

Some costs have been flexed to reflect the change in volume, whereas others have remained the same. This follows the distinction between fixed and variable costs. Materials are, for example, a variable or marginal cost whereas production overhead is a fixed cost.

(b) Reasons for the differences in the actual results shown on the report

The flexed budgetary control report is based on marginal costing lines, whereas the original statement was on a full absorption costing basis.

The marginal costing technique recognises that some costs vary with volume whereas others are fixed. Fixed costs are treated as time based costs and are written off against the period in which they are incurred.

Absorption costing matches fixed production costs to units produced and thus closing stocks, when valued at full costs, include an element of fixed costs. Therefore, a proportion of fixed costs are carried forward in the stock valuation to a further period.

The valuation of stock, marginal v absorption costs, is the factor which causes the difference in reported profits.

(c) Profit as a measure of performance

Distortions in profit are possible when absorption costing is used and depends on the amount of stocks held. Marginal costing focuses on those areas where control is possible, ie labour, material and some overhead, and treats fixed overheads, some of which are not controllable, as period costs.

This suggests that marginal costing is a better basis for measuring performance.

Please contact me if I can be of further help.

Yours sincerely

A Student

QUESTION 54 (December 2000)

Task 54.1

(a) Budgeted data

(i)	Budgeted cost of material per unit of Delta:		
	£600,000/100,000 Deltas	=	£6.00
(ii)	Budgeted variable cost of light, heat and power per Delta:		
	(£200,000 – £40,000)/100,000	=	£1.60
(iii)	Number of budgeted production employees:		
	£120,000/£12,000	=	10 employees

(b) **Flexible budgetary control statement for the year ended 30 November 2000**

	Flexible budget	Actual results	Variance
Volume (number of Deltas)	125,000	125,000	Nil
	£000	£000	£000
Turnover (@ £20)	2,500	2,250	250 (A)
Material (W1)	750	800	50 (A)
Light, heat and power (W2)	240	265	25 (A)
Production labour (W3)	156	156	0
Rent, rates and depreciation	140	175	35 (A)
Administrative expenses	110	110	0
Profit	1,104	744	360 (A)

Key:
A = Adverse
F = Favourable

Workings for flexed budget

(W1) Material   125,000 units × £6.00 = £750,000
(W2) Light, heat and power   £40,000 + (125,000 × £1.60) = £240,000
(W3) Labour   13 employees × £12,000 = £156,000

Task 54.2

REPORT
THE ROLE OF BUDGETS, FORECASTING AND VARIANCES AT PARKSIDE MANUFACTURING LTD

To: Judith Green

Prepared by: Management Accountant

Date: X-X-XX

Introduction

The purpose of this report is to provide a background and prior briefing on planning to be discussed at the Board meeting.

(a) **Budgets used at Parkside**

There are two types of budget used in the company. A fixed budget is one which is essentially a planning device and sets a target to which management are in the short-run committed. A flexible budget, however, is a control device. It is principally a revision of the original plan, whereby allowances are given for both cost and revenue, to match the level of activity actually achieved.

This enables a 'like with like' comparison to be made – the flexed budget v the actual results.

From this comparison meaningful variances can be reported, on which a measure of control can focus.

(b) **Factors to take into account before investigating variances**

It is not practicable to investigate all variances. Because of this, exception techniques are used by applying both a minimum absolute value and a minimum percentage variance before investigation is recommended.

A variance may be investigated if it is an element of a continuing trend.

Variances would not be investigated if the cause is a factor, of which management are aware. It is also not worth investigating variances if they are not controllable, eg insurances.

It is essential that the benefits of investigation, at all times, outweigh the cost.

(c) **Limitations of linear regression techniques**

- Assumption of linearity whereas sales volume might not follow that pattern.
- Use of historical data; past performance is not always a good guide to the future.
- Does not account for the effects of a product life cycle.

QUESTION 55 (June 2000)

Task 55.1

(a) Revised budgeted selling price:
(£1,760,000/11,000)   £160

(b) Material cost per unit in revised budget:
(£396,000/11,000)   £36

(c) Variable cost of production and administrative labour – high/low method:
Increase in budgeted labour cost (£630,000 – £580,000)	£50,000
Increase in budgeted volume (11,000 – 10,000)	1,000
Variable cost of labour per unit (£50,000/1,000)	£50

(d) Fixed cost of production and administrative labour:
Total budgeted cost of labour for 11,000 units	£630,000
Variable cost of labour (11,000 × £50)	£550,000
Budgeted fixed cost of labour	£80,000

(e) Variable cost of light, heat and power – high/low method:
Increase in budgeted light, heat and power (£164,000 – £160,000)	£4,000
Increase in budgeted volume	1,000
Budgeted variable cost of light, heat and power per unit (£4,000/1,000)	£4

(f) Fixed cost of light, heat and power:

Total budgeted cost of light, heat and power for 11,000 units	£164,000
Variable cost of light, heat and power (11,000 × £4)	£44,000
Budgeted fixed cost of light, heat and power	£120,000

Task 55.2

MEMO

To: Mike Green

From: Management Accountant

Date: 22 June 2000

Subject: Motivation and performance

I attach a budgetary control statement for Visiguard based on the flexible budget technique and wish to make the following observations.

(a) **Visiguard Ltd – Flexible budgetary control statement for the year ended 31 May 2000**

	Flexed budget	Actual results	Variances
Sales and production volume (units)	11,600	11,600	Nil
	£	£	£
Turnover (£160 × 11,600)	1,856,000	1,844,400	11,600 (A)
Variable materials (£36 × 11,600)	417,600	440,800	23,200 (A)
Production and administrative labour (£80,000 + [£50 × 11,600])	660,000	677,600	17,600 (A)
Light, heat and power (£120,000 + [£4 × 11,600])	166,400	136,400	30,000 (F)
Fixed overheads	240,000	259,600	19,600 (A)
Profit	372,000	330,000	42,000 (A)

(b) There is an assumption that a participative approach to budgets and budgetary control will improve management motivation and results. However, there is a number of situations where imposed budgets may be more effective than participative budgets. These include:
· Managers' objectives may not be those of the organisation as a whole.
· Managers do not have the training, skill or technical knowledge to set budgets.
· Managers would prefer not to set their own targets.
· Time constraint whereby full participation is not practicable.

(c) Setting of budgetary targets that are not achievable can be demotivating. If managers recognise this they are likely not even to attempt to achieve the target. Impossible targets can also bring into disrepute the whole planning process; and managers may question the validity and usefulness of the budgetary process.

This might have been the case in terms of the request to reduce material costs. If Visiguard do not have an alternative supplier, the managers may have little control over material prices.

(d) It does not always follow that improved performance compared to the original budget is because managers were motivated by the budget revision.

· Actual activity was greater than the agreed revision. This may have been due to the increased energy and motivation of managers. However, there may have been, outside the control of managers, a general increase in demand for the product.

· The only cost less than planned in the budget is light, heat and power. This may have been an inaccurate forecast or because weather conditions have been milder, thus reducing heating costs. It is unlikely that the power supplier has reduced costs.

QUESTION 56 (December 1999)

Task 56.1

(a) (i) Budgeted selling price:
(£960,000 ÷ 20,000 units)   = £48.00

(ii) Budgeted material cost per unit:
(£240,000 ÷ 20,000 units)   = £12.00

(iii) Budgeted marginal cost of light, heat and power per unit:
([£68,000 − £20,000] ÷ 20,000 units)   = £2.40

(iv) Actual marginal cost of light, heat and power per unit:
([£74,500 − £12,000] ÷ 25,000 units)   = £2.50

(b) **HFD Processes Ltd**
Flexible budgetary control statement – year ended 30 November 1999

F = Favourable   A = Adverse

	£	Flexible budget £	£	Actual £	Variance £
Volume (units)		22,000		22,000	Nil
Turnover (@ £48)		1,056,000		1,012,000	44,000 (A)
Marginal costs					
Material (@ £12)	264,000			261,800	2,200 (F)
Light, heat and power (@£2.40)	52,800			55,000	2,200 (A)
Fixed costs					
Labour	260,000			273,000	13,000 (A)
Light, heat and power	20,000			12,000	8,000 (F)
Fixed overheads	400,000			430,000	30,000 (A)
		996,800		1,031,800	
Operating profit/(loss)		59,200		(19,800)	79,000 (A)

Task 56.2

MEMO

To: Chief Executive

From: Management Accountant

Date: 2 December 1999

Subject: Flexible budget

(a) The flexible budgetary control statement I have recently produced differs from the original operating statement and results because of a number of factors.

The original operating statement is not a 'like with like' comparison as the original fixed budgetary target was 20,000 units whereas we achieved an activity level of 22,000 units sold.

The original plan did not include stockholding, whereas the actual figures take account of stock valued at absorption cost, ie full cost of production. Thus, some of the fixed costs are carried forward in closing stocks to the next period and not written off in the current period.

(b) It can be argued that certain fixed costs are essential to the manufacture of the stock and should therefore be included in its value. However, from a management control perspective this has a weakness.

It is possible for managers to distort their performance by increasing stock levels, thus carrying forward a greater amount of fixed costs.

The marginal costing technique, valuing stocks at total variable cost and treating fixed costs as a 'period cost', is more appropriate for measuring management performance and focusing on control of those costs which are within management's span of control.

QUESTION 57 (June 1999)

Task 57.1

(a) **Calculation of unit variable costs – high/low method**

	High original budget	Low revised budget	Range	Variable unit cost
Fasta units	24,000	20,000	4,000	
Variable costs	£	£	£	
Material	216,000	180,000	36,000	£9
Labour	288,000	240,000	48,000	£12
Semi-variable costs				
Heat, light and power	31,000	27,000	£4,000	£1

Analysis of heat, light and power

Variable cost (£1/unit)	£24,000	£20,000
Total cost	£31,000	£27,000
Fixed cost	£7,000	£7,000

(b) **Rivermede Ltd**
Flexible budgetary control statement for the year ended 31 May 1999

	Revised budget	Actual results	Adjustment	Revised actual	Variance
Production and sales (units)	22,000	22,000		22,000	
	£	£	£	£	£
Variable costs					
Material (W1)	198,000	206,800	7,520	214,320	16,320 (A)
Labour (W2)	264,000	255,200		255,200	8,800 (F)
Semi-variable costs					
Heat, light and power (W3)	29,000	33,400	(7,520)	25,880	3,120 (F)
Fixed costs					
Rent, rates and depreciation	40,000	38,000		38,000	2,000 (F)
	531,000	533,400		533,400	2,400 (A)

Workings for flexed budget:

(W1)	Material	$22,000 \times £9$
(W2)	Labour	$22,000 \times £12$
(W3)	Heat, light and power	$(22,000 \times £1) + £7,000$

Task 57.2

MEMO

To: Steven Jones

From: Management Accountant

Date: 16 June 1999

Subject: Flexible budgetary control

(a)   The original operating statement compares an actual level of activity of 22,000 units with a revised forecast of 20,000 units. This is not a 'like with like' comparison and is of little use for management control purposes.

The flexible budget, however, informs on a 'like with like' comparison by giving an allowance for costs and revenue in relation to the actual level of activity achieved. The variances reported are therefore smaller and also are more meaningful. The reduction in these variances is not attributable to participative budgeting.

(b)   There are a number of reasons why favourable cost variances may arise other than with the introduction of participative budgeting.
· A favourable variance may arise for a reason outside management's span of control.

The variance on fixed expenditure relates to rent, rates and depreciation which are costs that are not controllable.

A further example is that the fixed charge for heat, light and power may be different from planned.

· Managers may have inflated costs in the budget as a result of their participation.

(c)   Similar reasons could be argued for the increase in sales volume.
· There could have been a general increase in demand without extra sales effort.
· The revision to the budget may have been too low. This may have been a genuine concern that the original target was not achievable. However, it may have been intentional, since by understating forecast demand, the actual performance looks better.

We should continue with participative budgeting but based on the flexible budgetary control technique.

QUESTION 58 (June 2002)

Task 58.1

(a) **Variable costs per drum**

(i)	Material A:	£240,000/80,000	=	£3.00
(ii)	Material B:	£480,000/80,000	=	£6.00
(iii)	Material C:	£320,000/80,000	=	£4.00
(iv)	Power:	(£270,000 − £110,000)/80,000	=	£2.00
(v)	Water:	(£122,000 − £90,000)/80,000	=	£0.40

(b)

Alderford Ltd : Flexible budget statement – year ended 31 May 2002

	Budget	Actual	Variance
Number of drums	125,000	125,000	
	£000	£000	£000
Turnover (@ £30)	3,750	4,000	250 (F)
Variable costs			
Material A	375	425	50 (A)
Material B	750	680	70 (F)
Material C	500	500	0
Semi-variable costs			
Power (110 + 250)	360	440	80 (A)
Water (90 + 50)	140	200	60 (A)
Stepped costs			
Supervision (13 × 20) (W)	260	258	2 (F)
Fixed costs			
Rent and rates	250	250	0
Lighting and heating	120	118	2 (F)
Administrative expenses	200	240	40 (A)
Operating profit	795	889	94 (F)

(w) Original budget (80,000 ÷ 10) supervisors at £20,000 each
Actual (125,000 ÷ 10) = 13 supervisors at £20,000 each = £260,000

Task 58.2

MEMO

To: James Alexander

From: Accounting Technician

Date: 20 June 2002

Subject: Improved sales forecasting

(a) **Forecasting techniques currently available to Alderford**

    (i)   If the number of customers is small, it is possible to ask them what their likely demand will be over the next year.

(ii) Sales staff have a detailed knowledge of the market. They could be asked to provide a forecast based on their experience of demand from existing and prospective customers.

(iii) Market research is perhaps the best way of obtaining data where the market is large, where the market is unknown or where there is a large number of customers. Market research can be undertaken in at least two ways.

Primary research involves obtaining data directly from the customers either by sampling or the use of focus groups. Secondary research involves using existing data or data collected for another purpose. One example of this is the number of house starts, that is, the number of houses started to be built. Another would be the number of mortgages provided.

(iv) A further technique is to use some form of model that shows a linkage or pattern with the demand for the chemical prepared by Alderford. One example is the use of leading indicators where a change in one variable is associated with a later change in another variable. Rapidly rising house prices might be an early indicator of an increased demand for houses. Another example is a tool such as the product life cycle. This shows different growth patterns, depending on what stage the product is at in the product life cycle.

(b) **Forecasting techniques not currently available to Alderford**

Alderford and its product have only been in existence for twelve months. Because of this, it is highly unlikely that any form of forecasting based on past data will be appropriate. Techniques that rely on past data include linear regression and moving averages. Twelve months' data is insufficient to make these techniques meaningful.

(c) **Most appropriate forecasting techniques for the three strategies**

(i) **More sales to existing customers:** asking customers directly or asking the sales force is probably the best way of forecasting demand from existing customers.

(ii) **Sales to new customers:** this first requires identifying the potential new customers and so some form of market research will be necessary to discover who the new customers might be.

(iii) **Development of new markets:** some form of market research will also be required to help forecast the demand from new markets. Focus groups might identify if the product is acceptable to any new market. Surveys will then be necessary to estimate the potential size of the market.

QUESTION 59 (December 2002)

Task 59.1

(a) **Budgeted data**

   (i)   Selling price per unit   (£6,400,000/400,000)   =   £16.00
                                    or   (£7,040,000/440,000)   =   £16.00

   (ii) Variable cost of material per unit (£1,600,000/400,000) =   £4.00
                                    or   (£1,760,000/440,000)   =   £4.00

   (iii) Variable cost of labour per unit (£2,000,000/400,000)   =   £5.00
                                    or   (£2,200,000/440,000)   =   £5.00

   (iv) Variable cost of electricity:
         Incremental cost   (£960,000 – £880,000)   = £80,000
         Incremental volume   (440,000 – 400,000)   = 40,000 units
         Variable cost per unit   (£80,000/40,000)   =   £2.00

   (v)   Fixed cost of electricity
         (Total cost – total variable cost) = £880,000 – (400,000 × £2.00) =£80,000
                                    or   £960,000 – (440,000 × £2.00) =£80,000

(b) **Actual data**

   (i)   Variable cost of material   (£2,520,000/600,000) =   £4.20
   (ii) Variable cost of labour   (£3,180,000/600,000) =   £5.30
   (iii) Variable cost of electricity   (£1,200,000/600,000) =   £2.00

(c)

Actual expenses for the year on a marginal costing basis		
Variable costs		
Material	(450,000 × £4.20) =	£1,890,000
Labour	(450,000 × £5.30) =	£2,385,000
Electricity	(450,000 × £2.00) =	£900,000
Fixed costs		
Electricity		Nil
Depreciation		£300,000
Maintenance		£200,000
Other fixed costs		£800,000

(d)

Flexible budget statement - year ended 30 November 2002

		Flexed budget	Actual results	Variances
Volume (units sold)		450,000	450,000	
Turnover	(450,000 × £16.00)	£7,200,000	£6,840,000	£360,000 (A)
Variable costs				
Material	(450,000 × £4.00)	£1,800,000	£1,890,000	£90,000 (A)
Labour	(450,000 × £5.00)	£2,250,000	£2,385,000	£135,000 (A)
Electricity	(450,000 × £2.00)	£900,000	£900,000	£0
Contribution		£2,250,000	£1,665,000	£585,000 (A)
Fixed costs				
Electricity		£80,000	£0	£80,000 (F)
Depreciation		£500,000	£300,000	£200,000 (F)
Maintenance		£300,000	£200,000	£100,000 (F)
Other fixed costs		£700,000	£800,000	£100,000 (A)
Operating profit		£670,000	£365,000	£305,000 (A)

Task 59.2

MEMO

To: Robert Maxton

From: Management Accountant

Date: 5 December 2002

Subject: Budgets and results

Just over a year ago you imposed a budget on the senior managers of the Omicron division. The result was an actual profit for the year greater than even your imposed budget.

(a)   Sometimes it is better to impose a budget. There could be a number of reasons for preferring to impose a budget rather than developing one through the participation of the senior managers. These reasons include:
· urgency and lack of time for participation
· managers preferring to have budgets set for them
· managers lacking the technical knowledge to set budgets
· managers having different objectives from the organisation
· managers being prepared to distort budgets.

(b)   The original actual operating profit was improved by managers producing more than sold (and hence carrying forward fixed costs into another period); by charging less depreciation and by undertaking less maintenance than planned. In addition, the electricity supplier eliminated the fixed charge and so reduced costs for the division.

(c) The only difference between the original operating profit of £690,000 and the revised actual profit of £365,000 relates to the value of the closing stock. In the revised actual profit, the closing stock is valued on a marginal costing basis. In the original actual profit, a proportion of fixed costs was also included in the stock valuation. This had the effect of reducing the total expenses for the year.

QUESTION 60

(a)	**Budgeted unit Selling price:** £4,800,000/120,000		£40.00

(b) **Budgeted variable cost of material**
(i)	**A**: £480,000/120,000	£4.00
(ii)	**B**: £840,000/120,000	£7.00
(iii)	**C**: £360,000/120,000	£3.00

(c) (i) **Budgeted fixed cost of light, heat and power**

Total budgeted cost	£290,000
Variable cost: £2 × 120,000	£240,000
	£50,000

    (ii) **Budgeted variable cost of water**

Budgeted total cost	£212,000
Budgeted fixed cost	£20,000
Total variable cost	£192,000
Unit variable cost (£192,000/120,000)	£1.60

(d)

Shifnal Ltd: Flexible budget statement year ended 30 November 2003

	Flexed budget	Actual	Variance	
Omegas produced and sold	95,000	95,000		
	£000	£000	£000	
Turnover (95,000 × £40)	3,800	3,990	190	(F)
Material A (95,000 × £4)	380	456	76	(A)
Material B (95,000 × £7)	665	665	–	(A)
Material C (95,000 × £3)	285	266	19	(F)
Light, heat and power (W1)	240	249	9	(A)
Water (W2)	172	182	10	(A)
Labour (W3)	160	168	8	(A)
Maintenance (W4)	50	54	4	(A)
Rent and rates	360	355	5	(F)
Distribution expenses	600	620	20	(A)
Administrative expenses	300	280	20	(F)
Operating profit	588	695	107	(F)

Workings
1   £50,000 + (£2.00 × 95,000) = £240,000
2   £20,000 + (£1.60 × 95,000) = £172,000

3   Up to 3,000 units cost £5,000 of labour

95,000 units require $\dfrac{95,000}{3,000} = 31.67$ 'groups' of labour

This is rounded to 32 as it is a stepped cost and you cannot employ part of a 'group'.

Cost of labour = 32 × £5,000 = £160,000

4   95,000/20,000 = 4.75. Round up, therefore cost is 5 × £10,000 = £50,000

QUESTION 61

Notes for Mike Town (**Note:** only six are required in the answer)

The current report has a number of weaknesses that might make it more difficult for managers to manage. These include the following.

1   The report does not show the budget and actual for the month, only the cumulative for the year to date.

2   The 'budget to date' and 'cash expenditure to date' columns appear to have been put in the wrong columns.

3   The use of 'Cr' and 'Dr' is inappropriate and unhelpful especially for non-accountants. It would be better to use the more correct and understood terms 'favourable' and 'adverse'.

4   Capital and revenue items appear on the same statement.

5   The statement is produced on a cash paid basis rather than using accruals accounting.

6   The statement does not analyse the data into the different parts of the leisure centre, treating the whole centre as one cost centre.

7   There is no reference to revenue but it is reasonable to assume that the centre does generate income.

8   The 'budget remaining' column is unhelpful particularly given the cash basis of recording the expenses. It would be more useful to have a 'likely outcome' column for the whole year, although this may not be needed every month.

MOCK EXAMINATION – UNIT 8
ANSWERS

Section 1

Task 1.1

(a)   (i)   Actual price of material per litre:

£920,160/113,600   =   £8.10

      (ii)   Actual labour rate per hour:

£336,336/68,640   =   £4.90

      (iii)   Actual labour hours per tin:

68,640 hours/16,000   =   4.29 hours

      (iv)   Budgeted production for the year:

£5,040,000/£24   =   210,000 tins

      (v)   Budgeted production for the 4 weeks:

210,000 × 4/50   =   16,800 tins

      (vi)   Budgeted fixed overheads for the 4 weeks:

£5,040,000 × 4/50   =   £403,200

(b)   (i)   Material price variance:

(Standard price – Actual price) × Actual usage

(£8.00 – £8.10) × 113,600   =   £(11,360) A

      (ii)   Material usage variance:

(Standard usage – Actual usage) × Standard price

(112,000 litres – 113,600 litres) × £8

1,600 litres × £8   =   £(12,800) A

      (iii)   Labour rate variance:

(Standard rate – Actual rate) × Actual hours

(£5 – £4.90) × 68,640   =   £6,864 F

      (iv)   Labour efficiency variance:

(Standard hours produced – Actual hours worked) × Standard rate

(64,000 – 68,640) × £5   =   £(23,200) A

      (v)   Fixed overhead expenditure variance:

	£
Budgeted fixed cost	403,200
Actual fixed cost	410,000
Variance	£(6,800) A

      (vi)   Fixed overhead volume variance:

(Standard hours produced – Budgeted hours) × FORR

(64,000 – 67,200) × £6   =   £(19,200) A

Fixed overhead recovery rate (FORR) = 403,200/67,200 = £6 per hour, as on the standard cost card.

      (vii)   Fixed overhead capacity variance:

(Budgeted hours – Actual hours) × FORR

(67,200 – 68,640) × £6   =   £8,640 F

      (viii)   Fixed overhead efficiency variance:

(Standard hours produced – Actual hours worked) × FORR

(64,000 – 68,640) × £6   =   £(27,840) A

(c)   **Reconciliation statement for the four weeks ended 1 June 2001**

	£
Standard cost of actual production 16,000 tins × £100	1,600,000
Summary of variances:	
Direct material price	(11,360) A
Direct material usage	(12,800) A
Direct labour rate	6,864 F
Direct labour efficiency	(23,200) A
Fixed overhead expenditure	(6,800) A
Fixed overhead volume	(19,200) A
	(66,496)
Actual cost of production	1,666,496

Task 1.2

MEMO

To: General Manager

From: Management Accountant

Date: X-X-XX

Subject: Analysis of variances

Following our recent meeting on the performance of the new factory for the four weeks ended 1 June 2001, I outline revisions to a number of variances taking account of the additional information you supplied concerning certain elements of cost.

(a)   **Revised standard price of material**

Current standard price	£8.00
Additional transport costs (£8.00 × 1.25%)	£0.10
Revised standard price of material	£8.10

(b)   **Estimated labour hours per tin of X40 after the production workers are fully trained**

Current labour hours per tin	4.29
Inefficiency due to training (4.29 × 0.1/1.1)	0.39
Revised labour hours per tin	3.90

(c)   **Sub-division of labour efficiency variance**

Variance due to training

Hours actually taken (4.29 × 16,000)	68,640
Hours once fully trained (3.90 × 16,000)	62,400
Hours due to not being fully trained	6,240 A
Variance (6,240 × £5.00)	£31,200 A

Variance due to other reasons

Standard hours for 16,000 tins	64,000
Hours once fully trained	62,400
Hours saved compared with standard	1,600 F
Variance (1,600 × £5.00)	£8,000 F

(d) **Explanation of variance due to other reasons**

This shows a favourable effect of £8,000. The factors which cause this may include:
- the use of well qualified employees has increased the efficiency of labour
- factory layout and use of technology for movement of materials
- more advanced machinery.

Section 2

Task 2.1

(a)	**Gross margin** (£385,440/£560,640 × 100%)	68.75%
(b)	**Net profit margin** (£42,048/£560,640 × 100%)	7.5%
(c)	**Return on capital employed** (£42,048/£700,800 × 100%)	6.00%
(d)	**Asset turnover** (£560,640/£700,800)	0.8 times
(e)	**Average age of debtors** (£35,040/£560,640 × 12)	0.75 months
(f)	**Average age of creditors** (£14,600/£175,200 × 12)	1 month
(g)	**Months' expenses payable from cash balance** (£10,804/£518,592 × 12)	0.25 months
(h)	**Maximum capacity** 80 bedrooms × 365	29,200 room nights
(i)	**Occupancy rate** (17,520/29,200 × 100%)	60%

Task 2.2

MEMO	
To:	Helene de la Tour
From:	Management Accountant
Date:	5 December 2001
Subject:	Profitability of UK hotel

Further to our recent discussion regarding the profitability of the UK site, I wish to make the following observations.

(a) **Effect of discounting**
· Turnover ex discounts would have been:
17,520 × £40 £700,800
· Discounts given totalled:
(£700,800 – £560,640) £140,160
· Number of discounted room nights
(£140,160/£20) 7,008
· % of room nights discounted
(7,008/17,520) × 100% 40%

(b) **Revised financial statements assuming no discounts**

Operating statement

	£	£
Turnover		700,800
Variable costs		175,200
Contribution		525,600
Fixed costs		343,392
Profit		£182,208

Balance sheet

		£
Fixed assets		669,556
Debtors (700,800 x 0.5/12)	29,200	
Cash	3,000	
	32,200	
Creditors (175,200 ÷ 6)	(29,200)	
		3,000
		£672,556

(c) **Revised ratios**

Gross margin (525,600/700,800) 75%
Net profit margin 26%
Return on capital employed 27.09%

(d) **Discounting and profitability**

If the managers could have sold all the room nights at the full price then discounting would have clearly reduced profit.

The overall occupancy rate is fairly low at 60% after accounting for discounted rooms of 40% of the occupancy.

The business is a new venture and therefore initial demand is likely to be less until it is fully established.

It is highly likely that if the manager had not discounted the rooms, then the volume would have been less and profits lower than achieved.

As the business becomes more established the manager needs to have the flexibility of control in deciding when to discount and achieving a well balanced mix of prices.

MOCK EXAMINATION – UNIT 9
ANSWERS

Section 1

Task 1.1

(a) **Production budget – 4 periods to 21 October 2001**

Period	1	2	3	4	5
Sales volume	19,400	21,340	23,280	22,310	22,310
Add closing stock[1]	4,268	4,656	4,462	4,462	
Less opening stock	3,880	4,268	4,656	4,462	4,462
Good production	19,788	21,728	23,086	22,310	
Faulty production (3/97)	612	672	714	690	
Gross production (Gammas)	20,400	22,400	23,800	23,000	

Notes:

[1] Closing stock = 4/20 × next period's sales volume.
   Closing stock equals next period's opening stock.
[2] Period 5 shown to demonstrate calculation of period 4's closing stock.

(b) **Material purchases budget – 3 periods to 23 September 2001**

Period	1	2	3	4
Gross production	20,400	22,400	23,800	23,000
Material required (3 litres per Gamma)	61,200	67,200	71,400	69,000
Add closing stock[1]	16,800	17,850	17,250	
Less opening stock	16,500	16,800	17,850	17,250
Purchases (litres)	61,500	68,250	70,800	

Notes:

[1] Closing stock = 5/20 × next period's gross production.
   Closing stock forms next period's opening stock.
[2] Period 4 shown to demonstrate calculation of period 3's closing stock.

(c) **Cost of purchases**

Period	1	2	3
Total cost (£8 × purchases)	£492,000	£546,000	£566,400

(d) **Labour budget – 3 periods to 23 September 2001**

Period	1	2	3
Gross production	20,400	22,400	23,800
Hours (0.5 hours per Gamma)	10,200	11,200	11,900
Basic hours (70 workers × 40 hours × 4 weeks)	11,200	11,200	11,200
Overtime (surplus hours)	(1,000)	Nil	700

(e) **Cost of wages**

Period	1	2	3
Basic wages			
(70 workers × 4 weeks			
× £240)	£67,200	£67,200	£67,200
Overtime			
(£9 × overtime hours)			£6,300
	£67,200	£67,200	£73,500

Task 1.2

MEMO

To:　　　　Production Director

From:　　　Management Accountant

Date:　　　XX June 2001

Subject:　　Overtime payments and faulty production

Following our recent meeting to discuss the budgets, you questioned the need for overtime and made the observation that the 3% failure rate may be due to poor working practices on the shop floor.

(a) **Overtime payments**

There are 700 hours of overtime allowed for in the budget during period 3. There is however a surplus of labour capacity of 1,000 hours in period 1. If we produce an extra 1,400 units in period 1, the overtime hours in period 3 would be avoided.

This would result in a saving of (£9 × 700 hours) = £6,300.

(b) **Costs incurred in achieving the overtime saving (one only required)**
· Financing costs
· Storage costs

(c) **Advantages of sampling**

Sampling is likely to be much less costly than full inspection. In some industries there is no alternative to sampling, e.g. canned food, canned drink where testing the sample destroys the sample.

(d) **Types of sampling**

Simple or random sampling

Every item in the population has an equal chance of being selected.

Systematic sampling

Involves randomly choosing the first item and then the nth item thereafter, eg if in a population of 10,000 a sample size of 1,000 was required; if the initial item was, say, 5 then the next items in the sample would be 15, 25, 35 up to 9,995.

Stratified sampling

This is used where there are well defined groups within the population.

If, for example, a company wished to measure its staff morale across its range of categories of staffing; using systematic sampling might leave out a group. Thus, in stratified sampling the population is first split up into groups and a sample is taken from each group in its proportion to the population as a whole.

(e) **Sampling at Sandwell**

It is important to identify which production workers are causing the faulty production.

Therefore, a stratified sampling technique should be used as it would necessarily include all the categories of the workforce.

Section 2

Task 2.1

(a)	(i)	**Budgeted selling price**		
		(£1,440,000/36,000)		£40.00
	(ii)	**Budgeted unit material cost**		
		(£432,000/36,000)		£12.00
	(iii)	**Budgeted unit labour cost**		
		(£216,000/36,000)		£6.00
	(iv)	**Budgeted unit variable cost of light, heat and power**		
		(£92,000 – £20,000)/36,000		£2.00
	(v)	**Percentage of cost of production in stock**		
		5,000/40,000 × 100%		12.5%
	(vi)	**Actual variable cost of sales**		
		Material (£500,000 × 87.5%)	£437,500	
		Labour (£232,000 × 87.5%)	£203,000	
		Light, heat and power ([£96,000 – £12,000] × 87.5%)	£73,500	£714,000
	(vii)	**Total actual fixed costs**		
		Light, heat and power	£12,000	
		Depreciation	£70,000	
		Other fixed costs	£420,000	£502,000

(b) **Flexible budget statement – year ended 30 November 2001**

	Flexed budget £	Actual results £	Variance £	
Turnover (35,000 × £40)	1,400,000	1,365,000	35,000	(A)
Variable costs:				
Material (35,000 × £12)	420,000	437,500	17,500	(A)
Production labour (35,000 × £6)	210,000	203,000	7,000	(F)
Variable light, heat and power (35,000 × £2)	70,000	73,500	3,500	(A)
Variable cost of sales	700,000	714,000	14,000	(A)
Contribution	700,000	651,000	49,000	(A)
Fixed costs:				
Light, heat and power	20,000	12,000	8,000	(F)
Depreciation	100,000	70,000	30,000	(F)
Other fixed overheads	400,000	420,000	20,000	(A)
Total fixed costs	520,000	502,000	18,000	(F)
Operating profit	180,000	149,000	31,000	(A)

Task 2.2

MEMO

To: Harry Easton

From: Assistant Management Accountant

Date: 6 December 2001

Subject: Performance of Hall Ltd

(a) (i) **Difference between the two budgets**

The original budget was a 'fixed budget' or planning document. It was a target in which management were committed to achieve. The revised format is a control document and focuses on a different perspective.

The revised budget makes a 'like with like' comparison, a flexed budget for a volume of 35,000 units with the actual results for that level of activity, whereas the original target was 36,000 units.

(ii) **Difference between the actual reported profits**

The original planning budget and actual results were based on absorption costing which matches all costs including fixed costs against revenue earned. Therefore, any unsold production is valued at 'full' cost and some fixed costs are carried forward in the valuation of closing stocks.

The revised format is based on a marginal costing approach. This basis recognises that fixed costs are period costs and should be charged against the period in which they are incurred. The stocks are valued at marginal cost.

(b) **Why the actual operating profit was greater than budgeted despite lower sales volume**

Some costs in the original budget seem to be overstated.

The depreciation was budgeted at £100,000 whereas the actual charge was £70,000.

As 40,000 units have been produced, there has been a larger base on which fixed overhead has been recovered, some of which has been carried forward in the stock valuation.

The flexed budget also revealed a saving in the area of labour costs.

KAPLAN PUBLISHING

GLOSSARY

Term	Description
Activity-based costing	More accurate method of charging costs to cost units than traditional total absorption costing.
Attainable standard	Standard that can be achieved in reasonably good conditions.
Balanced scorecard	Approach to performance measurement that recognises that the business must be successful from several perspectives, not just in earning short-term profits.
Basic standard	Standard that is fixed historically and then not changed.
Benchmarking	Comparison of the performance of one's own business with the performance of competitors, in order to identify areas of possible improvement.
Budget	A plan expressed in quantitative terms for a defined period of time.
Budget centre	A department or area for which an individual budget is drawn up.
Budgetary control	The establishment of budgets prior to a period, with subsequent comparison of actual with budgeted results, in order to secure the objectives of a policy or provide a basis for its revision.
Cost absorption	The charging of the overhead costs accumulated in a production cost centre to the cost units relevant to that cost centre.
Cost accounting	Part of management accounting dealing with the ascertainment and reporting of costs.
Cost allocation	The charging of a cost to the single cost centre which has incurred the cost.
Cost apportionment	The splitting of the charging of a cost between the various cost centres for which the cost was incurred.
Cost centre	A location, function or item of equipment in respect of which costs may be accumulated and related to cost units for control purposes.
Cost of quality	The difference between the actual cost of producing, selling and supporting the company's products, and the equivalent cost if there were no failures during production or usage.
Cost reduction	A process to drive down the unit cost of products without reducing their suitability for the use intended.
Cost unit	A unit of product or service in relation to which costs are ascertained.
Direct costs	Costs that can be related directly to a cost unit.

Term	Description
Effectiveness	The degree to which an objective or target is met.
Efficiency	The relationship between inputs and outputs achieved.
Financial accounting	Provision of accounting information to parties external to the business.
Fixed budget	A budget which is not amended if actual volumes are different from budgeted volumes.
Fixed costs	Costs that remain unchanged whatever the level of activity.
Flexible budget	A budget which is amended if actual volumes are different from budgeted volumes.
Ideal standard	Standard that can only be achieved in perfect conditions.
Index numbers	A method of assessing growth by allocating an index number of 100 to a base figure in a series, and converting all other figures in the series to an index number using the formula: $$\text{Index} = \frac{\text{Current year's figure}}{\text{Base your figure}} \times 100$$
Indirect costs	Other costs. Also called overheads.
Interdependence of variances	The fact that different variances may be inter-linked by a common cause.
Investigation of variances	Examining the causes of variances with a view to introducing controls.
Limiting factor	The resource whose shortage limits the entire capacity of the business operation. Also known as key factor.
Management accounting	Provision of accounting information to parties internal to the business.
Management information system (MIS)	System providing managers at all levels of a business with the information they need to carry out their roles.
Marginal costing	Costing system under which stocks are measured at their marginal cost only. All fixed costs are written off as incurred.
Master budget	The budget into which all the subsidiary budgets are consolidated, normally comprising a budgeted profit and loss account and budgeted balance sheet (and possibly a budgeted cash flow statement).
PEST analysis	Analysis of the political, economic, social and technological environment facing an organisation.
Population	The entire set of data from which a sample is selected.
Primary data	Data gathered expressly for the purpose in hand.
Productivity	The efficiency of resource usage (particularly labour) and often measured in non-financial terms.

Term	Description
Random sampling	Sampling method in which every item in the population has an equal chance of being selected.
Sampling	Investigating less than 100% of the items in a population, in order to draw a conclusion about the population.
Secondary data	Data gathered for a purpose other than the purpose in hand.
Semi-variable costs	Costs having both a fixed and a variable element.
Significance of variances	Assessing the importance of variances with a view to their investigation, typically by expressing the variance as a percentage of the standard amount.
Standard cost	The planned unit cost of the products, components or services produced in a period.
SWOT analysis	Analysis of an organisation's strengths, weaknesses, opportunities and threats.
Time series	A set of values recorded for some variable over a period of time.
Total absorption costing	Costing system under which stocks are measured at their total production cost (including fixed production overheads).
Total Quality Management	A business philosophy dedicated to a continuous improvement in quality, efficiency and effectiveness.
Trend	The general direction in which a time series is going, once the short-term variations have been eliminated.
Variable costs	Costs that increase in line with the level of activity.
Variance	The difference between a planned, budgeted or standard cost and the actual cost incurred.
Zero-based budgeting	A method of budgeting which requires each cost element to be specifically justified, as though the activities were being undertaken for the first time.

INDEX

INDEX